The Mayfly Boys
SUMMER OF '63

Joseph Welch

Copyright © 2024

All Rights Reserved

No part of this publication may be reproduced, stored in a retrieval system, or transmitted in any form or by any means, electronic, mechanical, photocopying, recording, or otherwise, without the written permission of the author or the publisher.

Table Of Contents

Dedication i
Acknowledgments ii
About The Author iv
Preface 1
1. Waking Early 4
2. School Days 17
3. Pagan Babies 27
4. Sr. Bernard 40
5. River Pirates 46
6. After School 54
7. Night Prayers 61
8. Lucky 65
9. The Bayou 69
10. Meeting Royalty 77
11. Saturday Morning 85
12. Confessions 94
13. Sunday Morning 103
14. The Bundle 108
15. First Witness 113
16. Tempers 122
17. After The Inquest 132
18. Ms. Mame 137
19. The Cemetery 144

20. The Watch	147
21. Hoping And Praying	156
22. School Picnic	165
23. Last Day Of School	171
24. Free At Last!	178
25. The River's Rest	187
26. Filling Richard In	195
27. The Issues	202
28. Negotiating The Deal	212
29. The Title Company	221
30. Meeting At The Wall	229
31. Show And Tell	235
32. Car On The Bluff	236
33. The Oak	240
34. Showing Richard And Toby	248
35. Gunfight	254
36. John And Michael In	258
37. Transporting Materiel	262
38. The Retreat	271
39. Construction	282
40. First Friday	289
41. Figuring Tom	294
42. At The Hop	304
43. Mr. Hedges	311
44. Fr. Jim	320

45. Richard's Theory	329
46. The Visitor	334
47. Richard Hailed	341
48. Turtle Island	348
49. The Float	354
50. Meeting Sidney	357
51. Tools Of The Trade	362
52. Getaway Plans	369
53. Pirates	373
54. The Water Table	382
55. The Key	387
56. The Heist	394
57. Carly's New Friend	401
58. Serving More Masses	409
59. K.C. Picnic	411
60. High Adventure	416
61. Foiled Attempts	423
62. Replacing The Item	429
63. Sneak Peek	436
64. The Visitors	441
65. Fencing The Bar	444
66. Heaven	448
67. First Friday	452
68. Altar Boys Camp	455
69. The Pool	463

70. My First Campfire 467
71. Foiled Attempts 470
72. Lanyards And Bony Gus 477
73. Second Campfire 485
74. Target Practice 494
75. The Gainer 500
76. Time Out 503
77. Mrs. Buben And Buddy 509
78. Lots Of News 513
79. Plan B 522
80. Snooping With Urgency 528
81. Remnants 532
82. The Edges 536
83. Oom-Pow-Wow 541
84. Mrs. Washington 550
85. The Storm Breaks 557
86. Early Rounds 561
87. Liars 564
88. Telling The Truth 575
89. Fr. Jim 584
90. The Semis 594
91. Go, May Cats! 596
92. What Might Have Been 601
93. Richard's Discovery 606
94. Flashback: May 18th, 1963 610

95. Tribute Mass 618
96. Afterword 619
97. Deep Flashback: The Last Voyage 623

DEDICATION

To my family, with love and gratitude: to my sweet and patient spouse, Sharon, who inspires me to entertain her; and to my children and grandchildren, with whom I hope to share the wonders of my boyhood in a different time, in a town very much like Mayfly.

ACKNOWLEDGMENTS

So many people have provided support and inspiration during the creation of this book. Among many others, I particularly wish to thank:

Frank Rivers Golbeck and Eric Ryan Welch for their inspired cover design;

My children, who took time out of their busy lives to serve as *beta* readers and who have provided me with valuable counsel, advice and encouragement;

My brother, John, a true Knight of the Altar, for his painstaking and rigorous editing process, and for allowing me to poke fun at his staggering breadth of intellect, which is frankly the only way I can deal with it;

My brother, Michael, who good-naturedly allowed me to tell my version of "the unvarnished truth" (and who most days is actually nothing at all like a similarly-named character in the novel);

The "Little Boys," Mark, Stephen, and Tim, for the limitless hours of gloating superiority which can only be enjoyed by having won the birth lottery as an older brother;

Dave and Paula Hirner, d/b/a Flying Squirrel Aerial Optics, for their superb drone photography, which provided me with key details of portions of the river bluffs which are no longer safely accessible to me on "shanks' mares";

Leo Howarth, who had the patience to teach a snot-nosed neighbor kid how to execute a beautiful and deadly hook shot;

Dean Eichenberger, who refreshed my memory and my spirit by recounting for me the mysteries of Camp Oko-Tipi;

My heroes, the "Big Boys" whom we emulated: John and Jim and Bob and Bailey and Leo and Porky and Kerry and David and Richard;

Marian, and Marlene, and Greg, and John, and Bob, and Mark, and Kate, and Maggie, and Billie, and Barb, and David, and Donnie, and Ron, and Ronda, and Gail, and Scott, and Lisa, and Marvin, and Debbie, and Kathy, and Denise, and Jennie, and Judy, and Joan, and all my classmates, for the wonderful and vivid memories;

Cy Ritter for donating his newspaper subscription sales points to allow me to "win" a beautiful letter jacket;

Sr. Marie Caroline, and Sr. Kenneth Marie, and Miss Michaels, and Sr. Mary Carmé, and Sr. Arilda Marie, and Fr. Jim, for their many kindnesses;

Coaches Hedges, Buckman, Viorel, Sanders and Hall, for their dedication to us;

The Crane, St. Philip, Barbados, for providing me a venue of peace and unrivaled beauty in which to work and rework this novel;

And finally, to my sweet and patient spouse, Sharon, who has cheerfully shouldered more than her fair share of our daily duties to enable me to focus on this project;

Please accept my gratitude from the bottom of my heart.

ABOUT THE AUTHOR

Joseph Welch is a child of Hannibal, Missouri, and a product of the Mississippi River and the bluffs surrounding it. As a young man, he relived Mark Twain's *Life on the Mississippi* by floating a raft from Hannibal to New Orleans, where he was welcomed warmly, made an honorary colonel in the Governor's Militia, and awarded the key to the City of New Orleans. A  retired attorney, he is the father of five children and Papa to eighteen grandchildren. Joseph lives blissfully in Hannibal with his wife, Sharon. He has previously published a book of poetry and short stories entitled *Songs of Hannibal*. This is his first novel.

PREFACE

My name is Jamie Fletcher, but everybody calls me "Cy." I grew up in the small Missouri town of Mayfly, on the banks of the Mississippi River. I was raised in a very Catholic family, the second of six boys and no girls. I was small and not particularly exceptional, except in one thing: I could really play basketball.

Like many young boys, I was powerfully driven from my earliest recollections to become famous. In the Summer of '63, when I was twelve and just shouldering the burdens of boyhood, I strove for greatness in basketball. I dreamed of the respect and fame which would be mine if I could win a certain trophy, which gleamed golden in my vision like The Holy Grail. I craved the adulation which I was certain would accompany that trophy.

I was already a good player—to this day it amazes me to think of some of the moves I created, learning to score against an invisible defender. The hard part was getting other people to appreciate my talents.

Oddly enough, my brothers didn't show me the level of respect and admiration I knew I merited. And since I was with those guys most of my waking hours—bedroom and bathroom, meals, daily chores, basketball, family trips, and prayers—I had a lot to overcome. It was like trying to climb out of a well. Don't get me wrong—they were okay, those guys—a little different, that's for sure. But they didn't grasp the full extent of my greatness the way they should have—I could just tell.

In that long-ago summer, I also strove, along with my friends, to gain the rewards of Heaven—where I had every indication I might be refused admission—and to help a good mutual friend get there, too. And I strove to avoid the pains of Hell.

We also strove to send our pastor, a man we disliked intensely—to ... well, if not to Hell, exactly, then for a good stretch in the fires of Purgatory.

And my friend Toby strove manfully to do the best he could for his brother, and to find comfort for his parents, and peace for his mother.

And our friend Richard strove powerfully and persistently for knowledge, and for connection with his forebears.

And a chubby little dork we called "Sharkbait" strove for acceptance by us older boys.

And I also strove hopefully for a special kind of appreciation in the eyes of a certain girl I knew and liked, named Mary Ann Ventura.

I always believed in goodness, even when I was young. There were good people in our town, plenty of them—so many that I wasn't even aware of some of them until years later. But there was evil, too—enough that it couldn't all stay hidden. There were a lot of things I had to figure out as I went.

My boyhood in Mayfly in those years was very different from what it could be today. There are important things I need to tell you, while I still can—before I forget, before I'm gone. I understood some things at the time, and some I didn't. I was right about some of them, and some of them I got so very wrong.

Joseph Welch

In that long-ago summer of 1963, we all struggled mightily against colossal enigmas, myopically unaware of those magnificent days stealing past us, leaving our frantic adolescent pursuits unruffled by the passage of time, and now gone forever. This is that story....

1.
WAKING EARLY

Click. "Carson, Carson, Carson, Carson, Carson Pirie Scott…and Company," the smiling voices of a female vocal troupe gushed from our new bedroom clock radio. Six a.m. and I was basking in absolute joy to be the half-owner of an actual clock radio—that obnoxious buzz from our old alarm banished forever! And I loved that jingle—I sang it all day!

My older brother John and I swung our legs over the sides of our beds, sitting in our tighty whities and looking blearily across the room at each other. Golden shafts of sun peeked around the borders of Mom's handmade teal-and-white gingham café curtains, spotlighting our individual three-foot wide shelves—each of us had one—on which we had carefully stacked everything we owned—every single item—mostly toys and games. Our fleet of model airplanes glided noiselessly overhead, suspended impressively in action on two lengths of white cotton twine stretched from corner to corner by our Dad. Two NASA money banks stood silent sentinels on either side of our antiqued teal dresser, between which zoomed, in perpetual upward takeoff trajectory, our pride and joy: John's tabletop-mounted B-52 Stratofortress long-range bomber, accompanied by my own interplanetary Fireball XL-5.

Joseph Welch

"Good morning, Mayfly, Missouri," a jovial male voice erupted from the tiny speaker—it was obvious this guy knew something we didn't.

"It's your Mayfly Guy—62 degrees and sunny out there," he proclaimed, popping with pride that Mayfly had won the weather lottery. "And you know the early bird gets the worm, so listen up, all you worm lovers, while we bring you everything you need to know to get your Monday morning started just right. It's April 29, 1963...."

John reached over and smacked the "Off" button, then looked back across the room at me appraisingly, making sure I really wanted what he called my "money's worth."

"You ready?" he asked. "Yep," I replied, as he reached down under his bed and came up with a pair of huge red boxing gloves. An adrenaline jolt caromed off the insides of my temples—there was no time to lose. I hurriedly reached down for my pair. Bright and shiny red, white wrists emblazoned "Everlast," handy elastic cuffs so you didn't need a third person to lace you up—they smelled of new leather. Like our clock radio, the gloves were prizes that our parents would not give us, but allowed us to acquire if we wanted them badly enough to work for them.

We didn't pay cash for them, however—we earned them. They were our reward for selling sixty boxes of "All Occasion Cards" as members of the Junior Sales Club of America, an opportunity presented to us on the back of a Superman comic book, alongside pictures of the amazing rewards available to enterprising young men. Since we wanted most of that stuff: scuba gear, bow and arrows, Charles Atlas weights, a BB gun, and walkie-talkies, the hardest part was deciding which prize to go after first. We filled out applications to become members of the Club and were accepted—we even had colored cardboard name badges to prove it. We also received a suggested sales pitch, which we quickly committed to memory, before splitting up and heading in opposite directions to knock on doors north, east, south and west of our house:

Hello. My name is Jamie Fletcher, and I'm a member of the Junior Sales Club of America (showing my name badge.) *I'm selling All Occasion Cards....* (showing a sample box of floral-themed greeting cards).

It was surprisingly easy, because apparently the Junior Sales Club of America had never before extended its reach into Mayfly. I had no idea that All Occasion Cards were in such great demand—some women even bought multiple boxes!

Our career in the Junior Sales Club of America was productive but short-lived. Once we had earned everything we wanted, it seemed pointless to spend our time selling All-Occasion Cards. We had already acquired a beautiful thirty-pound pull laminated wooden bow with quiver and target arrows; a scuba set consisting of fins, mask and snorkel, which provided excellent underwater visibility in the pool and gave us leisure to gaze unsuspected and uninterrupted at some of the lovelier pool patrons (swimsuits did funny things when girls dived into the water—it opened up an entire world of exploration previously unknown to me); a Daisy BB gun with a thousand BBs; our prized boxing gloves, and a set of walkie-talkies with a three-mile range. Since our brother Michael insisted on keeping one of them with him all the time, I had to sell twenty-four additional boxes of cards to earn a second set, so John and I could each keep one with us—since I had sold the cards and Michael was already satisfied, I got to decide on the deployment of the fourth walkie-talkie, so I loaned it to my friend, Toby.

Now we were enjoying the fruits of our labor. Even though we didn't need to get up until 6:15, we had set our cool new clock radio fifteen minutes early, so we had time to fight for a while before getting ready for school. We even said our morning prayers the prior evening before we went to bed, because we knew Mom would check, so we could start fighting as soon as we woke up.

We punched our own fists together to settle the gloves on our hands, then vaulted off the beds, meeting in the center of the room, a cyclone of flailing arms and red leather, both of us throwing punches as hard and as fast as we could—WOP! WOP! WOP! Half a minute later, winded and realizing that neither of us could beat the other to the floor with pure brute aggression, we separated to arms' length and transitioned to a more sustainable approach: less slugging and more boxing.

John threw a left jab at my face, then another—then a vicious right cross. Wop-wop—WOP! Guard up; protecting my face—nothing hurt more than getting blasted on the end of the nose. I crouched, then exploded up with a haymaker left hook *a la* Floyd Patterson, then both of us were bobbing and weaving, left and right, circling barefoot in our undies, our feet dancing and sliding on the hardwood floor, warming the wax until we smelled it in our flaring nostrils, diving under the red incoming missiles, stepping just outside the reach of the big flying haymakers, then filling the room with uppercuts. We were in our glory. Nothing hurt. These were 16-ounce gloves—hard to break a nose with these—but we tried anyway. Besides, I would rather my brother break my nose than some stranger—and I bet he felt the same way. Blood brothers, for sure.

I hadn't made a public announcement yet, but I was going to become the heavyweight champion of the world. I had read all the great fighters' biographies from the Mayfly Public Library: Jack Dempsey, Gene Tunney, Rocky Marciano (the only man in history to retire as the undefeated Heavyweight Champion of the World), Joe Louis,

Floyd Patterson, Ingemar Johansson. This bedroom stuff was just a first step, necessary only because there was no gym to train a world-class prize fighter in Mayfly.

But I had other problems, too. Jack Dempsey had toughened his face by soaking his skin in leather tanning chemicals every day of his life so he wouldn't lose a fight on account of a cut. When I told Mom I needed to start soaking my face in alum, she wasn't very supportive. "We'll talk about it when you're 21," she said. I couldn't wait that long—Jack Dempsey started when he was 14. Heck, I wanted to be champion by the time I was 20. I told her that. "You don't even shave," she said. "You're too young." When I appealed to Dad, he just said, "Do whatever your mother says." *Sheesh! He's always saying that. It's like they're one person!*

My boxing partner, John, was my hero and confidant, not just my roommate. John was one year and a day older than me—nearly Irish twins. There were six boys in our family—no girls—six of us in eight years—my parents were so blessed! They kept us paired up by age, so John and I didn't have a choice about sharing a room. There was a lot of testosterone in our house, and Mom's strategy was to work us hard to keep it tamped down, so we did all the house work—but every time she got pregnant we prayed for a girl so we could stop doing the dishes. No luck so far, but we were still hopeful.

SMASH! John had just landed a huge right hook to my jaw, making my ears ring. I could taste the salt tang of blood, and my tongue felt the tooth cuts on the inside of my cheek. Not serious—nothing a little bit of Merthiolate wouldn't cure—the instructions on the bottle read "For External Use Only," but John said as long as you didn't drink it you should be okay. I was just glad it was John on the other end of that punch and not Michael.

Michael, now…Michael was another story. Michael is my next younger brother, and he was just plain huge, even at that age. He lived in another room down the hall, which was fortunate for me, because he played rough—I mean *really* rough. He was eleven, but his shoe size was a twelve—in men's. He could palm a basketball in each hand. He didn't worry about you much until you were nearly killed or paralyzed, but it wasn't because he was really trying to be mean—he was just too big for the area around him. Unless he was mad, of course—then he was a holy terror. The problem was, he was mad a lot. We called him The Archangel. We said a prayer every day to St. Michael the Archangel at the end of Mass, and it always made me think about Michael:

> St. Michael the Archangel, defend us in battle. Be our protection against the wickedness and snares of the devil. Do thou rebuke him we humbly pray….

I swear, if anybody really needed to be rebuked, The Archangel was the one you wanted on the job. He was what my friend Bad Billie Boyd called "one rebukin' sumbitch."

I don't admit this out loud to anyone, but Michael picked on me all the time. He didn't even think it was mean—he just thought it was funny. Once he put a rock collection under my pillow because he knew I liked to dive into my bed headfirst—until then, anyway. I could hear him laughing when I yelled. When I told Mom, he claimed he didn't do it—that I must've stolen it from him and forgot I hid it under my pillow. Some of my brothers lied so much that Mom never knew who to believe. Then she just punished everybody. Assuming she was in a good mood, that just meant more work. If she got in a bad mood, though, there were more immediate consequences.

But I keep losing my focus. That fighting time was my quiet time, when I could just let my mind go and react. Sometimes I got a little too philosophical, though—like right then, John was pummeling me across the room—philosophical issues didn't slow him down—water off a duck's back—they never even crossed his mental horizon. When I got knocked into the door jamb I yelled, "Time out! Watch out for the holy water font!" John paused his assault to let me move back into the center of the room. After all, we did have rules, and one of them was to not spill the holy water.

We had holy water fonts mounted on the doorway of every room in the house except the bathroom, so we could dip our fingers in and then make the Sign of the Cross as we entered the room. It was so automatic to us that we didn't think about it much. Mom always got mad when I let my parakeet Bobo loose, because he liked to perch on the edge of the holy water font in our room and drink from it, but I couldn't tell if it improved his behavior or not. I think probably not, because sometimes I would find little bird droppings in the font.

We also had a crucifix in every bedroom, so if we felt the need to kneel down right where we were and confess what wretches we were, we didn't have any problem feeling sorry about it, since right there in front of us, we had a three-dimensional sculpture of Jesus nailed to the cross with these huge spikes, His side lanced open and all His cuts and bruises realistically painted in, and every single one of us knew for damn sure that it was all our fault.

Because my Mom was religious—I mean *real* religious. Religious as in Catholic, with a capital "C." People trying to promote Catholicism tell you that "catholic" means "universal," but my mother was not one of those namby-pamby "universal" catholics. She was *Catholic*, by God, R.C., Roman Catholic, the One True Religion started by Jesus Christ Himself and passed down in unbroken succession from Peter, the first Pope, to Paul VI. And we had better be, too, if we knew what was good for us.

Joseph Welch

Our Mom believed the only reason we were here in this world was to "earn our place in Heaven," and apparently it didn't come cheap. Her sole mission on this earth was to drag her children there by the scruffs of our necks, no matter what the cost. She thought the Blessed Mother held the most sway with Jesus, so our whole family said the entire Rosary together on our knees every single night ("Hail, Mary, full of grace…" fifty-three times—I've counted) plus a whole host of other prayers. It made for a lot of kneeling on the floor.

Also every Tuesday night she really piled it on by adding a special Novena to Our Mother of Perpetual Help. Our Mother of Perpetual Help was the same person we prayed the Rosary to: the Blessed Virgin Mary, Mother of God. But since Mary's "intercession" was so powerful, we did lots of different devotions to her, and called her all sorts of exalted names. I had a list of twenty-one different names for her. She was sort of like our lobbyist in Heaven. If one complimentary title (like "Queen of Heaven") didn't convince her to cajole her son into giving us a break, maybe the next one would. Since Mom's first name was "Mary," though, I always wondered if she had a teensy bit of a conflict of interest in all this.

Mom thought we were eager to come to prayers, the way we all bolted into the living room at prayer time, but really we were just trying to get places on the rug—the last couple of us to arrive had to kneel on the hardwood floor, which could make for a long night.

But back to our morning fisticuffs: I could tell that our fighting time was almost up, because John's last punch just sort of smushed onto my face, and my forearms were starting to hurt like someone had frogged me there all over, caused by hitting John's sharp down-pointing elbows as hard as I could while trying to rearrange his facial features by throwing uppercuts past his guard.

Dad's knuckles rapped hard on our door jamb as he leaned into the room. "6:30, boys, time to get ready for school." We dropped our hands—keeping your guard up constantly with sixteen-ounce gloves could wear a fella down—then, crossing our arms in front of us, we both clamped our gloves under our own armpits to extract our hands before tossing the gloves back under our beds.

A thin cardboard backing from a boxed white dress shirt had been thumbtacked to the inside of our bedroom door. It had big block letters outlined and colored in blue ink. "THINK before you ACT," it said. Dad didn't lecture us much, but he had a way of getting his point across, especially if he was disappointed in you. He would just shake his head. Seems like he did that a lot. He understood us, though, at least part of the time. Like one time I was arguing with him and he just looked at me in disgust and said, "You don't even know what day it is." Right away I opened my mouth like a smart aleck to tell him, but then nothing came out—I was speechless—I just stood there like an idiot with my mouth open. He was right—I didn't know what day it was. But I still can't figure out how he knew.

As I headed into the bathroom, I could see Dad standing at the sink wiping the steamy mirror so he could finish shaving. "Shower's open," he said. "Three minutes, then your brothers," as he turned over the 3-minute egg timer. He had implemented the timer rule to keep us from standing around in the shower until the hot water was depleted.

"Thanks," I said, and ducked into the shower. It didn't take long, since I used Ivory soap all over, including my hair, which was cut as short as Mom could make it. We all had buzzes.

As the hot water cascaded over me, I quickly reviewed my plan to become heavyweight champion. Clearly, I was going to have to get better—lots better. I was not even the best fighter in my family, much less the world. John was still better than I was, and I wouldn't even fight Michael.

I guess I should mention that we all grew up mad—not angry—mad. We were our own solar system in miniature, all circling around our parents, our sun and moon, and trying to keep our safe distances. We were all so different, even our orbits, but we each exerted gravitational pulls on the others.

Last Christmas I had received an inflatable Popeye punching bag with a sand base, that you could hit as hard as you wanted, and it would smack the floor and then bounce straight back up. Michael and I were on opposite sides of it, really slugging it back and forth, when all of a sudden Michael hit me right in the nose as hard as he could! Of course, he told Mom and Dad it was an accident, that he had just missed, but I didn't believe him—I think he just wanted to see what it would do to my nose.

But my brothers weren't even my biggest problem. I needed to do lots more training to become champion: lift weights and run (we boxers called it "road work") and skip rope and put in hours each day on a speed bag. And I didn't even have a speed bag. But my biggest problem was that I didn't have time to do it all, because of all the other stuff I had to do every day.

Prayers took most of an hour every evening, and that didn't even include another hour going to daily Mass during school. Plus, I always had homework and dishes and the yard and basketball practice, and in addition to our regular chores, Mom was always coming up with extra work projects.

Dad didn't think much of my prize-fighting career plans anyway. "There's always somebody tougher right around the corner," he said. Also, he thought thugs were ruining the sport. I was delivering the early morning Globe-Democrat for a friend of mine the morning after

Cassius Clay defeated Sonny Liston. It showed a photo of Cassius Clay with his mouth open so far it took up half the picture frame—he looked like a crazy man. He was yelling, "I am the greatest!" The headline read, "The Mouth Was Big—So Was The Fine." Floyd Patterson had been revered—he was a gentleman. Now we had the likes of Sonny Liston and Cassius Clay—and Cassius Clay had a really bad case of "me-itis"—he was not a very good sport.

Mom came into the hallway from the kitchen. "Come on, boys—don't be late. Do you have your rosaries?" Nothing about clean underwear—if we were in an accident Mom would much rather we had our rosaries with us than clean underwear. "Yes, ma'am," we replied in unison, as she distributed brown paper bags containing our breakfasts to the four of us who attended school.

We grabbed our bookbags and headed off to school together, which was right next door to the church three blocks away. I think Mom talked Dad into buying our house so we could walk to church whenever we wanted to, not just on Sundays, but for daily Mass, too, as well as other things, like refilling our holy water supply from the baptismal font in church (we went through a lot of holy water) or stopping by the church "just for a visit" to Jesus in the Blessed Sacrament, who gets lonely when nobody comes to talk to Him.

It was a gorgeous spring morning. We had already snuck around the corner of the house to the front yard to check for Gunnar Green, our next-door monster, who might be lying in wait for us down the hill at the alley. His house was at the east end of our back yard, fronting on Ridgeline, but since his yard ran all the way down to the alley, he used to take the alley to Hill Street, and loiter at the mouth of the alley and wait for us as we came down the hill from our front door. But he was nowhere in sight and we knew he was too huge and too lazy to hide, so it was safe to walk down Hill Street, if we hurried, and as long as we stayed on the public sidewalk. Nonetheless, we loped to the bottom of our hill, telling ourselves that we were running because the hill was so steep, but we knew we were just afraid to spend much time near any of Gunnar Green's haunts. Even when it seemed like he was not there—you never really knew.

Gunnar Green was about eighteen, and he was still in the 8th Grade. He was what my mother called a "bad boy," but I've come to realize that he was actually a felon-in-training. He was 6'2" tall and *big*. He told us he weighed 280 pounds—and he was pretty proud of it. He picked on us little kids all the time. One time while my little brother Mark was playing in our backyard, Gunnar Green shot a hunting arrow from his front porch right past Mark's ear. It missed Mark by about an inch, but it stuck in the back of our house with a loud "thunk!" We were all afraid of him because he liked to hurt us and laugh about it.

I asked Dad if I could hit him with a baseball bat and he said yes if he was hurting us. I kept our Louisville Slugger standing in a hollow tree trunk close to Gunnar Green's yard. Just in case. The tree was still alive and dripped sap on the bat, but that was a small price to pay. Sometimes I carried it with me when I had to walk past his house to the store or for any other reason, even when I knew I wasn't going to be playing baseball. I had never had to use it, but the week before, my best friend Toby had rescued me by hitting Gunnar Green in the front of his thighs as hard as he could with the baseball bat because Gunnar was chasing me to put me in a headlock, so we were in somewhat of a hurry.

Although we could make it to school in three minutes flat if we ran the entire way, we still had plenty of time, so we strolled the final two blocks along the sidewalks lined with immense trees arching over the street. Squirrels dashed along the limbs sixty feet above us, cardinals sang their distinctive spring *aria*, the smell of warming earth permeated the air, and small discs of breeze-blown elm seeds showered us as we walked. God, Mayfly was Heaven!

2.
SCHOOL DAYS

Five minutes later we were at school. "Bye," we told one another as we summited the seven wide steps at the front door of Immaculate Conception School, then streaked to our respective rooms. Michael and Mark headed up the stairs, while John and I shot down the long, polished hallway on the first floor. Since there were no nuns in sight, we ran full out, but silently. John ducked into the Seventh Grade on the right, while I went on down the hallway to the Sixth Grade on the left.

"Morning, Sister," I said, as I quickly unloaded my book bag at my desk in the back of the room, then hung it on a hook in the cloak room. Sr. Ambrose glanced up at me, then looked meaningfully at the room clock, but I knew she was bluffing—I just ignored the implied threat, acting guiltless and nonchalant, confident in my safety because I was three minutes early. Nevertheless, I breathed a sigh of relief as I settled into my desk and tucked the aromatic brown paper bag containing my breakfast under my seat.

7:30. The electric bell blared throughout the building, loud and long, rebounding off bare blackboards, walls and floors. We Sixth Graders immediately rose in unison and stood next to our desks, all thirty-three of us, the girls in white cotton blouses and pleated Black Watch plaid skirts, the boys in navy slacks and short sleeve white shirts. Hands folded prayerfully in front of us, eight fingers pointing piously toward Heaven, our thumbs positioned in a cross, we watched Sr. Ambrose. She was hard to miss, a giant standing in the front of the room in a long black habit with long black sleeves. A huge white veil surrounding her head like a full moon projected outward six inches on each side of her face from just in front of her ears. She wore an enormous stiff white semi-circular bib under her chin over which a large black crucifix was mounted on a chain.

On her cue, we intoned the Morning Offering while contemplating the large crucifix hanging in the front of the room, and then recited a single Our Father, a Hail Mary and a Glory Be. Finally, hands over our hearts and eyes on the flag, we said the Pledge of Allegiance.

"Be seated," Sr. Ambrose said. "Take out a sheet of paper." I heard a poorly-stifled group groan—pop quiz—and in *catechism*, too, our first subject each morning. "There is no need to talk," she said. "Ready?" I was frantically identifying my paper as required: name on the top line, left side; date on the top line, right side, the subject "Catechism" in the center of the next line, and finally, the initials "J.M.J." at the very top center of the page.

This last bit was entirely optional, but it was scrawled and breathed by virtually all Catholic school students before every quiz, and I always figured it couldn't hurt to ask Jesus, Mary and Joseph for a little help. Recently I had even been drawing exclamation points right after it, first just one, and then, when Sr. Ambrose said nothing, I started adding more. I was up to three before she made me quit, claiming my exclamation points changed it from a prayer to a curse. I didn't think so—I thought it was kind of funny; I also thought it could still be a prayer, just an excited one, but apparently it didn't make any difference what I thought.

Sr. Ambrose advanced to the blackboard, picked up a piece of chalk, and began writing in perfect textbook cursive:

What is my conscience?

Who can help teach me to form my conscience?

How do I know if a thought, deed, word or omission is a sin?

as we hurriedly copied down each question, craning our bodies this way and that to see the blackboard around the huge all-black back of her veil. As required, we left two lines after each question for our answers. She finally stopped after number 6.

I hurried with my answers:

A voice in my head that tells me right from wrong;

The Church;

If it is against God's law; while Sr. Ambrose patrolled the room.

"Time's up," she announced. "Hand them in." We passed all the papers to the front of each row, then across to a girl at the front right corner, who stood up and handed them to Sister.

The bell rang again. "Line up in silence," Sr. Ambrose said. She was angry about something, but we had no idea what. The girls lined up in silence along the left wall and the boys lined up against the right. SNAP! Sister Ambrose snapped her fingers like the crack of a starter's pistol and the girls moved out the door in formation. She waited until they were well down the hall, then snapped her fingers again. SNAP! The boys moved out. "No running," she said.

We walked over to Mass in the Church next door, where we sat by class. The girls sat at the front of each class and the boys were ensconced behind them, which afforded the boys endless opportunities for gazing and daydreaming. Behind each class of boys was a full pew, empty except for a single nun.

Summer of '63

When I wasn't buried in my St. Joseph's Daily Missal during Mass, I mainly watched Mary Ann Ventura. She was a pretty girl in my class with light blue eyes and soft-looking brown hair. She was nice to everybody, and she made me want to be really nice to her.

The priest rang a brass bell mounted on a side doorway at the front of the church, a single authoritative gong, as he and two altar boys entered the Sanctuary, which is what altar boys called the front area of the church around the altar, separated from the congregation by the communion rail. The trio stopped at the bottom of the marble stairs leading up to the altar and knelt on thin red leather cushions.

Even from the back of church, I could see the priest's bald head surrounded by a ring of well-oiled and ridiculously standing dark curls. It was Fr. Reiser, whom I hated with a passion. I couldn't even say why I hated him so much. I think the main reason was that he made it so obvious that he was so much better than everybody else. I could have dealt with that, except he also thought he was better than me, which was really too much—it seemed intentional, like a direct slap in my face.

I think he may have been single-handedly responsible for what has since been called my Oppositional Defiant Disorder—which are just fancy words for hating his guts. If I had never known Fr. Reiser, I think I could have spent my entire life cheerfully compliant with the voice of authority. He sure ruined that for me—now I have a condition, and he gave it to me.

The Rev. Phillip John Reiser was actually a monsignor, which is a priest with some extra gold stars or something, and he wanted everyone to know it, but since nobody liked him or his superiority performance, we all just acted like we forgot and called him Fr. Reiser. That's not all we called him, either. His nickname at school was "P.J."—that stood for "Pompous Jerk."

We had been taught to respect the "holy priests" because they were "God's representatives on earth," and mostly I did. I respected almost all of them, and could even give the ones I wasn't crazy about the benefit of the doubt, but not this one—not P.J. He acted so far different from anything even remotely like Jesus, it was impossible for me to treat him as God's representative on earth. Jesus wasn't proud or pompous or always mad and didn't act like he was better than everyone else and wanting to rub your nose in it every chance he got. Anyway, not the Jesus I had heard about.

I detested P.J. We couldn't let my mother hear us call him P.J., though. She thought he was great; "a really spiritual man," she called him. The two of them were awfully tight. I noticed that all of the people who thought he was great were women. Maybe they were used to men who thought they were better than them. Maybe they even respected that—I don't know. Most of the men and all of us boys despised him.

"Oh, God, it's P.J.," I whispered to Richard Washington, kneeling next to me. He didn't react, but I could tell he wasn't comfortable calling the pastor names. Richard was what our grandparents called "a colored boy." They didn't mean anything insulting by it—they called my other friend, Toby Piper, "that red-haired boy"—but to the rest of us, Richard was just Richard. We liked him a lot. We liked him not in spite of his brown skin and not exactly because of it either, but it sure didn't hurt. He was like some exotic creature to the rest of us. We also liked him because he was honest and fair and smart as a whip, and he was nice—nicer than I was, for sure. I was best friends with Richard and also with "that red-haired boy," Toby.

Richard's father had died in the Korean War. His mother was a pleasant woman who worked in the office of our family doctor, Dr. Herbstreit.

"*Introibo ad altari Dei,*" Fr. Reiser intoned the Latin Entrance Rite. ("I will go to the altar of God.")

"*Ad Deum qui laetificat juventutem meam,*" we answered in unison. ("To God the joy of my youth.")

Until last year only the altar boys said the Latin responses. After the Second Vatican Council, however, the entire congregation was allowed to join in, which made it kind of fun even when you weren't serving Mass. The altar boys still had to be proficient, however, because there were very few people at the 6:30 a.m. early Mass, and some of them were almost too old to hear or be heard, so the altar boys still had to be able to shoulder the laboring oar with the Latin responses.

Also, after Vatican II, the Epistles and Gospels were read in English instead of Latin, so the people could actually understand them for the first time, which led to some interesting discoveries by the faithful. For instance, the story of Susannah, the wife of Joachim, telling her maids, "Bring me oil and washing balls, and shut the doors of the orchard, that I may wash me." Who would have ever thought that long old Latin Epistle contained the delightful story of a beautiful young woman taking her clothes off in her garden while two perverted old judges hid in the bushes and watched her? And then they tried to make her "lie with them," and it didn't really say, but I don't think they were talking about taking a nap together either. No wonder they kept it in Latin for so long.

I loved this story so much. It became one of the foundations of my early scriptural formation. I read it several times each day during Mass—I knew most of it by heart. If I dropped my St. Joseph Daily Missal it opened automatically to the Epistle on Saturday of the 3rd Week in Lent. Plus, there was a young boy who was the hero of the story, and that gave me hope. If Susannah weren't already married to

Joachim, I bet she would've married Daniel after he saved her from the perverted old judges.

Every day I wished I had a chance to save Mary Ann Ventura, or even to save anyone, as long as Mary Ann could see me do it. Like if some black-leather-clad assassin came into the back of the church and I was the only one who saw him and he was going to shoot the priest with a big bow and a razor-tipped hunting arrow because one of them gave him a too-hard penance in Confession but he wasn't sure which one did it so he was just going to kill whichever one he found first, and I waited until I saw him aim the arrow and then just as he let go of it I jumped up and threw my arm up in the air and the arrow went right into my arm instead or maybe even part way out the other side but nobody else was hurt and everyone was saved and Mary Ann looked at me with her mouth open in wonder of how brave I was and how fast, too, and she could see I was hurt pretty bad and then I could see a tear falling down her cheek as they took me to the hospital. I thought about that scenario a lot, and even though I kept my eyes peeled for an opportunity, no black-leather-clad assassin ever showed up in the back of our church wanting revenge on the priests, at least not while I was there.

Actually, I had no great desire to save Fr. Reiser from anything. He thought he was so important, and we were so beneath him, even when we were helping him out by serving Mass—his idea, not mine. His and Mom's, that is. You'd think he would have been grateful, but he wasn't. Like during Mass when he washed his hands just before the Offertory, the server held a water pitcher and poured the water over the priest's hands into a bowl, and every time he did it, all I could think about was how P.J. looked like Pontius Pilate, washing his hands in front of the people because he didn't have the guts to set an obviously good man free, so he was going to have him crucified to curry political favor.

And Fr. Reiser always gave this pompous snap of his wrists when he was finished, instead of just nodding in gratitude for our washing his hands, like the water we were pouring was too filthy for him to be associated with any longer, and like we were his slaves, and he didn't want to be associated with us either. I had a hard time putting up with this day after day. So once when I was serving Mass and was just seething, watching him, and had enough of his arrogance to last me a lifetime, I pretended not to know what his stupid wrist snap meant and just kept on pouring the water over his hands. And he really went ape shit. "Stop!" he yelled, totally mad. I just looked at him, all shocked and open-mouthed, doing my best wide-eyed-innocence act.

Fr. Reiser thought he was entitled to order everyone around, and when he said "Jump" he expected all of us to just genuflect and ask "How high, Most Reverend Monsignor?" but just looking at his face got my back up. Everyone else was afraid of his temper, but I wasn't—his temper was nowhere near the top of my chart—I lived in the same house as The Archangel. So that sissy pompous jerk with the bullshit oily curls didn't scare me at all—he just made me mad. In fact, just watching him made me mad.

So, if I were going to save a priest at the altar, I would prefer that it would be a good one, someone worth my time, because I wouldn't go out of my way to save that pompous jerk from anything—he was not a "spiritual man" to me—he was a fraud. Although I'm usually a "live-and-let-live" person, even with chronic assholes, P.J. merited special treatment because he inflicted his assholism directly on me. If it weren't for the fact that I would get in big trouble, I would probably clap if the assassin actually hit him.

"*Orate, fratres*...," P.J. intoned. ("Pray, brothers....")

"*Suscipiat Dominus sacrificium de manibus tui....*" ("May the Lord receive the sacrifice from your hands....") we responded. The Offertory prayers continued, leading up to the Consecration and then Holy Communion.

After every Mass, Fr. Reiser knelt at the foot of the altar and said in a real pompous fake-charitable tone, "Let us pray for the conversion of Russia." We had been doing this for as long as I could remember and it didn't seem like it was working, but we were all game anyway—not because it was P.J.'s suggestion, but if we could help the Russians, we would keep praying for them. After three Hail Marys, he stood, then he and the servers all genuflected one last time and left by the same side door of the sanctuary.

The rest of us filed out to our classrooms, the youngest first, girls then boys, under the eagle eyes of the nuns. The only sound was that of shuffling footsteps.

Breakfast time was next—my favorite part of the school day. Crates of four-ounce milk cartons had appeared in our classrooms while we were at Mass, courtesy of a local dairy. We ordered today's milk yesterday: 32 chocolate and 1 white—3 cents each. Also visible on Sr. Ambrose's desk were fragrant stacked white boxes from the bakery two doors down the street, containing glazed twists. Fifteen cents each, also ordered yesterday. Thirty-two of them—one for every kid in the room except me.

I was the only one in the class who brought his own breakfast. Mom didn't think a glazed twist was a nutritious meal. So, every morning she fried one large egg in bacon grease for each of us, sandwiched it between two slices of white bread, cut it into halves, wrapped it in aluminum foil, and placed it in a brown paper bag, together with a peeled orange and a paper napkin. For dairy, we also got chocolate milk at school every day.

We always had to wait until after Mass to eat breakfast, because we couldn't receive Holy Communion at Mass unless we had fasted from at least midnight the night before. And all of us were expected to receive Communion at every Mass, unless we had not fasted or unless we had committed a Mortal Sin, which of course no one would want to admit in public—and not going to Communion would be a dead giveaway. We fasted from everything—even chewing gum—because the flavoring on a stick of gum was enough to "break your fast." The only exception was water. Also eating snow was okay, since it was just water. I even had to ask P.J. in Confession once, but he said it was okay. But not snow cones—eating a snow cone would break your fast, since it had flavoring in it. So, we couldn't have snow cones before Mass, which seemed like an awful hardship at the time, but now when I reflect on it, I realize we couldn't have bought a snow cone before Mass anywhere in Mayfly.

Finally, I was able to focus on the mouthwatering aroma of my sandwich. As I opened the foil carefully, I found the bread soggy and delicious with bacon grease, just as I hoped. I was so glad my Mom was serious about nutrition!

3.
PAGAN BABIES

Sr. Ambrose read at her desk as we finished our breakfasts. We were allowed to leave our desks to throw our napkins and milk cartons in the trash can.

"Alright, students," she said, "does anyone have money for the Pagan Babies?" A large colored poster at the front of the room showed a group of dark children with dusty faces and arms and torn clothing, holding bowls and looking pleadingly into the camera with puppy eyes. I just wanted to help those children, especially when Sister told us that not only did they need food, but they were so abysmally ignorant that they didn't even know about God. If we gave twenty dollars, we could "buy" a Pagan Baby, and then they would be raised properly and learn all about God and Heaven and Hell and get baptized Catholic, and get some catechism classes, for God's sake, so they could get to Heaven. Although, frankly, it was hard to imagine anybody so ignorant that they didn't know about God. What did they think holy water fonts were for—a quick sip as you entered the room? (Not with Bobo around, you wouldn't, and by the looks of things, those Pagan Babies probably had all kinda birds flying in and out of their houses.)

So, when Sister announced that the class would have a race, girls against boys, to see who could buy the most Pagan Babies, I was more than ready to pony up. I had $32.27 in my NASA money bank at home when the race started. Every time we boys put twenty dollars together, we got to buy a Pagan Baby, which also meant we got to name it, and we boys were totally fired up for that. So far, we boys had bought three Pagan Babies and had named them Bart Starr and Dick Butkus and Deacon Jones. The girls always named theirs after saints: Mary and Theresa and Ann, which seemed like such a waste—they should've named them after somebody really famous. The girls were getting awfully close to another baby, and the boys were still pretty tapped out on the last one—we only had $2.12 in the boys' kitty as of the day before—and I was determined not to let the girls beat us, so I had brought in $17.88, the remaining contents of my NASA bank.

I went to sleep that night musing about what Mary Ann would think when I handed in that much money, but when I looked at her after plunking down the deciding contribution, I was disappointed to see that she wasn't paying attention. Anyhow, we decided to name him Johnny Unitas. And the girls still needed almost three more dollars, so there would be no girl Pagan Babies getting a ticket to Heaven that day—they would just have to wait and hope. All night long I had been feeling mighty virtuous about myself, but after Mary Ann missed the whole thing, I felt sorta like I had wasted my money.

Reading was next, then English. Getting a little dozy, my eyes on the clock, I was jerked out of my lethargy by Sr. Ambrose advancing to the blackboard and writing a sentence across the top: "The mischievous young puppy barked noisily in the yard."

Oh, no! I hated diagramming sentences. I looked across two rows at Richard Washington, seeking commiseration, and found him staring at me fixedly, elbows on his desk, hands folded in front of his face, his chin resting on his right index finger. I raised my eyebrows in surprise, then adopted the same posture, acknowledging his sign for a secret meeting, and waited. I watched him raise three fingers from his left hand and lay them casually on his left jaw. Our signal for the Three Musketeers—he wanted Toby, too.

Sr. Ambrose turned back to the class and began calling us up to the blackboard, one at a time, to diagram the sentence. She always made the boys look stupid. Usually that wasn't very difficult to do, especially since she never played fair. Her routine was boringly predictable—first, she called on one of the dimmest boys in the class, then when he made a mistake, she called on one of the sharp girls.

"John Brooks," she announced. The room was deathly quiet. We all knew what was going to happen, and so did John Brooks. We had seen this show before. He might have had more hope if he were being carted off to the guillotine with his head shaved and his hands tied behind him.

As he shuffled to the board, I looked up the next aisle at Toby. He was easy to spot—his red hair floated a full twelve inches above anyone else in the room, and he was still sitting down. His head swayed on his long skinny neck as I eyeballed him. Obviously, I was not the only one having trouble staying awake. He had to be desperately tired to be losing it with Sr. Ambrose in the room—she loved to get hold of a boy who had been asleep in her class. Right then, however, she was mercilessly abusing John Brooks. Her eyes were fixed in pre-strike mode, a cobra who had just spotted a mouse trapped in a corner.

I rested my left ankle on my right knee under my desk. Quietly picking up my Bic pen, I popped off the tiny blue button from the top and then pulled out the brass tip, extracting it and the filler, leaving only the hollow plastic tube. I slid the blue button into my shirt pocket and the more incriminating naked filter into the ankle of my left sock. Quietly tearing off a small piece of scrap paper, I rolled it tight and then worked it between my front teeth, compressing it on each side until it was tight and tiny, hard as a BB, then loaded it into the hollow tube.

Sitting on the side of her desk and facing the board, Sr. Ambrose was circling her prey.

"Begin at the beginning. What is 'the'?" she asked.

"Pardon me, Sister," said the hapless John. "What is what?"

"'The'; what is 'the,' the article 'the'?" she asked, warming to her task.

He looked at her helplessly while she stared back at him, seething at his cluelessness, the anger plainly visible in her eyes. He was hypnotized, staring into the eyes of the cobra.

"Well?" she asked.

Finally, he said, "I don't know, Sister."

"*Sit* down," she hissed. Her tone left no doubt as to his inadequacy, which went far beyond his lack of command of the parts of speech. Completely defeated, he was no longer interesting to her.

"*Mis*-ter. Wickens." She had obviously not yet slaked her thirst for humiliating boys.

Bill Wickens jumped up and hurried to the board.

"What is 'the,' Mister Wickens?" she asked again.

"An article, Sister," he replied immediately, desperate to please.

"Correct, an article. 'The' is *always* an article. What is 'always,' Mr. Wickens?"

"An adjective, Sister."

"An adjective," she said, a look of kindly-smiling mock agreement on her face. "Interesting. And what do adjectives modify, Mr. Wickens?"

"Nouns."

"Nouns, *what?*"

"Nouns, Sister," he added, abashed.

"Yes, nouns," she said, partially mollified. "Give me an example of a noun, Mr. Wickens."

"What about 'desk,' Sister"?

"Yes, 'desk' is a noun. So then," she said, a cat waiting to pounce, "Do you have an 'always' desk? Does *anyone* have an 'always' desk? *Can* anyone have an 'always' desk?"

The class giggled. *Pffft*. My projectile hit Toby in the side of his long neck, making him snap awake, freezing as he caught Sr. Ambrose's dagger eyes sweeping the room, alerted no doubt by Toby's sudden movement, cutting off the class mid-giggle. He looked startled. He ought to.

Sr. Ambrose turned back to her prey of the moment. "Is it an 'always' desk, Mr. Wickens?" she asked again.

"No, sister."

"*Sit* down." A pause, as she debated strategy. Prolong this delicious episode or go for the *coup de grace*?

"Miss Camp," she called, having reached her decision, her voice suddenly musical. The boys breathed a sigh of relief. Their public humiliation was over for the moment, except of course for being completely shown up by a girl—again. But there were certain offsetting benefits.

"Yes, Sister," Catherine Camp said, hurrying to the board. I loved it when she called on Catherine. She was an excellent student, but her primary reputation had nothing to do with scholarship. Catherine was universally acclaimed as the most developed girl in our class. She was very bouncy. Every person in the class, Sr. Ambrose included, watched Catherine's progress toward the blackboard. I knew for a fact that I was not the only one watching the outline of her bra under her white cotton blouse and wishing I had x-ray vision.

"What part of speech is 'always,' Miss Camp?" Sr. Ambrose asked, in a "let's-show-these-morons" tone of voice.

"An adverb, Sister?" Catherine asked, a question in her voice.

"Are you asking me?" Sr. Ambrose inquired, face now bright, with just a whisper of camaraderie in her voice. The class giggled—everyone liked Catherine.

"No, Sister; an adverb."

"'Always' is an adverb?" Sr. Ambrose asked. "Is 'always' *always* an adverb?"

This was too much—the entire class laughed at Sr. Ambrose's cleverness as she allowed the sudden merriment to bubble up and fill the room with good humor—at least that of the girls. The boys were just hoping she'd leave them alone.

"Yes, Sister."

Toby looked around at me. I gave him the secret meeting sign while looking nonchalantly toward Catherine at the board, then back at Toby. I saw recognition dawn, then he returned the sign, swiveling so that I couldn't help but see his chin perched on his right index finger. I lightly scratched my left jaw with three fingers. He immediately looked over at Richard and saw him also showing Three Musketeers, while gazing trancelike at Sr. Ambrose. Toby's head swiveled back to the blackboard, then nodded several times in exaggerated super slow motion, like he had just internalized the fact that "always" was always an adverb. Anyone watching would have thought that was one of the watershed parts-of-speech-enlightenment moments of his young life.

"Correct, Miss Camp," Sr. Ambrose announced. "Please complete the diagram."

The tap and squeal of chalk filled the room. The three of us nodded slowly as though agreeing with Catherine's diagramming decisions, then turned our full attention to the lure of her ripening twelve-year-old charms as she drew, then energetically erased, neatened and finally completed the sentence diagram. She was a young gymnast at the blackboard—it was an exercise in beautifully animated artistic efficiency, and Catherine was completely oblivious to the visual perfection of her performance art. Stunning.

As Catherine returned to her desk, the ten o'clock bell blared throughout the building. *Recess!*

"Put your books away and line up quietly," Sister directed. We grabbed the balls and lined up quickly. I carried the basketball. We were on our best behavior because we knew Sr. Ambrose would delay taking us to the playground if anyone talked.

Surveying us imperiously, she finally said, "Proceed. No running." We were a hot tea kettle, poised one degree south of boiling, waiting to erupt in screaming steam, which we did as soon as we passed the playground gateposts.

Most of the girls ran to either the four square or the volleyball court where the Seventh Grade girls were already playing, or divided up into kickball teams.

"Wanna play kickball today?" Toby asked.

"Nah, I wanna work on my moves," I replied. *If I'm not gonna become the Heavyweight Champion of the World, I think I'll be the best basketball player in Mayfly and then play in the NBA.*

We both looked over at Richard, but he was busy choosing a kickball team. Another friend of ours, Cecil Ritter—everybody called him "Critter"—was choosing the other team, pointing at kids who then lined up behind him.

"Looks like Richard and Critter are captains today," Toby said. "Wonder what time we have our meeting."

Without another word, Toby and I headed to the basketball court, dribbling and passing the ball to each other as we went.

Toby's family lived at the River's Rest Motel, half a block past the school on Broadway. His parents owned the motel, and they all worked there. Toby's dad and mom were always on call. His dad maintained the property and his mom worked the desk, paid the bills and kept the books. Toby's older brother, Tom, worked as the janitor. They had one employee, a house maid named Carly Stolte. She was very thin, but incredibly strong. Eighteen years old, she looked about thirteen, with small high breasts, a glossy dark pageboy and long bangs partially shielding her big brown eyes. Sometimes when the motel was crowded, Tom and Toby also had to help her clean the rooms.

Toby would probably prefer to play kickball at recess, a sport I regarded as beneath me because it didn't require any real skill, but he always came over to the basketball court because he knew I needed someone to pass me the ball and rebound my shots. Toby was a somewhat goofus-looking guy—he looked almost exactly like his older brother, a carrot-topped bean pole. I played point guard and he played post man, well, sort of—at least he was tall and could catch the ball.

I passed him the ball, and he sent it right back. I popped the net. He rebounded and tossed the ball to me out front. I dribbled a few times, then fired the ball to him at the top of the lane. He faked a pass to an imaginary teammate while I cut for the basket, then hit me for a layup. We did it again, but this time I broke the other way. Again, but this time he hit me with a bounce pass and I drove the lane. Again, but I stopped abruptly and hit a short jumper. Again, but I broke out to the corner and drained a long shot. I just loved shooting from the corner—that was my spot—I owned it. I was deadly from there. At that moment, I was "in the zone" there on the playground with Toby, a budding legend, at least in my own mind.

There was a simple reason I did all the shooting—I was the best shot in our class. I could *really* shoot. We both understood that. He helped as much as he could by yelling, "Hit it!" and "Pop it!" and "Take it!" and "Drill it!" and "Drain it!" and "Boom!" while I was shooting. Sometimes he ran up to me pretending to be a defender and tried to block my shot. I always tried to burn him when he played defense on me—even though he was trying to help me, I still took it as a personal affront—the very idea!

Pop! Perfect from the corner again. I looked over to the volleyball court to see if Mary Ann saw that one. Apparently not, but once I located her, I watched for a few seconds while I caught my breath. She looked so beautiful, particularly when her pleated skirt jumped around as she ran after the ball. Pretty—and so sleek!

"You wanna play or what?" Toby asked, pulling my attention back to our court and passing me the ball.

"Wonder what Richard wants," I said, as if I had been looking over there because of Richard and not because of Mary Ann.

"Yeah, me too—bet we find out soon, though," Toby said.

"There's a pretty good-looking girl who checked into the motel last night," Toby told me, "in town for her aunt's funeral. Room 111." I look at him, interested. You would think people just go to a motel when they are traveling overnight and need a place to sleep, but a lot goes on there besides sleep.

Toby and Tom were always telling stories about things people did at the motel. Their mom smoked, and Toby and Tom were always stealing her cigarettes. They smoked them down in the basement next to a round opening where a stovepipe used to hook into an old chimney. There was an aluminum foil pie plate covering the old opening, and it lifted off easily. They just stood next to it and all the smoke was drawn up into the chimney like there was a fan blowing it up and out above the roof.

The basement of the River's Rest Motel was long and narrow. It had a low ceiling with an aluminum cold air return running its length and passing right next to the old chimney. The cold air return worked like the simple homemade telephones you make by stretching a string between two tin cans—only better. When the furnace wasn't running, you could hear sounds from all the rooms coming through the cold air return. The best way was to listen with a glass jar pressed against it and your ear glued to the bottom of the jar. Sometimes the boys invited me over to listen with them. Toby and Tom kept three glass jars on top of the cold air return.

Toby's big brother, Tom, was 17, five years older than Toby, but the two looked like identical twins. Tom was still as thin as Toby. He looked like the 98-pound weakling on the back of the comic books, the guy the beach bully kicks sand at, before he turns into a real he-man using the Charles Atlas weight-lifting program. But Tom was a great guy. He had his driver's license and a black '57 Chevrolet convertible Bel Air Coupe with silver wings in the back. It was a real beauty. Tom was a funny kind of guy. You'd think he'd have a lot of girlfriends, or at least one nice one, but they didn't like him very much, and he didn't seem to care.

Except for Carly, the house maid—"Crazy Carly," he called her—she had it for Tom bad—I mean real bad. Tom told Toby and me that she was really a nymphomaniac, that she cornered him in a room and locked the door and took her clothes off, and just threw him on the bed and attacked him, and she was really wild and nasty and did everything to him, and she was also beautiful, even more beautiful without her clothes on, and her breasts were bigger than Tom had ever noticed before, but Tom didn't want to do it anymore because she was just too nasty, and that made her really mad at him. She was a big problem for Tom—she acted mean to him, and kept calling him names and bumping into him, but she was also always trying to catch him alone in a room. He couldn't tell his parents about it because then they'd know what he had done, and they might make him marry her.

Tom was a natural spy—he spent a lot of energy finding out what people were up to, and Toby wasn't far behind—he was always on the lookout for a pretty girl checking in—even older women out of high school. Usually, he told me about it and I came over and shared one of his Mom's cigarettes with him in the basement. Most of the time we just heard stupid stuff, but occasionally we heard something more interesting, mostly giggling and once some kinda stupid moaning that didn't even sound real. Tom was never very interested, though. He always said he had work to do, then he'd vanish upstairs and sort laundry in the linen closet, if he could get in without Crazy Carly seeing him. He oiled the hinges, so he could come and go without making any noise.

The linen closet had once been a closet inside the Bridal Suite—Room 111, the largest and nicest room in the Motel—"Fun, fun, fun in 111," Toby used to say. But years ago, they had installed a wardrobe in the Bridal Suite and converted the closet to a hallway linen closet, sealing off the old closet doorway into the room and building a new closet door opening into the hallway. They took out the old transom window between the linen closet and Room 111 but left the framework in place to provide ventilation to the linen closet. Inside Room 111, the old transom opening had been covered up with a register grate, so it looked normal.

The brothers used the linen closet as a handy place to stash stuff they didn't want their parents to find, like alcohol and cigarettes and copies of magazines which people left behind in the guest rooms. Toby kept his stash under the old winter blankets on the bottom shelf. Of course, when storing Playboys, he had to take the chance of going to Hell for all eternity, but he said he was playing the percentages and he should be okay because he probably wouldn't die for a long time. It didn't seem to bother him as much as it did me—the risk was just too high.

They also snuck stuff out of the linen closet and took them half a block up the alley to the church where they could enjoy them at their leisure without anybody seeing them. The Church was unlocked all day and all night so people could come inside whenever they felt like it and "make a visit" to Jesus in the Blessed Sacrament.

Usually there was no one in the choir loft during the day, except maybe Ray Lee Po. Ray Lee Po was a strange man who walked around Mayfly by himself. He had no family anyone knew about, and no one knew where he lived, and no one bothered him. He was about 6'4" tall with real long hairy arms and long legs—rangy and strong. He couldn't speak, but he could grunt. He just loped around town in dirty bib overalls and a dingy white T-shirt and went wherever he wanted to. People gave him food. His mouth always hung open and his eyes always looked vacant and he always needed a shave. He looked just like a painting of a cave man. He didn't like people and didn't want you to speak to him or even look at him, but he never hurt anybody as far as anyone knew. He knew all the quiet and comfortable places to hang out, though, and a lot of times he sat up in the choir loft in the dark at our Church. He might have even slept there. I know for a fact that he used the restroom in the back of church. Tom was always trying to befriend Ray Lee Po, but you could tell that Ray Lee didn't like it. Tom tried to treat him like a normal person, but he wasn't a bit like a normal person. He always gave me the heebie-jeebies.

Tom did a lot of volunteer chores around the church, because P.J. was always calling him and asking if he could come up and move church furniture or climb up a ladder to change light bulbs in the chandeliers, basically whenever he "needed a young man." The church had a custodian, but he was old and frail and P.J. wouldn't let him climb ladders or move heavy things. Once P.J. asked Tom to shoot a bat that had gotten into the church, which Tom was happy to do—he hated bats. Once he found one while working on the motel sign and it scared him so bad that he fell off his stepladder.

Tom even had a key made to the bell tower. It opened a door at the east end of the vestibule next to the restroom, behind which was the stairway to the tower. There was another door into the tower stairwell from up in the choir loft, behind which were three additional flights of wooden stairs, ending in a trap door into the bell tower, which was never locked. Sometimes Tom went up there just to be by himself and sit in the big open-air windows with his legs hanging down over the edge, and sometimes he smoked and drank while he watched traffic going by below him, or just looked at the Playboy collection he kept up there in a plastic bag. He loved being up there by himself.

4.
SR. BERNARD

10:20 a.m. Recess was over. The bell reverberated off the walls of the playground, as well as every building within a three-block radius. It was safe to assume that none of the neighbors worked nights, because if they did, they would have to live in another neighborhood. We captured the balls, lined up quickly and headed back inside. Richard hustled over and we made room for him in the line between us. He looked serious.

"Captain's," he whispered loud enough for Toby and me to hear. "Right after school." We both nodded. The Captain's Place was a large cave in the base of Castle Bluff, a sheer bluff that rose above River Road immediately south of downtown Mayfly. We named the cave after Captain Kidd, since it was such a perfect pirate hangout. It was super-close to town, which made it handy for meetings, but unfortunately we were not the only ones who knew about it. It was also very dark, and parts of it were damp, and all of it was spooky. Toby especially disliked it, because he was sure there were bats in it, but you couldn't see well enough to know where they were. He would never touch the walls, because he was afraid of reaching out and putting his hand on a bat. Also, when you first went in, you never knew who or what might have gotten there before you, and there were branches and tunnels that we had never fully explored that ran off in several directions back into Castle Bluff. On the top of the bluff two hundred feet above River

Road was Fr. Reiser's Rectory. He had lived there by himself ever since a parishioner gave the property to the church.

We reentered our classroom to find a nun sitting motionless at the teacher's desk in the front of the room. Her huge veil projected on both sides of her head, preventing us from identifying her until we were well on our way to our desks. *Oh, God—it's Sr. Bernard!* Sr. Bernard was really old—she was really old when our parents had her for class and she still looked exactly the same. She had to be in her eighties at least. She had wire-rim glasses and a prominent mole on the left side of her chin. She was also very strong and extremely fast and had a brain like a computer. Her face was a permanent bright red. She was mad all the time, not just angry—explosively mad.

Unlike Sr. Ambrose, Sr. Bernard didn't seem to enjoy hurting children—in fact, she didn't seem to enjoy anything—but that didn't deter her from dishing it out—she apparently considered it her duty. Nor did it deter our chubbiest classmate, Little Crickett Quinn, from getting in trouble because he couldn't keep his big mouth shut. Little Crickett was average in just about everything, except one—he was so pathetically desperate for notice that he was willing to be savagely beaten every school day in exchange for some one-on-one attention from Sr. Bernard. And he always made a big production of it—he loved it!

"Sit down," she barked. "First boy to the board," pointing to the blackboard on the right wall of the room. "First girl," pointing to the blackboard on the front wall. She didn't know our names and didn't care. Obviously, we wouldn't be getting grades on our performances at the board.

"396 times 27." The first set of victims hurriedly scribbled the problem onto the boards. "Answer!"

"11,484," announced "First Boy" David Runner after a quick and chalky calculation, the accuracy of which was doomed by his copying the problem so fast that his "27" looked like a "29." If he had been listening to the class instead of working so frantically, he would have immediately realized his error by the little gasp which escaped from the sympathetic mouth of Gail Hayden, who liked David in a special way, but David missed that cue, as oblivious of Gail's fondness as he was of his transcription error.

"Wrong! Sit down!"

"10,692," announced "First Girl" Joan Battista."

"Correct," said Sr. Bernard, trilling her "Rs," "stay there!"

"You win and you have to stay for another?" Little Crickett expostulated from his desk in the front row. "Geez, I'd rather lose," then ducked his head and covered up as, predictably, his outburst launched Sr. Bernard from behind her desk. She was on him in a flash, wailing away on his head and face with both hands while Crickett held his arms up in defense.

"You heinie, you jack, you ike, you brass tack," she yelled, swinging away for a baker's dozen blows, until she was too winded to continue. Although all of us had heard this litany on many occasions, none of us knew what any of the terms meant. As she regained her seat at the desk, she said, "No more wisecracks out of you today, Mr. Quinn."

"Cracks?" he said. He couldn't leave it alone. "Speaking of cracks, I need a new butt—mine's cracked." We had all heard this one before. Many times. From him. Sr. Bernard, however, did not seem to be as bored with it as we were, because it served to precipitate Round Two—more of the same, but this time it didn't last as long. She was getting worn out beating him. The rest of us were so used to this scenario that we had ceased to be appalled. We all fervently wished Little Crickett would just shut up.

"Take out a sheet of paper," she said. *Oh, God, now he's done it.* We hurriedly extracted a sheet of looseleaf from our binders and supplied our personal information.

"Ready?" she said. "396 times 25. Start. You have ten seconds." Then, two breaths later: "Time! No more writing. Turn them in."

"Mr. Craventz," she said, pointing to a blonde kid with glasses sitting in front of the row nearest the window, "open the windows." Arwain Craventz was really smart, but he had the most unusual name in the class—probably some sort of European extraction—maybe distantly related to The Green Knight, but, seriously, who ever heard of St. Arwain?

"Yes, Sister," Arwain replied. He retrieved the long oak pole used to unlock the windows and dutifully began to open the row of windows along the left side of the room.

"Wrong... wrong... wrong...." she said, sifting through the papers and throwing them on the floor. "One person got it right—one! Jenny Jones," she said to a sweet blonde girl with a cherubic face, "tell these lazy boobs how you did it."

"Well, Sister," Jenny said, "I used a shortcut. I know that four 25s equal one hundred, so I just divided 396 by 4 to find out how many hundreds and got 99 hundreds."

"Correct," Sr. Bernard said, with a long trill. "Did any of the rest of you think of that? No, of course not, because you didn't *think*," she said, tapping her desk loudly with her extended pointer finger. "You lazy Americans are going to learn to think if it kills you. All the rest of you are going to do it the long way." Advancing to the board, she writes: "Homework: Start with 9900 and subtract 396 as many times as it takes until you get to zero. No remainders," then returned to her desk.

Arwain, finished with his window duties, replaced the window pole in the front corner of the classroom, and started back to his desk. He paused, however, at the side of Sr. Bernard's desk, hidden from her eyes by her enormous veil. Then, to the wide-eyed horror of the rest of the class, he mimed tommy-gunning her up and down until he was satisfied, while Sr. Bernard continued, "And I'll be checking your work. Due tomorrow."

Content with the thoroughness of his completed effort, Arwain returned nonchalantly to his seat as Sr. Bernard reached into her desk and came out with a thick stack of lunch tickets. Removing the rubber band, she flung the entire stack into the center of the room, yelling "Pass them out!" as they fluttered onto heads, shoulders, desktops and floor, and we scrambled to retrieve them. Reading the names on each, the entire class was up and in motion, attempting to deliver each to its proper owner before lunch, still twenty minutes away. "Silence!" yelled Sr. Bernard.

Hearing the shriek of Sr. Bernard's chair legs scraping on the floor, we looked up in alarm. Sr. Bernard, however, darted unexpectedly to the left side of the front blackboard, where she seized a wooden and wire contraption which held five long pieces of chalk in evenly spaced parallel lines. She had apparently been overcome by an immediate need to indoctrinate our heathen group into the fine arts. *Oh, no! Music class.*

Starting high on the blackboard, she dragged the contraption from left to right, creating a long musical staff transiting the front of the room. Deftly, she drew a perfect treble cleft by hand, after which she notated the proper time (2/4). Then, while holding an open book in her left hand, she began filling in the chalked staff with quarter notes, eighth notes, dotted quarters, half notes and a pair of rests. She continued down the board, drawing three similar staffs below the first one and populating them with notes. She was done with the entire affair in two minutes.

Having finished the musical notations, she began chalking the lyrics below the four staffs, completing the project with a chorus at the bottom of the board:

> *Spring once said to the nightingale*
> *I mean to give you birds a ball*
> *Pray then tell the birdies all*
> *The old and young, the great and small*
> *Tra La La La La, Tra La La La La*
> *TRA La La La La, Tra La La*
> *[REPEAT CHORUS]*

She then turned to face the class with a frown, as if daring us not to participate in the upcoming joyous ode.

"Alright, all together," she said. Standing beside the blackboard with the oak pointer in her left hand, she suddenly threw both arms wide in an operatic gesture intended to assure a uniform start, simultaneously cracking the pointer against the blackboard and blasting out the opening lyrics with an aggressive trill of the "R" in "Spring." Aghast at the horror of this musical spectacle, we tried to follow, hesitating on the unfamiliar tune, as Sr. Bernard's apoplexy increased visibly.

Mercifully, the bell blared for lunchtime.

5.
RIVER PIRATES

John, Michael, Mark and I ran all the way home for lunch. We continued running, even up our incredibly steep hill. Mayfly is extremely hilly—a lot like Rome, only smaller. And not as old. And not Italian—but we do have a pizza place on Market Street. Three minutes total, according to my trusty stainless steel Timex wristwatch with Twist-O-Flex band, a gift from Santa. We gulped lunch and blasted out the door again, downhill this time. We didn't want to miss a minute of recess. We knew Gunnar Green was at his school—wherever that was—probably Reform School, so we didn't even hesitate. We arrived sweaty and out of breath two minutes forty-five seconds later. No matter how early we got there, though, some of the kids were already on the playground.

More of the same—basketball. I had a reputation to uphold. Toby wasn't too bad, either, but he wasn't much of a shooter—he really needed to practice his shooting more, but he needed to do it on his own time—when we were together, I needed him to do the rebounding for me.

Next we had Sr. Arilda Marie for art. She was a sweet soul. We were currently making mosaics out of seeds and corn. We had each created our own unique individual design first, without benefit of color or medium (types of seeds), drawing the shapes out on stiff cardboard, then using crayons to color the shapes to indicate which seeds would go where. Finally, we had arrived at the point where we were allowed to glue our seeds into place with lots of Elmer's glue. We were nearly finished. And we had hope—"The mark of a true artist is knowing when to stop," she told us, and I was feeling every bit the true artist.

Following art class, Sr. Ambrose was back for history and science. All I could think of was whatever Richard wanted to talk to us about. It must have been awfully important if he didn't want to talk about it at school, even to tell us what it was about. I didn't feel particularly worried about it, though, because Richard didn't seem worried. He seemed excited.

Finally, the bell rang at 2:57. We quickly closed and stashed our books, stood next to our desks and prayed in unison: "Hail, Mary, full of grace...." Then, "Glory be to the Father, and to the Son, and to the Holy Spirit....world without end. Amen."

"Dismissed," Sr. Ambrose said. "You may leave in silence," which we were careful to do until we reached the front steps, when joyous whoops broke out, and everyone talked at once, several of us jumping down all seven steps to land on the wide concrete sidewalk with foot-stinging slaps.

"Bye," I yelled to Mary Ann, who told me "bye" back, smiling shyly but sweetly. I looked around for John and Toby, then remembered John had a Knights of the Altar meeting.

Toby and I started for The Captain's Place. As we approached the River's Rest, a black Lincoln Continental pulled across the driveway in front of us and into the parking lot. Toby and I watched the driver get out of the car. He was dressed in a white shirt, with black chest hairs sticking out of his unbuttoned shirt collar, sleeves rolled up to just below his elbows, and no necktie or hat. He pocketed the car keys and opened the back door, releasing a cloud of cigarette smoke. A small dapper man dressed in a sharp gray business suit and necktie, and wearing a hat, exited the car, took a last pull on his cigarette, and flicked it onto the driveway, then ground it out under the sole of his Italian leather shoe. They both walked toward the office.

"Unusual guests for Mayfly in spring," said Toby, as we continued walking toward the river. I deferred to his professional judgment in such matters, but to me they looked like unusual guests for Mayfly in any season.

Mayfly was an unpretentious town. Unlike many New World towns which optimistically named themselves after grandiose cities across the pond, (New London, Paris, Memphis, Rome, Cairo), Mayfly is named after the huge swarms of insects which hatched in enormous numbers, often at the same time, and usually in a period of two or three days in May. Frightening to look at, they resembled enormous mosquitoes, approximately two inches long, spindly and primitive—except they didn't bite. They didn't even have a working mouth.

Their sole business on this earth was to mate and then die. Females only lived for about five minutes, but they laid between 400 and 3,000 eggs in that time. Males could live for up to two days. Male and female, they all died in droves. In some years their bodies were so thick on the bridge over the Mississippi River that the State Highway Department had to use snowplows to push them off, just so cars could drive across. Sometimes their swarms even showed up on the local weather radar. So this was not the best time to visit Mayfly unless you were seriously interested in bugs, and these two didn't look the type. They looked like mobsters in a movie.

Toby and I walked quickly toward the south end of downtown Mayfly, toward River Road, which ran both north and south alongside the Mississippi River. As we entered the road at the foot of the bluffs, a light breeze bore the mingled scent of fecund vegetation, mud and fish to our nostrils. We headed downriver, walking the ancient roadbed carved into the side of the huge bluffs which formed the western cradle of the Mississippi riverbed. River Road was a nightmare to maintain. Cut into the foot of the bluffs thirty feet above the water, parts of the road continually caved away into the river and parts of the bluff above it collapsed onto the road—not only rocks and huge trees, but sometimes entire sections of the bluff.

As we approached The Captain's Place, we saw Richard hanging around on the outside, just behind the curtain of kudzu and grapevine which hid the mouth of the cave. He was holding a flashlight.

"Bat!" Richard said, as we pushed aside the viny curtain. Toby ducked his head, trying to hide his ears with his shoulders, and looked around, terrified. "Batter late than never," Richard continued. Toby looked at him angrily.

"That's not funny," he said, righteous now. "Bats carry rabies."

"Sorry, man," Richard said, apologetically. "I just couldn't resist."

The cave was not really our own secret—it had a wooden gate across the mouth. The large cavern behind it had been used as an occasional warehouse for as long as anyone living could remember. Richard had already checked the main cavern with a flashlight to make sure we were alone, but that didn't include all the tributary tunnels and branches, which was why he wanted to talk outside, instead of inside.

"What's going on?" I asked.

"I've been trying to find some treasure," Richard said, straight-faced.

"Oh, great, you found out that pirates really were here, then?" asked Toby, donning his best "my mama didn't raise no fool" expression.

"Yeah, maybe," said Richard, with just a hint of superior knowledge playing around his eyes and mouth.

"Oh, come on, Richard," I said, "what's this about really?"

"Really, it's about pirates, but not Captain Kidd. Different pirates—river pirates."

"River pirates! For real, man?!" Toby said, trying to sound totally skeptical, but you could tell by his tone that he wanted to hear more.

I looked Richard in the eyes. I had known him long enough to know he was not just pulling our legs. He always played it close to the vest. He was a little bit mysterious—he didn't usually announce theories until he had them figured out.

"What do you mean?" I asked.

Richard came closer to us. We leaned in.

"It's about the *Flying Eagle*," he said, his voice above a whisper, but just.

"What's the *Flying Eagle*?" both Toby and I hissed the question in unison.

"It was a river boat that sank here."

"I've never heard of it," said Toby.

"It was before you were born," Richard answered, low and slow.

"When was this?" I asked.

"1865," Richard said.

"1865! And it had pirate treasure on it?" I asked.

"I don't know," Richard said.

"Then why are we talking about it?" I asked.

"There are two men in town trying to find it," Richard said.

"How do you know?" Toby beat me to it.

Joseph Welch

"I was at the Mayfly Free Public Library when these two men came in. I was back in the fiction section, but I heard them ask the librarian if she had the old newspaper records for the Civil War, and she said 'yes.' I peeked over the top of the row of books—they were dressed really strange. One of them was a small guy, dressed in a suit and tie and shiny black leather shoes. The other one was huge and real tough-looking with a gold tooth. He had on a white shirt."

Toby and I looked at each other. "I think we saw them at the motel," Toby says.

"So," Richard continued, "Miss Lizzie took them downstairs in the elevator and showed them how to find the newspaper records on microfilm. I tiptoed down the stairs and stood behind a row of shelves and watched them. They asked her if all the articles were there from the Civil War period between 1861 and 1866. She said yes, they were, and showed them how to search and then went back upstairs. And after she left, the tough-looking guy said to guy in the suit, 'So we're looking for a boat called the *Eagle*?' And the other one said, real impatient-like, 'The *Flying Eagle*, sunk in 1865. Explosion on board.'

"So they messed around for a while and it was obvious they didn't know what they were doing with the microfilm reader, and I was getting really tired just standing there and wondering how I was ever gonna get out of there without them seeing me, but finally they found an article in the Mayfly Courier-Post and the guy in the suit pulled a notebook out and copied it down, then he just said, 'Okay, let's go,' and they left. And as soon as the elevator doors closed, I ran up the stairs super-quick and quiet and beat them upstairs by a mile and I was hidden behind the stacks when the elevator door opened, and I just stayed there until I heard them go out the door. Then I went to the door and saw their car, and it had New Jersey plates. So I went right back downstairs and looked up the same article and I copied it, too," he said, holding out a folded sheet of looseleaf.

We both grabbed for it, but I got there first. I snatched the paper and unfolded it and started reading. "Read it out loud," Toby said.

"Here, you read it," I said, "it's your writing," and handed it back to Richard.

"Okay," he said, then read:

(Mayfly Courier-Post Monday, April 16, 1865):

Flying Eagle Sinks at Mayfly: Explosion on Board

The *Flying Eagle* sank just north of downtown Mayfly shortly after midnight on April 15, after passing upriver through the draw span of the Burlington Northern Railroad Bridge. Witnesses reported hearing a loud explosion, and then seeing the boat floating downriver under the railroad bridge completely engulfed in flames. It sank quickly, just downriver from the bridge, in 55 feet of water. The *Flying Eagle* had departed from Memphis at 3:00 p.m. on April 11, carrying 170 Union Soldiers, all but three of whom had disembarked at St. Louis two days prior. There were thought to be seven people remaining on board, including three Union officers. There are no known survivors. Four bodies, all boat crew, have been recovered. The search continues for the bodies of the three Union officers. According to the captain of *The Alton Belle,* the boat had completed a wood lot stop at Cottonwood Point south of Mayfly shortly before the explosion. The final intended destination of the *Flying Eagle* is unknown.

Joseph Welch

Finished, Richard looked up at us expectantly. His eyes were gleaming, his mouth slightly open, barely able to hold himself in check. He was on the verge of something.

"Okay, but it doesn't say anything about treasure," Toby said.

"Yeah, why are we interested in this now?" I asked.

Richard closed his mouth and glanced quickly down, then looked up, somewhat chagrined.

"I know," he said, "but I've been thinking about this. Listen to this: number one, they don't look like history buffs to me—they look like mobsters, and they even talk like mobsters, and they lied to Miss Lizzie about what they were looking for. Plus, New Jersey is a long way to come to look up a little history, and why would they need to keep it secret from the librarian, unless it was something pretty important and, well…secret. And also, they don't know anything about research—you should have seen them—they didn't have any idea what they were doing. They're definitely not history buffs."

We all stood there looking at each other, wondering what was so important about the *Flying Eagle* a hundred years before.

"I wonder what was so special about the *Flying Eagle*," Toby said, finally.

"Yeah," I answered. "And I wonder why it sank."

"And what it was carrying," Toby continued, warming to the excitement.

"And where it was going," I added.

"I'm going to find out." Richard said.

6.
AFTER SCHOOL

The three of us hiked north on River Road, back into Mayfly and our homes. On the southern edge of downtown Mayfly, we passed a familiar tumbledown house built up against the foot of the bluff. It squatted behind a high concrete porch running the entire width of the structure. The front side of the concrete bore a legend painted by hand with a very large brush. The bright red letters were irregular, but the message was perfectly clear: "DON'T PARK ON THE DAM SIDEWALK," it said.

As we passed the house, we heard a voice call to us through a ripped screen door.

"Hey, queers! Watcha doin'?" It was Bad Billie Boyd.

"Hi, Billie," we said.

"Just heading home," said Toby, trying to preempt questions about where we had been.

"I've got chores to do," I said.

"Too bad," said Billie. "I was just about to go score me some pussy."

Bad Billie had a good heart, but he had a really dirty mind. His father was an alcoholic who had pretty much worn himself out beating on Billie's mother and two older brothers. And Billie's older brothers were mean—I mean *real* mean. Both of them had been in jail and one of them was still in the penitentiary. We felt sorry for Bad Billie, and we were always nice to him and sometimes even let him hang out with us, but we never told our parents.

Bad Billie was always going on about pussy. I don't think he really knew anything about it, but he talked like he did. He thought about it a lot. He touched himself plenty, too, and I don't mean just taking a shower—I mean impure acts—and he was always trying to get the rest of us to admit we did it, too. Since Billie wasn't a Catholic, he didn't know it was a Mortal Sin. He didn't even know what a Mortal Sin was. He was like one of the Pagan Babies. I thought he was pretty lucky in that regard, because if you didn't know something was a sin, then you couldn't commit that sin. One day Bad Billie decided to see how many times he could do it in one day—I won't say what he called it, but it's close to what you do with a car before you can change a flat tire—thirteen times, according to him! Still the world record, as far as I know.

As for the rest of us, since we were Catholic, we all knew that any kind of "sin against purity" was not only a sin, but a Mortal Sin—the worst kind—as bad as killing someone—the kind that will send you straight to Hell if you die without first going to Confession and having your sins forgiven. So touching yourself was awfully risky business for Catholics, because we *knew* it was a Mortal Sin. Bad thunderstorms were especially worrisome, lying in bed with maybe your 16th woodie of the day, and going through the nightly struggle of trying not to have any impure thoughts (because any impure thought is a Mortal Sin, too, just as if you had done some impure act), and knowing that God is flinging lightning bolts around over your head at that very moment and no doubt has plenty to spare.

So on the matter of "scoring us some pussy," we all just expressed our deep disappointment because of other pressing obligations, wished Bad Billie good luck, and continued our trek home.

"Where have you been?" asked my mother as I came in the back door. Luckily, I didn't have to tell her, "Scoring some pussy."

"Talking with Richard and Toby," I answered instead, omitting my visit to The Captain's Place and our pussy-scoring invitation from Bad Billie. My Mom just wouldn't understand.

"The vegetable garden needs weeding," she said. "We had almost two inches of rain last night—it's good weeding weather and it won't last forever. Change your clothes and get to it. Work fast, because at 4:30 you're going to start your homework for one good hour before dinner."

That was the thing with Mom. There were always extra projects to do, besides the regular daily stuff. And we did lots of regular daily stuff. We all folded our clothes and put them away and cleaned our rooms and made our beds and kept the holy water fonts filled. Plus, I took care of Bobo, my parakeet, cleaned his cage every day and fed and watered him, and shopped for his food, and covered him every night to keep the drafts off him. And after dinner we divided up the chores six ways, so we all had something to do, taking turns a week at a time, washing the dishes, drying them, putting away the food, wiping the stove and counter tops, sweeping the floor, and taking out the trash. And that was just the daily stuff.

Then there was the weekly house-cleaning every Saturday, using another six-way division of labor: each of us was tasked with either cleaning the bathrooms, or else mopping the linoleum floors, dust mopping the hardwood floors, vacuuming the rugs, dusting the furniture or edging along the baseboards.

Plus, the seasonal stuff: raking leaves, hulling walnuts and picking apples in the fall, washing windows, cleaning out our closets and planting gardens in the spring, cutting the grass and weeding the gardens in the spring and summer, and shoveling walks in the winter. We lived on a corner lot high up on a hill surrounded by a bunch of old people that Mom felt sorry for because they didn't have anyone to do their labor, so she volunteered us—all the time. We shoveled seven walks every time it snowed, and three of them were corner lots like ours, so their sidewalks were three times as long as a regular lot, since the sidewalks also ran along the lengths of their back yards and not just the width across the front. But the sidewalks were the easy part compared to the steps, a significant disadvantage to living on a steep hill. Besides our own seventeen front steps and seven in our back, we shoveled dozens of neighbors' steps.

And our weeding projects bordered on insanity: considering a brick walkway the length of our house, an all-brick patio, Mom's herb garden, the rock garden, the mint patch, two huge myrtle beds, the vegetable garden, and our twenty-four bushes, we could pull weeds every day and never finish. We also weeded our Grandma's vegetable garden, which was so big it should have been done with a tractor. We used an old hand plow between the rows and our hands up close. And we had to make sure we pulled them all up by the root, since we were held to the standard of professionals.

I had a vested interest in weeding as quickly as possible because I knew what two inches of rain did for weeds—they practically pulled themselves. The next day would be a completely different story. And I was not working by the hour—I was working until the job was finished. So I resolved to get out there and do as much as I could before my pre-dinner homework hour.

Summer of '63

Even when I started my homework, I continued to work as fast as I could, because I knew I'd have to stay up late and finish whatever I didn't get done, and then that would make it harder for me to get up early the next morning and fight. I was learning to beware the slippery slope.

Dinner was great, as usual: a huge half-inch-thick ham steak cut into eighths like a pizza, mountains of mashed potatoes, peaches, steamed broccoli, and rhubarb for dessert. After dinner we all cleared the table, then hustled through our chores. John washed, I dried, Michael put the food away, Mark cleaned the stove and countertops, Stephen swept the floor, and Tim took out the trash and compost. We always raced each other and usually finished everything within twelve minutes.

I heard a car horn honk and looked out the window. Tom Piper was sitting there behind the wheel of his black '57 Chevy, with the top down; Toby was riding shotgun, and Richard was stretched out in the back.

"Wanna go for a ride?" Toby asked, as I ran out onto the porch. I stuck my head back inside the screen door.

"Mom, can I go for a ride with Tom Piper and Toby and Richard?" I asked.

"I guess so," she said, "but be back by 7:15. No later."

"Okay," I said, "I will." I couldn't be late because we started the Rosary at 7:30.

Thrilled, I ran down the steps and hopped into the back seat with Richard. Tom drove along Ridgeline as he turned on the radio to 1070 AM, the familiar voice of Smilin' Dick, who was in rare form, his radio-timbre voice "sending one out for Porky from Ann." The first few bars of "Roses Are Red (My Love)" poured into the evening air, courtesy of the sweet voice of Bobbie Vinton.

As we passed the end of our back yard and the front of Gunnar Green's house, I saw the curtains part in the front window and Gunnar Green's face peering out from behind them. He was fuming with hatred—he looked like the incarnation of evil. I didn't wave at him.

"Let's drive down Broadway," Toby said. Tom didn't say anything. Maybe it wasn't quite as cool for him to "drive Broadway" with three Sixth Graders as it was for us to be seen doing it, especially in this car.

"Yeah, Tom, can we?" I asked.

He hesitated, apparently thinking, then, "Sure, why not?" he said, and turned the wheel in that direction. We were at the absolute height of quintessential Sixth Grade Cool, bebopping our heads and snapping our fingers in time to "Tossin' and Turnin'" as we drove up and down Broadway in a long line of cruising teenagers, waving at all the oncoming cars and trying to look appropriately laid back as we sat at red lights next to guys with one hand on the wheel and the other arm around the shoulders of a girl scooted over really close.

After a couple of passes, Toby asked, "Anybody need fireworks? There's a new stand right across the bridge and Tom is taking me there to get some M-80s."

"M-80s!" I yelled, "Whoa! M-80s are illegal in Missouri!"

"There might be a reason for that," Richard says. "They're a third of a stick of dynamite. One of them will blow your whole arm off if you don't get rid of it fast enough."

"I didn't bring any money," I say, not mentioning that I didn't *have* any money—the Pagan Babies got it all.

"Me either," Richard chimed in.

"I'll loan you some," Toby said. "I brought six dollars—we can go thirds—I'll loan you each two dollars."

"Great! Okay!" Richard and I said, as we turned up the road to the bridge approach. Six dollars brought us untold riches in explosives. Twenty-four M-80s! We told Toby to keep them, since we hadn't paid for our shares yet. Also, Tom and Toby had all sorts of great hiding places around the motel—Richard and I were considerably more limited.

"Okay—I'll keep them in the linen closet under the blankets," he said. "People won't be using those for a while, and it's a good dry spot with no flame." That was a prime consideration, alright.

I had been watching the time. 7:05 p.m. "I have to go home, Tom," I said. "Mom says I have to be home by 7:15 so I won't be late for prayers." And I wasn't. Good thing.

7.
NIGHT PRAYERS

On the next evening, securing a place on the carpet for Tuesday night family prayers carried enhanced importance. We began with the Sign of the Cross, then warmed up with the Rosary.

We took turns "leading" the Rosary, which meant the leader said the first half of each prayer out loud, and then the rest of the family said the second half in unison. But an important qualification for the leader was the ability to memorize and recite the "Mysteries of the Rosary." The Mysteries were supposed to give you something to meditate on while you said the same prayers over and over, if for some reason you couldn't focus on the prayers themselves. Because sometimes your mind might wander a little, since there is a lot of repetition in the Rosary. You only say the Apostles Creed once, but you also say six Our Fathers, fifty-three Hail Marys, and six Glory Bes, and then some adjunct prayers which aren't really a part of the Rosary but might as well be, since they are said in conjunction with the Rosary almost every time.

So whoever led the Rosary had to be able to recite the Mysteries of the Rosary in order, a different mystery for each decade of ten Hail Marys. I liked the Sorrowful Mysteries best—they were the easiest to remember since they followed a story: The Agony in the Garden, The Scourging at the Pillar, The Crowning with Thorns, The Carrying of the Cross, and finally The Crucifixion. The Joyful Mysteries were easy, too: The Annunciation, The Visitation, The Birth of Our Lord, The Presentation in the Temple, and The Finding of Jesus in the Temple. The Glorious Mysteries were my least favorite because they always seemed a little fuzzy to me when I tried to picture them: The Resurrection, The Ascension, The Descent of the Holy Ghost" (we were still praying to the "Holy Ghost" in those days—now we pray to the "Holy Spirit," ghosts having gone out of fashion in spiritual circles), The Assumption, and, finally, The Crowning of Mary as Queen of Heaven.

After the Rosary we always prayed "The *Memorare*":

> Remember O Most Gracious Virgin Mary, that never was it known, that anyone who fled to thy protection, implored thy help, or sought thy intercession was left unaided. Inspired by this confidence, we fly unto thee, O Virgin of Virgins, our Mother. To thee do we come, before thee we stand, sinful and sorrowful. O Mother of the Word Incarnate, despise not our petitions, but in thy mercy hear and answer us. Amen.

This was followed immediately by the "Hail, Holy Queen":

> Hail, Holy Queen, Mother of Mercy; hail, our life, our sweetness and our hope. To thee do we cry, poor banished children of Eve; to thee do we send up our sighs, mourning and weeping in this vale of tears. Turn then, Most Gracious Advocate, thine eyes of mercy towards us; and after this, our exile, show unto us the blessed fruit of thy womb, Jesus, O clement, O loving, O sweet Virgin Mary.

Pray for us, oh Holy Mother of God.

Joseph Welch

That we may be made worthy of the promises of Christ.

Then, having sufficiently warmed up, we began our special Tuesday Night Devotions to Our Mother of Perpetual Help, which were lengthy all by themselves.

Some of the time my mind wandered—I couldn't help myself. "I've got to find a way to get out of some of this work," I told myself. "How am I ever going to become Heavyweight Champion of the World? I don't have enough time."

I considered various possibilities: Injury? Illness? That wouldn't work—I wouldn't be allowed to train if I were pretending to be sick or injured. Nothing seemed like a good solution. I remembered how I had once figured out how to trick Mom into agreeing that I could be a cowboy when I grew up. I knew she wasn't a big fan of gun fights, or even fist fights, for that matter, and she knew as well as I did that those were just part of the job description, so I was concerned that she wouldn't give me permission to pursue the life's work that I was cut out for. So when I finally worked up the courage to ask, I made sure to describe my career path as being more along the lines of a "singing cowboy," like Roy Rogers, than a real gun-totin', shoot-'em-up, fisticuff-deliverin' cowboy. It seemed like she fell for that one hook, line and sinker—I can't remember if she definitely said "yes," but at least she didn't say "no." In fact, she didn't seem to care that much. Go figure. The thing I considered one of the biggest issues in my life was not even on her radar. There must be some kind of lesson in this—women are different, I guess.

Family prayers finally came to a close. I was ready for bed, beaten into submission by our devotions, but I had to finish my homework first. Fortunately, I had done the hard work first and saved English for last, which I could do even brain dead. After twenty questions, I closed the book and brushed my teeth, decided that I had already prayed enough for one evening, then finally crawled into bed.

My next conscious awareness was the tiny audible "click" preceding the clarion call to combat: "Carson, Carson, Carson, Carson, Carson Pirie Scott...and Company."

8.
LUCKY

The next afternoon, John was off on his paper route, and Michael, Toby and I galloped over to the Train Park playground, hoping to play some serious basketball with the high school players. Unfortunately, I didn't see anyone I knew. I was disappointed—I always looked forward to choosing sides with a group of older players, since I usually got picked right after the players on the high school team. A tall, thin kid with straight blonde hair was lying on the grass next to the court with his head resting on a basketball.

"That must be the new kid," Toby said, indicating.

"What new kid?" I asked.

"Oh, yeah," Toby said. "I forgot to tell you. Joan told me about him. He just moved in next door to Mary Ann. He has a horse, too. Joan went trail riding with him and Mary Ann."

This was news.

"Come on," I said, "let's go meet him. The three of us walked across the court toward him. As we approached nearer, I was startled by the bluest eyes I had ever seen, framed by lashes that were almost white.

"Hi," I said. "I'm Jamie Fletcher. Welcome to Mayfly," extending my right hand. He reached up and shook my hand.

"Lucas Crane," he said, standing up. He was tall and lanky—closer to Toby's height, almost a full head taller than me. "Just call me 'Lucky.'"

"Okay, Lucky. This is Michael and Toby," I said, indicating. "I heard you play basketball."

"Yeah, I was starting point guard for the St. Clement Crusaders," he said. The St. Clement Crusaders were famous, even in Mayfly. They frequently won the St. Louis CYO league and were a dominant force in it every year. They had also won the Mayfly tournament multiple times.

"You're kinda tall for a point guard, aren't you?" I asked, picturing him more as a possible rival for Toby's position as starting post man.

"Not in St. Louis," he said. "Plus, I really like to handle the ball and be in charge of the offense. I can make things happen when I'm out front." *Ha! Lucky for me, so can I, Lucky!*

"How about a little two-on-two?" he asked, walking onto the court.

"Sure," I said, "let's shoot free throws for sides. The first two who make it are a team. Winners take the ball out. You go first," I added, trying to be gracious to the new kid, even though I already had a big reason not to, and her name was "Mary Ann."

"Okay," he said. He walked up to the free throw line, dribbled three times, then popped the chain net.

Stunned, but trying to act nonchalant, I tossed the ball to Michael, who did the same thing. That was it. Lucky and The Archangel were a team, taking on Toby and me.

"You guard Michael," I said. "I'll take him," wanting to show this kid how well I could play defense.

"No, I'll take him," Toby said. "I don't wanna guard The Archangel. He gets too mad if I block him," he whispered.

"Okay," I relented—I knew what Toby was scared of. "You take him, and I'll take Michael," I said, tossing the ball to Lucky, who tossed it inbounds to Michael out on the point, then broke suddenly across the lane. Michael hit him with a pass. Lucky stopped on a dime and shot a short jumper, popping the net again.

"Make it—take it," Michael announced. That meant they got to take the ball out again each time they made a basket. We counted baskets by ones: "1-zip."

I retrieved the ball and tossed it back to Michael, who threw it inbounds to Lucky out on the wing, then Michael broke down the lane for a pass. I stuck to him like glue, even though if he had the ball, he could have shot over me easily. I was determined to get the ball back, so Toby and I could go on offense and I could do some shooting of my own. Lucky, however, declined to pass the ball. Instead, he dribbled it casually with his right hand, then broke to the right, fast. Toby, who was pretty quick and no slouch on defense himself, immediately slid over sideways, blocking him, determined to make Lucky pick up his dribble. At that instant, Lucky dribbled the ball between his legs, corralling it with his left hand and simultaneously cutting hard left so sharply that Toby actually fell down trying to make the adjustment, while Lucky continued dribbling lazily into the basket for a left-handed layup. I was dumbfounded.

"Here," I said. "Let me take him." Toby didn't argue. He was red in the face. But it didn't matter much who took him.

Next, he drove right, toward the basket, then took a quick step back, shot and popped. In my effort to stop his drive, I was so far away from him that he could have used a set shot if he had wanted to. Twenty minutes later, it was 21-6. Lucky almost never missed, and the few times he did, The Archangel got the rebound. The only way we even got the ball was our rule in "Make it—Take It" that if a team scored three consecutive baskets, they had to let the other team take the ball out. So we got some "pity possessions." I could still hit, though. The few times we had the ball, I was 5 for 7 from the field. Toby was 1 of 2.

I was in shock as we left the playground. I felt hateful. The experience was completely demoralizing. The Archangel was not happy, either. Lucky had not thrown him a single pass. The only thing which saved Lucky from the wrath of The Archangel was the fact that The Archangel was so shocked he hadn't yet had time to think about vengeance, but he was getting closer.

"Holy smokes!" Toby said, "I'm glad he's gonna be on our team." I wasn't.

That night after family prayers and finishing my homework, I climbed into bed, exhausted. Instead of dropping off into dreamland as usual, however, I lay there tossing and turning, reliving some of the playground scenes of the afternoon. I was still in shock. I had to admit that Lucas Crane was truly a great basketball player, possibly even better than me. And to make matters worse, he lived next door to Mary Ann. And he had a horse, which I knew was the most important thing in the world to Mary Ann, and they had already been horseback riding together. And the worst part of it all was that there was nothing I could do about it. I would have to practice harder, and keep my eyes open, and see if there was any way I could get Mary Ann to like me better than "Lucky" Lucas Crane.

9.
THE BAYOU

On Friday afternoon, the Three Musketeers left downtown Mayfly behind us in high spirits, traveling south along River Road by foot, talking about the snakes we hoped to see. Our Science teacher, Sr. Cletus, had given each of us a way to get a guaranteed "A." All we had to do was to go outdoors and arrange to eyeball the required number of a certain type of animal.

Sr. Cletus was super ancient. She fell asleep in class almost every day. When she was awake, though, she was a great teacher, and we really didn't mind her going to sleep every day. We figured when you were that old you just needed your rest.

As soon as she started nodding off, we used our unsupervised time to pass around an order sheet for how many doughnuts we wanted from the neighborhood bakery. After the orders were tabulated, our most agile and athletic classmate, Marcus Privet, would slide quickly and silently out the window and then climb down the bricks and lower himself to the ground below. Fifteen minutes later he would be back, carrying large white paper sacks stuffed with a couple dozen donuts, then stand up on the building footing outside our classroom and signal his return from a location where Sr. Cletus' veil would prevent her from seeing him if she happened to be awake. As soon as he received the "all clear" sign from his accomplice in the back row, he climbed up the side of the building one-handed, passed the large white paper bakery sacks in through the open window, taking care to minimize any rustling, then slipped back inside. We were happy little mice, our cheeks stuffed, all eyes on the sleeping Sr. Cletus, careful not to wake her up until we had demolished all of the doughnuts, checked one another for powdered sugar trails, and quietly disposed of the paper sacks.

Sr. Cletus thought that interacting with our natural environment was important. We were required to keep a field notebook in which we recorded the date, time of day, location, and species identified. Each sighting, to be valid, had to be attested in writing by a witness. The number of sightings required for an "A" varied, based on Sr. Cletus' appraisal of the difficulty of viewing each particular species. The animals must all be different species—you couldn't just see twenty-five red squirrels, for instance, but you could get an "A" if you spotted and logged twenty-five different bird species, or twelve different types of moths and butterflies, or six different species of reptile.

So the three of us had all chosen reptiles because we figured it would be fun to do it together. We intended to go find snakes, but frogs, turtles and lizards would also count. Richard knew where we could see loads of snakes, so the three of us walked downriver, notebooks in hand, pens in our pockets, each of us carrying a long straight stick, specially selected with a fork in the thin end, for holding the head of the snake out of harm's way—our harm—while we collected enough detail to properly identify it. I also had binoculars hanging around my neck.

We were headed past Scipio, an old icehouse, a remnant from the days when men cut huge slabs of ice off the surface of the frozen river in winter. They used mules to drag the slabs up an iron ramp into the old concrete structure. There they sat for months, layered in sawdust, waiting to be sold in warm weather to the citizens of Mayfly for their iceboxes and cool drinks. Scipio Ice House was located on a long shallow chute of the river. It was only a few feet deep, and was protected from the west wind by woods on the shore and from the east wind by the island which separated it from the main body of the river. The ice slabs cut from this protected chute were smoother on top than those cut out in the open channel. Also, the current in the chute was much slower than it was in the open river, so it wasn't nearly as dangerous as cutting ice out in deep water, where, if you happened to fall in, you could be quickly swept under the ice where no one could rescue you or even find you. But if you fell into the chute that ran past Scipio, you would basically end up standing thigh-deep in the muddy bottom until someone pulled you out—you could probably even crawl out on your own or walk over to the shore and climb out.

The snakes didn't much care how deep the water was or how fast the current was. They were excellent swimmers and very quick and they liked fish and frogs.

A quarter mile past Scipio we followed a truck track across an old bridge that led into an enormous swamp. Much of it was still wet from the spillover of rain and snow melt in the spring. Dead trees stood in the water, their trunks ghostly, limbs devoid of leaves—some were just rotting vertical trunks with no branches. The living trees with big canopies were all species largely dependent on a continuous supply of water.

"This is the northernmost bayou on the Mississippi River," Richard said. I wondered, not for the first time, how he knew stuff like that. "We want to just stay on the edges—there's a lot of wildlife in here."

Trying to stay on higher ground so we wouldn't have to actually enter the snake-infested bayou, we followed deer paths among white trunks and broad limbs of sycamores draped in gray moss. Fluffy white seedlings carried past us on the light breeze, released from seed pods on towering cottonwood trees with enormous trunks, whose roots siphoned enough water to evaporate a hundred-thirty gallons per day into the heated air, creating their own humidity zone. This was pure snake habitat, and they were everywhere—all we had to do was keep very quiet and watch.

"If Sr. Cletus saw this place, the requirement would be much higher," I whispered—too loudly—the grass moved just ahead of us. We changed trajectory to avoid the area.

I was glad that Richard was going first. "Be careful back there," he said, as if he could read my mind. "It's always the second person in line who gets snake bit—the snake pulls back and watches when the first person goes by and then strikes the second person." *Great. Is he serious or just messing with me?*

We advanced silently, tiptoeing through the high grass, weeds and cattails, and watching carefully to make sure we kept on high ground, skirting holes made by God-knows-what.

"Wonder what lives in these holes," Toby whispered.

"Snakes, muskrats, foxes, some of these are even crawdad holes," Richard said.

"This place looks like The Land That Time Forgot," I say. "I wouldn't be surprised if Tyrannosaurus Rex came parading around that clump of trees right in front of us."

I was secretly glad I was with my friends. I would hate to be in this place by myself. I would also hate to be here after dark, even with my friends.

"Hope we see a cottonmouth," Toby said, real brave.

"Hope we don't," I said. "They're really poisonous."

"There are no cottonmouths north of the Missouri River," Richard said, like he was talking to some dimwits, which he was, but we didn't want to admit it, even to ourselves.

"I don't believe that," I said. "What, they can't swim across?"

"Let me know the first time you see one," Richard responded. "I won't hold my breath."

When he said that, I realized that I was holding my breath. This place was not what I would call homey. We kept walking through waist-high grass and rushes, trying to be quiet, even when the grass moved right in front of us, or the water suddenly showed ripples from God-knows-what that just dived below the surface. The problem with the place from a snake-watching perspective was that it was so overgrown you couldn't really see anything—until maybe it was too late. Except the birds.

And birds were everywhere. We watched a bald eagle lift off from the top of the tallest cottonwood in our field of vision. A flock of thirteen turkey vultures sat, scattered among the limbs of a huge dead tree, watching us. Redwing blackbirds rose in alarm from small trees overhanging the water as we passed. Purple martins and indigo buntings cut and dived and hovered, hunting flying insects. A great blue heron perching on long legs in the still water emitted its prehistoric *"grawk"* as it left its silent fishing station, laboriously flapping its five-foot wings, their tips just dimpling the surface of the water as its huge body fought to gain elevation. Two mallards floated together companionably, apparently unconcerned by all the predators in the region. *Don't they know there are snapping turtles here which would love to snap off a duck leg?*

"We should've chosen birds," I said. "At least we could see them."

A pair of iridescent blue dragonflies floated past us on the breeze. As we moved further along the margin of the bayou, the insect trill became just short of deafening. I could smell river mud mingled with the sweetness of plant material decaying in the warm sun. *Lots of other things besides plants are dying in droves in this place, but the flesh is no doubt being consumed rapidly by other residents.*

"Richard, this isn't working," I said. "We haven't seen a single snake."

"They're all around us," he said, "but we're making way too much noise. They can hear us coming a mile off. I'll show you a place where we can sneak up on them. But we have to be completely quiet from here on in—that means our steps, too."

We left the high grass and headed down into a low clearing between some pussy willows and a stand of cattails. Richard motioned us over closer. He pulled our heads in right next to his mouth and said in our ears, almost too low to hear: "Quiet, move very, very slowly. Peak around this clump and look at the logs in the water. One at a time."

I went first. Moving my head and shoulders in super slow motion, I peeked around the stand of cattails, then stood frozen, mesmerized. Out in the main body of backwater, small-mouth bass were breaking the glassy surface in aerial arcs as they seized low-flying insects. A very long tree trunk stretched across the surface of the water. Two dozen turtles of different sizes and shapes were arrayed along the top of the giant trunk, basking in the sun.

In slow motion, I ducked back behind the cattail screen and raised the binoculars to my eyes, then peeked out again. The view was dramatic. I saw two huge alligator snapping turtles with bony ridges running down their backs like a stegosaurus, five or six ornate southern painted turtles with distinctive red stripes down their backs, and numerous low-profile spiny softshell turtles. I was halfway finished the assignment, if I could only get a good witness sighting for each of them.

Very cautiously I pulled back and reported my findings. I handed over the binoculars. Toby was next, then Richard.

"I thought we were gonna see snakes," Toby whispered, frowning, as Richard moved his head back behind cover.

"I saw one," Richard said.

"What? Where?" from Toby.

"Shhh. Look on the top of the second big stump to the right of that huge log," Richard said, handing Toby the binoculars.

Toby stuck his head out slowly, held still for a good thirty seconds, then brought it slowly back in, his eyes wide.

"What is it?" he asked.

"Black rat snake," Richard said.

"Lemme see," I whispered, grabbing the binoculars and moving Toby aside while stretching out my head in slow motion. Sure enough, there it was, a big one.

Having now harvested all the reptile species visible to us from our hiding place, we approached the water. A huge bullfrog leapt off the bank and floated submerged, only the eyes visible above the waterline, watching us watch him. That made five.

"I sure thought we'd see more snakes," Toby whispered as we moved back away from the still water.

"We can," Richard says. "That was just the low-hanging fruit. They're all around us. They're just bashful and we're crashing around and making too much noise. Let's try another place. I know where we can see a northern water snake, but if it hears anything or even sees any motion, it'll be gone in a flash."

We left the strip that bordered the bayou and moved into the neighboring grassland. By now we were ignoring the scamperings around us in the tall grass, most of which were probably just rabbits—we hoped. We couldn't see anything in the grass anyway—all we could do was scan the fallen logs and stumps. Our change in strategy was rewarded—Toby saw, fifty feet away but distinctive on a rotting stump, a very long cream-colored snake with dark brown markings. Silently, he pointed, freezing us in our tracks. We traded the binoculars back and forth.

"Western fox snake," Richard said. "Its size is the first clue—longest snake in these parts—except for the black snake. If we caught it, we could see that its belly is marked like a perfect checkerboard."

As we left the bayou area, we stopped for a few minutes to duly log and attest our five sightings, then followed Richard's lead as we headed back upriver. Just south of Scipio we passed an old boat ramp which dipped into the Mississippi. Richard motioned us quietly onto a high grassy promontory just downriver from the ramp. From our high perch, we could see the river's current washing over the ramp, creating a small swirl at the end of a tiny waterfall where the water fell off the edge of the ramp. Lurking there just outside the swirl was a submerged northern water snake, half his head protruding above the surface of the water, reptile eyes focused intently on whatever prey might come over the falls. We were above and behind him and could see him clearly. We lay there on the grass and watched him for a couple of minutes until he vanished under the water—our 6th reptile, and our "A" in Science, the entire adventure courtesy of the ancient Sr. Cletus.

10.
MEETING ROYALTY

As we walked River Road back towards Mayfly, we looked up at the bluffs rising almost vertically on our left, two hundred feet to the top. Their sides were blanketed with trees and vines, including numerous trunks of fallen trees which remained suspended precipitously above us, held by other stout trees which grew out of the side of the bluff and overhung the road and the river. Two bald eagles, disturbed by our approach, appeared to fall out of the top of the tallest of these trees, then spread their wings and glided over the river, beginning the slow powerful strokes required to propel them to the top of a great cottonwood on the far shore.

We approached a break in the bluffs, formed by an ancient streambed which had emptied into the river for eons, its tiny delta providing sufficient level ground to perch a single residence and a cluster of outbuildings. The pillared, white stucco plantation-style house was inhabited by Old Man Milchard, who raised chickens. We could hear them, back in their coop, clucking in alarm. Suddenly, the front screen door of the house banged open, and Mr. Milchard came running out. He was wild-eyed, his hair was askew and one strap of his overalls was undone. He stopped at the top of his front steps and leveled a shotgun, as a huge deer-colored animal with a barrel chest came flying out of the chicken coop, holding a chicken in its mouth, which clucked hysterically. Mr. Milchard aimed the shotgun and let go: BOOM!

We stood frozen, watching the animal rocket away across Mr. Milchard's yard, not even pausing as he vaulted the fence, a long, graceful arc showing a streak of red, our mouths wide open as the wounded animal landed on River Road, still holding the chicken in the jaws of what from a distance appeared to be a very large dog.

"I got him," Old Man Milchard yelled. "I shot that son of a bitch!" He ran down the porch stairs to the front gate, yelling, "I'll kill ya, ya son of a bitch!" and raised the shotgun to fire again.

I was running, too, as fast as I could. "Don't!" I yelled, "that's my dog!"

Mr. Milchard lowered the shotgun and looked at me. The dog was out of range by now, just a brown streak on the road, getting smaller by the second. Mr. Milchard turned on me with a snarl.

"Your dog, huh?" Mr. Milchard barked. "Then you owe me for one chicken. What's your name, boy?"

"Jamie Fletcher," I told him.

"Well, Jamie Fletcher, that was a four-pound chicken. Twenty-nine cents a pound, means you owe me $1.16 plus 4 cents tax. $1.20. Pay up, boy."

"I...I don't have it, sir," I said, my mouth open. And I didn't know how I could get it. *I wonder if I can get a refund on some of my Pagan Baby money.*

"Better get it, then, boy," he said, "or I'll come by your house and get it from your parents."

Oh, no! That would be a disaster. My parents would know I lied about the dog, and they'd also have to pay Old Man Milchard. "Yes, sir," I said. I turned and headed back toward town.

We Musketeers looked at each other, wondering if the dog would live, wondering if and how I would pay Old Man Milchard, and what he would do if I didn't. Halfway back to The Captain's Place, we saw some scattered chicken feathers near the base of the bluff. The big dog was lying back against the bluff, under a veil of kudzu, with what was left of his prize.

"Hi, boy," I said, lifting an armful of draping kudzu, "are you hurt?" He just looked at me. "It's okay, boy," I said, "let me look at you." He put his head down on the ground and whimpered.

"Watch out, Jamie," Richard said. "Wounded dogs are dangerous."

Toby was just staring at the dog. "He's beautiful," he said softly. "It's okay, boy. We want to help you."

The dog allowed me to come closer, talking to him low and soft. "Good boy," I said. "You were just hungry, weren't you?" He raised his head to watch me as I ducked under the kudzu drapery and sat down three feet away from him. He put his head back down on the ground, apparently comfortable with my being there.

"What are you gonna do?" asked Toby.

"Take him home," I said.

"Can he walk?" asked Richard.

"I dunno," I said, "I'm gonna stay here with him until he can."

Richard and Toby sat down with me to wait. After a few minutes, the dog resumed his meal.

Fifteen minutes later he stood up. I called him, "C'mere, boy—let me look at you." He came over and stood next to me while I looked at him.

His left hind leg was injured. I could see his raw, dark muscles. I could even see the white of his bone in places, where the buckshot had stripped the skin and muscle off his leg. I could see his tendons, but they were still attached. He was a young animal, healthy-looking except for his injury. He was a big dog, powerfully built, with a huge barrel chest on the body of a mastiff, and the friendly face of a boxer, but without the saggy jowls. He had large, expressive dark brown eyes and a very broad head, good for patting. His fur was short and deer-colored, and he had the shortest stub of a tail, little more than an inch long—it was virtually non-existent, just a tuft of raised fur, but, oddly enough, his ears were not clipped.

"You're a good dog," I told him, offering my hand for him to sniff, which he did thoroughly. When he had finished, I raised my hand slightly and patted him, and he allowed me.

"Let's go home," I said. He walked right next to me as we continued north on River Road, into downtown Mayfly, and all the way to my house. I walked around our house to the back door, so he wouldn't have to walk up our long front steps with his injured leg.

"Mom!" I yelled from the door, "I have a dog! He's hurt." My brothers came tumbling out of the house *en masse*, followed closely by my mother.

"He was shot," I said. I told them the whole story. "He doesn't have a home, Mom. Can we keep him?"

Mom approached him and let him smell her hands. She patted his broad head, then stood back and looked at him appraisingly. "He seems like a good dog," she said. "We'll see what your father says when he gets home. Better get him a pan of water in the meantime. I'll see if we have any food for him."

My brothers and I spent the rest of the afternoon lying on the ground next to the dog and talking to him. Mom made us all stay an arm's length away from him. We older boys made sure the little ones were not allowed near him, especially his back legs. It was after dark when Dad got home. We bombarded him with the story. "I'll go take a look at him," Dad said.

"He's a good dog, Dad—can we keep him?" Dad could scarcely get through the kitchen to the back door because of all the supplicants of various sizes pulling at him.

"Be careful, Bob," Mom said, looking at Dad. He stopped and looked back at her. "He's hurt. It's his hind leg on the left side. And I don't know if he likes men."

"I will," he said, taking the flashlight off the shelf and turning to go out the door.

"Can we come, too?" we asked.

"No, you just wait inside. All of you," she said, looking around at each of us so that we had no doubt that we were included in the prohibition. Her look brooked no argument.

We ran to the two back windows. All six of us leapt onto the two beds and pulled the curtains open. Mom stood behind us in the darkened room.

It was like a movie. We all watched Dad come out into the yard with his flashlight. We distinctly heard him call, "Here, boy!" then he stood still and waited. The dog was holed up in a window well just below us. We watched him get up and slowly approach Dad, who knelt on one knee as the dog approached him. We could hear Dad encouraging him.

"That's right, boy; you're a good dog. Come on over here and let me look at you."

We watched Dad hold out his hand and offer it to the dog to smell. He was talking lower now, and we couldn't hear what he was saying, just the low hum of his voice as he talked to the big dog. After a long while, Dad put his hand on the dog's broad head and neck and shoulders while he continued to talk to him intermittently. It seemed like Dad was listening to the dog. We never knew exactly what the dog said to Dad, but it seemed like he told Dad his whole story right there in the dark in our back yard, where he was from and how he came here and what had happened to him, and Dad just listened to him and responded from time to time. It was obvious they understood each other.

After a while Dad got up, and we all ran to the kitchen, waiting there at the back door, every one of us holding his breath. The door opened and Dad entered the kitchen, then looked around at the group of us, graduated in size, all eyes open in attention and anticipation. He gave a short laugh, then looked up at Mom, who stood behind us, her hands wrapped in her apron. Their eyes met for a long second, then he looked back down to us.

"He seems like a good dog, boys," Dad said. "You can keep him."

Our house exploded—the kitchen could not contain us. Stephen and Tim bolted into the dining room, ran the complete interior circuit of the house, and were back in ten seconds. "Can we see him now?" we asked.

"No, boys, he's hurt," Mom said, "and he needs rest. And he needs to get to know all of you better before you go ganging up on him. Right now, he knows Jamie best, so Jamie will feed and water him..." A chorus of groans and disappointment erupted before Mom continued, "for now— and in a few days you may start taking turns."

I looked around the room. Five glowing faces were stretched in astonishment, ten eyes opened wide, eyebrows raised almost to their buzzed hairlines. A stranger walking in at that moment would assume we had just struck gold in our kitchen.

"Boys," Mom added after a moment's consideration, "you need to stay away from his hind legs. He might bite you if you get too near him where he's been hurt. Never touch his back legs."

"That's right," Dad agreed. "He will need to protect himself. That doesn't mean he's a bad dog. And stay away from him while he's eating, too, boys. Dogs bite if you get too near them while they're eating."

"And, boys," Dad added after a moment, "if anyone comes and tells us he belongs to them, we will have to give him back." Stunned silence. Then twenty questions.

"What if he's not really theirs and they just want him?" Stephen asked.

"We'll be able to tell if he really belongs to them," Dad said.

"How?" Mark asked, his eyes narrowed.

"We'll see if they know his name, then watch what the dog does when they call him—we'll be able to tell if he knows them."

"What if they're mean to him?" Tim asked.

"We'll be able to tell that, too," Dad said.

"Speaking of names," Mom said, "we have to give him a name."

"Yeah," Mark said, "what shall we call him?"

The kitchen walls vibrated with shouted suggestions: "'Rover'! 'Brownie'! 'Buddy'! 'Max'!" my younger brothers shouted almost simultaneously.

"Boys," Mom says, "I have never seen a more handsome dog or a stronger-looking dog or a prouder dog. I watched him coming up the hill next to Jamie and I said to myself out loud, 'That dog is a prince and he knows it'. I think that's the perfect name for him, the only name: 'Prince.'"

And "Prince" he was, from that moment forward.

Prince was so grateful to have a dry place to sleep and food brought to him every day that he began presenting us with prizes which he captured after dark: rabbits and possums and raccoons and, especially, disemboweled cats. He was certainly eliminating the neighborhood varmints, but we were afraid he would get rabies, so we started chaining him up at night. I built him an insulated doghouse with wood paneling on the inside, and made sure he had a fresh bowl of water each morning, and we let him off his chain again early every day when we brought him his breakfast so he could sniff around in the cool of the early morning.

And just like that, Prince joined our pack—or we joined his, because I think he was actually the leader. We were keeping him, but it seemed like he had decided to keep us—he had chosen us as his family. I knew he could live anywhere in the world he wanted to, except maybe Mr. Milchard's.

11.
SATURDAY MORNING

Saturday morning—no school! The opportunity to sleep late conquered even the lure of early morning fisticuffs. John and I had set our clock radio for 7:50 a.m., and woke up to the prices of corn, soybeans, and pork bellies, whatever they were. Since we were not going to Mass on Saturday, we fell off the sides of our beds onto the floor on our knees in our underwear, and said a quick Morning Offering:

> Dear Jesus, I offer you all my prayers, works, joys and sufferings of this day, for the intentions of your Sacred Heart, in union with the Holy Sacrifice of the Mass throughout the world, for the salvation of souls, in reparation for my sins, and for the reunion of all Christians.

Then we bounded up and quickly donned our robes. After a fast pit stop in the bathroom, we hustled immediately to the kitchen. I tossed two pieces of bread into the toaster, which was already hot, grabbed a plate and knife, and started for the living room.

We were allowed to watch Saturday morning television, virtually the only shows permitted us other than "The Wonderful World of Disney" on Sunday night. Saturday morning featured "Captain Kangaroo" and "Circus Boy," followed by "Mighty Mouse," "Fury," "Rin-Tin-Tin" ("Yo, Rinny"!), "Roy Rogers," and "Sky King."

All six of us sat in our bathrobes on the floor of the living room in front of our black and white TV, jumping up at every commercial and racing each other barefoot to the two-slice toaster in the kitchen. Among us, we devoured three full loaves of bread. Toast with butter, toast with grape jelly, toast with strawberry preserves, toast with honey, cinnamon toast, and on and on. We were bottomless, the capacity of the toaster our only limit. Once it got properly warmed up, though, it could really hum.

During a commercial break, I ran into the kitchen and asked Mom if we could bring Prince into the living room with us. "It will help him get to know us better," I said, "and keep the flies off his leg."

"I guess so," she said, "but just this once." That was the beginning of our Saturday morning ritual with Prince, who enjoyed it at least as much as we did.

I opened the back door and called Prince in. He didn't have to be asked twice. My brothers were thrilled when he bounded into the room, wagging his entire rear end and moving from one of us to the other to allow us to pet him and say hello. I saw Mom standing in the doorway observing, satisfied. We smothered him with pats and affection, and finally got him to lie down on the rug in the middle of all of us. He rolled over playfully and looked at us with big dark eyes. We snuck him pieces of toast, which he gobbled in one bite. Despite his serious injury, he never growled at any of us—not even once.

Mom spread a layer of newspapers out over the kitchen linoleum. She perched the tall metal kitchen stool in the middle of the floor and plugged the hair trimmer into an outlet. "Who wants to be first?" she called from the kitchen doorway. "Me," I said, undoing the belt on my robe as I ran into the kitchen for my haircut—I wanted to be finished before "Fury" and "Rin-Tin-Tin." Mom pinned the barber sheet behind my neck and buzzed me to a uniform length. It didn't take her long—this wasn't her first rodeo.

"Alright," she announced, "you're finished. Send in one of your brothers," as I tossed two more pieces of toast into the toaster and scampered back to the living room floor, my scalp now gray and shorn where the sun hadn't touched. My toast retrieval and buttering operation would just have to wait until the next commercial. When I jumped up at the next break and ran barefoot to the kitchen to claim my prize, Tim yelled, "Jamie, will you put two pieces in for me?"

"How do you ask?" I yelled back automatically, since Tim was one of the "Little Boys." I wouldn't have made John say "please," and certainly not The Archangel—there would have been a price in pain to pay later on.

"Please," he said.

"Okay, then," I said, satisfied, and extracted my own toast before dropping two more pieces into the hot toaster.

We had somehow created a descriptive division of the six of us into the "Big Boys" (John, Jamie and Michael) and the "Little Boys" (Mark, Stephen and Tim), three of each. Even though Michael The Archangel doesn't room with John and me, you certainly couldn't call him one of the "Little Boys," and not just because of his size, either—we never wanted to risk setting him off.

Finally, Mom made us turn off the TV and get dressed. She had chalked the list of chores on the large kitchen blackboard, which included cutting the grass and pulling the weeds out of the joints in our brick sidewalk. Because it had rained hard during the past week, we were spared having to carry a two-gallon bucket of water to each of the two dozen foundation bushes.

John had his own afternoon paper route, Route #38, one hundred papers on both sides of Broadway. Every Friday, after delivering his papers, he was required to collect from his customers, 40¢ from each household. Collecting usually took him two or three hours. He needed the money to pay his weekly bill at the Courier-Post every Saturday. I also intended to walk downtown with him because Bobo was almost out of bird seed.

"Do you have a clean handkerchief and your Rosary in your pocket?" Mom asked as we left the house.

"Yes, ma'am," I replied. I had also brought a dime and a nickel in my pocket, since the bird seed box was clearly marked "15¢."

On the way downtown, we stopped at the Pastry Box and entered the back door, where they sold day-old pastries. John bought a dozen day-old donuts for twenty-five cents. We continued our walk, eating as we went, oblivious to the powdered sugar cascading invisibly down the fronts of our white T-shirts.

Once at the Courier-Post office, we joined the queue of boys lined up in front of the counter. Two women on the other side counted money and issued receipts. When John's turn came, he showed the clerk his bill, then placed his stack of paper money in front of him. Next, he dumped his money bag onto the long counter, and he and the clerk opposite began gathering coins into stacks of a dollar each, then moved them off to one side and ranged them in rows. When they finished, the clerk took the precise amount from the piles in front of her and marked the bill "paid," while John scooped the remaining change back into his money bag, to be used during his next Friday collections.

We started for the dime store, passing an ancient fieldstone building and two darkened storefronts that served as the back-room warehouse for Haydon Hardware, then lingered to look inside a

Joseph Welch

window of a closed storefront labeled "A & M Amusements," through which could be seen some old pinball machines. We entered Mayfly's most prosperous business district, including some surviving Victorian storefronts with ornate cornices and pressed tin facades, a Florsheim Shoe shop displaying a patterned tile floor in the entranceway, and The Famous women's clothing store. We directed our steps toward a long, buff-brick two-story building squatting on the corner of Main and Broadway. Newer than most of the buildings in this section of downtown Mayfly, the words "S.S. Kresge Company" appeared in large red letters across the second floor. To us it was simply "The Dime Store."

We approached one of the big glass doors framed in gleaming blonde wood, and I pushed against the double brass bar running horizontally across its center. We walked past a long lunch counter, behind which an aproned waitress in a crisp light blue service blouse smiled while chatting and wiping counters. Half of the red rotating stools were occupied. A black woman behind the counter, dressed in all white and wearing a hair net, monitored a griddle and deep fryer, while chopping and dicing ingredients for luncheon menu items. A chalk board proclaimed "Today's Special: Ham salad sandwich, cottage cheese, coffee—65¢."

The pet department was in the back of the store. We took our time, looking at the goldfish, the fancy guppies, the tropical fish, and the aquarium paraphernalia: bubblers, coral arches, plastic seaweed, a sunken treasure chest. We examined the baby turtles—there were forty or so, each an inch and a half long, 10¢ apiece. Then, finally, the birds: island-bright canaries, yellow, orange and flame; parakeets of many colors, their tan or blue ceres sporting gender. I reviewed the cuttle bones, then investigated the cage toys item by item, picturing Bobo as the beneficiary of my possible future *largesse*. He was pretty well-fixed right then, however, and I only had 15¢ with me. I finally picked up a box of "3V" seed ("Vim, Vigor & Vitality," the box explained) and we walked back to the front of the store and stood in the checkout line.

"I'm gonna look at bikes while you wait in line," John said. "See you later."

The cashier was pleasant, conversational and efficient. When I put my box of bird seed on the counter, she said, "16¢, please." Shocked, I looked up at her.

"It says 15¢," I said, pointing to the obvious price marked on the front of the box.

"There's a penny tax," she explained.

I just stood there with my mouth open. I didn't know what she was talking about. Finally, I said, "I only have 15¢."

Without missing a beat, she said, "I'll bet Mr. Wilson has a penny he'll give you," flashing a smile at the man behind me. I turned to look up at him—I was obviously out of my depth here.

"Why sure, what do you need?" he asked, fishing a handful of change out of his pocket. "A penny? Here you go," he said, putting it down on the counter.

"Thank you, sir," I said. "I'll pay you back."

"No need to, son. It's a gift," he replied.

I thanked him again as the cashier put my box of bird seed in a brown paper bag with the receipt.

Still thinking as I walked home about how nice both Mr. Wilson and the cashier were to me, I wondered how you could ever know if someone was really good. What if someone like Mr. Wilson went to hell for some reason? John just pooh-poohed the idea.

"But what if he did?" I persisted. "What if George Washington or Davey Crockett are in hell? How can you ever be sure? What if they were good almost all their lives, but then they died with a Mortal Sin on their soul?" I knew how easily something like that could happen.

Apparently, even this didn't bother John, but then he was never very big on the what-ifs. I think he had an aversion to abstract thought. With him, if you couldn't see it, touch it, eat it or drink it, it wasn't real, or at least not very important. I tried to encourage him to expand his mind a little, to engage in the process of trying to figure stuff out, but he never seemed very interested. Ignorance is bliss, I guess. Sometimes I wished I could just ignore some of the really big issues, but I guess that is the price you pay for having an inquiring mind. This "going to hell" thing seemed pretty important to me, and to Mom, too, and it bothered me a lot!

Arriving at the house again, we began the afternoon chores, which for the Big Boys meant cutting the grass with our old-fashioned rotary push mower. It hadn't been sharpened in my lifetime and none of us boys knew how to adjust it so it could actually cut anything, so we just basically rolled the weeds down and hoped they stayed rolled down for a few days. Our scissors-style hand trimmer also needed sharpening, but we were too clueless to even know that, so we just wailed away at the tall buckhorns and dandelions until we basically rubbed the stem in two. The finished project was nothing to write home about, but at least it was finished.

It wasn't really such a big job, because we didn't have much grass, having stomped into extinction every blade in the area of our basketball court, which took up virtually our entire back yard, so we only had isolated patches of buckhorns and dandelions on the very edges.

We knew we had to go to Confession later, but until then, it was basketball time. The fact that we would have all our sins forgiven that very afternoon allowed us a certain license on the Saturday afternoon basketball court—it was the opportune time to hone our cursing skills.

Summer of '63

If we hadn't been such basketball fanatics, the afternoon hours might have been better employed in other diversions, but we lived in a small house with shared bedrooms and one bathroom.

We had broken so many shingles on the back of our house playing ball that Dad had covered the entire back wall with a high protective chicken wire fence. It ran all the way from the ground to the roof line and was fastened to two huge telephone poles buried in cement footings and projecting fourteen feet above the ground, to which he had bolted our painted, white 4' by 8' basketball backboard. It was a formidable array. The poles were on the out-of-bounds line, dead even with the backboard. They were completely unforgiving—they had no padding, which encouraged us to retain bodily control as we drove toward the hoop. We got a new net every Christmas, because we wore the old one out completely—we could all hit, and there was a lot of net-popping in our yard—you could hear it snap, even after dark—shooting by the light of our single yellow porch light, even in the snow.

The court was not paved. We played on bare dirt, packed so hard it was great to dribble on—it felt like concrete, except for the layer of dust which we produced every day as we vibrated the top dirt molecules off the hard pack. So, every day before we played, we swept the loose top layer, a quarter inch of dust, off the hard pack. Basketball in our yard was serious business—it was *the* venue for blocks in any direction. There were only two playgrounds in Mayfly that could field more or better personnel than the Fletcher boys in our own yard. After Prince came to live with us, though, we had to chain him up with a big logging chain whenever we played basketball, because he took a dim view of other kids playing defense against the Fletcher boys. He never hurt any of them—he just grabbed their ankles and held them rooted to the spot until we came over and convinced him to let them go.

Injuries and fights were always part of the game, and no one took it to heart. But woe to the uninitiated that fouled one of the Fletcher boys a bit too hard—especially if the situation warranted fetching The Archangel. The Archangel was famous for his persuasive ability. He didn't need a lot of time to bring people around to his point of view—he believed in the economy of words. Most of the heart-to-heart talks he had with miscreants were short and to the point.

"C'mere, punk," he'd say. "Listen up. You bother my brother again I'll make you a cripple, you understand? Now, go over there and apologize to him—like you mean it."

So the other players always tried to get the offender to make amends before that point was reached. Because as another local tough once told me about The Archangel, "The thing about him is he just gets too mad." *Yup, that's it, in a nutshell. 'Nuff said.*

12.
CONFESSIONS

At 5:15 Mom called us in to clean up and get ready to go to Confession, which meant fresh white T-shirts and school pants. Dad always went with us, and we walked the three blocks to church, where we knelt down while performing our "Examination of Conscience." That meant going through the Ten Commandments silently in our minds to determine if we had violated any of them in any way. Fortunately, our Catechism had taught us all the ways we could violate the Commandments, and there were tons more than the Commandments actually said.

For instance, "Thou Shalt Not Kill" prohibited not only killing, but being mad at someone, or talking to them in a mean way, or saying mean things about them, even if they were true, and even if they never found out you did it. And "Thou Shalt Not Commit Adultery" covered way more than adultery; there was a whole panoply of "sins against purity," including any "impure thought, word, or deed"—and touching yourself was an "impure deed"! Of course, you had to touch yourself sometimes, but one of the high school boys gave us the rule on that: if you shake it more than three times, it was a Mortal Sin, but you could get around this by peeing a little, then shaking it three times, then peeing a little more, then shaking it three more times, and so on. We Catholic boys were apparently renowned for well-developed kegel muscles, but I didn't know what that was.

Joseph Welch

And the worst part was that *all* the *"sins against purity" were Mortal Sins!* Even looking at ads of women's underwear in the Sears catalog or wondering what a pretty girl looked like under her dress or looking at Annette Funicello's legs and breasts in a swimsuit. And this made staying away from Mortal Sin completely impossible. When I was in the First Grade, I knew for a fact that I would never, never, not even once in my life, not under any circumstances, commit a Mortal Sin— I would choose martyrdom—I would even be burned alive, rather than commit a Mortal Sin. But by the end of the Second Grade, I didn't know how I could ever *not* be in a "state of Mortal Sin." I had a whole long list of things to confess, and the numbers were pretty staggering. By the summer before Seventh Grade, it had gotten so bad that the only way I could begin to keep track was to use a daily average, and the only way I could get a daily average was to take an hour's worth of sinning (and even that had to be estimated—I couldn't keep up with it) and then multiply it times the fifteen hours of the day I was awake— then I rounded up, because the waking hours didn't tell the whole story—I even committed Mortal Sins in my sleep!

I stood in line along the side aisle of the church, waiting my turn. The west-facing stained-glass windows over my head were ablaze with depictions of Jesus, Mary and Joseph, as well as other saints who had conquered temptation in all its forms. The Confessional was divided into two small rooms. I saw the red light glowing above the priest's section, indicating that a priest was sitting in his armchair on that side. A similar red light glowed above the other section, indicating that some poor sinner was occupying that side, kneeling on the bare wooden rail, which helped to instill a penitential mood.

When my turn came, the departing sinner, now forgiven and once more "in a state of grace," but looking duly contrite and abashed, held the door to the sinner's cubicle open for me. I entered, the door closed automatically behind me, I knelt on the rail, and the priest opened the sliding wooden panel next to our heads, leaving between us only a translucent screen which allowed us to hear each other. Although I couldn't see the details of his face, I could see by the outline of the silly ringlets standing up from his head that it was P.J. again. *Nuts!*

"Bless me, Father, for I have sinned; it has been seven days since my last Confession," I began. "I lied twice," I continued, opting as usual to start with the small stuff. "I was mean to my little brothers four times. I had impure thoughts six hundred-thirty times," rounding it off at six times per hour, ninety times per day, but wondering if that really covered it—I was probably on the low side, but I would have been embarrassed crossing into the seven hundreds range. And so on—because that was only the beginning—I figured once you had one impure thought, you might as well just let 'er rip, since I was doomed to hell at that point anyway—unless I could get to Confession right before I died, and what were the odds on that? Every night I prayed that I wouldn't die right then.

Finally I wound down. Then P.J. said, "Have you ever confessed these sins before?" like he didn't already know.

"Yes, Father," I replied. I wanted to tell him, "No, this was just something that came up out of the blue," but I didn't think he'd believe me. Also, lying during Confession makes it a "bad Confession," which is another Mortal Sin. So then, not only are the sins you came in there to confess not forgiven, but now you had another one—a Really Big One.

"And you're not able to stop yourself from committing these sins over and over?" he asked.

"No, Father," I said, hoping he'd say, "Well, that's all right, then," or something to that effect. No such luck.

"Alright, I am going to give you a prayer to say to Jesus about your sins. I'm going to tell you the prayer—it's very short—you can remember it. It's this: 'Lord, be merciful to me, a sinner.' Repeat it," he says. I did.

"I find that this prayer helps with sins against purity," he said. "Can you remember that?"

"Yes, Father."

"I'm going to give you a copy of the prayer to carry with you. It's written out on a strip of paper underneath the church bulletins. Take a copy before you leave. Fold it up and keep it with you. And when you are tempted to sin, say that prayer. And even if you fall into that same sin again, you say that prayer. You understand? We are all sinners, and we are all in need of God's mercy."

"Yes, Father."

"That prayer is your penance," he said. "Now make a good Act of Contrition."

> Oh my God, I am heartily sorry for having offended Thee, and I detest all my sins, because I dread the loss of Heaven and the pains of Hell, but most of all because they offend Thee, my God, Who art all good, and deserving of all my love. I firmly resolve, with the help of Thy grace, to confess my sins, to do penance, and to amend my life. Amen.

While I said the Act of Contrition out loud in English, he prayed in a Latin undertone the prayer by which Jesus Christ had empowered him to forgive my sins and grant me Absolution:

> *Deus, Pater misericordiárum, qui per mortem et resurrectiónem Filii sui mundum sibi reconciliávit et Spiritum Sanctum effúdit in remissiónem peccatórum, per*

ministérium Ecclésiæ indulgéntiam tibi tribuat et pacem. Et ego te absólvo a peccátis tuis in nómine Patris, et Filii, et Spíritus Sancti.

"And if you keep having problems with that sin, you come to the Rectory and see me, okay?" he said.

"Yes, Father," I said, knowing I would never do that. I tried to picture standing at the front door of the Rectory and ringing the bell and then telling P.J. that I was still having problems with sins against purity. I just couldn't do it—it sounded way too creepy. *What would he do about that, anyway, tell me he had to take a look at it?*

But since I was again in the "state of grace" and had made a "firm purpose of amendment" to stay in that condition as long as I could, I went over to the table where the church bulletins were kept as I exited the Church, and looked underneath them, and, sure enough, there was a stack of thin strips of paper, reproduced in purple mimeograph ink: "Lord, be merciful to me, a sinner." The pile had been knocked slightly askew, but I could see that some of the older copies near the bottom were written in cursive, while the newer ones on top were typed out. He must have been expecting quite a run on sins of impurity, because he had made at least a dozen of them. I imagine that pile was considerably reduced, however, by the time the Fletcher boys left the church. I selected a typed copy from the top of the pile, folded it quickly, and put it in my pocket.

After dinner that evening, we went through our Saturday night ritual, bringing all our dress shoes into the dining room while Dad spread newspapers over the table. We each polished and buffed our own shoes, trading back and forth the tins of brown and black Kiwi wax polish, the applicator rags and the one buffing brush, before night prayers and then off to bed. But after John got into bed, I sat at my desk for a minute, tore off the bottom of a piece of looseleaf paper, and wrote out my prayer in my own handwriting, so I could keep it with me—it would be less incriminating than the strip P.J. was handing out in Confession. I tucked the church copy into my St. Joseph Daily Missal, alongside the thirty or so "holy cards" which I kept in there. These were small cards showing copies of beautiful artwork of Jesus, Mary and Joseph or other saints and angels. Some were gifts from nuns as a reward for good work, and some were remembrance cards given out at funerals.

"What are you doing?" John asked, annoyed that the light was still on.

"Just making a note for tomorrow," I said, then dipped three fingers into the holy water font and flicked the water onto him, saying "Baptizz, baptizz," before hitting the light switch and leaping across the room into bed, racing the vanishing light, and trying to get there before the room turned fully dark. It was a close thing, but I never quite made it.

"Hey, John, you wanna build a clubhouse?" I asked, lying there in the dark.

"What for?" John asked.

"Just so we have a place to go," I said.

"We have plenty of places to go," he said. And that was it. I didn't even have to ask Michael. Whatever John said was what Michael agreed to—and everybody else, for that matter.

I had a problem getting people to take my ideas seriously. Probably because of John. He was so perfect—everybody listened to him—Mom and Dad did, too. Whenever we had an argument, they always took his side—even when he was lying and I was telling the truth! They just trusted him. *Wait 'til I'm Heavyweight Champion of the World. I bet people will listen to me then.* But until then nobody seemed to give a whip what I said or wanted or did.

My older brother was famous. He was the Mayfly Newsboy of the Year last year. Even got to go on a trip to the State Capitol in Jefferson City and meet the governor! Came back with a big trophy, which was all polished up behind glass in the living room, alongside a picture of him shaking hands with the governor. The picture was even in the newspaper!

There was a framed document on the same shelf. It had the Papal Seal on it and certified that big brother John was also a Knight of The Altar. I was going to try for it, too, so I was studying the Handbook:

> It is of the utmost importance to choose the right type of boys to serve at the altar. The future Knight of The Altar, first of all, should be a boy of superior character, pure of heart and soul. He should have a special love for Our Lord in the Blessed Sacrament. He should show his love in a practical way by often visiting Our Lord as He waits in the silence of the tabernacle and by receiving Him frequently in Holy Communion.
>
> Secondly, he must be intelligent. He must learn the Latin prayers and be able to recite them from memory.
>
> He must always be trustworthy and reliable. When an altar boy is scheduled to serve early Mass, he must be on time. Some mornings it requires a certain amount of self-sacrifice to keep an appointment, but the true knight remembers what his Master sacrificed for him and any sacrifice an altar boy may be required to make is small in comparison. "Be on time" is an ironclad rule for any true Knight of The Altar.

But I wasn't sure if I would make it. I was pretty much just an "also ran" next to John. Plus there was no room on that shelf for another certificate and I didn't think I would get my own shelf—what else would I put on it?

Nobody seemed to like my ideas much—and this went all the way back. Heck, I remember when I was really little, collecting entire armfuls of box elder bugs. I can still picture those calm black bugs, outlined in thin orange margins with deep red balls for eyes, loading them into my toddler wheelbarrow by the armload to take them for a ride. They didn't even act grateful. If I were a bug and someone went out of their way to take me for a ride I would appreciate it. Bet if John took them for a ride, they'd all be fluttering their wings and chirping their thanks, or whatever they do.

Then another time right after 3rd grade I came up with a great idea to start a Military Club. I spent the entire morning hauling big boards up our seventeen front steps onto the porch, then carried up a bunch of huge rocks to support the boards so we could sit on benches. Nobody would help me—John and Michael weren't interested in my idea. Undaunted, I invited all the kids in the neighborhood to the first meeting. I was the boss of the club. Everybody talked at once. Even when I told them to shut up, they didn't pay any attention—even though it was *my club*. The club never really got off the ground. After a while, people just drifted away. Maybe I should have had some club business or an agenda of some kind, but that wasn't the point—I just thought it would be neat to start a club that I was the leader of. We didn't vote on that—I was afraid they might vote for somebody else, like John.... Probably not The Archangel, but who knows? I still shudder to think what could have happened.

I never called another meeting. Then Mom made me carry the boards back down the steps and put them "back in the shed where you found them" and haul the big rocks back to wherever they came from in the rock garden. Looked like I couldn't count on anybody else. But that was gonna change when I was Heavyweight Champion of the World—in fact, I was counting on it.

13.
SUNDAY MORNING

The next morning was Sunday—we were up early, showering and dressing to attend early Mass at 6:30. We all wore white shirts and ties, even Tim, who was only five. We boys wore the clip-on variety, which saved a lot of time getting ready, since Dad only had to tie one necktie instead of seven. I patted Prince good morning and let him off his leash. He leapt up and down, hoping I was taking him somewhere fun. I felt especially guilty to abandon him as he was doing his play bow. *He probably thinks I'm too stupid to figure out what he's telling me.*

On Sunday, we always drove the three blocks to church in our nine-passenger station wagon. As soon as the door closed on the eight of us, Stephen turned around in the rear-facing third seat and yelled, "First half first, second half second, buy and carry the paper." *Darn!* Everyone else was too sleepy to be on the ball, but Stephen had it all planned out—he was talking about the funny paper, which came in two halves. The rule was you couldn't call it before everyone else was all together in the car for early Mass.

"First half second, second half first," Tim yelled.

"I already called it," Michael says.

"Oh," says Tim. He hadn't, but no one argued—you didn't want to set The Archangel off before Mass, especially in a confined space like the car.

Summer of '63

We arrived at the Church parking lot at 6:25 a.m., disembarking like a SWAT team as four car doors plus the back tail gate sprang open at the same moment and disgorged the eight of us. We dismounted, hustled into the church and walked up the center aisle to the front pew. Mom thought it was good for us to sit where we could all see, so we could "participate more fully" in the Holy Sacrifice of the Mass, but I'm sure the rest of the congregation appreciated it at least as much as we did.

The Fletcher Circus was the weekly entertainment at early Sunday Mass: Dad and Mom and six freshly buzz-headed boys. John waved left and right to his many fans and admirers, real and imagined, as he walked up the aisle. Michael had been on a recent walking-stick jag, and Mom, also unwilling to rile him up before Mass, allowed him to bring his fanciest stick. It had an ornate gold knob at the top, and The Archangel was nothing short of imposing as he tapped his way up the long marble center aisle. Mark, who had never forgotten that a pigeon had once escaped from the belfry and gained entrance to the sacred precincts, meandered this way and that in the wide center aisle, his neck craned hopefully as he scanned the rafters and choir loft for any fresh signs of aviary incursion. Stephen, perhaps more goal-oriented than the majority of his siblings, had all he could do to pick his way through the bobbing and weaving group of brothers without bumping into them or tripping on them. The smallest entrant, youngest brother Tim, had used so much Brylcream on his quarter-inch-long buzz that it glistened in a golden halo in the light of the overhead chandeliers. No one made the mistake of confusing him for a saint.

I sighed and dragged myself up the aisle with the rest of them. Sometimes it seemed I was the only normal one in the family.

I carried my St. Joseph's Daily Missal, eagerly anticipating some quiet time to meditate upon the Scriptures, particularly the story of

Susannah. This strategy, however, required me to enter the pew surrounded by Little Boys, because if I sat too close to Mom or Dad, they might notice that I was reading the Epistle from the Third Saturday in Lent instead of today's Mass. When you were required to be as good as we were, trickery and duplicity were essential tools of the skillset.

Sixty seconds after we were all ensconced in the pew, the entry bell rang from the side doorway at the front of church, and it all went south. It was P.J.—again. I thought I saw him look searchingly at me as he came out into the sanctuary, and again when he approached the pulpit prior to the sermon. As the sermon began, half a dozen men in the congregation rose from the ends of their pews, genuflected toward the tabernacle, and walked to the back of the church. They didn't like P.J. any more than I did and refused to listen to his sermon. I wondered why. We heard the big front door open as they left the church for a smoke. I wished I were old enough to smoke—in public, that is. No one appeared surprised; the mass exodus was expected—it replayed itself every Sunday morning, and the sermon was not a necessary part of our duty to attend Sunday Mass.

In the Catholic Church, you don't get to fire your priest, even if you can't stand him. I asked God the same question about P.J. that I asked about mosquitoes: why did He create them? What was He thinking? The same reason He created smallpox and polio and the bubonic plague, I guess. But I hated Fr. Reiser more than mosquitoes or disease. I hated him because he thought he was better than me, better than everybody else, and better than the animals that God created—but I'll get to that part later. Anyway, being saddled with a total jerk like P.J. could really put a person off his feed, spiritually speaking. He was Christ-like in one way, though, I reflected—"he was a worm, and no man."

Summer of '63

"My dear people," P.J. said from the pulpit. He was at it again, playing the Big Man, the Good Shepherd, opening his arms wide and figuratively embracing his "flock," many of whom hated him. When his eyes passed over me, I got the distinctive feeling that he knew who I was in the Confessional and was trying to gauge whether I had made it through the night. I kept my face blank as he talked about sin and Judgment Day. He went on and on about the evil of sin, and the penalty that we would have to pay for sin. He even quoted Jesus at the Last Supper, saying that it would have been better for Judas if he had never been born. I couldn't imagine myself ever doing anything quite on the scale of Judas, but I did have my issues, and even my best attempts seemed to morph into Mortal Sin at alarming intervals, so even though I tried to ignore him, I was wondering whether I would be among the sheep or the goats and whether I would be gathered into the sweet barn of heaven or burnt in unquenchable fire, and he almost had me right there, because once I burned my wrist on the oven door, and it hurt something terrible, and what if it hurt like that all over, and what if it just went on forever, so I thought maybe I really better go see him about my problem. I wondered what he could do that would really help me. But after a few minutes the impulse went away when I remembered how much I hated his guts.

After the sermon, the smokers, who had been watching through the big double doors at the church entrance like juvenile delinquents, walked back up the aisle, genuflected, and re-entered the pews where their families sat, back in full attendance for the mandatory parts of their "Sunday Obligation."

At the end of Mass, immediately after the Prayers for the Conversion of Russia, the priest intoned the first few words of yet another prayer, an oldie but a goodie:

"St. Michael the Archangel," he said, and we immediately answered together:

Defend us in battle; be our protection against the wickedness and snares of the devil. Do thou rebuke him, we humbly pray; and do thou, O prince of the heavenly host, by the power of God, thrust into hell Satan and the other evil spirits who prowl about the world for the ruin of souls. Amen.

Michael looked smug. He loved what St. Michael the Archangel stood for—kickin' ass for God. In his bedroom, he even had a colored statue of St. Michael the Archangel with a long spear, preparing to run it into the devil—*en route* to thrusting him into hell.

As we left the church vestibule, Stephen held out his hand and Dad dropped a quarter into it. Stephen and Tim hurtled down the steps to where a newsboy had left his hand truck standing upright, contents open toward the church steps, containing a stack of newspapers—the St. Louis Post-Dispatch. The newsboy was not there, but Stephen deposited the quarter onto the pile of change left on top of the kid's money bag and picked up a copy of the paper.

When we got home, Stephen and Tim retired to the living room floor with their prizes, while Mom started heating two cast-iron skillets for our regular Sunday breakfast extravaganza: a huge platter of eggs with bacon, piles of toast with jellies and preserves, a delicious home-baked St. Timothy coffeecake, and cantaloupe. Dad began toasting and buttering the two loaves of bread, and the rest of us set the table, selected the jellies, and poured the juice, which was always either grapefruit or homemade tomato juice (great unless you had a sore throat). I wiped the skillet out with two slices of white bread and slipped out the back to give them to Prince. He was appreciative. Life was good.

14.
THE BUNDLE

On Sunday evening, our telephone rang, startling the entire household out of Sunday evening quiet. The dishes were done, the shoes were shined, "The Wonderful World of Disney" had just ended, and the television set was turned off for the night. It was 7:30 P.M. I got to the phone first. It was Toby, excited.

"Hurry over; you've gotta hear this!" he said.

"Really? You want to work on our science project this evening?" I asked, enunciating perhaps more than usual. "I'll ask."

Five minutes later, during which time I hopped around like I had to go to the bathroom while I waited for Mom to get out of the shower, and finally having lied my way into the required permission, I busted down our hill to Broadway and turned right for the four-minute sprint past the church toward the promise of juicy eavesdropping at the River's Rest.

Immaculate Conception Church was built on the corner of Hayden and Broadway, right next to our school. Even from blocks away in the deepening dusk, it was distinctive by its corner bell tower of contrasting brick and limestone, which rose fifty-two feet above street level. Majestic by Mayfly standards, it boasted eight arched open-air windows, two on each side of the tower, separated by white stone pillars and supported by huge carved white stone lintels, window frames and ledges.

As I approached the church, I caught sight of an object at the foot of the bell tower which slowed me down—something odd. There was a person bent over a bundle on the ground. Puzzled but in a hurry, I continued running toward the church quickly and quietly, now jogging silently in my canvas shoes, curiously attentive, but hoping to slip by without being seen. I was on a mission, and I couldn't afford to be delayed by some elderly person who had dropped their groceries, even though under non-emergency conditions I would have stopped to help. But as I drew closer, I could see a man with a small-brimmed hat kneeling on the ground just downhill from the corner. He was looking down at the bundle and talking angrily.

"I warned you! I warned you!" he was saying. Then several things happened in quick succession. First, I recognized the voice from under the hat. It was Fr. Reiser. *Oh, my God—what's wrong with him? What is he talking about? And why is he kneeling on the ground?* By this time, I was frozen motionless, wishing that I could just disappear, that God would somehow make me invisible, at least until I got past the corner of the building. Then I looked at the bundle and saw, to my horror, what it was—it was a man lying there, not a bundle, or at least some weird form of a man, because the man didn't look right—he lay all wrong, spraddled out in unnatural angles, and Fr. Reiser was bent over it, talking to it, or to him.

My mission forgotten, I stood rooted to the sidewalk, mouth open, staring. I could feel the hair on the back of my neck rising. Then I saw something that literally scared the bejesus out of me—I went rigid in absolute terror—that familiar mop of red hair. But his skull was horribly cracked open like an egg and gray matter was spilling out. It formed little oily islands in a big pool of blood on the concrete sidewalk, which ran downhill before rolling off the edge of the sidewalk. That familiar face that I knew so well, frozen in fright or pain or both, with his recognizable blue eyes open, surprised and sightless there on the concrete, left me too stunned to form a single coherent thought. But not too stunned to feel horror in every pore.

And then I smelled the powerful appalling fresh fecal stench which hung over him, and vomit rose in my throat, and I stood there with my hand in front of my mouth, staring in shock and disbelief and disgust at the body of my best friend whom I had just talked to on the phone ten minutes before, and knowing he had no inkling of this and no warning—but in all that terrible sight, of my best friend lying there in a heap, completely destroyed, irretrievable, thrown away like trash, in pain and horror and ugliness and total waste, it was his shoes which gave him away, which riveted my attention, which turned me to staring stone—because they weren't Toby's shoes at all—they were Tom's Converse sneakers.

Fr. Reiser hadn't heard or seen me. He was going through his pants pockets. I crept in soundlessly beside him.

"What happened?" I asked. "Who is it—is it Tom?" Tom, whom I had seen only hours ago, smiling and coming out of Church when I went in for Confession.

Fr. Reiser started at the sound of my voice right next to him, a single jerk of his entire body, then he froze. He didn't acknowledge me for the longest time. When he finally looked up at me, I could tell that he didn't know who I was. His eyes were deep and wide and far away, lost in some other world. They were as dead as the eyes of the man at his feet. Finally, he started to come back, pulled back, slowly, a long journey of a return, and he looked at me for several moments without a word, a guilty look—but defiant, the look of a vandal caught spray-painting a wall, and then, as I stared at him, a protracted grapple for words, and finally he said, so quiet I had to strain to hear him, "I don't know what happened to him. He must have fallen." And I don't know why, but something about his answer, I don't know if it was what he said or the way he said it, something was wrong—I felt like he wasn't telling the truth, that he was covering something up.

I stood with my mouth open, staring at this pompous, contemptible man I so hated, bent over the mangled and shit-smelling body of my friend, and tried to digest all that this statement imparted, when the huge oak front door of the church exploded open with a startling bang, propelled forcefully back on its big bronze hinges until it smacked the brick façade, a sound like dead wood hit with an ax, and Ray Lee Po came loping down the front steps, two at a time. He showed no sign that he saw us or even knew we were present, but merely walked over to where Tom's body lay smashed on the concrete, then stopped short and pointed at it with his long index finger and grunted repeatedly while he continued to point, then turned and pointed, grunting, at the church doors he had just come out, then turned away and left.

My mouth hung open. *What in the name of God is wrong with him? What did he mean by it?* There was so much expression in those grunts. *Did they say something to him? Did he know that he couldn't speak any language we could understand? Or did he think we understood him? Did even he understand what he meant?* I thought so. *But what did he mean? Why was he grunting? And why was he pointing?*

I wanted to run after him, to ask him, but as soon as the impulse occurred to me, I knew that it was useless. *Was it a warning? Of what? Amazement at Tom's condition? An "I told you so"? "I hope you get better"? "You need to call the police"? "Get up"? What?* I looked at Fr. Reiser, who was watching Ray Lee Po's long strides as he receded rapidly into the distance, then looked back at me.

"What happened?" I asked, "Is it Tom?"

He didn't answer either question. "Is it Tom?" I asked again.

He just ignored me, then said, "Run home and call the police."

And tell them what? I looked at him, nonplussed, anger flaring inside me. I wasn't going anywhere.

"What happened? Is that Tom?" I demanded, louder now. Even though I thought I knew, I wanted to make that pompous jerk answer me.

"Now," he said. "Go," then turned back to the body.

So I did—I left, because he was a priest and he told me to, but I turned around and looked back as I ran away. Fr. Reiser was still kneeling next to Tom's body, and he was mumbling something, but I couldn't make it out—any of it.

15.
FIRST WITNESS

On Tuesday afternoon, Toby and I stood in a stuffy old office room on the second floor of a commercial building on South Main Street, listening disconsolately to the drone of flies. They were buzzing angrily against the dirty upper windowpanes, too stupid to notice that the lower panes were wide open in a vain attempt to capture a breeze. In one corner, a door stood open to reveal an ancient bathroom with a stained toilet, an empty wire toilet paper holder and a dirty pedestal sink. Street noise provided the only other sound. No words were said.

A filthy drinking glass, its inside crusted with some long-evaporated liquid, hosted its own collection of dead flies as it perched on a sagging wooden windowsill. An empty Pepsi Cola bottle stood on the floor below it. The only seating in the room consisted of an unmatched pair of rickety wooden chairs set against the back wall, which were occupied by Toby's parents. Mr. Piper's red-rimmed eyes stared out of dark, sunken sockets at a floor layered in years of dust and littered with old candy bar wrappers. Mrs. Piper sat with her hands clenched in her lap, one hand covering a balled-up Kleenex, which she daubed at her swollen eyes sporadically. Her eyes searched the room wildly—she was a trapped animal looking for a way out.

Toby and I were waiting to testify in front of the Coroner's Jury, which was meeting in another room down the hall. The Coroner was

George Randall, an obese former politician who liked to feel that he was still important. We had been officially notified by a telephone call to our parents from the Coroner that our attendance was required. He had taken pains to make it clear to them that, if we did not show up, the sheriff would bring us in.

Footsteps sounded on the bare wooden stairwell outside the door of our room, and four pairs of eyes swung to the doorway, expectant. It was Fr. Reiser. I guess I should have anticipated that he would be there, since he was the first to find Tom dead, but the sight of him shocked me as he leaned his head into the doorway.

"Good morning, Father," said Mr. and Mrs. Piper immediately, followed by Toby and me, for whom civilities to P.J. had always been less than automatic, and were even less so now.

"Good morning," he said, then withdrew his head and walked down the hallway to the jury room. Nothing more. We looked at each other. That was very weird. Why was he avoiding the Pipers? We listened to his footsteps as he walked away.

I tiptoed down the hall and went into the new bathroom next to the Inquest room. I could hear the Coroner's big voice.

"Hello again, Rev. Reiser. We haven't seen you since the hearing on that Dalton boy's suicide three years ago. What's gotten into these young people?" I left the bathroom and hurried quietly back down the hall to the front room.

After an unintelligible rumble of voices, the Coroner came down the hallway and stood in our doorway. His girth was enormous—he completely filled the doorway.

"Good morning, folks. I'm George Randall, the Coroner," he announced. "You can all come in now; we're ready to begin. Follow me."

The four of us followed him down a long hallway smelling of dry wood and covered in ancient, yellowed linoleum. The floor creaked loudly under his weight. Halfway down the hall, a dim and dirty bulb hung from the high ceiling on a single wire, illuminating the old woodwork. It was tongue-and-groove wainscotting, painted with thick industrial pea-green enamel and topped by a full-thickness crown molding covered with the dust of ages. Overhead, an unpainted aluminum cold air return ran out through the transom in our waiting room and down the full length of the hallway before turning left into the back room, which was being used for the Inquest.

The Inquest room was an addition to the rear of the building. Fluorescent lights glowed feebly in competition with the glare from the windows. The room was warm. It smelled of coffee and stank powerfully of rotten eggs, and the windows on three sides had been thrown open. On our right, stretched across the front of the room, stood two old wooden spindle-legged tables, placed lengthwise, end-to-end. Three chairs had been placed behind each table, facing the room, and all six were now occupied by the jurors, six men with dead eyes, one of whom nodded soberly to us as we entered—the others didn't acknowledge us at all. A carafe of ice water stood on each table next to a stack of paper cups, and a coffee maker stood on a small table behind them.

The middle of the room was bare, except for a single witness chair facing the jury, which was already occupied by Fr. Reiser. His coffee cup rested on a plantstand which had been placed in front of him. There was no podium, no bailiff, and no court reporter. To our left in the back of the room stood a scattering of metal folding chairs facing off in various directions.

The Coroner slid behind a big desk on the far side of the room facing the doorway and picked up his coffee cup.

"Have a seat, folks," he said, indicating the collection of folding chairs with a sweep of his massive right arm. "We don't stand on ceremony here." According to Toby's parents, he was an unemployed undertaker by trade, with no other medical training and no legal training. Since he had been the only candidate on the ballot for the last sixteen years, however, he had presided over a number of inquests. He paused until we were seated, then picked up a gavel and thumped it on his desk.

"We're here to inquire into the death of Thomas John Piper, age seventeen years," he began. "This Coroner's Jury has been assembled and charged with their duty and sworn in, and you witnesses have been summoned, and I see that we are all here. This hearing is not on the record, but I will make notes of the testimony. Also present are the decedent's parents, Mr. and Mrs. Piper. And I believe that Rev. Reiser asked to make a statement before we begin taking evidence, so go ahead, Rev. Reiser, the floor is yours."

Fr. Reiser rose. "Thank you, Mr. Randall. Without going into the evidence, I wanted to remind all present of the priest/penitent privilege, which, as you are aware, is recognized by Missouri law and which prohibits inquiry into my knowledge and communications with a member of my church regarding any spiritual matter."

"Thank you, Rev. Reiser. We will keep that in mind," said Mr. Randall. "Now, if we could begin with you, I'm sure you have a lot of other duties this afternoon."

"Yes, I do, thank you."

"Alright," said the coroner. "Raise your right hand and be sworn," as he raised his own right hand in demonstration and recited, "Do you swear to tell the truth, the whole truth and nothing but the truth, so help you God?"

"I do, subject to my reservation of any items covered by the priest/penitent privilege," answered Fr. Reiser.

"We understand that. Very good. Please have a seat, Rev. Reiser. You're the pastor of the Catholic Church here in Mayfly, aren't you?"

"Yes, I am."

"How long have you lived in Mayfly?"

"Eighteen years."

"Do you know Thomas John Piper?"

"Yes, I've known him all his life. I baptized him." A whimper escaped from Mrs. Piper, who stifled herself with her hand, her shoulders shuddering in silent sobs. After a brief pause, he continued, "He and his family are members of my parish."

"I understand you are the one who found the body, correct?"

"Yes."

"Can you tell me how you happened to find the body?"

"Well, it was about 8:30 p.m. last Sunday evening. I had just finished saying my Office and I decided to walk around the outside of the Church while I finished my prayers."

"I'm sorry, what was that about your office?" one of the jurors asked.

"The Divine Office, the Liturgy of the Hours, a series of prayers that priests say every day, based on the Psalms. I often walk while I pray the Office."

"So you were walking around your church?" the Coroner asked.

"Yes, praying, and it had gotten dark, because it was overcast that day, but I could see by the streetlight that there was something on the ground, and as I got near to it I could see that it was a body."

"What did you see?"

"Well, he was lying all wrong, but I could see his head and his legs and one of his arms sticking out—one of his arms was under him, I guess."

Silence.

"Anything else?"

"Well, I could see a large pool of blood spreading out around the body and there was a footprint next to it that was being covered by the blood. Someone had already stepped in the blood. And I hurried over to see if I could help stop the bleeding or help the person in any way, and I had to step in the pool of blood to get near him and I had to just kneel down in it and when I leaned over him, I saw that he was clearly dead."

"You could tell that by looking?"

"Yes."

"How could you be sure?"

"His head was split open and I could see his brains lying on the concrete."

I looked over at Mrs. Piper, who had just pushed both hands in front of her mouth. As I watched her, I heard a high wail. It took me a moment to figure out that it had not come from her—it had come from Toby.

I watched Mr. Piper trying to console his wife. Toby had tears running down both sides of his face. His chest was heaving, but he was at least silent. I couldn't look at any of them. I looked back at Fr. Reiser. Fury boiled up inside me. I wanted to kill him. The arrogant jerk didn't get it. He didn't know what it felt like to love someone, to have a son. A brother. Clueless jerk. Asshole. I wanted to shit in his coffee. I hated him so much that my vocabulary was inadequate to the task at hand—I had only been cursing for a year, and I wasn't very good at it. "Screw you, butthole!" I finally said in an explosive whisper, a bit too loudly. Several of the jurors looked at me. It infuriated me even more to know that now I had to go to Confession and tell him that I had used bad words and that I had been angry.

"Mrs. Piper," said the Coroner, apparently under the impression that the wail had come from her, "I'm sorry, but we have to go into this. Would you prefer to wait in the other room?" An emphatic shake of her head. No.

Turning his attention back to Fr. Reiser, the Coroner asked, "Rev. Reiser, do you know what happened to Thomas Piper?"

I watched him carefully. He didn't even hesitate. It was like he had practiced the answer. "No, I don't know how he ended up on the ground. I don't know why he was in the bell tower. It looked like he fell," he said, but something about his answer didn't ring true with me. He was under oath. *What was he hiding? What did he mean by 'it looked like'?"*

The Coroner continued, "And just so everyone here is aware, Rev. Reiser, I understand from the police that you leave the church unlocked twenty-four hours a day, is that correct?"

"Yes, we always have, and virtually every other Catholic church in the world is open twenty-four hours a day," he said.

"And why is that?"

"We believe that Jesus Christ is actually present physically in the tabernacle in every Catholic church. People like to visit with Him. In case anyone would like to stop in, day or night, the doors of the church are always open."

"Juror, take this over to Rev. Reiser." A pause, while the nearest juror disentangled himself from his chair, hitched up his pants, and walked across the room to the Coroner, who handed him a transparent plastic bag containing several small pieces of paper, then delivered it back to Fr. Reiser, who looked up questioningly at the Coroner.

"You may examine them inside the plastic bag, Rev. Reiser," said the Coroner. "Please do not open the bag or touch the paper inside the bag directly."

Fr. Reiser looked down at the bag for a couple of seconds, then blanched visibly. He turned the bag over in his hands and examined the back sides of the fragments. Then his eyes changed again, subtly. He looked almost furtive.

"Did you look at the pieces of paper?" the Coroner asked.

"Yes. Where was this?" Fr. Reiser asked quietly.

"In his shirt pocket," the Coroner answered. "Do you recognize that?"

"If I did, I wouldn't be able to talk about it, because of the sacred bond of the Confessional," P.J. said.

"You will agree that those pieces of paper show the letters 'l,' 'o,' 's,' 'e,' and 'r,' though, won't you?"

Fr. Reiser looked back at the bag, turning it over in his hands. "Yes," he said, after a pause.

"And the "L" is capital, correct?"

"Yes."

"We have a lot of questions about this boy's personal life, Rev. Reiser. I assume you won't be able to talk about that for the same reason?"

"I'm afraid not."

"I see. Alright, then," said the Coroner. "Do any of you jurors have questions for Rev. Reiser? If not, I'm going to excuse him."

No response. They just looked at him.

"None? Alright, Rev. Reiser, you are free to go. Thank you for coming in."

Fr. Reiser stood up, head down, shoulders hunched like he was carrying the weight of the world. I figured he was acting. "I think I will just stay and observe, if that is permissible," he said.

"Of course. This is a public hearing," said the Coroner.

16.
TEMPERS

"James Fletcher," the Coroner called, looking directly at me.

"Yessir," I said, standing up, suddenly on high alert. I didn't know what I was afraid of, but my body was in full flight mode—my ears rang and my eyes strained open. I must have been standing still for a while, because I heard the Coroner say, "Please take the witness chair, Mr. Fletcher," and I noticed for the first time that everyone was staring at me. I started moving toward the witness chair.

"Raise your right hand and be sworn," he said, demonstrating. I did.

"Do you solemnly swear to tell the truth, the whole truth and nothing but the truth?"

"I do."

After eliciting my full name, date of birth, address, and phone number, the Coroner asked if I had also seen the body that night.

"Yes."

"What were you doing at the time?"

"I was headed down to visit his brother Toby at the River's Rest Motel."

"Kinda late for a schoolboy your age to be out, ain't it?"

"Yes, we had been working on a project for the Science Fair." Telling the whole truth meant confessing that we were going to smoke some cigarettes in the basement, while hopefully eavesdropping on some juicy stuff going on in the room of this pretty visiting coed, but obviously I couldn't tell any of that. *Oh, nuts! Perjury already, and only the second real question. Still, I can't rat out my best buddy, no matter what. And it's not any business of this fat old bastard what we were doing anyway.*

"And you saw the body lying on the ground just as Rev. Reiser described?"

"Yes."

"What was going on when you arrived?" I could feel P.J.'s eyes boring into the back of my head.

"Fr. Reiser was bending over the body." I didn't mention that Fr. Reiser was talking to Tom, that he was really angry, that he said, "I warned you" over and over, that he was searching his pockets, that I didn't see the other footprint he claimed was there, that Ray Lee Po came blasting out angry and upset and pointed at him and grunted at him over and over, or that Fr. Reiser sent me away—none of it. *So much for the whole truth. But then that fat bastard didn't ask me, did he? I'm not a mind reader.*

"And could you tell if he was alive?"

"Yes—he was dead."

"How do you know?"

"The same way. I could see some of what looked like his brains on the sidewalk."

"How well did you know Thomas Piper?"

"Very well. He's a good friend of mine and my best friend's big brother." *Or was.*

"I understand he owned a car."

"Yessir."

"A '57 Chevy convertible."

"Yessir."

"Did you ever go riding with him?"

"Yes."

"Where did you go?"

"Mostly up and down Broadway."

"Ever go to Central Park with him?"

"No."

"Why not?"

"He didn't take us there. He went to Central Park when he wanted to be alone."

"Who's 'us'?"

"Toby and Richard Washington and me. He usually took us all riding together."

"So you knew he spent time in Central Park?"

"Yes."

"At night?"

"Yes."

"That he sat in the bandstand there?"

"Yes."

"Above the public restrooms?"

I just looked at him. *What is he insinuating?* I didn't answer.

"I asked you a question," he said.

"What question?"

"You knew he sat right above the public restrooms?"

Without warning, there was a massive explosion just inside my temples. My peripheral vision vanished, replaced by roiling walls of fat gray smoke. I had tunnel vision, and all I could see at the other end was this fat, greasy, insinuating bastard staring at me. *Prying Fatboy.* His new name energized me. Suddenly I didn't give a good goddamn about Prying Fatboy and the entire Dead-Eyed Fart-Sniffing Jury. In fact, I hated the whole lot of them and I didn't care if they knew it. I looked him right in the eye, down the length of my tunnel: "You know more about the public restrooms than I do," I said, flinging it out as a challenge. "I think your name is on the wall there."

Long pause.

"Son, do you realize you are under oath?"

"I'm not your son." *Dad would have been proud of me.*

Another pause while he eyed me, then, "Did Tom have a girlfriend?"

"Not that I know of," I spat. *Well, maybe Crazy Carly, but Tom hardly considered her his girlfriend.*

"Would you know if he had a girlfriend?"

"Prob'ly."

"Why do you think he didn't?"

"He just wasn't a hit with the girls—it didn't seem to bother him," I said dismissively.

"Did he have any men friends?"

"I don't know."

"You never saw him with other men?"

"I don't know what you mean by 'men'; I don't know if he had friends his age. Tom was my friend, and he was a great friend to Toby and to Richard Washington."

"Who is Richard Washington?"

"A friend of ours."

"Is that someone your age?"

"Yes."

"How did they know each other?"

"Same as me. Friends with Toby. Tom took us riding sometimes."

"Did you know that Thomas Piper drank alcohol?"

"Yes, some."

"What do you mean, 'some'?"

"He didn't drink very often. Only if a customer left a bottle in the room when they checked out."

"And Tom would drink it?"

"Sometimes." *I'm certainly not gonna "tell the whole truth" by mentioning that Toby and I did, too.*

"Do you know how Mr. Piper got into the bell tower of the church?"

"I think he had a key."

"How did he happen to have a key?"

"He had one made at Haydon Hardware when he was helping out around the church."

"Did he go in the bell tower often?"

"Yes, well, maybe once or twice a week."

"What did he do up there?"

"He mainly sat and watched the traffic. He just had a quiet place to think. And a place where Carly couldn't bother him." *I'm not going to mention in front of Mr. and Mrs. Piper all the smoking and drinking he did up there—not telling the whole truth again.*

"Who is Carly?"

"Carly Stolte. She's a maid at the motel and she has it real bad for Tom. She's always trying to trap him in a room."

"And Tom wasn't interested?"

"No, he tried to keep away from her."

Toby was next, and they started in on him with the same questions about Tom's personal life that they asked me. Toby started off merely sullen, but it progressed predictably from there. You don't have to wonder what Toby is feeling—you can tell by looking at him. He has real pale skin, and when he gets angry it gets all blotchy. He had already reached that stage when the Coroner asked, "Did he drink up there?"

"Sometimes," Toby answered. *Like, whenever he could get his hands on it.*

"What did he drink?"

"Whatever he found lying around." *I glanced at Mr. and Mrs. Piper. They didn't look surprised. I guess this wasn't news to them after all. When you grow up in a motel, there may be a whole list of acceptable "boys will be boys" behavior that wouldn't fly in the Fletcher household.*

"Have you ever seen him drunk?"

"Yes."

"How many times?"

"I don't know."

"More than a dozen?"

"No."

"More than five?"

"Maybe about three."

"*About.*" *Wonder what he calls drunk,* I mused, immediately calling to mind far more than three occasions that would qualify under my definition.

"Did you ever visit him in the bell tower?"

"He showed it to me once."

"Why didn't you go up there with him after that?"

"It was his quiet place, where he went when he wanted to be alone. He could just think, and watch the traffic go by below. I didn't want to bother him."

"Was there a place to sit in the bell tower?"

"Just the windowsills."

"Did he sit on the windowsills?"

"Yes. I did, too. They were safe, really wide and comfortable."

"Did you know that Tom was up in the bell tower the night he died?"

"Not then—I do now."

"Do you know whether, on the night he died, he had any alcohol with him?"

"No."

"Did your brother have any enemies?"

"No, everyone liked him."

"Anyone you can think of that might want him dead?"

"No." Crazy Carly came immediately to my mind, and I imagine to Toby's, too, but I could see he didn't want to bring that up in front of his parents. Since she figured out that he was avoiding her she had been on a tirade. I wasn't sure how they would take knowing that their son had been seduced by their maid right under their noses.

But Toby had apparently been debating it, because then it just popped out, but thankfully not in all its glorious detail: "Well, there was this one girl who wouldn't leave him alone."

"Who was that?"

"Carly Stolte. She works at the motel. She thought Tom should be her boyfriend, but he didn't want to. She was always chasing him around, trying to get him alone. He just wanted to get away from her."

"Did she know he used the bell tower in the church?" the Coroner asked.

"Not that I know of, and Tom didn't want her to find out, either."

"Okay, anything else your brother talked to you about?"

"Not really. Just his car, his work at the motel, customers and stuff." *Customers and stuff. Nicely put.*

"Was your brother happy, do you think?"

"Yeah, normal happiness—not too happy, but not sad either."

"Did he ever act depressed?"

"No."

"Did he ever talk about suicide?"

"No!" Toby's face had turned bright red.

"Did he ever mention anything about being a loser?" I watched the muscles in Toby's jaw tighten, the cords on his neck straining.

"No. He wasn't a loser," Toby answered through clenched teeth, challenging the Coroner to contradict him. Their eyes locked for several seconds, then the Coroner asked another question.

"Have you seen the note that was in your brother's pocket?" he asked.

"No," Toby said.

The Coroner looked toward the juror. "Hand him the note," he said.

Toby took the plastic bag and stared at it. He fidgeted with it, turning it over and over in his hands. "It's not his," he said, finally.

"What do you mean it's not his?" he asked.

"Tom doesn't write like that," Toby answered. The Coroner just looked at him.

"It was in his pocket," he said, as if that settled it. Then he turned toward the jurors.

"Alright, anybody got any more questions for any of these people?" the Coroner asked.

Silence. Six pairs of dead fish eyes stared out of six poker faces at Mr. and Mrs. Piper and Toby.

"Okay," he continued, "the jury is going to deliberate now, and no one else is allowed to be present during deliberations, so you all are excused. You'll need to leave the note here with us while we deliberate. We'll let the family know when we've reached a verdict. And please accept our sympathy, Mr. and Mrs. Piper, and you, too, son, on the loss of your brother. I know this is very difficult to accept."

"Oh, and folks, can you please close the door on your way out? Thank you. I'll be in touch."

Fr. Reiser was out the door and gone while the rest of us were still sitting there looking at each other and wondering what we should do now. We heard the sound of his footsteps as he walked down the long hallway. He sounded like he was in a hurry.

Finally, Mr. and Mrs. Piper rose and walked toward the door. Toby and I followed.

"I'm not his son, either," Toby said into my ear as we left the room, giving me a quick nod of approval. "Hang back—I've got an idea."

Joseph Welch

As we neared the front of the building, Toby said to his parents, "You go on ahead, I'll just be a few minutes. We can walk home; I need to use the bathroom."

"I'll wait and walk with Toby," I told them, and we both ducked into our former waiting room.

Toby walked toward the bathroom, closed the door loudly, and waited until we heard his parents' steps on the stairs, then ran over to the windowsill, grabbed the empty glass, dumped the dead flies, and sprinted back to the hall doorway with it. I seized one of the rickety chairs for him to stand on, but as tall as Toby was, he was still way too short. Desperate, I looked around the room. Nothing. Toby grabbed the top of the door with both hands and pulled himself up until he could stand on the doorknob with one foot. Still short.

"Here. On my shoulders," I said, holding onto the edge of the door with both hands, then wedging a foot on each side of it to steady it.

"Alright. Hold the glass," Toby said. I stuck my left arm up to take it, like passing a baton, while Toby climbed from the now wavering doorknob onto my shoulders, then reached down for the glass and pressed it to the cold air return, his ear against the bottom of the glass.

"They're getting ready to vote," he whispered. "He's makin' a speech."

Silence, except for occasional street noises and the squeaking of the door hinges as I leaned against it for support, then I heard in disbelief the two words which he spat out with the utmost of his concentrated vehemence: "It's suicide!"

17.
AFTER THE INQUEST

"Those bastards! Those idiots! Morons! Assholes!" Toby swore as we left the building.

"Shhh!" There were other people on the street. "They'll hear you," I said.

"I don't give a shit!" Toby said. "Screw them! Assholes!" he yelled up at the windows. Toby usually didn't swear at all, but he was swearing like a sailor.

"I know, Toby; I don't believe it either. How is that possible? Tom wasn't even depressed," I said. "I saw him that afternoon coming out of church when I went in to go to Confession and he was smiling."

"The last time I saw him was that evening," Toby said, "right after I called you to come over and listen to that girl making out in 108. He was coming out of the linen closet in a big hurry, and I tried to tell him what was up, but he just waved me off. 'Not right now,' he said. 'I gotta tell you something—later.' He didn't even stop—he was in such a big hurry. So I just ran back down to the basement as fast as I could and that was the last time I ever saw him alive. He didn't look like someone who was getting ready to kill himself—you think he was in a hurry to commit suicide? Bullshit! How is that even possible?" Toby was really wound up, and I didn't blame him. I just let him continue.

"You wanna know what that fat bastard said? What I heard through the duct?" He didn't wait for me to answer.

"Look people," he said, doing a creditable imitation of Prying Fatboy's good-ol'-boy intonation, "Ah'm a big impo'tant muckity-muck and ah've got a total load o' shit ah wanna lay on y'all, so just listen up, heah? Ah've got a golf game to get ta and ah sure as hayull want to be theah at the 19th hole bah fahv o'clock. Looks like we're purty far inta the weeds here."

I just stared at him, open-mouthed, but impressed and interested.

"Y'all tryin' ta tell me that some sissy-boy who spends his evenin's lurkin' 'round the public restrooms in Central Park," he continued, "who's got no real friends 'cept whatever other *per*verts he meets in the stinkin' public stall, got no girlfriend or apparent *in* trust in even *havin'* one, goes up into a church steeple all by hisself, who bah the way is *in*'tamuhtly familiar with that steeple," (rolling his eyes knowingly) "and then just happens to fall fo'ty-six foot to his dayuth, with a note in his pocket that says "Looza" and it was a accident?"

I just shook my head.

"Shit, ah'd kill mahself too," he went on. "Ah've heard enough—let's vote," he finished, as he lifted one knee and mimed farting.

"That's exactly what that fat bastard said. And I'm never gonna forget it—ever," Toby continued.

I just stood and looked at him, agog. I was all in for joining the profanity parade. "That stupid shit! He rushed it so he could get to his golf game," I said, unbelieving.

"Golf game! That means the bar! The 19th hole is the *bar*!" Toby informed me.

I stopped dead on the sidewalk, staring at him. "*That Asshole! That big, fat turd!*" I said, joining Toby in giving it my very best. We walked on in silence.

"Wait," I said suddenly. "I gotta stop at the Dime Store. I need a Magic Marker."

"Good idea," Toby said, as we headed in that direction. "We don't want to make a liar out of you." Ten minutes later, we were paying the clerk for the marker.

As we headed toward Central Park, Toby asked, "What about the footprint? What was P.J. talkin' about?"

"Toby, I was there early on, and I didn't see any other footprint," I said.

"P.J. is the only one who saw it, and there's somethin' really weird goin' on with him."

"Yeah, for instance, how come he was avoiding us?" Toby asked. "We've had him over to the motel for dinner for years, even on Christmas Day. Plus, Tom helped him around the church—for years—since he was eight! He always called Tom whenever he needed something—even little things that the janitor could have done. And Tom always went over, whenever P.J. called him."

Shortly after, I was printing the words "Prying Fatboy" with Magic Marker on the freshly painted masonry wall in the men's restroom underneath the bandstand in Central Park. Then just for good measure I printed, "For a good time, call George Randall," vowing to add his phone number the next time I was in the neighborhood—I had to look it up first in the telephone book.

Having completed our restroom project, neither of us had much else to say when we parted, each to our own home. But I couldn't stop thinking about it, and I was sure that Toby couldn't, either. I felt like I couldn't leave it alone.

I called him after dinner.

"Listen, Toby," I said, "can you get the note that was in Tom's pocket? They don't need it anymore," I suggested.

"Good idea," he said. "I'll get my dad to ask him for it; tell him we'd like to keep it because it's Tom's writing."

"Is it Tom's writing?" I asked.

"I didn't think so, but I can't be sure. My parents haven't even seen it."

"We need to look at that note," I said.

"Actually, there's a lot we need to look at," said Toby.

"Yeah, but I don't see what good it can do. What difference does it make, anyway?" I asked.

"Well, for one thing," said Toby, "if Tom committed suicide, he can't be buried in hallowed ground. P.J. told Mom and Dad. He called and told them about the inquest verdict because that bastard politician didn't have the guts to call them himself—he just called P.J. instead."

"What's hallowed ground?" I asked.

"The Catholic cemetery is hallowed ground. It's specially blessed. Tom can't be buried with the rest of our family—he'll have to be buried someplace else.

"Some place else?"

"Yeah. And the worst part is, if you're not buried in hallowed ground, you can't go to Heaven."

My mouth dropped open—I was completely speechless. "*Are you serious?*" I asked, finally.

"That's what P.J. told my parents. It's a rule of the Church. There's a specific Church Canon on it. Number 1180."

I was stunned. In shock.

"Oh, shit, Toby, this is terrible! We'll never be able to prove he didn't commit suicide—especially before the funeral. It's almost impossible to prove that something didn't happen!"

"There won't be a funeral, either, at least not a Catholic funeral. No Requiem Mass. You can't have one if you commit suicide. My parents said there won't be a wake, either—no one would come. We're burying him tomorrow in the public cemetery. Dad found a single grave in Riverside Cemetery, on a bluff overlooking the river. Mom keeps crying because he won't be in Heaven and he won't be with the rest of the family. She hasn't slept at all. She keeps going down on her knees and asking God to let him into Heaven anyway. You should see her—it's terrible—she' just crying and praying out loud, 'Please, God, let my boy into Heaven with you. Please, God, I'll do anything.' Dad has to pull her back up. He's really worried about her."

Tom's death was horrible, but this was even worse, if that were possible. I kept thinking about Tom. He was so good-hearted, so nice to us kids, so generous with his time and his car and…Just everything. Didn't that count for anything?

Did he really kill himself? Because he didn't have a girlfriend? Because he was queer? I didn't know if he was queer or not, *but if he was and wanted to change, wouldn't Carly be awfully helpful with that? But that would be a Mortal Sin, too. But so is being queer. I wonder if it's a worse Mortal Sin to have impure queer thoughts than impure thoughts about girls. But how can any Mortal Sin be worse than another? Any one of them will send you straight to hell. Oh, God, I hope and pray that Tom's not in hell—please, God, let Tom come into Heaven with you!*

18.
MS. MAME

The newspaper headline read, "Piper Death Ruled Suicide." As Toby and I approached a Y-shaped intersection called "The Wedge" the next morning on foot, we could see two black men squatting on the sidewalk, their backs against a building. The front picture window identified the place as "Little Africa." One of the men turned and swung his head into the doorway, still squatting, and yelled to someone inside. A moment later a very large and very dark man came out onto the sidewalk, wearing a small white cotton apron and white shirt with sleeves rolled up to the elbow. He looked at the two of us approaching, then pointed a big finger at Toby.

"Your name Piper?" he asked. We both stopped.

"Yessir," Toby said.

"The brother of the boy that died?"

"Yessir," Toby said again.

"Ms. Mame wants to see you," he said. We just stood there rooted to the spot. I felt the sun blazing down on us from overhead. "It's about your brother," he said.

"Who...who is Ms. Mame?" Toby asked.

"She's upstairs. I'll show you." Toby and I looked at each other nonplussed, then followed the man through the open doorway. It was cooler inside, dark and smoky, a shotgun layout, one large room all the way to the back of the building. An antique bar with carved leaves and scrollwork in some dark wood ran down the left wall. Other than the large plate glass window, the only light came from three overhead fixtures, a handful of fluorescent beer advertisement signs, and the long mirror behind the bar. We were the only white people there. A nicely dressed elderly woman wearing a flowered hat sat on a stool at the bar with a tall glass of beer in front of her. She was so tiny her feet didn't touch the floor. One table was occupied by three men wearing suits, one of whom was smoking a cigar.

"This way, boys," said the bartender, leading us the length of the wooden floor to a dark stairwell rising from the rear of the room. He pointed up the stairs, then stood aside as we mounted them, holding onto the wooden railing in the half light. "Knock loud four times when you get to the top, then say, 'Ms. Mame, it's the Piper boy,' and she'll let you in," he said, as he turned to go back to the bar.

I didn't know about Toby, but I had no idea what we were getting into. I wanted to go to the bathroom. We climbed the stairs in the half-dark, then hesitated. "Go ahead," I said. "Four times, loud." Toby turned and knocked. "Ms. Mame, it's the Piper boy," he said.

"Come in," someone called. Toby turned the doorknob, pushed the door open slowly, then walked in. I followed him, looking around so busily that I bumped into him.

The room was extremely warm, and it was foggy—the air was blue. Ms. Mame was standing at a large round oak pedestal table in the middle of the room, facing the door. The table was littered with black and white photographs, tiny bones, coins, skeleton keys, piles of dried flowers and leaves and seeds, and several small patches of cloth. A stack of willow twigs lay next to a small fire which burned in an iron bowl mounted on a tripod.

The most striking piece in the room was a large, extremely ornate wrought iron bed with dust ruffles. It was covered with a shiny red satin duvet and had lots of fluffy pillows scattered on it. The decorative ironwork was hung with trinkets and shells and little bells that tinkled as we walked into the room. Standing next to the bed was a three-panel screen depicting a lovely oriental woman in various poses of undressing in the outdoors and bathing next to a waterfall. Hanging over the top of the screen were tiny swaths of satiny cloth in various colors, many of them bordered with black or white lace.

Ms. Mame was thin and dark, and her skin glowed with a pearlescent sheen. Her tiny bare arms were covered with multiple bracelets and bangles which caught the light as she moved. The veins showed prominently on the backs of her hands. She wore a flowing pink gown wrapped and tied around her waist, and a matching scarf shaped like a turban around her head and knotted in the front. A necklace of coral beads surrounded her throat, and large gold hoops dangled from her ears. Her facial bone structure was beautiful—she had virtually no wrinkles anywhere, except for tiny crinkle lines on the sides of her large dark eyes. Her age was anyone's guess, but her eyes were ancient.

She was holding what looked like a small tea ball over the fire with a pair of tongs, from which rose thin tendrils of sweet-smelling gray smoke. As we stared at her, she waved it back and forth under her nose and inhaled, eyes closed.

A beautiful tropical parrot with blue tail plumage the length of my arm watched us from the back of one of the chairs. After several seconds, she opened her eyes and spoke to us.

"Which one of you is young Piper?" she asked, her eyes on Toby.

He raised a finger, "I am, ma'am."

"I thought so. I am so very sorry about yo' brotha," she said.

"Thank you, ma'am," Toby said.

"And who is this young man?" she asked, looking at me.

"This is my best friend...."

"Jamie Fletcher, ma'am. Pleased to meet you," I said, holding out my hand.

"Well, well, such nice manners," she said, taking my hand and holding it in both of hers, while she looked at me. Her hands were soft. I stared back into her eyes and felt myself relaxing completely as her eyes took in all of me. I felt myself expanding, aware that her eyes were sweeping through my exterior, deep into me, even into my secrets and dreams, all of which I willingly opened to her as she gazed at me. Finally, she released my hand and turned back to Toby, and the spell of her eyes lifted, and my mind slowly reentered the room.

"I saw yo' brotha in a dream," she said, turning abruptly to Toby. "He look like you."

Both of us stood there gaping—neither of us could reply. *How could she possibly know that?*

"And he did *not* commit suicide," she continued. We stared at her for several seconds before either of us could speak.

"How do you know, ma'am?" I managed, finally.

"Ah tol' you—ah saw him. In a dream."

"What happened to him?" Toby asked.

"Ah cain't tell you that. Ah just knows that when *ah* saw him, he was not wearin' no Hangman's Noose—he wasn't nevah at the end a' *his* rope. An' that' *all* ah know."

"And you can tell from that?" asked Toby. "You can tell he didn't kill himself?"

"Yes, chil'."

"Does everyone who commits suicide wear this noose? This Hangman's Noose?" Toby asked.

"Yes, chil'. Ah don't know jus' *how* he died, but ah *can* tell you that he din't kill hisself."

"We need to prove it; we need to prove that he didn't commit suicide," I said.

"Easy to prove to yo'selves. Hard to prove to somebody else," she said.

"How do we prove it to ourselves?" we both asked.

She paused as she waved the tea ball under her nose and took two long, deep breaths. We watched the gray tendrils race into her nostrils. Finally she spoke again, in a heavy, langourous voice, her eyes closed, pausing as if watching an image in a dream.

"A suicide...be condemned...ta rise...at midnight. He gotta walk th' earth...until his sin...be paid." We could hardly hear her now. "He walk ever' night. Some walk fo' years." A long pause, then she opened her eyes. Her voice gained sudden strength. "Watch yo' brother's grave," she said. "If he don't rise at midnight, den you know fo' sho' that he din't kill hisself."

"Is this true, ma'am?" Toby asked excitedly. "Is this for real?"

"As true as the gospel," she said, apparently returning to the present, then sighing deeply. "Is there anythin' else I can do for you boys?"

"Just one more question," Toby said. "You said it was hard to prove to somebody else, but not impossible, right? How do we prove it to somebody else?"

"You gotta prove how yo' brotha died."

"But we don't know that," I said.

"Nor either do I; so you gots ta fahnd out."

We stared at her, then at each other.

"Oh, boys, there is one mo' thing."

"Yes, ma'am?" we both said together.

"In mah dream ah watched a man put a spell on yo' brotha's grave." We jerked upright, then stood stock still, looking at her.

"What do you mean?" Toby finally asked.

"He look like Papa Legba," she said.

"Who did?" I asked, confused.

"Dat man," she said.

"Who is Papa Legba?" Toby asked.

"He talk to Bonye," she explained.

"Who is Bonye?" I asked.

"You call him 'God,'" she said.

We continued to stare at her, completely clueless.

Finally, "What kind of spell?" Toby asked.

"Ah don't know. All *ah* know is ah watched him do it. He warn't talkin' to yo' brotha—he said a spell—in a strange tongue. But he warn't talkin' to Beelzebub either. Ah *do* know that."

"Are you sure?" asked Toby.

"Oh, ah'm sure," she said, the whites of her eyes enormous. "Ah *knows* what ah saw. He be sprinklin' somethin' on yo' brother's grave. Might be blood, mebbe not, ah don't know. An' that's *all* ah know, but ah knows that. Ah also knows that yo' parents gone be lookin' for you two. Goodbye, boys," she said, her voice musical, waving her fingers toward the door in a walking motion.

Joseph Welch

In slow motion, still full of questions, we half-turned to leave, disappointed that we had been dismissed, unable to take our eyes off her.

"Ms. Mame," I asked, "can we come back?"

"If you like," she said, pleased that we had asked. "Ah allus be glad to see you boys. Don't let Phay-roh out when you leave—ah have a devil of a time catchin' him if he git downstairs. It's been nice meetin' you boys."

"Thank you, ma'am," I said. "It was very nice to meet you, too."

"Yes, thank you, ma'am, for your help. I appreciate it," Toby said.

We walked out in a dream, our eyes the size of saucers. Luckily, Pharoah made no attempt to escape. The men at the table sniggered as we passed, perhaps at us—we didn't care—we were floating.

By the time we got home, though, we had questions ricocheting around our brains. We couldn't settle on anything, except we agreed we couldn't waste any time. Tomorrow was the burial. We would meet tomorrow night before midnight at Tom's grave. Since my house was on the way, Toby would come by at 11:00 and do his catcall, and I would climb out my bedroom window.

Brother John agreed to watch out for me coming and going. He would leave the screen out of the window after I left, so I could just reach in and tap him when I got back, and he could check to see if the coast was clear before I climbed back in. He thought our idea was totally crazy, though, and he might have been right, but then he hadn't met Ms. Mame.

19.
THE CEMETERY

The burial was at 11:00 a.m. the next morning. I was glad I wasn't going to school—I didn't want to talk to anyone else about Tom's death. Mr. and Mrs. Piper and Toby rode together. Richard Washington and I rode with my parents. My mother had carried a note to Sr. Ambrose telling her I would not be in school that day so I could attend Tom Piper's burial—she didn't ask for permission. No one else attended. Crazy Carly had asked for time off so she could attend, but Mrs. Piper told her that they really needed her at the motel, since everyone else would be gone.

The cemetery sat on the third bluff south of Mayfly between two highways. The east face of the bluff rose above River Road and overlooked the Mississippi. The west end of the bluff had been dynamited away for the new State Highway, leaving a high wall of naked rock rising above the new roadbed. The only vehicular access to the cemetery was a natural break in the southern end of that naked rock wall, where a gravel cemetery road left the State Highway. It was marked by two cut stone pillars supporting an archway which spelled out "Riverside Cemetery" in wrought iron.

We left downtown on the State Highway, driving south past the back of Castle Bluff, which loomed over downtown Mayfly. Next, we passed Lover's Leap, the second bluff south of Mayfly. Tall and sheer with a distinctive anvil rock overhanging the Mississippi River, it was a popular scenic view and lovers' parking spot.

When we got almost to the tail end of the third bluff, we turned left off the State Highway, and began the long uphill trek on the unpaved and heavily rutted cemetery road. My father winced as we repeatedly dragged our undercarriage, passing through a series of switchbacks, and detouring around the deepest ditches which cut across the road, until we reached the main loop at the top of the bluff. Here we saw some truly spectacular views of the Mississippi as we drove past the graves of many prominent names in Mayfly history. At the south end of the loop lay the Jewish Cemetery, its boundaries fenced and walled off from the rest of the cemetery, its gateway marked with a Star of David. We continued, following the road as the loop turned back to the north.

At the far north end, a branch road consisting only of two rutted tire tracks departed from the main loop and ran further north, and even further uphill. We followed the ruts as far as they went. When they turned south again in a hairpin turn, we left our vehicles and began walking.

We followed a narrow strip of lawn past a thick copse of trees, after which our vista broadened out, allowing us to see Tom's grave sixty yards away and still further uphill. The open grave had been dug in the last patch of grass in a little clearing which jutted into the woods on the north end of the cemetery. The woods hung somberly over the little grave, and the bluff's sheer side fell away to the east, two hundred feet to the river.

As we gathered around the grave, Toby whispered, "Lover's Leap is just on the other side of these woods. Coming through there would save a ton of time, but there's no road across the top of the bluffs—just these woods."

At 11:00 a.m., P.J. showed up with his breviary, but he didn't need it, since Tom was not entitled to a Catholic funeral. He merely prayed that "God forgive Tom his sins and, if it be your will, admit him into the joys of Paradise with you and your son, Jesus Christ." Then we all said an Our Father, a Hail Mary and a Glory Be, and then P.J. said, "My sincere condolences, Mr. and Mrs. Piper, and Toby, too, and don't give up hope—the Lord works in mysterious ways, and often His ways are inscrutable to us."

We all just gaped at him. *What in the hell does that mean?*

"Now," he continued, "kneel down and I'll give you my blessing." Mechanically, we all knelt there on the ground, next to the fresh grave, as he intoned: "May the blessings of Almighty God, the Father, the Son and the Holy Ghost, be with you and remain with you forever," to which we all responded, "Amen."

But I didn't feel blessed, and I doubted very much if the Pipers did, either. *"He's acting very weird. There's something funny about that man,"* I thought, as he hurried out of sight, down the hill, and around the copse of trees to the road, where he had presumably left his car.

20.
THE WATCH

I couldn't sleep a wink, waiting for Toby. The clock on the mantel counted out the hours in slow motion, chiming on the quarter hours. After everyone went to bed, I discovered to my irritation that I could also hear it ticking the minutes.

Dad passed by our doorway on his way to the bathroom. I pretended to be asleep. While playing basketball after dinner, John had chased a ball outside our fence and surreptitiously removed the full-size wooden window screen from our window.

I lay there in the dark, scared. Dad's big flashlight was hidden under my pillow. I was already dressed except for my canvas shoes, which lay in readiness under my bed. The heat was oppressive—my pillow was soaked. My ears were attuned to every sound that came through our window. An elderly man out walking his dog shuffled past our window. I wanted to bring Prince along, but was afraid other dogs would see him or smell him and start barking at us.

Rain was predicted overnight. Lightning flickered through the cotton curtains, but I couldn't tell if it was heat lightning or if it meant a storm.

Bong. 10:15. I waited. Was Ms. Mame pulling our leg? Had she known no one would rise from the grave, so she told us that to make us feel better when it didn't happen—was she just trying to comfort us? Did Tom actually commit suicide because he thought he was a loser? What about me—what if I didn't become famous? Would I be so humiliated that some day I would eventually want to end it, too?

Bong. Bong. 10:30. Tick, tick, tick, tick. I got up and went to the bathroom, just a fidget pee. I didn't flush—no sense waking anyone. Back to bed. Waited.

Bong. Bong. Bong. *How do I know that isn't really three a.m.?* I checked the luminous dial of my Timex. 10:45. *Interminable! Come on!* I went to the bathroom again.

Eleven bongs! *Where is he? We're doing this for his brother, not mine! Is he asleep? Did he get caught?* I checked my Timex: 11:04. Quietly, I walked over to the open window, parted the curtains, and stared out at the towering clouds outlined in gold by the recent full moon. Just then Toby's long-drawn-out "meeeooowww" cut through the humid air. I hurried back to the bed and slipped on my shoes.

"John, I'm leaving," I whispered. "I'll tap you on the shoulder when I come back."

"Okay," he mumbled. "Be careful."

I stepped through the open window and dropped the short distance to the ground. The world was different out of doors in the summer night. Crickets sang in the heat, and the scent of honeysuckle permeated the night air. I crouched at the foundation wall and ran, bent over, smelling the prickly juniper bushes which assailed my legs as I tried to skirt around them. Reaching the corner of the house, I lit out across the back yard to the alley, where Toby waited, crouched behind a rock wall, and surrounded by lightning bugs which hovered above the tall grasses.

"You get out okay?" I asked.

"Yeah, they're out cold. I could hear them snoring—both of them. I think they both took a sleeping pill."

"Great, let's go," I said, heading through the alley toward downtown and Highway 79. "Minor's curfew is 10:00 p.m. so we'll have to keep out of sight. If a policeman sees us, he'll take us in and call our parents."

"Oh, God," Toby moaned. Neither of us wanted that.

We hustled along the alley, stopping at cross streets and checking for cars.

"Richard was probably smart not to come," I said.

"Yeah, he says it will be different for him if he gets picked up," Toby agreed. "He says they'll think he's out stealing, and they'll keep an eye on him as long as he lives here."

"Yeah, plus he didn't meet Ms. Mame," I said. "I don't blame him for thinking this is pretty crazy."

"I know," Toby agreed. "I still don't know if I believe her. You gotta admit it sounds kinda nuts, walking into a graveyard in the middle of the night to see if Tom rises from the dead—I mean, do you believe that?" Toby asked.

"I don't know what to think," I said. "I think it's something we just have to do ... you know ... just in case...."

"Just in case what? In case it's *real*? The only way we're gonna know for sure is if he rises from the grave," Toby said.

"I know," I said. "And how would he rise? In his body? Oh, God, all broken up.... As a ghost? As a soul?"

"Yeah, will it be like vapor? How will we even recognize him?" Toby asked.

"Yeah, and will he know us?" I asked. "I hope he's friendly, at least, and we can talk to him."

"I hope we don't see him." Toby said, as I pitched forward onto the cobblestone with a yelp, a sharp pain in my right ankle.

"Oh, oh, oh, oh! Damn!" I said.

"What's wrong?" Toby whispered.

"I sprained my ankle. There's a big hole in the alley, a missing cobblestone," I said, trying to stand up again.

"Can you walk?" Toby asked.

"I think so," I said. It hurt, but I was already blocks from home and either had to walk home on it or go ahead with the plan. "I think I can walk," I said, standing on it gingerly.

"Oh, shit!" I said. "I forgot my dad's flashlight."

Just then a car roared into the far end of the alley behind us, pinning us in its headlights. The driver hit his brights, blinding us.

"Act natural," Toby said. "Just walk over to this garage like it's our property." I walked as naturally as I could until the two of us passed the corner of the garage, then we turned right out of the headlights and hid along the far side of the garage. We heard the car approaching, then grind to a sudden stop as its headlights passed us. A spotlight snapped on, the light circle right above us on the wall, then he adjusted the beam, so we were lit up like the midday sun.

"Hey, you two, what are you doin' messin' around my garage? I'm callin' the police," he yelled. My ankle pain forgotten, we ran around to the front corner of the garage and turned right, around the corner and out of the beam, then up toward the house, running across the back of it to the far side. Someone turned on the back porch lights just as we turned at the back corner of the house and ran up the side of the house toward the street.

"This way," I said, limp-running back toward home. We heard the car coming around the block just as we made the corner. We turned left, then crossed the street and ran down between two houses to the alley, where we hid behind a big hedge. Dogs barked in our wake. We watched the headlights turn the wrong way at the corner, then ran three blocks as quietly as mice, until we rested again, panting, between two cars parked in a back yard. Looking up between the houses, we saw a police car drive past us heading west on Broadway, but by this time we were blocks away from the place where we were spotlighted, and we had not roused any dogs to our current whereabouts.

My ankle was killing me—it throbbed. We could hear voices coming from the nearest house.

"Let's go back and get the flashlight," I said.

Suddenly the back door flew open, showing a stocky man dragging a young woman by her arm out of the house and onto the back porch.

"Come on, baby, ya know ya wanna come with me," he said. "We'll go dancin', then I'll take ya someplace really special," he said.

"No, Biff, don't. It's a weeknight and Mama won't want me out 'til all hours," she said.

"Come on, doll, you'll love it; it's called Polliet Boulevard. It's beautiful, baby. I wanna show it to ya."

"Not tonight, Biff, please. I'll go with you, just not tonight. I'm not feelin' so good—I'll go next week." Lightning flashed. "Look, it's gonna rain."

"Ah, nuts!" Biff said, letting go of her arm. "Next week! What ahm ah s'posed ta do in the meantime?"

"Come on back in the house, baby. I'll help you. I know my baby has needs," she said, kissing him and then pulling away, giggling.

They vanished inside and the door closed.

"Come on, let's go. It's getting late," Toby said. "Forget the flashlight. We need to get to the graveyard." The two of us started off at a trot, me limping all the way, wondering if I could make it there and back.

The thunder was coming nearer—the lightning flashes were by now clearly storm-related.

"Let's move over one block to the right when we get to the corner," I said. "I know that alley." I had walked home on it frequently after my brother John's paper route. We did, then turned back toward downtown and the river, hustling now.

We made good time, even though my tiptoe running was modified by a major limp. I knew which yards had dogs, and we crept past those places, then ran as fast as my condition would allow through safer territory. We paused at each cross street and looked for cars before moving on. Within minutes we were at an alley running parallel to the State Highway which left downtown past the back of Castle Bluff, Lover's Leap and the graveyard. We had to cross Bear Creek on a bridge, but we couldn't risk walking the highway bridge, so we detoured one block east and crossed the creek on an old railroad bridge next to the river.

Once outside the city limits on the railroad track, we cut back to the State Highway and ran past Castle Bluff to the foot of Lover's Leap, then scrambled up the back side, over the rocks and through the tall grasses and brush until we found the rutted gravel road which ran up to its knoll through a series of switchbacks.

"We need to stay off the road," I said. "There's no place to hide from cars. Let's just shoot through here," ducking into the brush and feeling my way blindly up the steep back side of the bluff toward the next switchback. Lightning flashed. I memorized the trees in front of me, then hustled through them, still blinded by the stark after-image. I could hear Toby cursing behind me.

"This way," I said. "Watch out for the wild roses—they're mean." Moments later, Toby was beside me.

"Listen, this is nuts," he said. "Let's use the road and just watch for headlights."

"And then what?" I asked.

"We'll see them a long way off. Then we just look for a place to hide." I was dubious. "We're not gonna make it," he said. "We've lost too much time." I looked at my watch. It was 11:43. He was right. We had seventeen minutes to climb to the top of Lover's Leap, then make it through the woods without a flashlight, and find Tom's grave in the dark.

"Okay, let's go—and let's run. But hide on the inside of the curves. The headlights will shine onto the outside, but not the inside."

"Right," he said. "Hurry!" And we did. We ran uphill, huffing and puffing. We were completely winded by the time we reached the first switchback. We couldn't run any more, but we didn't stop—we walked as fast as we could, huffing and puffing, me limping mightily. Finally, we reached the last hairpin and saw the top of the bluff open out into a grassy knoll in front of us. Luckily, there were no cars at the top. The sound of tree frogs was deafening. Lightning was fairly constant now, and very close, and peals of thunder followed the lightning flashes almost immediately. The storm was nearly upon us.

We ran across the knoll into the face of the wind, cowering under the deafening peals of thunder and praying that we would not become living lightning rods. We were stunned by our own idiocy, conscious of the bluff edge which fell away dramatically on our left, over two hundred feet to the dark river, trying to veer away from it, the two of us running loose on the top of the bluff, which was now near the center of the storm.

Summer of '63

As we crossed the knoll, a sustained, multi-flash lightning burst revealed a solid gray storm front approaching us, pushing a huge gray roller, an upside-down breaker of surfing storm cloud which spanned the sky, plunging toward us on the naked knoll.

We ran toward the woods, running uncomfortably close to the edge of the bluff, then waded into the tall grasses, which were now bent nearly horizontal in the storm. Wild privet and autumn olive flattened in the wind. Trees danced and swayed, their limbs flailing back and forth, whipping and slapping as we stumbled through the dark woods, cursing the forgotten flashlight, cursing our complete idiocy. Leaves, torn loose by the wind, smacked us in the face, and airborne branches tumbled past us. One hammered my shoulder, scratching my neck and arms.

The lightning continued, now directly overhead. My hair stood on end. I could smell ozone. The peals of thunder were deafening, the reverberations booming out over the immensity of the Mississippi River valley.

Toby had vanished. I bent all my energy toward moving south through the woods, alert to the danger of walking off the edge of the bluff in the dark, when a huge flash of lightning shattered the sky, turning the area brighter than daylight. I only saw it for an instant—a single break in the blackness that lasted a fraction of a second, but the scene burned itself into my brain, leaving an after-image from Hell. Off to my right, to my absolute horror, stood Toby, frozen at the edge of the clearing, ten feet away from Tom's fresh grave, both of his hands up in terror, his mouth wide open in a scream which was still audible when the huge crack of thunder died away, staring in that intense strobe at a large human figure standing facing the grave, fully dressed, in an identical posture of shock and terror, both arms in the air, in fear or supplication or both, and even before the lightning flash bled out fully, running downhill away from Tom's grave in the high wind and the flying debris.

"Jesus!" I said—it was a prayer, not a curse. I heard another wail of terror from the blackness and sank down to the ground, unable even to stand. I fell forward, grabbing a tree trunk with both my arms—either for help or protection or in prayer, I didn't know—as the wind surged and the sky split in a roaring deluge of biblical proportions that hammered me to the earth.

I don't know how long I knelt there, my elbows and forearms sinking in the mud and the drenching rain, weeping in stunned and senseless fright and agony and bewilderment as the storm mounted me, a living thing, a vengeance, whipping me into complete submission as it took possession of the bluff. Finally, grudgingly, it moved slowly over the bluff—I felt it look back at me, ensuring I was still compliant, that I knew the Fear of the Lord.

It was a long time later. At some point I knew I had to look for Toby. I gathered the courage to get up. I could barely put weight on my injured ankle. I couldn't bring myself to go near the grave, and I prayed I wouldn't have to. I figured that Toby would have to go back to Lovers Leap—if he were alive, if he were able. Leery of falling over the precipice to my death, I partly crawled back to the top of the knoll and waited there in the downpour, looking for him in the blackness. Eventually I started calling for him, softly at first, and then louder, as the storm moved off further across the great valley, leaving only the cold and the downpour and my fear, abject and tangible.

21.
HOPING AND PRAYING

In terror and absolute depression, I waited in the cold rain at the top of Lovers Leap. Time slowed to a near stop. Imagination figments abounded as I peered into the drenching darkness. A shrouded figure moved toward me out of the blackness. When it vanished, I heard twigs snapping. I jerked my head left, then right, my eyes straining. I turned around. Nothing. Where was Toby? What had happened to him? Who or what was that figure, the one etched in my brain by a lightning flash, the one I saw for that mere fraction of a second, the thing at Tom's grave? It couldn't have been real—except that I saw it.

Was that Tom? Had he risen to walk the earth until his sin was expiated? Was that the person Ms. Mame had warned Toby about, the one putting a spell on Tom's grave? God help me—help all of us—help Toby—help Tom. Who was it? Or what was it? Is Toby even alive? What had that creature done? Fear overwhelmed me, and not just for myself. I felt the cold dread of Toby's death, and his parents' devastation at the loss of their other child, their only other child, their last child. *Please, God. Please.* "Toby!" I called. No answer. "Toby!" Louder this time. No answer. Slowly I worked up the courage to call louder, and louder yet, until I was yelling at the top of my lungs, screaming in desolation and abandonment. But it was no good—there was no answer. All I could do was pray. And I did. I prayed and cried, my tears joining the rain running down my face. *Oh, God, please help Toby. Please let Toby be alright. Please, dear God. Please.*

Other prayers came to me, there in the darkness, in my hopelessness, my terror, my despair. *Hail, Mary, full of grace, the Lord is with thee....pray for us sinners....*

"Yes, pray for us sinners," I prayed aloud. Slowly, I became calmer. I knew what I had to do. I became reconciled to necessity. I gathered up my courage and went to look for Toby where I had left him—at his brother's grave. I moved back through the woods for the third time that evening, my injured ankle screaming at every step, praying out loud as I again felt my way south through the trees on the top of the cliff.

There was no sense of urgency this time, only dread. I was cold, and injured, and scared, but not of the apparition; instead, I was scared of whatever had happened to Toby. My personal fear had abated—in a distant part of my mind I no longer cared what happened to me—my parents had lots of other sons—they would be okay. I was just so cold, so hurting, so forlorn, so depressed that I had lost some of my terror of the supernatural. I had to find Toby, but I dreaded what I would find.

How could I ever explain to Toby's parents that their other son was lost on the same day, and in the same place where Tom was buried?

When I emerged from the woods at the edge of the graveyard in the cold and steady rain, it was too dark to see where I was. I had to find Tom's grave. I decided to trace the perimeter of the woods, walking away from the cliff, and staying in touch with the woodsy undergrowth below the tree line. When I felt the tree line curving back to the south, I retraced my limping steps until I calculated I was in the neighborhood of Tom's grave, then stumbled out onto the lawn, crisscrossing and calling for Toby. Suddenly, I sank into a sodden mess of freshly dug earth—Tom's grave. I froze, motionless for some time, and waited. Was it open or closed? I didn't know.

My feet ankle-deep in the mud, I bent over and felt around, then extricated one foot at a time, as I moved down the length of the fresh grave, feeling as I went. It was closed, as far as I could tell. Was I walking next to the grave on the fresh earth? Was there an open chasm on either side? I moved sideways, several feet in each direction. No hole. So where was Toby? I limped around the grave in widening circles. No Toby. I called again, peering around me in the blackness for some sign of the creature I had seen in the lightning flash, then cautiously called again, then several more times. Nothing. I waited quietly, listening. Still nothing. I looked at the wet fluorescent dial of my Timex—12:50.

"He's not here," I said aloud, suddenly determining to look for him heading home. But just as I tried to leave the grave, something grabbed my left shoe, hard, causing my ankle pain to explode against the inside of my skull and freezing me in a silent screaming agony. I pulled—there was no answering tug. Finally, I was able to lurch forward, leaving my shoe behind. I stopped, frozen, my heart pounding, and waited a full minute. Nothing. I knew I couldn't walk home barefoot on my injured ankle. There was no one to help me. I had to have my shoe back. I waited two full minutes, expecting any moment to feel something seize my leg. When nothing else grabbed me, I reached back, whimpering, desperately hoping I would not encounter a slimy hand protruding from the earth. Finally, I touched something—my shoe, abandoned, in the grasping mud. Hurriedly extricating it and putting it on, I limped back through the woods, breathing heavily and shaking my head, more confident now in the dark lay of the land, but still taking care to avoid walking off the edge of the cliff. "Toby!" I yelled. "Toby!" as I reached the top of Lovers Leap. Still nothing. By now, the wind had died down, and the rain had slowed.

I took the rutted gravel lane down the back side of Lovers Leap toward the State Highway as fast as I could manage, repeatedly wrenching my swollen ankle on the rolling rocks and the erosion gulleys, pain shooting up my leg and blasting into my skull with every other step. Soon, I was creeping down the switchbacks sideways, stepping first with my good leg and then dragging my injured leg behind, calling as I went. No Toby.

Finally, I reached the highway and started the long, wet journey, limping home without Toby, hoping with all my being that Toby was safe, and that my absence had not been discovered at home.

Hail, holy Queen, Mother of mercy, hail, our life, our sweetness and our hope. To thee do we cry, poor banished children of Eve. To thee do we send up our sighs, mourning and weeping in this vale of tears. Turn then, most gracious Advocate, thine eyes of mercy toward us...O clement, O loving, O sweet Virgin Mary! Pray for us, oh holy Mother of God.

Walking down the shoulder of the steep road toward town, my ankle hurt so badly that I decided not to make the detour to the railroad bridge, rationalizing that it was so late I could gamble on using the highway bridge without being discovered.

I was wrong.

As I approached the bridge, I suddenly heard the crashing of underbrush on my right. A dark form rushed out at me from the undergrowth on the shoulder of the road, illuminated by the headlights of a car that had just turned off Union Street onto the highway, its headlights swinging over me in an arc. I froze in terror, my hands up in front of me.

"Jamie!" it yelled.

My breath caught for a half-second only. "Toby!" I roared as it exploded out of me, relief flooding over me.

"Where have you…" we both started simultaneously, just as the car stopped alongside us. *Oh-oh*. We turned simultaneously, mouths open. *The police*, I thought, resigning myself to being hauled down to the station while they notified our parents.

The passenger window rolled down, and we heard a familiar voice say, "Hey, queers! Want a ride?"

Bad Billy Boyd! I couldn't have been happier to see him if he had been my patron saint. *Absolutely, we wanted a ride.* "Hi, Billy! Yes, please—it's wet out here," I managed, stepping into the stream rushing down the highway curb off the big hill and letting it gush over my shoes and muddy socks, creating a thigh-high fountain and picking them clean, while I bent down to look at the driver. It was Bad Billy's big brother, Deano, who I thought was still in the penitentiary. He was sporting a buzz cut and a white T-shirt with the sleeves torn off. On the seat between his legs was a brown paper bag with the neck of a bottle sticking out the top.

"You two look like drowned rats. Okay to give them a ride, Deano?" Billy said, turning to the driver. "They're friends of mine."

"Sure," Deano said, his voice low and gravelly. "Why not? Hop in."

"Thanks," we said, looking at each other, both of us shaking our heads almost imperceptibly in a silent pact not to tell details. It was just too weird. Plus, we didn't even know the details ourselves. We weren't telling anyone until we had a chance to talk this out.

"Deano just got paroled today," Billy said, "so we're havin' a little celebration. He took me with him in case he needs me to drive him home."

"Congratulations, Deano," I said. "Good to have you on the loose."

"Thanks, man. Where you boys headed?" he asked in a growl.

"Home," we both said. I continued, "Toby lives on Broadway in the River's Rest Motel. I live on Hill Street, but I'll get out on Broadway, because I don't wanna wake up my parents."

"I bet you don't," Deano said, taking a pull from the bottle without bothering to remove it from the bag. "What're you two boys up to, anyway? It's kinda late to be out."

"It's a secret," I said, "but we can tell you two. Toby's brother was buried today, and we've been up at his grave, hoping we could just visit with him, but it didn't work out, then the big storm came, so we just kinda struck out." I looked at Toby, who nodded at me almost imperceptibly.

"Will you guys not tell anybody, please?" asked Toby. "I know it sounds crazy. And we don't want it to get back to our parents."

"Yeah," Deano growled, "it does sound pretty crazy, but I get it. It's cool, man. Sorry about your brother, man," he said to Toby. "I didn't know him very well, but he seemed like a nice kid."

"Yeah, man, I'm sorry, too," chimed in Bad Billie Boyd.

"Thanks, guys," said Toby. "And thanks awfully for the lift. You have no idea what a godsend you are."

"Ha!" Deano said. "First time I've been called that. But you're welcome, man. And don't worry—this little episode'll just be our secret. Right, Billy?" His voice sounded like a purring lion.

"Right," Billy agreed.

"I'm not going to school tomorrow; gonna tell my parents I'm sick," I told Toby.

"Me, too," he said.

"You're gonna have to come up with somethin' better'n that," said Bad Billie. "You look like shit. You got scratches all over your neck and arms, and you're limpin' pretty bad."

"I'll come up with something," I said, but I had no idea what could possibly explain all my injuries without telling the truth—and the truth wasn't even an option. Running around town in the middle of the night was not acceptable under any circumstances. I'd be grounded for years, and the extra work would be unbearable. I'd be better off as a Russian political prisoner in Siberia.

Moments later, I exited the car at the foot of Hill Street. "Thanks, Deano," I said, "and thank you, too, Billy."

"No charge, man," Deano said.

"See ya," said Bad Billie Boyd.

"See ya later, Toby," I said, wishing we had gotten a chance to talk about whatever had actually happened at the grave, especially who he saw, and whether that was Tom, and what happened after I left. And also, of course, to get our stories straight. But under the circumstances, we just had to go on home.

I know Toby was thinking the same thing, but we couldn't talk in front of the Boyd boys, and we were really lucky to get a ride, and it was late. "Yeah," he said. "Talk to you whenever—and good luck," he said, as I began the painful climb up the hill.

By the time I got to the top of the hill, the rain had slowed to a drizzle. I had to detour into the street to get around a large maple tree that had blown down in the front yard next door to us, the branches crossing the sidewalk. Prince heard me, though, and started barking as he rocketed out of his doghouse. He was jerked to a halt at the end of his chain, still barking.

"Prince!" I yelled in a whisper. He stopped barking immediately. I limped over to him and patted him while he jumped around me, celebrating my visit, oblivious to the rain.

"Hi, Prince," I said, "good boy. Calm down." And then it occurred to me—Prince was the answer. He was also a godsend—the second one that night—Prince explained everything.

So the next morning, when John woke me up, and I limped into the bathroom, holding onto the wall and then the doorknob and the side of the bathtub, scratches showing on my neck and arms, my T-shirt dotted with streaks of seeped blood, my ankle purple and blue and three times its normal size, and Dad looked at my reflection through the oval section of the medicine cabinet mirror that he had wiped clear of steam, his face covered with shaving cream, and nearly dropped his badger-bristle shave brush, and said, "Good God Almighty, boy! What happened to you?" I was ready.

"Prince was whining last night because of the storm, so I went out to let him in, but when I unhooked him, he just took off down the street, and I ran after him, but I tripped on a tree that was across the sidewalk and sprained my ankle and fell into the branches and got kinda scratched up." Amazing how glibly the lies rolled off my tongue! (But lying is just a Venial Sin, punishable only by some extra time in Purgatory—so I knew I wasn't going to Hell—not for that sin, anyway—and I was pretty sure that, under the circumstances, the extra time in Purgatory was absolutely worth it—later on I could worry about whether I had just told eight lies or only one longish one, but I couldn't worry about those kinda details right then—I had to keep my head about me.) *And thank you, too, Holy Ghost, for enlightening me in my hour of absolute need with the inspiration it took to create that whopper,* I prayed silently. *It's true—the Lord truly does work in mysterious ways.*

"Mary!" Dad yelled. "Look at this boy!"

It wasn't long before Mom was fully informed, "You shouldn't leave the house at night," she pronounced. "Let this be a lesson to you."

"I know," I said, "I just felt sorry for him." *Darn! The longer we talk about this, the more lies I have to tell—my Purgatory burn time just keeps adding up.*

"You should have told us you were hurt," she said.

"I know," I said, "but I didn't want to wake you." *Lucky for me—that one is probably not really a lie.*

And that was all, but only because she didn't know I really *had* left the house at night, and in a very big way. I shuddered to contemplate the level of punishment that would have been meted out if all the facts were known, not the least of which was the best part of the night—getting into the car of a convict who was drinking while he was driving.

"I don't think I can walk," I said.

"Alright, young man," she said, "you just get back in your bed, and as soon as the doctor's office opens, I'll call and get an appointment."

"Yes, ma'am," I said, obviously dejected. *Do I have to?* I limped back to bed, mouthed "I'll tell you later" to John, who just shook his head at my luck. I was sound asleep in seconds.

22.
SCHOOL PICNIC

My ankle was not broken, just sprained. I stayed on crutches for several days, then limped around, wrapped in an ace bandage.

Six days later, I was at Riverview Park for our school picnic. The ground had finally dried hard after the big deluge, and it was hot.

I was disappointed that Toby was a no-show, even for the school picnic. He had come back to school on the Friday after the funeral, and before he even walked in the front door, all the kids started asking him about Tom, and he just turned around and left. He hadn't been to school since then, and I didn't blame him.

Rumors abounded. Kids had been asking me, too, but I just acted dumb and told them I didn't know anything about it, which was close to another lie, because I actually knew a lot about it, but I still didn't know what happened, so I started saying I had no idea what happened. I tried to couch it so it wasn't technically a lie, because, let's face it, there's no sense in being stupid about stacking up time in Purgatory. I mean, you do get burned there—that's what you're there for, and any time I can shave time off that, I'm all for it—especially if it's me who's gonna be getting the torch treatment.

Summer of '63

So, I was just sitting on top of a picnic table with Richard, talking about Toby and how he was going to get by now that his big brother was dead.

Just then, our friends Bob Beard and Marva Lynn Mailer came running up to us. Marva Lynn was a very pretty girl in our class with soft blue eyes and feathery lashes. She was so sweet and kind and had soft brown hair. I knew just how soft it was because she sat right in front of me in First Grade, and her hair hung down her back and over my desk, and I spent most of every day playing with it—it was the softest thing I had ever felt—softer than my pillow, softer even than my teddy bear. She didn't seem to mind—she was so nice she didn't even complain to our much-loved first-grade teacher, Sister Mary Michaels.

"Come on," Bob said, "we're going exploring. Wanna come?"

Richard and I looked at each other. If he thought I was gonna pass this up, he was crazy. Marva Lynn was fun just to look at, much less talk to. In my wildest dreams, I never thought I would ever go wandering in the woods with her.

"Sure," I said.

"Nah," Richard said. "Better not." Then, turning to me and saying confidentially, "People find me in the woods with a white girl, I might get hung," his eyes fakey big, half joking, but I knew there was some old truth behind it.

"You're always tellin' us you *are* hung," I replied quietly, deadpan.

Richard licked his finger and mimed chalking one up for me, then turned to go. "Have fun, kids," he said to all of us. "Don't do anything I wouldn't do," which made Marva Lynn giggle. The three of us walked around the curve in the road, then ducked into the woods.

"Watch out for poison ivy," I said, eager to demonstrate my survival skills. "It's everywhere, especially here. It likes the edge of the woods, where it can get some sun," I added, casually demonstrating the extraordinary depth of my woodsman experience.

"I don't get it," said Bob, dismissively, like he was way too tough for poison ivy.

Marva Lynn looked at me. "I don't know if I get it or not. What's it look like?"

"This is it," I said, "here and here. See? 'Leaves of three, let it be.' Just walk around it. Follow me," I said, holding out my hand, helpfully, I thought. She took it, completely unaware of what a scrapbook event this was for me, and I led us safely into the interior of the woods. The undergrowth grew sparser as we moved deeper in, and the exuberant yells and squeals of our picnicking schoolmates became fainter, finally disappearing as we crested a hill and traipsed down the other side. Cornflower-blue petals on tall, thin stems dotted the ground. Occasional shafts of sunlight pierced the high leafy canopy, illuminating clouds of insects, which whirled in close mad dances in the shafts of warmed air. We passed through cool pockets next to banks of ferns and smelled the faint beckoning of multiflora roses and sweet briar as our senses adjusted to the shade and the quiet.

Huge Tarzanesque grapevines hung from the upper limbs of mature oaks, hackberries, walnuts and maple trees.

"I wonder what animals are watching us right now that we can't see," I said in a dramatic undertone.

"I bet there are lotsa snakes around here," Bob said out loud. I looked at Marva Lynn and saw the alarm in her eyes.

"Probably," I said, matter-of-factly, "but they'll stay away from us. They're more afraid of us than we are of them," repeating words I'd heard my father say. "If we don't bother them, they won't bother us," I added, hoping that were really so.

We meandered on together, kicking up last year's dead leaves from the deep carpet.

"I'm little, but I'm really strong." It just burst out of me without thinking about it. Marva Lynn looked at me in surprise. Bob probably did, too, but I couldn't tell you—I wasn't looking at him. "Watch this," I said, holding my right arm up in a Charles Atlas muscleman pose while surreptitiously holding my left arm up level behind my right bicep, hoping she didn't notice that one, as I used my fingers to push my tiny right bicep up from behind. She just giggled. Maybe she thought I was joking. Or maybe she could see my left hand, in which case I was willing to pretend it was a comedy routine. I smiled at her, playing it either way. She smiled back. She had a very pretty smile.

Suddenly I ran over to a huge grapevine dangling down from a treetop, as big around as my wrist, and started climbing it like a monkey. As I reached a long curve in the vine thirty feet in the air, moving decidedly slower than when I had begun, my body weight swung the vine over next to the gnarled limb of a tall oak tree. Seizing the opportunity to perform yet another act of derring-do—and also, incidentally, rest for a moment—I hooked a leg over the limb and climbed onto it, releasing the grapevine, then looking down to see what she thought about *that*. I expected to hear applause and see her clapping wildly. What I saw, however, was that there were no lower limbs on the oak tree, just a straight trunk far too large for my arms to encircle—there was no way down the tree. The grapevine was now fifteen feet away from me, swinging in the air. I was stuck.

"How're you gonna get down?" Bob yelled up at me.

"You think I should jump?" I asked, pretending to really consider it.

"No, you'll kill yourself," said Bob. Marva Lynn just giggled. "Here, lemme see if I can get the grapevine back over to you," Bob said, grabbing and swinging it, but it wouldn't come nearly far enough before the tail end rose higher above the ground than he could reach—if he ran as far as he could with it, it was still ten feet away from me, far too far to jump. Plus, I would have to catch it on the fly and be able to hold onto it—my life would depend on it.

"It'll come over here if you climb up it," I said.

"Not a good idea," Bob said. "How do we know it will hold both of us at once? The fall would kill us."

"Here, guys, try this," Marva Lynn said, going over to some fresh young grapevine a quarter inch in diameter and breaking it off at the ground, then pulling with all her might until she pulled thirty feet of long green vine down from a tree.

"That'll never hold us," Bob said.

"It won't have to," she said. "My aunt makes wreathes out of grapevine—watch this." She walked over to the bottom of my huge vine, wrapped the green vine in a spiral around the last foot at the tail end of it, and then bound the overlap with supple green tendrils while we watched. "Now try running away with it," she said to Bob, handing him the other end of the newly spliced green vine. He did, changing direction several times, until he was able to bring the old vine over next to me. I took it, relieved, and scampered down, a little too quickly, resulting in some painful burns that served to remind me of the event many times each day for a week, even though I didn't need the reminder. Another episode that I would remember for the rest of my life.

Chagrined, I thanked Marva Lynn for her great idea, and we resumed our walk. I was considerably more abashed than before my glorious ascension. Soon, however, we came out of the trees onto a broad, easy slope. A light breeze carried lily-of-the-valley scent that wafted through the tufts of early grasses and wild onion, and the sun smiled down, beaming on our exposed skin and warming our faces and arms. A rocky outcropping beckoned to us.

Marva Lynn seated herself on the warmed limestone slab, pulled a long foxtail and bit the bottom end, sucking out the sweet moisture. Her irises, partially shaded from the bright daylight by her lashes, matched the sky. Her skin glowed, highlighted by only the barest hint of a sprinkling of freckles, as she lay back, seemingly oblivious to us, luxuriating in the perfect weather. A perfection of tiny light-colored hairs on her shins shone in the early summer sun. Bob and I just looked at each other in wonderment, stupefied. Knowing it would be bad form to whimper aloud, we nonetheless did so silently.

We were hot and tired and quiet by the time we left the woods, heading back up the park road toward soda and food. We had been gone a long time, and I was hungry and thirsty. As we neared the pavilion, I saw Mary Ann Ventura talking to Lisa and Jenny and Denise, all friends from our class. Their faces turned toward us as we walked up the road. Mary Ann was facing in my direction, but she apparently didn't see me, because when I waved at her, she didn't wave back. Maybe her distance vision wasn't that good.

23.
LAST DAY OF SCHOOL

The next day was the last day of school, the end of a months-long countdown. We were scheduled to be dismissed at 11:00 a.m. I hoped Toby would at least show up for the final day, but he didn't. I really needed to talk to him, but I had other problems on my mind right then, like Sr. Ambrose. She had a reputation for ending the year with a bang, at least for the boys.

So after morning Mass and breakfast, we only had time for the last religion class of the school year before we checked in our textbooks and were dismissed. Sr. Ambrose said that Fr. Reiser would come by our room just before dismissal with a special announcement for the boys.

"Students," she announced, "for our last religion class this year, let's have some fun, shall we? We'll have a little contest between the girls and the boys," she said, smiling in anticipation. *Uh-oh. Something was up.*

"Everyone take out a sheet of paper and put your name on the top." We dutifully supplied our names as well as the other required data. I put a big "J.M.J." at the top of mine, following it up with nine exclamation points (my lucky number: 3 times 3) but with the point of my pen retracted, so that it left no visible evidence unless she used a microscope—I wouldn't put it past her, so I pressed lightly. I hoped it would be sufficient to alert the Holy Family to the fact that their divine intercession was needed.

Sr. Ambrose then advanced to the board, picked up a piece of chalk, and wrote in perfect penmanship: "Name in their correct order the Seven Gifts of the Holy Ghost."

"You have three minutes," she said, returning to her desk, where she sat looking out at the classroom, like a very large tiger watching her caged prey. I could hear the swish of her tail.

I didn't need three minutes; thirty seconds was a lavish abundance. "The Seven Gifts of the Holy Ghost are Wisdom, Understanding, Counsel, Fortitude, Knowledge, Piety and Fear of the Lord," I wrote, in not-so-perfect penmanship, but it was the best I could muster. I read it back, checking my work, including my spelling. I looked up. Richard and Arwain Craventz were apparently finished, too, but no other boys were. Only a few were writing sporadically. I looked at the girls. A half dozen of them were sitting with their hands folded on top of their papers, pens down, obviously finished and looking smug. Several of them were arrested in mid-answer, deep in thought, and Gail even had her pen in her mouth, apparently stuck. I looked from one to the other of the boys, to their sweating faces, as they made false start approaches of pen to paper before pausing again.

"Time," Sr. Ambrose announced. "Put your pens down and pass your papers forward. Boys first." We did, some anxiously, others casually, sighing in relief that the last quiz of the year was finally over. "Boys' papers here," she announced, indicating a front corner of her desk. "Now girls' over here," indicating the other corner. "You may take out your books and check your answers while I grade the papers. No talking." She went quickly through the two groups, sorting each group into two stacks. *The sheep and the goats.*

As we checked our work, the silence began to erode as students felt compelled to share their answers with others. Sr. Ambrose looked up. "Boys," she said, "I said 'no talking.' Do you hear the girls talking? No, it's only the boys. Come up here, boys. Line up across the front of the room," she said, as she resumed correcting the papers. We lined up across the front of the room, looking at one another nervously. Finally, she finished correcting and sorting her papers and looked at the class.

"Alright, students, we have the results," she said. "Boys, three correct, twelve incorrect; girls, fifteen correct, three incorrect. Congratulations, girls."

"Boys, I don't know what to do with you," she said, proceeding to the blackboard and grabbing her pointer. It was a formidable weapon, especially when wielded by an angry nun, 6'1" tall and built like a bricklayer, who brought unusual vigor to her task. "We have been over this question time and again. We have recited it in class; we have written it on the board; you have had it assigned as homework; you have written the answer down in your religion notebooks," she said, her anger rising as she recited each squandered learning opportunity. "I even told you it might be on your final exam. Now, I don't think like a *boy*," she said, making "boy" sound like a dirty word, "but it occurs to me that even a very *stupid* boy would have studied this, would have memorized it, would have created a memory device to help him remember. But no, it appears that you have more important things on your mind, like playing ball and talking in class."

"So today I am going to do you boys a favor. I am going to share my own memory device with you. I am going to help you remember the Seven Gifts of the Holy Ghost. Bend over and grab your ankles, Mr. Moore," she said to the first boy in the line, advancing behind him with the pointer, then laying into him like she was swinging for the bleachers. WHACK!

"Oh! Oh! Oh!" Eddie Moore said, hopping around the front of the room and holding his bottom with both hands.

"Now, sit down with your book and memorize the answer, and repeat it as many times as you need to until you know it by heart, and then I'm going to give you another chance in a few minutes. Do you understand me?"

"Yes, Sister," Eddie said, tears in his eyes.

"Mr. Benz, you're next. Bend over and grab your ankles." WHACK! The big rosary at her waist rose horizontally at the force of the impact. And so it went on down the line. But when she came to me, she said, "Congratulations, Mr. Fletcher, you had the correct answer. You may take your seat," she said, but you could tell she was not very happy about it. I could see by the way her eyes lingered on me that she hoped there would be another opportunity. *Better luck next time.* Richard and Arwain Craventz also got passed over—but all the other boys got the advantage of her "special memory device."

After Round One was over, the boys were allowed to raise their hands when they thought they knew the correct answer, and each one was allowed to stand up by his desk and say it out loud. Two of them missed it again and had to go up front for another application of the memory device. Davey Abbott didn't really miss it—he just froze when he stood up, and then he wet his pants when he had to go up for the second round. I was so embarrassed. I looked around at the girls. No one laughed—their eyes were enormous. Sr. Ambrose, however, was finally satisfied.

"Get a rag from the janitor and clean it up, Mr. Abbott," she said.

I can still see him kneeling there on the floor in his wet pants, wiping up his pee on the last day of school. That was the last time I ever saw him.

Then, turning away from the mess, "I'm going to collect your textbooks before Msgr. Reiser gets here," she said. There was a collective sigh of relief. I watched Davey trying not to cry as he wiped up the floor. "Bring up your Religion books first. Catherine, you're in charge of stacking them properly on the table, five stacks across, only six books high." We shuffled through our desks for our religion books. "First row," Sr. Ambrose said, and the entire row stood up. "Bring them forward." And so on across the room until Math, English, Reading, Spelling, Science, and History texts were all stacked and counted on the table. Ten minutes to spare.

"You may all sit quietly for the next ten minutes. Pray that you will do better next year." We prayed fervently—that we would not have Sr. Ambrose again next year.

At 11:52, P.J. came in, three minutes early. At first sight of him, we immediately jumped to our feet next to our desks and recited in unison, "Good morning, Father."

"Good morning, students," he said. "Good morning, Sr. Ambrose. I have an announcement for the boys. We will have a day-long spiritual retreat next Friday, a week from today, just for the boys entering Seventh Grade. Your attendance is mandatory. It will be held in church, starting at 8:00 a.m. Inform your parents. Also, we are going to be holding a week-long camp for Altar Boys at Camp Oko-Tipi in July. Details will be posted in the Sunday Bulletin."

"Thank you, Monsignor," Sr. Ambrose said, in her "visitor" voice, all sweetness now. "We have a few minutes before dismissal; does anyone have any questions for Msgr. Reiser before we leave for the summer?" *Of course not—who could possibly want to ask that arrogant jerk a question?*

But I saw motion out of the corner of my eye, and when I turned my head, I was absolutely shocked to see that it was Mary Ann, holding her hand up, her clear-eyed gaze on P.J.

"Yes, Miss...."

"Ventura," Sr. Ambrose supplied.

"Miss Ventura, yes," he said, "what would you like to ask?"

"Father, I have a horse that I really love; she's a good horse, a very nice horse. When I get to Heaven, will she be there, too?"

P. A. smiled indulgently. He looked like it was painful for him, like trying to smile was giving him an attack of gas. "No, Miss Ventura," he said. "I get this question a lot, but a horse doesn't have a soul, so there is no way it can go to Heaven."

Mary Ann's jaw dropped. "But she's a *good* horse," she managed, finally. "She *tries* to be good. She comes when I call her, and she never kicks or bites...."

"She may be a good horse," P.J. pronounced, "but a horse is just a dumb animal. Jesus didn't die to save animals—he died for us. You won't want your horse when you get to Heaven anyway."

I looked at Mary Ann. Her cheeks were flushed and she looked like he had just slapped her. She was dumbfounded—apparently, she really did want her horse in Heaven. I wanted to help her, to get her horse to heaven with her. But I didn't even have a horse. I couldn't argue about that—it would be silly. P.J. would slap me down in a minute, and laugh about it, too. But I had a dog—surely I could argue that point. My hand shot up.

"Mr. Fletcher," he said.

"What about dogs? Dogs can go to Heaven, can't they?"

"No, Mr. Fletcher. Dogs don't have souls either," he said, "so there is no way a dog can go to Heaven."

Looking back now, I think that was the moment when I first knew for certain, for an absolute fact, that he was a liar. I mean, I hated his guts before that—I always had, as far back as I could remember. But right then is when I knew he wasn't on the level. I'm not sure how, but suddenly I was certain he was lying. *Of course God allowed dogs into Heaven! I didn't have to be a Doctor of the Church to know that much.* "My God, Who art all good and deserving of all my love" had Himself created dogs when "He created the Heavens and the Earth." Surely He had also created them "in His own image and likeness." Surely His Heaven had room for His own dogs—at least the good dogs. And good horses, too. I was gonna stand with Mary Ann, not with him. P.J. could go to Hell.

"But when I get to Heaven, I'm gonna want my dog," I protested.

"You mean *if* you get to Heaven," he said, chuckling.

I felt like I had been gut-punched. I sucked in a mouthful of air. He wasn't funny—not to me. I was really worried about getting to Heaven, and probably he knew exactly why. So what did he mean by that? And now, what did my classmates think? Did they know that I had a problem with Mortal Sin? I couldn't talk about it, especially in public, especially then and there, and I was too angry and too proud to plead with him. I just turned away from him. And as I did, suddenly the images came flooding back into my mind, images that I had seen the night I found Tom's body, images that were walled off into a separate cubicle in my brain because they didn't make sense to me, but they weren't forgotten, just hidden—from me. I started remembering other things, too, things I had heard him say when he didn't know I was there. *I'm not the only one here with secrets.* I needed to talk to Toby—and Richard, too.

I knew he was a liar and a fraud—what did he have to lie about?

24.
FREE AT LAST!

I walked home with Michael and John. I could hardly wait to tell them about Sr. Ambrose.

"I'd like to make her name the Corporal Works of Mercy, and smack her big butt with her pointer for every one she doesn't know," I said.

"Yeah, I know," John said, matter-of-factly, "she did that to us, too."

"What? Why didn't you tell me?" I asked, sitting down on the wall at the foot of our hill. My brothers sat, too, John in the middle.

"She always has to have an excuse. She only does it to boys who don't know their catechism. She didn't do it to me, and I knew she wouldn't do it to you, either."

"What are the 'Seven Gifts of the Holy Ghost'?" Michael asked.

"Wisdom, Understanding, Counsel, Fortitude, Knowledge, Piety and Fear of the Lord," John and I said together.

"No, I mean, what *are* they?" Michael asked.

"Presents from the Holy Ghost," John said.

"Did you get them?" The Archangel asked, suddenly on the alert. In our family, you had to make sure you got your share.

"I dunno; I don't think so," John said.

"Me either," I said. "I don't even know what most of those things are. I might know about the Fear of the Lord part, though."

The three of us looked at each other, then down at the sidewalk, pondering, wondering if we would ever know what they were, and if we would ever receive them, and, if we did, whether we would even know it.

We heard a bark and looked up the hill to see Prince barreling downhill directly at us. He had heard us or smelled us and knew we were coming home early. He arrived, a skidding furball, wagging his stump of a tail and jumping up on us as we patted and pushed him, laughing as he dashed from one of us to the other. I'm not sure who was happier we were out of school, Prince or us.

Finally, John said, "Oh, man, I can't believe that school is out."

"Me either!" Michael and I echoed.

Prince plunked himself down between John and Michael, sitting proudly as they patted him.

"The entire summer ahead of us—with nothing to do," John said.

"Total freedom," Michael offered.

"What are you guys gonna do?" I asked.

"Sleep late every day," John said. "And ride my bike."

"Read comics," Michael said.

"Shoot our bow and arrows," John said. Our bow and arrow equipment was another prize from selling all-occasion cards. The arrows were not the razor-tipped type used for hunting big game, but they did have metal tips and would bring down rabbits or squirrels or other small game. Our end of Ridgeline was cut into the side of a very steep hill. Although the street was passably level by Mayfly standards, the side of the street opposite our backyard was a nearly sheer cliff that stretched a story and a half up to a public sidewalk above it. Each house on that side of the street was accessed by two separate sets of twenty steps each, one from the street to the public sidewalk and one from the public sidewalk up to the house. John and I used to stand on the curb on our side of Ridgeline with a quiver full of arrows slung across our backs and shoot across the street at a cardboard box perched in the weeds below the public sidewalk on the cliff opposite. It was an ideal backdrop for target practice, and we got pretty good with a bow.

We had lots of fun and adventure with our bow and arrows. Our backyard was ninety feet long by half of that wide, and we could stand in the middle of it and shoot our arrows straight up into the air, almost completely out of sight, where they would slowly turn over and fall straight back into the yard, tip first. Sometimes, they would miss the yard and fall into the street. I can still hear the sound of the metal tip hitting the concrete as the arrows bounced up into the air a dozen feet before coming back down. We didn't worry about the arrows penetrating the tops of our skulls, simply because it had never happened.

"Yeah, and I'm gonna practice with my slingshot," Michael said. "But not if Gunnar Green has his out." Gunnar Green used to shoot anything he wanted, whether it moved or not. He sat on his front step, his mouth loaded with BBs, one held at the ready in the leather web of his slingshot, while he knocked round glass bullseyes out of the side windows of passing cars. There was always a loud "CRACK!" as his BB hit a car window, and it was a source of continual wonder for the Fletcher boys why none of the drivers ever stopped to confront Gunnar. Probably because of his size, and maybe also because they heard he was crazy, and so was his old man. The Hubbard house, across the street from us on the high side of the street, was vacant after both Mr. and Mrs. Hubbard died, and there was a window in the attic gable sixty-five feet above street level. Gunnar shot it so full of holes that eventually it just fell out.

"And also," John said, "get Dad to take me out to the country so I can shoot my BB gun." We were allowed to use the bow and arrows and the slingshot without supervision, (although if they knew everything we were doing with them, we wouldn't have been), but not the BB gun. Only the BB gun was considered "dangerous," which was ridiculous, considering the things we got up to with the bow and arrows, the slingshot, matches, and rocket fuel. We could only use the BB gun in company with Dad, and only out in the country. For some reason, they were terrified about us getting into a BB gun fight and getting an eye shot out. Both my parents had told us to "never get into a BB gun fight," and both my grandparents had as well. They didn't really have to worry about that, though—since we couldn't even imagine being tempted. We all knew that only an idiot would get into a BB gun fight.

"Build model cars," Michael said. "I'm gonna tape a CO2 cartridge onto the roof of a model car and make a rocket car out of it and shoot it up the street."

"And I'm gonna build rockets," John said. "Real ones with rocket fuel that blasts off." David Dye, an older boy who picked up his newspapers at the Market Street Fire Station where my brother John's papers were delivered, was a rocket maker and bomb assembler *extraordinaire*. He was also a great advocate for bombs and rocket fuel in general, as well as an excellent instructor.

He had a penchant for describing the huge craters left in the ground, excavated by explosions from bombs and rockets that he manufactured. He used potassium chlorate as the rocket fuel, which he energized by mixing it with an oxidant. Each day, he would describe in graphic detail, his eyes glowing while he gesticulated wildly, the various explosives that he had ignited in his neighborhood. John and I were apt pupils.

In those days, you could order potassium chlorate directly from the chemical company with no silly questions about how old you were or what you intended to use it for. We mailed off a hand-written letter for a pound of the stuff, enclosing $4.65 in the envelope, and two weeks later it came through the U. S. mail in an amber glass jar in its "safe" unoxidized state—solid rocket fuel in powdered form. The stuff was so explosive that you could use virtually anything as an oxidizing agent. We used powdered sugar because it was inexpensive and easy to obtain and measure—an entire box cost nineteen cents.

Our parents did not wholeheartedly embrace our rocketry projects at first. They had some doubts. Before giving their okay, they assigned me to write a paper on the properties of potassium chlorate to see if it was safe. Our World Book Encyclopedia claimed that it was highly volatile, subject to accidental explosion, and that many people had been burned, injured, and blinded while using it in explosives and amateur rocketry. However, since my brother John and I had secretly been using it for several months already and were veterans of numerous rocket constructions and blast-offs with a perfect safety record, I felt justified in leaving that probably inaccurate claim out of the research paper. The paper that I presented to my parents was rather bland, concluded that the stuff was safe as sand, and recommended its use in amateur rocket-building. *Where there's a will, there's a way.* Needless to say, our experiments continued.

"Number, please," the operator had said, one evening during the past winter.

"4692," I answered, My grandparents' number, one of three phone numbers I knew by heart. While rocketry was not our grandmother's cup of tea *per se*, our grandfather had a more adventurous spirit. He understood boys. John and I were eager to show him how his grandsons were gearing up to assist President Kennedy in "putting a man on the moon in this decade."

"Why, sure, boys, I'd be honored to come over and watch your launch. I'll be there right after dinner."

Our rocketry skills were just in their infancy at the time—we had no real fuselage or nose cone or engine. We basically took a single newspaper page, folded the top down to the bottom, folded the half page into thirds left to right, then opened it back up, located the middle of the center strip, dumped a large quantity of already-oxidized (i.e., fully explosive in reaction to any spark, including friction) "rocket fuel" into the center, folded the left and right sides of the newspaper over the center, folded the bottom half over the top again, then rolled it up like a cigar with an explosive core. Next, we folded the "nose" section over once and scotch-taped it against the side of the rocket, then taped a dried reed, carefully selected from the dried stalks of weeds in the woods, onto the side of the rocket (which converted it into a crude version of a bottle rocket and held the back end up off the ground so it could be lighted—we didn't bother with fuses). Next, we cut off a section from a paper drinking straw and taped it along the side the rocket to act as a launch guide apparatus, assuring that the rocket went up instead of sideways, then took an ice pick and jammed it up the interior of the rocket to create an exit tunnel for the explosive gases—otherwise it would just blow up like a bomb once it was lit (or possibly when some idiot jammed an ice pick up inside it—but we had faith). Assembly completed, we then paraded to our launch pad in the back yard. The launch pad was a wooden block, into which we had inserted a vertical launch guide in the form of a straightened coat hangar, and over which we threaded the straw tube until our weed reed rested on the wooden block, supporting the rocket until the instant of launch.

"Ready?" John called.

"Ready," I confirmed, then began the countdown, which was as much fun as the launch—the countdown was novel to us in those heady days, the inherent drama almost as exciting as the blastoff itself. We argued over who got to say it: "10...9...8...7...6...5...4...3...2...1...0...blast-off!" while John lit a match and applied it to the bottom of the rocket until the thing fired. It went immediately from a single spark to a long white flame, its outer edges outlined in orange fire, as huge quantities of white smoke barreled out of our carefully engineered central exhaust tube, and the rocket rose vertically along the coat-hanger guidance system. When it reached 5'8" of elevation, however, it suddenly veered ninety degrees from the vertical and shot absolutely horizontal above the ground. As if it were an enemy missile with eyes, it sped across the yard in a fraction of a second, directly at Grandpa's head, a mere twenty feet away. Although my grandfather had a reputation long before I was born as a good minor league baseball player, I had never thought of him as quick, but as he stood there in his hat and suit coat with his cigar in his mouth, and that rocket crossed the yard in one-half second flat, I watched my Grandpa duck his head, cigar, hat, and all, as the rocket whizzed over his left ear and exploded against the side of our house, leaving a large black blast scar on the white siding. So we had some reason to think that we needed to perfect our technique, and the summer was an opportune time to do it.

"What're you gonna do this summer?" John asked.

"Practice basketball," I said.

"All summer?" Michael asked.

"Yeah," I said, "I'm gonna win the Mayfly Future Famer Trophy and get a college scholarship at Notre Dame and play for the St. Louis Hawks." The Future Famer Trophy was awarded each year at the end of the CYO Summer Tourney to the most promising player in junior high school.

"For real?" Michael asked.

"Yep, and I need you guys to practice with."

So spirits were soaring at the Fletcher house as we headed into the regular Saturday and Sunday routines, which were unchanged by summer vacation. Monday morning, however, was going to provide us with the first real occasion for celebration, and I was so eager that I considered getting up early just to exult in the fact that I didn't really have to get up.

During dinner on Sunday evening, however, Mom told us that she had volunteered John and me to serve 6:30 Mass for the month of June, "since we live so close to the Church and Father has trouble getting servers in the summer." *Gee, I wonder why that is.*

"And, boys," Mom went on, "there's a lot of work that needs to be done around here this summer, and there's no reason why you big, strong boys can't pitch in. The brick sidewalk needs to be weeded, and those weeds need to come up by the root, you'll have to do it again next week. Also, the myrtle and ivy beds need to be weeded. You don't have to do them all at once. You can each weed one hour per day until you finish, and you can teach the little boys how to do it while you're at it. Also, I want a two-gallon bucket of water carried to each of the young bushes and trees every day it doesn't rain. That's twenty-four buckets of water per day. Just fill them half full so you don't spill any. That's too heavy for the little boys, so it's up to you three to do it—that will be eight buckets per boy per day. You can take Sundays off. If it rains, you won't have to do it that day."

Summer of '63

It hadn't rained in a long time—since the night of Tom's burial.

"But Mom," I protested, "I gotta practice basketball."

"And you may, just as soon as your work is done," she replied. "This will make you stronger, and that will help your basketball. Think of it as part of your training."

The summer euphoria had been instantaneously dampened. I felt like a slave.

25.
THE RIVER'S REST

I waited until after dinner and chores were done, then asked Mom if I could go down and see Toby. "I haven't seen Toby since the way home from the cemetery," I told her. This was carefully phrased so as not to add another lie to my list of sins—at this point, I needed a calculator to keep up with them—maybe I should carry a little "sin notebook" in my pocket, but I couldn't risk Mom discovering it in the wash. Hell wasn't the only thing I lived in constant fear of.

"Good idea," she said. "Tell him we are praying for his family, all of them." We had, in fact, added the Piper family to our list of nightly prayer intentions, and had also been closing our prayers with a request for the repose of Tom's soul:

> Eternal rest grant unto him, O Lord, and let perpetual light shine upon him. May his soul and the souls of all the faithful departed, through the mercy of God, rest in peace. Amen.

"Alright if I take Prince with me?" I asked.

"I guess so. Keep your eye on him—Broadway is a busy street."

"I will," I promised. Prince was extremely well-behaved. He was wise about traffic, and so attentive that he seemed to understand intuitively what I wanted him to do, often without my telling him. I wasn't terribly concerned about taking him with me to the River's Rest, even though I knew we would be walking along the busiest street in Mayfly for several blocks.

As Prince and I approached the River's Rest, however, Prince suddenly dashed straight out into the street. "Prince! I screamed, watching terrified as his trajectory intersected with the front wheel of a large black car. "Prince!" I screamed again, but he ignored me. He began running alongside the car, snarling at the front tire, his head down, matching its speed.

Graaawwp! Graaawwp! Graaawwp! My God! What is he doing? The sound was so loud it reverberated off the walls of the building behind me—I had never heard anything like it. *Graaawwp! Graaawwp! Graaawwp! Oh my God! He's biting the tire!* Prince was attacking the car viciously while it was moving. He was trying to stop the car so he could tear it apart. That unearthly sound was the tire twisting loose from his teeth every time he bit it and clamped down, trying to hold it in his teeth.

"Prince!" I yelled again, as loud as I could, scared to death for him. He finally pulled off and came back to me, looking angry. I watched the car turn into the River's Rest side parking lot and suddenly recognized it as the black Lincoln Continental that Tony and I had seen the gangster-looking men in before.

As I came around the front of the building into the side lot, the two men had just exited their car. Once again, the large driver who looked like a bodyguard was wearing a white shirt, muscles bulging under the thin material; the smaller man was wearing a dapper gray suit and smoking. They both had their backs to us as they walked toward the office. Toby came out of the door to the office, and I saw the muscle guy stop in his tracks. Puzzled, I stopped where I was and gave Prince a hand signal and a quiet "Shhhh." Prince immediately dropped into a perfect sit on the pavement next to me, but his eyes never left the two men.

"Boss, look!" Mr. Muscle hissed.

"What?" Dapper Man said quietly, obviously annoyed.

"It's him," Mr. Muscle said in a hoarse whisper.

"Nah, he had a brother," Dapper Man said in an undertone, continuing to walk toward the office. Prince and I followed quietly, twenty feet behind them.

"Hi, son," Dapper Man said to Toby. Toby looked him in the eye.

"I'm not your son," Toby said. He looked sullen. The three of them stood for a second, just staring at each other.

Finally, the Dapper Man said, "Listen, I'm sorry to hear about your brother."

Toby's face turned instantly red. "What did you hear?" he demanded.

"We heard he jumped off the tower at the church," Dapper Man said, tossing his cigarette on the pavement and crushing it out. "Very sad."

"No, that's not what happened," Toby said, his tone challenging Dapper Man to contradict him. I could tell he wanted to fight.

"It's not?" Dapper Man asked. "What did happen then?"

Toby's teeth were clenched in defiance. "None of your goddamn business," he said. Prince and I quietly moved up behind the mobsters, unbeknownst to the two men.

"Hey, boy, don't get smart with Mr. Napolitano," Mr. Muscle said, taking a step toward Toby. Just then, Prince leapt forward to Toby, planted himself squarely in front of him, and snarled at Mr. Muscle, deep and deadly, his back up, his teeth bared. Prince was a lit fuse. The blood in my body braked instantly to a halt, stopped by the sheer menace of that rumble from deep in his barrel chest. I was frozen, vaguely aware of the office plate glass window vibrating behind him. I had never seen him like this.

Mr. Muscle took a step back, and Prince took a step forward, barking in short, fast, explosive dog curses of four or five barks each, alternated with horrific snarls, which only seemed to make him angrier. The ruff on his back stood up stiff, forming a perfect mohawk all the way down to his stub of a tail. He was so angry that he was snarling while he was barking. No one doubted that he was seconds away from tearing Mr. Muscle's throat out.

"Get your dog, boy, or I'll shoot him," Mr. Muscle said, quietly, as I came up alongside the two mobsters.

"Better not, mister, or my Dad'll kill you," I said.

"Don't make me laugh, boy," he said.

"I'm not jokin', mister—I'm just tellin' you."

"It's alright, Rocko, let it go. The boy's been under a lot of strain," the little Dapper Man said. "Grab your dog, young man; he's not going to shoot anybody." No one moved an inch until I had my arms around Prince.

"Good boy, Prince," I said, kneeling beside him. "It's alright, they're not gonna do anything. You're a good dog," I crooned to him while I patted him. His body continued to vibrate with a low rumble, almost inaudible.

"Is your mom here?" Dapper Man asked Toby, trying to end the standoff by turning to open the office door. I continued to hold Prince. His eyes never left Mr. Muscle, and his back was still up. "Good boy," I said, trying to pat it back down. As they walked into the office, I leaned toward Toby and whispered, "Bastard doesn't know how lucky he is—I mighta brought The Archangel."

When they opened the office door, I got a glimpse of Toby's mom. She looked thin and drawn, her eyes rimmed with red. I had never seen her looking so old.

"Evening, ma'am," we heard him say through the screen door, "I think we might've left some papers here—do you have them, by any chance?"

"No, but the room hasn't been cleaned since you left—you can look for yourselves," Mrs. Piper said, handing him the key.

Toby grabbed my arm. "Quick! To the basement! We'll use the outside door off the alley. I have the key."

Prince and I ran with Toby around the corner of the building to the back door, closed it quietly behind us, and each grabbed a glass from the top of the long duct.

"This is under their room, right here," Toby said.

I looked at Prince. His big, dark eyes looked back at me, waiting. "Shhhh," I whispered. "Quiet, boy." He didn't exactly nod, but his expression changed. I could swear he understood me.

We listened intently, but there was no conversation. We heard things being moved around above us as they searched. Prince lay down on the floor and watched me. *What are they looking for?* Finally, we heard Dapper Man say, "Check the closet," and then heard Mr. Muscle's heavy footsteps move out into the hallway to the linen closet next door. Toby and I looked at each other, our eyes wide. *What are they doing in there?* We could hear him shifting things around above us, then fast, heavy footsteps. Prince sat up, ready.

"Shhhh, boy, it's okay," I told him.

"Boss! I found the map," we heard. "And look what else!" Silence, then Dapper Man's voice, the clearest and loudest we had heard yet, said, vehemently, "That bastard! That nosey dipshit bean-pole bastard!" Then, "Anything else? What about the report?" and Mr. Muscle said, "No, that's all that was in there, except a couple of Playboys."

"Okay," Dapper Man said, "he must've taken it to his room."

"Want me to look, Boss?"

"No, it will just cause suspicion, especially since we already told the old lady we were looking for some papers. They won't know what it is even if they find it. I can get another copy," Dapper Man said, "it'll just take a few days. We need it to check out Cottonwood. Put that thing back where you found it, but wipe it off first."

We looked at each other. Toby was mouthing, "Cottonwood," his face screwed up in a grimace. I just nodded.

We heard the closet door open, then both doors close, one after the other, and two sets of footsteps going down the hallway back toward the office.

"I wonder what those guys found," Toby said. "Let's wait a few minutes and go look in the closet."

"I thought those guys were long gone," I said.

"Gone from here. They moved to the Laze-E-Daze the day after Tom died."

"That dump? Your place is much nicer!"

"I know, but it's okay. Tom never liked them anyway," Toby said.

"Why not?"

"He thought they were up to no good. I just don't know what," he said. "Crazy Carly left, too. Business is terrible. We haven't even cleaned the rooms. Don't need to–nobody's staying here."

"Why did Crazy Carly leave?" I asked.

"No idea. Probably because she was in love with Tom, and he's gone." We were both silent for a while.

"Toby—we need to talk about that night in the graveyard," I said, finally.

"I know. I've wanted to talk to you about it, but I just can't make sense out of it," Toby said.

"Did you know I saw it, too?" I asked.

"Saw what?" he asked.

"Saw someone leaving Tom's grave."

"Oh, my God! You saw it, too? How could you see it?" he asked.

"I was just coming out of the woods on your left when that big lightning flash hit. Who *was* that?"

"I have no idea. I'm positive it wasn't Tom, though," he said, looking at me to see if I disagreed.

"I didn't think so either," I said, "but I don't know who it was or even who it could have possibly been."

"This is really important," Toby said. "I've gone over and over it in my mind. I even dream about it. I'm not sure I even know anymore what I actually saw and what I didn't see."

"Think they're gone yet?" I asked. "Let's go look in the closet and see what they were talking about."

We peeked around the back corner of the building—their car was gone. What we found in the closet was a broken rear-view mirror fastened with electrical tape to the end of an old broom handle. It was standing in a small vertical space between a wall stud and the stud framing the closet door. Toby held it up to the register grill—both of us had a perfect view into Room 111. He inadvertently hit the register grill with it, causing a dull clunk and making both of us cringe.

"Oh my God!" Toby said. "I just remembered, the last time I saw Tom, he was coming out of the linen closet real fast, and he said, 'I gotta tell you something—but later,' and he had a real serious look on his face."

"We need to get Richard in on this," I said. "And we need to tell him about the night of the storm. We can all take the oath first."

Toby just looked at me for several seconds, taking this in. "You're right, but there's a lot more to tell; it's gonna take a while. Let's meet at The Captain's Place. Tomorrow afternoon—two o'clock? I'll tell Richard," he said.

That night, I tossed and turned. I dreamed that I was bent over, grabbing my ankles while Sr. Ambrose beat me with her pointer, seven times because I couldn't remember the Seven Corporal Works of Mercy. I tried to tell her that I knew them, but I just couldn't remember right then—and every time I tried to recite them, all I could think of was a flaming ring with curls of smoke coming off the sides, like the hoop that clowns jump through in the circus. And P.J. was there in the doorway, nodding and saying, "Go ahead—he deserves it." And Bad Billie Boyd was walking by and he was waving for me to hurry up, like we had someplace we had to go. When I looked around, I saw Mr. Muscle standing there with a gun, and I hated him because I knew he was looking for Prince, and I didn't want Prince to get to heaven if I wasn't there—he would just keep looking for me.

26.
FILLING RICHARD IN

The next afternoon, Toby and I were at The Captain's Place early, waiting for Richard. We lifted the heavy green blanket of kudzu, causing several predatory daddy-long-legs to scatter across the foliage. Under the blanket, I smelled the moist limestone and felt the cool exhalation of the big bluff.

I had brought Dad's good flashlight, but I also brought Prince along to warn us if someone else was there, hiding in any of the passages that spun away from the large entrance chamber. I flashed the beam around the interior and up the side passages as Prince wandered about, apparently unperturbed, getting a snootful of the people and animals which had been there before us, and discovering what they had been doing. He seemed satisfied, and as far as I could see, there was no one inside but us. We sat in the middle of the big room in the dark, on the cool cave floor, our eyes drawn toward the opening and the light, while we waited for Richard.

"I wouldn't know a cottonwood if I saw one," Toby said. "What are they?"

"Enormous trees," I answered. "Huge, sort of like the Mississippi River version of the giant sequoia. They're the real tall trees you see towering above all the other trees along the river and on the islands. The bald eagles roost in them."

"How big are they?"

"They all get to be a hundred feet tall—a big one can grow close to two hundred feet, and their trunks are so big it takes three grown men touching hands to get their arms around them. And the bark ridges are two inches thick. They grow along the river because they need to be plugged directly into a water source. A big one will evaporate a hundred-thirty gallons per day on a hot day. They produce those little puffs of cotton that you see floating around in the air. Those are their seeds."

"But there must be cottonwoods all up and down the river. How will we know what cottonwood they're talking about?" Toby asked.

"I think they're talking about Cottonwood Point," I say. "Remember? It was mentioned in the article those guys looked up in the library—the wood stop that the *Flying Eagle* made before it exploded. It must be around here somewhere, or they wouldn't be here. So, I think we should just start by asking around. I heard it's a good place to fish," I said, after a pause, looking at him in the dim light until he looked back, then winking. "And now you have, too," I said, smiling.

He nodded—he got it. The fishing comment wasn't meant to be believed—I had only said it to protect Toby, and me too, from the wages of sin, because each of us, having now heard this inane comment, would not be lying if we told someone we had heard it, since we both had—after all, we didn't have to say who told us or whether they were serious or if we believed it. And the wink even covered my first lie to Toby, since it clearly indicated that I was just kidding. So not only did that seemingly meaningless remark provide a good cover story for our investigation, it also provided spiritual cover, saving us a bit of burn time in Purgatory which would otherwise have been earned by lying—killing two birds with one stone. I tried to use my head about these things—the good Lord helps those who help themselves—and God knows I needed all the help I could get in that department. There were so many lies I was forced to tell that it was just silly to add to my burn time needlessly by telling ones that weren't strictly necessary.

Richard arrived, and we brought him up to speed. I insisted on the oath, which we all took together, left hands touching the cool stone floor and right hands raised:

I swear by the trees and earth and stone,
I swear by my skin and blood and bone
I swear not to tell by my head and behind,
And if I ever do, I'll walk around blind.

We said it in unison, covering our eyes during the final line, and finishing together.

Then, while Prince walked around the perimeter, sniffing at whatever he found interesting, we sat on the cool floor, Indian style, our heads leaning close in toward one another, still worried that we might be overheard by someone in the cave or even outside the entrance.

"Richard, you're not gonna believe what just happened," Toby said. Richard raised his brows, waiting. "Those mobsters were back at the motel, looking for something."

"What do you mean 'back'?" Richard asked. "I didn't know they had left."

"Oh, yeah, they left the day after Tom died. They moved over to the Laze-E-Daze," Toby said.

"Tell it in order," I said. "Tell about Prince in the parking lot." So Toby did.

"I wonder why Prince went crazy?" Richard asked.

"No idea," I said. "I've never seen him like that."

We took turns then, filling Richard in on Mr. Muscle thinking Toby was Tom, and telling Mrs. Piper they were looking for some papers, and eavesdropping on them, and their knowing to look in the closet, and finding the map and the mirror taped to the stick, and calling Tom a "dipshit bean-pole bastard," and wiping the mirror off and putting it back, and talking about not wanting to create suspicion, and having to get another copy of something because they couldn't find it.

It took a long time. Finally, we ran down.

"Do you know what they were after?" Richard asked.

"No," we both said.

"Have you checked Tom's hiding places?"

"Every place I could think of," Toby said. "Nothing."

"There's more," I said. "We need to tell you about the night of Tom's burial." Toby looked over at me and nodded. His eyes were far away—I couldn't read his expression. Richard was looking at both of us.

Finally, Richard said, "Guys, I want to hear this—I *really* want to hear it, and I want to hear it right now, but I can't—I have to get home for a family dinner. It's my aunt's birthday," (but he didn't say "ant"; he said it 'ahnt'). "We have lots of work to do on this, but I can't stay any longer."

"I know," I said, "but we've gotta do it fast."

"Why's that?" Richard asked.

"Lots of reasons," I said. "What if we're right and Tom didn't commit suicide, and because he's not buried in hallowed ground, he can't get into Heaven, and the only way we can get him buried in hallowed ground is to prove that he didn't commit suicide? I think we have to do everything we possibly can to get him into Heaven as soon as we can."

"Right!" Toby said.

"I agree, then," Richard said.

"And," I continued, "what if those mobsters had something to do with Tom's death? We don't know how long they'll even be around here."

"Right," Richard and Toby said.

"And what if P.J. had something to do with it? Because Tom is the second boy in the last three years who was connected to him, who supposedly committed suicide. And he's still in business."

Richard looked surprised. "Who else?" he asked.

"The Dalton boy," I said.

"Oh, yeah," Toby said, "I forgot about that." Richard looked a question at the two of us. "The coroner mentioned it at the Inquest," Toby said.

"He died three years ago, and P.J. was also called as a witness at his Inquest," I said. "We need to find out what happened to him."

"Yeah," Toby said, "and P.J. is acting really strange since Tom died. He won't even look my parents in the face, and we've had him over to the house for dinner lotsa times. Tom helped him lotsa times, too, whenever he'd call and say he needed a young man."

"And also, Ray Lee Po is walking around loose, and what if he did it?" I said.

"Did what?" Toby asked, startled.

"Pushed Tom off or threw him off," I said. "He was completely mad when he came out of the Church. He was pointing at Tom and grunting, really upset. He acted like he was crazy."

"Good grief," Richard said. "We're gonna have to start meeting regularly. Let's meet back here tomorrow afternoon at 2:00, okay? Right now, I gotta run!"

When I got home for dinner, I was in the bathroom, washing my face, hands and arms so I could set the table, when the doorbell rang. I heard Stephen say, "Mom, it's someone for you."

Curious, I cracked the door and listened as I dried off.

"Is Jamie Fletcher here?" I heard someone ask. *Oh, God, it's Mr. Milchard—I forgot all about it!*

"Why do you ask?" Mom said. I could tell she wasn't impressed.

"That boy owes me $1.20," Mr. Milchard said. "His dog killed my chicken, a four-pound chicken. Twenty-nine cents a pound makes $1.16 plus 4 cents tax is $1.20." My Mom was silent for a moment.

"So, you charge tax, do you?" she said. "I'll go see the City Collector and make sure your tax calculations are correct. But since you're so good at math, you must already know that a four-pound chicken is only a pound and a half dressed," she said. "So you're trying to sell him the head and feet, too. Sounds dishonest to me. Fraud is a crime—so is extortion—you can go to jail for it. What's your name?"

"Milchard. Harold Milchard," he said, somewhat abashed.

"Well, Mr. Milchard, it sounds to me like he saved you having to clean the bird, which at $1.20 per hour is 40¢ even if you work fast, plus you shot the boy's dog, so if you take us to court we'll countersue you for that. He's an awfully good dog—I bet shooting him will cost you at least twenty dollars—and then we'll end up owning all your chickens and your whole chicken coop plus your house, too, if it comes to that.

"Now I'm going to call the dog," Mom continued, "and I suggest you get along pretty quickly, because I imagine he'll remember you when he sees you. And on your way home," she said, her voice rising, "you can pray for forgiveness, and pray to God that he won't send you straight to hell for all eternity. And if I were you, Mr. Milchard, I'd take better care of my chickens in the future." SLAM!—that was the front door—the conversation was apparently over.

Mr. Milchard had gotten some food for thought—that's what Mom was good at.

27.
THE ISSUES

After Sunday Mass and breakfast, I played some basketball shooting games with John and Michael, then headed toward downtown and River Road. Since there was no school, I knew Gunnar Green was home. Most other non-Catholic kids were at Sunday school, but Gunnar Green wasn't just non-Catholic—he was non-God. There was a special word for it, but I forgot what it was. Apist, maybe. I just thought of him as Satan.

Once, when I was in the First Grade, he grabbed me just as I left our yard—he had been hiding behind an enormous ball yew which marked the beginning of his property.

"C'mere, punk, I wanna show ya somethin'," he said, lifting me up with one arm. I was scared to death, frozen even after he put me down. I was afraid to run—I thought if I tried to get away from him and he caught me, he might kill me. "Look at this," he said, reaching into his back pocket and pulling out a tooled leather wallet. I was curious—maybe he had some foreign money or something interesting he wanted to show me—he didn't really have any friends he could show it to. He pulled out a piece of paper and shoved it under my nose. *Oh, no!* It was a picture of a woman with no clothes on—a Mortal Sin to look at.

"No," I shouted, turning away, "I'm not gonna look! It's an impure picture! I don't wanna go to hell!" He just grabbed me and kept holding it under my nose, laughing until I looked at it—that's the kind of boy he was.

Today I was taking no chances, however—I had Prince with me. He was happy to run alongside my bike. As we entered River Road and passed Bad Billie Boyd's house, he yelled through the screen door.

"Hey, man, where'd you get the dog?"

"I found him," I said. Billie came out and patted him.

"What's his name?"

"Prince."

Prince and Bad Billie seemed to get along famously. Prince seemed genuinely glad to meet him—you'd have thought they were soul mates.

"I'm just taking him for a run," I said.

"Great, man—see ya later. See ya, Prince," he said. Prince wagged his rump at him.

Minutes later, Prince and I were at the entrance to the Captain's Place. I hadn't brought Dad's good flashlight, because it was harder to sneak it out of the house on a Sunday. As I approached the mouth of the cave, I could hear conversation spilling out through the kudzu blanket at irregular intervals, and it was not Richard or Toby. Stopping just short of the cave mouth so as not to darken the opening, I listened to two uncouth male voices speaking low, occasionally raised in volume, frequently punctuated by cursing. Prince began a low growl, listening intently while registering his disapproval.

"Come on, boy," I whispered. Retreating silently back up River Road toward downtown, I waited for Richard and Toby.

The two of them showed up together, Richard carrying a shopping bag.

"There's someone inside the Captain's," I told them.

"Who?" Toby asked.

"No idea," I said. "Two men. I just heard their voices and left—I didn't go inside. They might just be hobos sleeping there."

"Let's hang around and see if they come out," Toby suggested. We crossed the railroad tracks, hugging the foot of the bluff to a thin strip of land next to the river. We directed our steps toward an old rock foundation wall, a vestige of a warehouse built on the riverbank a century before, veteran of many inundations. The timbers were all missing; some carried no doubt to New Orleans, some to the Gulf of Mexico, and some perhaps salvaged downstream and living another life in the south.

Random honeysuckle vines grew up on the sides of the ancient foundation. Heavy crowns of lush green foliage rose intermittently above the top of the wall, covered with elongated white and yellow flowers that enveloped us in nearly unbearable fragrance. Hundreds of bees of all sizes buzzed around in the foliage. A large black snake ruffled the grass as he slid past us, close to our feet. Prince followed it for a few feet, sniffing and snapping at it playfully, but it didn't want to play and soon vanished.

The stone wall had been laid in an era when men knew how to build walls out of rough field stone, and build them straight, with no lean—true and strong enough to withstand a hundred Mississippi River floods. Now, a century later, it beckoned to us. We walked over to a stretch of bare wall, brushed away the spiders, and plunked ourselves down on the top row of stones, appreciating the warmth of the sun on the irregular surface.

"I brought a notebook," Richard said, pulling it out of his shopping bag. "to keep track of all the issues we need to investigate. First, let's make a list," he said, producing a pen from his pocket.

"Well, first," Toby said, "we need to prove that Tom didn't commit suicide."

"That's right," I said. "That's the main reason we're here."

"I agree," Richard said, writing in the notebook, "and that issue gets complicated." Prince gave a long whimpering moan and lay down in the long grass.

"I know," Toby said, "how can we prove it?"

"I've been thinking about this," Richard said. "There are only three possibilities. Either he committed suicide, or it was an accident, or someone killed him."

Toby and I just looked at him, trying to absorb these possibilities. We couldn't think of any others. I nodded slowly.

"Alright," Richard said. "Let's take suicide first, since that was the verdict of the Inquest. What evidence supports Tom committing suicide? Be honest, now. Why did the coroner rule that Tom had committed suicide?"

Toby and I were both silent. Finally, I said, "He kept harping on about Tom's personal life, that he used to hang out in the Central Park bandstand, that he didn't have a girlfriend. What was it Prying Fatboy said, Toby?"

Turning to Richard, I said, "Toby heard the entire speech. Say it again, Toby."

"Look, y'all," Toby began by getting himself into character, "Y'all tryin' ta tell me that some sissy-boy lurkin' 'round the public pisser who's got no friends 'cept pree'-verts, who don't even want to *git* a girlfriend, who goes up a fo'ty-six foot towah with a note in his pocket that says 'Looza,' din't kill hisself? Hell, ah'd kill mahself, too. Ah've heard enough. An' ah don't wanna be late fo' the nineteenth hole, 'cause ah just love gettin' drunk on mah fat ass."

"Nice job," I tell Toby, nodding at him. Richard just stared at Toby, then at me, then gave a short laugh and shook his head.

"Okay, so it looks like they thought he was queer, and he thought of himself as a loser," Richard said, writing in the notebook, then looking up. "Was there any evidence that Tom thought he was a loser besides that note?"

"No," Toby said, "that was the only thing."

"Did your Dad ever get the note back from Prying Fatboy?" I asked Toby.

"Dad said he was gonna ask for it, but I don't know if he ever did. I'll ask him when I get home," Toby said.

"That reminds me," I said. "I need to look up Prying Fatboy's telephone number when I get home." Richard looked at me quizzically, then went on, apparently unwilling to chase every squirrel that ran by.

"Okay, that's another one for the list: was the note in Tom's handwriting?" Richard said, writing it down.

"The note was in pieces," Toby said. "Three pieces. It spelled 'Loser'."

"The note was in pieces?" Richard asked.

"Yeah, it had been torn up—they had the pieces inside a plastic bag, like an evidence bag," Toby said.

"We really need that note," I said.

"Okay," Richard said, "if he didn't commit suicide, then it was either an accident or he was killed."

"I think Reiser did it," I said.

"What!? Why do you think that?" Toby asked.

"Lots of reasons," I said.

"Let's just make our list first," Richard said. "We can investigate each of these possibilities one at a time later. We just need to get them all down first."

"Okay," I said, grudgingly. "Then I guess we just need to put down: was it an accident? And was he killed? And did P.J. kill him?" *Why was everybody so inclined to give that jerk a break? We could save ourselves a lotta time by skipping all this other bullshit and just investigating him.*

"Done," Richard said, writing them all down. "What else?"

"Why was P.J. the first one to find him? Why was he talking to him? Why was he saying, 'I warned you' over and over?" I said.

"Yeah, and why was he going through his pockets?" Toby asked.

"Hold on, hold on," Richard said, writing furiously. "Okay."

"Why did he start acting so weird right after?" I said.

"Who was the Dalton boy and what happened to him?" Toby said.

"And why was Ray Lee Po grunting and pointing at him?" I asked. We waited until Richard paused from his writing.

"And why didn't P.J. tell them about that at the Inquest?" Toby said. "Or mention that he had warned Tom about something?"

"And why did Prince go nuts on that gangster, Mr. Muscle?" I asked.

"And what did those guys lose at the River's Rest?" Toby asked.

"And how did they know to look in the closet?" I asked. "And why did the Dapper Man tell Mr. Muscle to wipe it off before he put it back?"

"There's something else, too," I said. "Something big." I had Richard's full attention, but I didn't know what to tell him. I looked over at Toby, who just shrugged, willing me to continue. Both of us were afraid to talk about what we had seen. *Was that Tom? And if not, who or what was it?* I was certain I hadn't just imagined it.

"Richard," I said, "We gotta tell you something, but first you gotta swear you'll never tell this to anyone else or even talk about it with anyone, except Toby and me."

"Okay," he said.

"We gotta all take the oath on this part, too," I said.

"The oath?" he said. "You serious?"

"Very."

"Must be something really important."

"It is," I said.

"Okay, then," he said, as we all bent down and picked up a small rock.

I swear by the trees and earth and stone,
I swear by my skin and blood and bone,
I swear not to tell by my head and behind,
And if I ever do, I'll walk around blind,

we finished, closing our eyes as we recited the last line.

"Good," I said. "You're not gonna believe this." So I told Richard all about Ms. Mame and what she told us.

"Oh, bullshit!" Richard interrupted.

"We swear," both Toby and I said together.

Then I told him about going to the graveyard the night of the burial and everything that happened. Richard just listened, his eyes getting progressively larger as the story went on.

"You're makin' some of this up!" he said at one point.

"I swear to you, this is the gospel truth," I said.

"Okay," he said, "go on." And I did—I told him the whole thing, down to the Boyd boys and my lies about how I got injured and blamed it all on poor Prince. While I was making this admission, I looked at Prince guiltily. He looked sorrowful, but then he got up and came over and leaned against my legs. He knew he had taken the rap for me, but it was obvious he understood why he had to—he didn't hold it against me.

Finally, "What did he look like?" he asked.

"I don't know. It was so fast, and his arms were up, and his mouth was wide open. But I don't think it was Tom. I don't know who it was—or what it was. I was too far away, and I only saw it for a split second. I'm not even sure Toby knows what he saw."

Toby just shook his head ruefully. Richard looked amazed.

"And you have no idea who it was?" he asked Toby.

"No, I was scared shitless," Toby said. "But I'm sure it wasn't Tom. I just don't know who it was or what he was doing at Tom's grave."

"Okay," Richard said, adding to the list in his notebook, "who was the strange apparition at Tom's grave, and what was he doing there?"

Both Toby and I thought that just about covered it. We waited until Richard finished the list. "Okay," he said, "let's take these issues one at a time, starting with 'Did Tom commit suicide?' the next time we get together."

We heard a train whistle and then the approaching train, the volume increasing as it grew nearer. A minute later, a freight train thundered past us on the track, hugging the base of the bluff between River Road and the riverbank. We were cut off from the bluff and from Mayfly. Conversation stopped as the towering brick-red steel cars rushed past us, causing me to sway in the slipstream, the smell of hot diesel in my nostrils. The massive structure roared its roar of steel and rust, deafening me, and filling me with awe and a sudden fear of derailment. My entire body alert, my ears bombarded with screeching, I pictured the carnage that would ensue—however unlikely a derailment was, I would be crushed instantaneously by the enormous steel boxes gouging into the ground where I sat, if only God willed it. Surely this was "the Fear of the Lord."

"My Jesus, mercy!" I prayed, falling back in my moment of terror on one of the easiest ejaculations which met with Church approval. I liked this one not only because it was easy to learn and didn't take much time to say, but also because I got a free "Get-Out-Of-Purgatory-For-300-Days" card every time I said it. Pope Pius IX had announced this indulgence in 1846, and he was infallible, so this one was a sure thing, an absolute lead-pipe cinch. And, yes, I knew that goat Martin Luther had made a big stink out of indulgences, but that was just because people were *selling* them, not because they weren't legitimate ways to eliminate some scheduled burn time. Indulgences were real—all you had to do was learn about them and do the work—one of the many tricks of the sinner's trade. I pitied the early Christians who had no way to find out about them and had to serve all their purgatory time just getting burned, with no time off for good behavior.

So I would have been a total fool not to take advantage of learning this indulgenced ejaculation and saying it every chance I got—saying it twelve times would get me out of my scheduled burning for ten years, which had to be worth a lot, although I had no idea what percentage of my pre-Heaven burn time ten years would amount to by the time I was done stacking up all my sins in this vale of tears. And it was so quick and easy to say, especially if time was short for some reason. And let's face it, if that freight train derailed all of a sudden, time would definitely be short.

"Listen, you guys," Richard said when we could hear one another again, and I found myself still sojourning in the land of the living, "we really need to find a better meeting place—somewhere completely private. We're gonna have to meet practically every day for a while, and we can't count on the cave, and this place is pretty public. People are bound to start asking what we're up to. Let's all keep our eyes open for another place."

"Yeah," I said, "and we need a good cover story, one we can tell our parents." Looking for the perfect lie—again.

"Also, Richard, we need to find out where Cottonwood Point is. I hear it's a good place to fish," I told him, winking. He looked at me for a second, then nodded. He got it immediately.

"It's gotta be downstream," he said. Toby and I just looked at him. I hadn't thought of that.

As we walked home with Prince, I realized that we had never seen the men who were in the cave. Maybe they were sleeping in there. Since nobody had come up with an idea for a good hangout, we agreed to meet at the stone foundation wall again the next day.

28.
NEGOTIATING THE DEAL

So on Monday morning, the day of my previously anticipated summer vacation exultation, I was up at dawn, scheduled to serve early Mass. For me, that meant getting up by 6:00 a.m. at the latest—my roommate, the Knight of the Altar, was on duty, too, but he had decided to sleep in until 6:15, knowing he could count on me to cover for him by lighting the candles and filling the cruets with water and wine. All he had to do was show up, don his cassock and surplice, and kneel on the *prie dieu* in the sacristy at 6:29 a.m. for the "Prayer Before Mass." Then he would pull the rope on the hanging brass bell at the arched doorway to announce our entering the sanctuary from the side of the altar, so that the congregation would know to stand.

I knew I could get up at 6:00 and be dressed and at the church by 6:15 if I hustled, and I had it down to a science. I went to the bathroom, washed my face (well, okay, my face-washing was fairly abbreviated, consisting of a few drops of water to rinse the sleep out of the corners of my eyes), brushed my teeth—some of them at least—and dressed, all in four minutes. Getting out of the house, reconnoitering Gunnar Green's ambush area and getting safely past it took another minute. I knew I could run the three blocks in three minutes, allowing two minutes to climb the steep back outside stairs into the sacristy, find and don my correct-sized cassock and surplice, and still have five minutes leeway for emergencies—like someone else getting to the bathroom ahead of me, or a Gunnar Green sighting, which would require a three-block detour.

"Do you have a clean handkerchief?" Mom asked as I dressed.

"Yes, ma'am," I said.

"Do you have your Rosary in your pocket?" she asked as I left the house.

"Yes, ma'am," I replied dutifully, ducking out the back door and carefully reconnoitering Gunnar Green's lair. I knew he wouldn't be up this early unless he were still up from last night, in which case he would be loud and obnoxious, but slow. All was quiet, so I blasted down the steep incline of Hill Street, running as fast as I could to keep from falling onto my face, then braking at the foot of the hill to navigate the turn onto Broadway. As I ran west, my legs pumping in the footsteps of my elongated shadow stretched out in front of me, I could see the windows of the church bell tower bathed in the golden rays of early morning. It looked like a postcard—not at all like the place where my friend was killed.

Weekday Masses didn't take very long. Six days of the week, there was no sermon. These were typically "Low Masses," which meant a plain liturgy, as opposed to "High Masses," with pomp and circumstance, sung responses, more candles, and occasionally even incense, which I loved. Since the congregation couldn't understand the Latin Mass prayers anyway, any priest worth his salt could blow through the Latin prayers at a Low Mass clearly enunciated but very fast, and everyone in attendance, including the altar boys, appreciated it. Twenty-eight minutes, as opposed to a full hour at a High Mass on Sunday. Nevertheless, after putting out the candles, stowing away the sacred vessels, and hanging up our cassocks and surplices, it was almost 7:20 when we arrived home.

Summer of '63

The three "Little Boys" had already eaten breakfast and were out in the big six-sided sandbox under the apple tree in their pajamas. Mom woke Michael, too, since she wanted all three of the older boys to eat breakfast right away so we could clear the table and put the food away.

"It's too hot to leave the milk out," she said.

"I want you boys to do your chores first thing every day," she said. "First things first. That way you can do your work in the cool of the day, and it won't be hanging over your head all day long. You should be finished by 9:30 and have the rest of the day to play." *Sounds good to me, all except the getting up early part.*

"Tell me when you're starting, and I'll set the timer on the stove," she said. The stove timer was the final authority on deadlines and work durations. And Mom controlled it. "And I want a good hour's work—no stopping, resting, getting drinks, going to the bathroom—you do that before you start. If you want to talk while you're working, that's alright. But if I look out there and your boys' hands aren't busy, I'm going to start the timer over, do you understand? So go on, all of you—go to the bathroom and get a drink and then tell me when you're ready to start, and by that, I mean on your knees on the sidewalk." So we did. *Sigh. The salt mine.*

Since this wasn't our first rodeo, we also grabbed our one dandelion digger, a paint scraper, and the old, non-matching table knife which had been relegated to yard work, and then we all headed out to the brick sidewalk.

"Okay, we're ready—start the timer," John yelled.

"How do you ask?" she yelled back.

"Please," he said.

"Alright, boys, I'll let you know when your hour is up, and then you can take turns watering the trees and bushes."

We talked about important stuff while we worked, mostly about how great it was going to be to get our work done early and then have the rest of the day to do whatever we wanted.

"It's getting pretty hot," Michael said. Concerned, I looked over at Prince. He seemed unfazed by the heat, but then he was lying on the ground in the shade under the elm tree. *What a smart dog!*

"Yeah," John said. "Good thing we're doing this in the cool of the day." I couldn't tell if he was serious or being facetious. A little bit of both, probably.

"Yeah," I said, "can you imagine kneeling on this sidewalk this afternoon?" Then, assuming the voice of Mom, "Do you boys ever stop to think how lucky you are? I bet none of your friends get to do their work in the cool of the day."

After weeding and watering, it was time for basketball. John and Michael were pretty good, too, but they mainly just wanted to play for fun. Okay by me—I just needed people to play with—I had a dream.

So we played lots of H.O.R.S.E. with "provin's," which simulated the pressure of having the game on the line, and when we were short on time, we played P.I.G. with "no provin's" required. We played "Around the World" and "Around the World and Back," and we always gave The Archangel two opportunities to "chance it" if he missed, instead of only one, partly because he was younger than us, but mainly because one day he just announced that he got two chances, and we certainly didn't want to argue with him. We played "1-on-1", and "2-on-2", and "3-on-3" when we could get enough other players, and we played "3-Man-21" when we couldn't, and "Make-It-Take-It." Sometimes we even played regular rules where we took foul shots.

Summer of '63

All of us were getting pretty good, but even though John and Michael had decent skills and made some nice shots, and fairly frequently, too, no one drilled the absolute eyes out of the basket like I did. I was starting to feel pretty positive about my prospects for the Future Famer Trophy. Heck, Michael might even win it after me, if he wanted to, but I'm not sure it mattered much to him—the way he was headed, it looked like if he could stay out of prison, his career was gonna be in personal security, like a bodyguard for the President or something.

So, yeah, I was just getting better and better, but nobody knew it yet, and the point of this entire effort was to become famous. I'm not sure what drove me harder—I had detailed visions of universal acclaim, the coolest car, worship by my beautiful wife, tons of money, living in a mansion, everyone loving me and knowing my scoring records by heart, kids all wanting my autograph. But it made me feel ill when I thought about the humiliation I would feel if I failed, if I were forgotten, or, even worse, talked about as a "pretty good player" who wasn't good enough for the big time, or if I had to stay in Mayfly and work in my Dad's business.

I needed to be so great that everybody knew it. I had already told my brothers, so I had to do it. If I didn't, I was just a fraud, an also-ran, somebody who talked a big game, and that was all, "all hat and no cattle," as my aunt used to say. I wanted nothing less than universal acclaim, like Wilt Chamberlain, or Bob Cousy. I wanted to be known as *the* on-court *maestro*, and I would have to make it happen without being seven feet tall. So there was no other option—I had to win that trophy—it was the first big step—but it was an important one. In fact, it was absolutely necessary.

So, I made a deal—not with the devil, and not with God, either—I made it with the Poor Souls in Purgatory. Those were the souls of people who had committed sins during their lives—which was every person who had ever lived, except Jesus. Oh, and also except Mary—because God couldn't bear to be born to a woman who had sinned. So He made it so Mary not only never committed a sin, but she didn't even have Original Sin—that black stain that every person has, every other person who has ever been born, that is, and the only way to get rid of it is to be baptized. Even Catholics didn't know for ages that Mary was born without the Original Sin, which all the rest of us had on our souls from the moment of conception, but fortunately, Pope Pius IX announced it to the entire world in 1854. Better late than never. And we happen to know this is true, because of Papal Infallibility. So people who want to complain about how come we didn't know this for almost two thousand years can just shut up.

But anyway, back to the Poor Souls—some people called them "the Suffering Souls." Basically, all the people who ever lived, except Jesus and Mary, had to suffer in the fires of Purgatory to get purified before they could go to Heaven, and the more sins you committed, the longer your time in the fire. Going to Confession could forgive your sins, so if you were in Mortal Sin, Confession could keep you the hell out of Hell, but it didn't reduce your time in Purgatory by one jot—you were still gonna have to pay in fire—otherwise, Confession would just be a free lunch if it took away not only sins, but also the penalties.

I didn't know where we would be without Purgatory. It looked to me like Purgatory contributed to peace on earth, because if you didn't have the assurance that your adversary would be burned all over in fire for mistreating you, even for little things like sticking out their tongue at you, you might have to resort to more immediate punishments, like mayhem and murder. It looked to me like the world would be a better place if everybody knew about Purgatory the way we Catholics did—but maybe it didn't really make us better, just a lot trickier.

For instance, sometimes when I got into an argument with one of my brothers and I knew he was lying, I'd say, "That's not true," and then of course he'd have to say, "Yes, it is," and I would just keep insisting it wasn't true, so he would have to just keep lying and insisting it was, and I knew that every single lie he told meant additional time in the fire for him, so the entire argument could be pretty satisfying. *The Lord truly does work in mysterious ways.*

Anyway, the thing was, there were thousands of Poor Souls, hundreds of thousands, probably even millions, and nobody knew how long they had to stay there before they could go to Heaven. And since they were in such horrible pain from the flames all over them, they were really eager to help any way they could, if you just promised to say a few prayers for them so they could get out a little sooner. And they had no bargaining power at all—none. Because being burned really, really hurts! It hurt like Hell, except you knew you wouldn't be there for all of eternity, so you still had hope.

So, when this scheme occurred to me, I knew I had an ace in the hole. Because those guys would do anything—I mean *anything*—for some relief from the burning. And I didn't even need to sell my soul to the Devil. I could just make a deal with the Poor Souls and get what I wanted and still have my soul and be free to go to Heaven—if I could manage it otherwise, that is. I wasn't sure exactly how the Poor Souls got things done, but they were pretty incentivized, so they had obviously figured out something.

I needed a quiet place to cut the deal, so the next time I had to go to the bathroom, I locked the door and sat on the toilet, then I closed my eyes and whispered very slowly and clearly, *"If you help me win the Future Famer Trophy, I promise to say some extra Rosaries for the relief of your burning."* Then I had a sudden inspiration that I thought would really clinch the deal. *"And just so you don't have to wait for the trophy presentation before you get some relief, I'm going to pay you in advance—I'll say an extra Rosary for you every night this summer. Did you all get that? An extra Rosary—every night!"* I figured this type of *largesse* would make me one of their prime customers and get them all working really hard for what I wanted. *I should get VIP treatment for this.* They would have to work out among themselves how they were going to split up the relief from suffering, but I assumed they had some type of system. I knew it was a lot to pay, but it was going to be worth it—I would reap the benefits my entire life!

So I had the supernatural help all lined up, but I knew the Poor Souls couldn't do it by themselves. They couldn't make a silk purse out of a sow's ear, so to speak, and besides, the good Lord helps those who help themselves, so I knew I still had my work cut out for me. I would hate to invest the time and effort in all those extra Rosaries and not get the benefit of my bargain.

Nonetheless, as I gave the bathroom a quick shot of deodorizer, I was feeling pretty good about my prospects, grateful to the Holy Ghost for inspiring me to come up with that idea, and also glad to be able to help those poor bastards in Purgatory. In fact, I was so glad that I started my first Rosary right there, instead of making them wait in fire all day long until nighttime for the cooling mercy my prayers were going to win for them, however much that was. I just said one decade then, though—*No use spoiling them*—I'd say the other four decades once I got into bed that night.

Then I went back outside, considerably lightened at heart, and got into a great game of "3-Man-21" with John and Michael. Since I almost always won, we played the rule that I had to hit twenty-one right on the nose, and if I "busted" (went past 21), then I had to go back to zero. Also, I had to do all my dribbling left-handed, and shoot all my free throws left-handed, which always gave my brothers a better chance—they even managed to win a few, once in a blue moon. I also got pretty decent using just my left hand. I wanted to get all my practice in as quickly as possible, because I had a meeting at The Captain's Place at 2:00 p.m.

29.
THE TITLE COMPANY

That afternoon, Toby and I were hanging around the foundation wall, throwing rocks into the river while we waited for Richard, when he came running down River Road.

"Guys," Richard said, his voice somewhat frantic, "I have to tell you something." We both looked at him—he was gasping. "I found out what they're up to."

"Who?" Toby asked, his eyebrows up near his hairline. "What are you talking about?"

"The mobsters!" he said, leaning over with his hands on his knees, huffing and blowing before he continued. "This morning, I rode my bike over to the title company to ask if they had ever heard of Cottonwood Point," he said, taking a deep breath—he was starting to recover his wind. "The title company is in the basement of the courthouse, and the entrance is right off the front sidewalk.

"My mom was a classmate of the manager there, Mr. Mills, so I asked the woman at the counter if I could talk to him, but he was upstairs in the courthouse, and she said he'd be back in just a few minutes and I could wait for him if I wanted, so I just grabbed a magazine and sat down and waited. I hadn't been there five minutes when I heard footsteps outside and almost jumped out of my skin when I saw Dapper Man walking down the stairs carrying a briefcase, with

Mr. Muscle right behind him. I started to hightail it out of there, but then I realized that they had never seen me before and had no idea who I was, so I just sat there, hoping they would get waited on and leave before Mr. Mills came back. And right then, Mr. Mills walked in through the back door just as they came in the front and walked up to the counter. Lucky for me, he asked them if he could help them. I just kept my head buried in the magazine.

"The little guy, Dapper Man, did all the talking. His name is Anthony Napolitano. He said he represented a gravel company, and he was looking for a place with a good supply of river gravel and it had to be near a deep-water channel so they could load the gravel onto barges. He had a map, and he pulled it out of the briefcase and showed it to Mr. Mills and pointed to a place on it and asked Mr. Mills if he knew who owned it."

"Could you see the map?" Toby asked.

"No," Richard said, shaking his head side to side as if his favorite dog had just died, "I even thought about getting up and acting like I needed to borrow a pencil or something so I could get a good look at it, but it seemed too obvious, and I figured if he had a map with Cottonwood Point on it, I could find one, too, so I just sat there quiet as a church mouse and listened."

"So," I said, "what happened next?"

"Well, Mr. Mills said, 'Oh, that's Cottonwood Point. I think I know who owns it, but let me make sure,' and he went over to a file cabinet, and pulled out a folder and leafed through it."

"Did you get the name?" Toby asked.

"Yep," Richard said. "Mr. Mills said, 'That's part of the Armani farm. It's down in the bottoms. It's in the flood plain, and it's not very valuable land because it floods about every other year, mostly in the spring, but sometimes in other seasons as well, so you can't count on getting a crop off of it even if you put one in.'

"And Dapper Man said, 'That's okay; we're not going to farm it anyway. Do you think she'd be willing to lease the land out so we could mine gravel off the sand bar there?' and Mr. Mills said, 'I don't see why not; it's not very dependable for farm income because of the flooding. I expect she might like to have some income off it.'

"And then Dapper Man asked if she were married, and Mr. Mills said he didn't think so, 'Young widow, I believe,' he said. 'No man in the picture, so far as I know,' and you should've seen the two mobsters look at each other. Then Dapper Man asked if he knew her first name."

We waited.

"'Angela. Angela Armani,' Mr. Mills said. 'Pretty girl—grew up here. Moved away after high school, then moved back a couple years ago when her mother died and left her the farm. Don't know anything about her husband. She uses her maiden name, which is what everyone around here calls her by. Has a young son, keeps to herself mostly,' he thought, but he said he didn't really know her very well."

"Angela Armani," Toby said. "Oughta be an actress."

"There's an Armani kid in our school," I said. "Anything else?"

"Yeah," Richard continued, "then Mr. Mills told him that the Mississippi River is a navigable waterway, which means the State of Missouri owns the riverbed up to the high-water mark, so they would need to get the state's permission to mine any part of it that was below the high water mark."

"What did they say to that?" Toby asked.

"Mr. Dapper made it sound like that was no big deal. 'Oh, sure,' he said, 'we'll have our lawyer look at that.' Then Mr. Mills said, 'Who is your lawyer, anyway?' and neither one of them said anything for a second, and I could tell they were just trying to make up a lie, then the little Dapper Man said, 'It's nobody local; our lawyer is back home,' and Mr. Mills said, 'Fine, where is home?' and looked at Mr. Muscle and he said, 'Joisey' at the same time that Dapper Man said 'N'yawk' and the two of them just looked at each other while Mr. Mills looked at the two of them, and then Dapper Man said, 'He's from New Joisey and I'm from N'yawk,' and Mr. Mills said 'Well, where is your business located?' and Mr. Muscle just looked at Dapper Man with his mouth tight shut and Dapper Man said, 'Delaware.'

"Then Mr. Mills said, 'Delaware! Well, you're pretty far afield here. What did you say was the name of your company?' and Dapper Man says, 'The Mississippi River Gravel Company, Incorporated.'"

Toby and I just looked at him, spellbound, as he paused. This was better than a movie—we felt like we were right there. Richard could really tell a story. He certainly remembered details. I couldn't stand it any longer. "So then what?" I asked.

"Well, Mr. Mills just said, 'Delaware!' again, like he just couldn't believe it, and I don't think he really did, and then the little Dapper Man said, 'That's right. That's where our head office is located.' And then Mr. Mills said, 'Do you fellas have a business card?' and then Dapper Man looked really surprised, and so did Mr. Muscle, and then Dapper Man put his hands in his pants pockets and then made a big show of checking all his suit pockets and then he said, 'Looks like I left them on the dresser.' You should've seen it!

"Then Mr. Mills says, 'When are you lookin' to start, then?' just like he believed them, and Dapper Man said, 'Just as soon as we can get a lease signed and get our equipment and our boys...I mean, some of our employees, out here from Delaware.'

"'Well,' Mr. Mills said, 'you have your lawyer contact me if he needs anything,' and he handed Dapper Man a business card and then said. 'Anything else I can help you gentlemen with?'" Richard said, as he mimed a very proper and somewhat snooty British-butler-style handing-over of the business card.

"'Uh, no, thanks for the information,' Dapper Man said. 'We'll talk to the owner, and our man will get back to you if we need any title work,' and he turned to Mr. Muscle and jerked his head toward the door, and the two of them left. And as soon as they walked out the door, Mr. Mills turned to a woman at the desk and said, 'We better call her and warn her about those birds.' I assume he meant Mrs. Armani.

"Then Mr. Mills looked over at me, kinda curious-like, and the desk clerk said, 'Oh! Mr. Mills, this young man is here to see you,' nodding over at me.

"So what was I supposed to do now? I couldn't very well ask him about Cottonwood Point—'Hello, Mr. Mills, I'm here to ask you about Cottonwood Point because I hear it's a real nice place to fish?' so I just stood up and introduced myself and told him my mother is Ruby Washington and she told me to drop in and meet him sometime and I was just riding by and thought I'd stop and see if he was in.

"'I'm Richard,' I said.

"'Richard Washington,' Mr. Mills said, shaking my hand. 'I'm Loren Mills, and I'm very glad to meet you, young man. I've always admired your mother.'

"'Thank you, sir,' I said. 'So is there really any money in mining a sand and gravel bar?'

"'Sure, there is,' he said, 'if you're a good manager. And if you have enough financial backing. But it takes a lot of equipment; it's a big investment. First, you have to dig out the sand and gravel, then you have to load it onto trucks or barges, then you have to process it somewhere; you have to separate it by size, different aggregate for different uses, mostly making concrete or mortar or laying road beds, and you have to sift the sand out of it—of course, you can sell the sand separately as long as it's clean, and you have to have a big piece of land to do all that processing and store the processed aggregate in huge piles until you load it onto train cars or trucks or barges when you sell it, so you have to own trucks or barges, too. It's an enormous investment to buy all that machinery and land and transportation, and you have employee costs for your labor, and then of course you also have to buy or lease the land that you're going to mine, and you have legal fees involved in that. It's very expensive.'

"Then he said his granddaughter told him I was a good student and if I were ever interested in working in a title company to come and see him because he was gonna need some help around there someday, and not everybody could do that type of work. He said at least you don't need a million dollars to start, and you don't take the risk that the sand bar will just disappear in a flood, and there will always be title work.'

"'Disappear in a flood!' I said. 'Do they do that? Disappear?'

"'Sure,' he said, 'they appear and disappear all the time, especially on the Mississippi. The floods move them around, wash them downstream, and deposit them in other places, sometimes in the middle of the river. Here, I'll show you something,' he said, grabbing a map from a desk behind the counter. 'See this huge sand bar here? Cottonwood Point; that's the one they were talking about. Well, it wasn't always there—I'll show you,' and he pulled out this huge leather-bound plat book. It was so old that brown particles of leather as fine as dust fell from the cover as he opened it.

"'Look here,' he continued, 'this map is from 1860. It shows the Mississippi riverbed and the shore as it was at that time. No bar there

Joseph Welch

at all,' he said, pointing to a bend in the river downstream from Mayfly. 'Now watch—I'll show you 1870. See it? It's starting to build up right here,' he said, pointing to the same spot, and sure enough, there was a small sandbar there. 'And then by 1900, look at it now,' he said, pulling out another plat book, this one with a dark green cloth binding, and, sure enough, it had grown considerably. 'And look at it today,' he said, showing me another map tacked up on the wall behind the counter, 'now it's built up so far it's created this bayou behind it.' It was the bayou where we had gone snake hunting, but we had stayed along the edges, because we didn't want to actually go into it.

"I asked him what made it start growing in the first place, and he said that was an interesting question. 'I asked an old barge man the same question once,' he said. 'He had captained towboats on the river all his life. He said sometimes something just got stuck there—might have been a big tree trunk, perhaps, and it started catching other stuff that floated down the river, and it just piled up there, and before you knew it, it was catching sand and mud and silt and gravel that washed down the riverbed, and it builds up into a sand bar or an island.

"He said there's an island upriver that got started when some old man drove a junk Model T into the riverbed during a drought and just left it there, and it started catching stuff, and the next year there was an island there, and it's still there. He said usually these bars build up in shallow water, but I asked him about the riverbed down at Cottonwood Point and he said the channel is thirty-five feet deep there, that it just sheers off into deep water.

"I asked him why it was called Cottonwood Point, 'I guess because there's a lot of cottonwoods there?'

"And he said, 'No, not that I know of. That's the funny thing. I haven't been there in years, but the last time I saw it there weren't any cottonwoods there at all, except the ones that are washed up on it. The point just sticks out into the river on the outside of a bend, and it just naturally catches big stuff that floats down the river.' Anyway, he didn't know why it was called Cottonwood Point unless the bar got started when a big cottonwood got stuck on something there in the riverbed.

"He said he thinks there's gotta be somethin' really big holding that bar together right out in the current all these years. 'And anything buried underwater won't rot because there's no air and no sunlight. But if I were those men,' he said, 'I'd be mighty careful about what I pulled up from the bottom of that bar. That entire thing could wash away in minutes, out in the current like that, in deep water, with them and their machinery on it, if they disturb whatever's anchoring it. But they must know that—it's their business,' he said, and he winked at me.

"'That's really interesting, Mr. Mills,' I said. 'I'll remember that. Thank you. It was nice to meet you, sir."

"'Nice to meet you, too, son. Tell your mother 'hello' for me. And remember what I said if you're ever interested in a job here.'

"So I just told him I would, and thanked him again and left."

30.
MEETING AT THE WALL

Two days later, the Three Musketeers got together again at the wall on a Wednesday afternoon.

"I know our main goal is to prove that Tom didn't commit suicide," Richard said, as he pulled out his notebook, "but the thing about suicide is that we can never really know, since there were no witnesses, so maybe we should start with the other stuff first."

"There are some things I need to tell you," Toby said.

"I have some things I need to tell you, too," Richard said. "You go first."

"Well," Toby began, "I didn't feel like I should be sharing Tom's secrets before, but now I think I have to."

It all came out in a rush, Toby barely pausing to breathe: "Tom was thinking about becoming a priest. He was even talking to P.J. about going to the seminary in the fall. He hadn't told Dad and Mom yet—he was still trying to figure out his vocation. He thought it would be really keen if he had the power to forgive sins. It was a hard decision for him, and he was always looking for a quiet place where he could be alone with his thoughts and think about whether he really wanted to do it. But he felt like he was a sinner, and he didn't know if he was holy enough to become a priest, and it really bothered him a lot."

Neither Richard nor I said anything. *How does anyone know if he's holy enough to be a priest?* I stared thoughtfully at Toby.

"And when he thought about what his life would be like if he didn't become a priest," Toby continued, "I think from some things he said that maybe he was afraid if he didn't become a priest, no girl would ever marry him, and he'd just be a lonely old man and never have any fun or any friends to have fun with, and then when Crazy Carly seduced him, the whole experience was just really nasty, and she talked really dirty about it, and he didn't like it, and maybe he thought he wasn't cut out to be married either."

"But one time, he told me that if Reiser was holy enough, then he was holy enough, too, especially if he had the power to forgive sins. And he wondered if he would be able to forgive his own sins, too, or, if not, at least confess them to someone who had the same sins, and they could just forgive each other's. He said, 'Heck, we could do it every day.'" Toby finally wound down.

Richard and I were quiet, absorbing all of it. I was thinking of the agony that Toby had to go through in deciding whether or not to tell us, then picturing Tom with his huge decision, how he would have felt, and how he could ever really know. Because once it was done, it was done for the rest of his life. He couldn't change his mind if he didn't like it. "You are a priest forever, according to the order of Melchizedek." And you have to vow never to have a girlfriend, or a wife, or even a prostitute. Really high stakes.

Finally, Richard spoke. "Okay," he said, "but that doesn't mean he committed suicide." I looked back at Toby. Tears were running down his face.

"God, I hope not," he said. "I worry about him being in hell. I pray that he isn't, but if he is, there's nothing I can do about it."

"I know," Richard said, "but I don't think he is." He said it with conviction, like he was pretty darn sure. This was incredibly comforting, not only to Toby, but to me, too. Richard was usually right. And he didn't speak until he had made up his mind.

"Do you think he was depressed?" he asked Toby.

"No," Toby said, "not depressed, just trying to figure things out."

"Right. Same thing we're all doing," Richard said, "but not with something as important as entering the priesthood—something truly irrevocable. But everyone struggles, every day."

Listening to Richard, I couldn't imagine what struggles he was having. Maybe I wasn't the only one who had a problem with sin. Maybe I wasn't the only one with impure thoughts. I knew for a fact that Toby had them—the entire basement eavesdrop system was a testament to impure thoughts—we had high hopes for impurity—we planned for it—we did everything but pray for it. I wondered if Toby had thought of that, if he confessed it. I wondered about Richard. What if every one of us were just one unlucky lightning strike away from going to Hell for all eternity? The only good thing about that was at least Prince wouldn't have to go to Hell with me.

Richard broke into my reverie: "I did a little research on suicide," he said. "Basically, no matter how bad a person's life is, no one ever kills themself on the spur of the moment. It's a really big, really hard decision, and it takes time. There are common warning signs, like being sad and withdrawn, feeling depressed, sleeping all day or not sleeping at all, talking a lot about dying, giving your property away, and feeling like you aren't valuable to anyone. And I gotta tell you, unless I didn't know Tom at all, that just doesn't sound like him, none of it. Am I wrong?" he asked, looking at Toby.

"No, I agree," Toby said, "that doesn't sound like Tom to me, either—not at all—not any of it. He was a great sleeper, but he also jumped right up when the alarm went off."

"What was it you said at the Inquest, Toby?" I asked. "Normal happiness—not too happy, but not sad, either.' I thought that was a pretty honest answer."

"They made a big deal about Tom not having friends," Toby said. "And it's true he didn't have a girlfriend, but that didn't seem to bother him. And he didn't really have friends his own age, but he had us. We've gotta count for *something*."

"Yeah, and Tom had fun with us—he was really good to us. If he didn't, he wouldn't have taken us riding with him," I said. "And he didn't care what other people thought. He didn't care that it wasn't cool driving Broadway with a buncha kids."

"Yeah, and he loved his car," Richard said. "What a beaut! Did he ever talk about giving it to you if anything ever happened to him?"

"No, never once. He never talked about giving me *anything* if something happened to him. And he was *generous* with me—he let me borrow anything he had. He even told me once that I could borrow his car when I started dating." Toby was silent, then looked away, his eyes misting. Richard and I looked away, too. "He said, 'borrow it,' not 'I'm gonna give it to you.'" After a while, he said, "I'm pretty sure he didn't know he was gonna die."

"Exactly!" Richard said.

"Except for that note that said 'loser,'" I said. "That's the only thing that might support the suicide theory—that Tom thought he wasn't valuable to anyone. And that's what the coroner relied on, too."

"Dad is gonna go by and pick up the note today," Toby said. "I'll let you know if he gets it."

"Okay," Richard said, "then let's look at this realistically. We think the inquest people were wrong. They thought Tom was queer, and we don't think he was. And we think if he was, we would have known it or at least suspected it. We knew him, and they didn't. They also didn't know Tom was happy, that he had friends, that he had a good life, that he loved his car, that he was thinking of becoming a priest, none of it."

"They didn't know because they didn't ask," Toby said.

"So, if he didn't commit suicide," Richard continued, "he either had an accident, which is possible, or he was murdered. Normally, the odds would be much higher that it was an accident, that something happened that he didn't expect, that he lost his balance, whatever. Except that Tom had spent a lot of time in that bell tower and was very familiar with it—it was almost like his own room—and it's hard to imagine him suddenly just falling out of it. Add to that the fact that there were some bad people not only showing up with Tom close to the time of his death but also doing some pretty strange things right after. So, let's look at the possibility that Tom was killed. Let's make a list of all the people who could have killed him and what their motivation might have been."

"I think P.J. did it," I said.

"Why?" Richard asked.

"I caught him, remember? I caught him going through his pockets, and he was really angry with him, talking to him like he was alive. And he didn't mention any of that at the Inquest."

"Yeah, but neither did you," Toby said.

"I know, but they didn't ask me," I said. "And you've gotta admit that he's been acting totally weird since then. He won't even look at the Pipers or talk to them—why? You'd think that now he'd go out of his way to be comforting to them. My God, they've all been good to him. I just think he's acting awfully suspicious, that's all. I don't trust him."

"I don't either," Toby said.

"Alright," Richard said, "I've got that down. We'll see what we can find out. We need to make a complete list right now. Who else could have killed him?"

Toby and I were silent.

"Okay, I'll start," Richard said. "Ray Lee Po might have thrown him off. But we can never prove that because there are no witnesses. Ray Lee Po couldn't tell us even if he wanted to—even if he remembered doing it."

"Why was P.J. telling him 'I warned you,' over and over? And why was he searching his pockets?" I insisted, unwilling to move on to any other suspects. "Was he afraid Tom was going to tell something?"

"Yeah," Toby said, "or was he searching for the same thing the mobsters were?"

"You're right, the mobsters are suspects," Richard said. "They certainly had a motive, and we know they were looking for something that Tom had, and now we know that somehow they found out he had been spying on them."

"Right," Toby said.

"And we have to include Crazy Carly, who was really mad at Tom—and she also moved out the day after his death, which is weird by itself," Richard added, "and we have no idea why she ran off or where she went."

31.
SHOW AND TELL

"**G**uys!" Toby said. "C'mere! I've got the note," pulling a plastic bag out of his pants pocket. "They were in Tom's shirt pocket when he died."

We were at the school playground the next afternoon, supposedly there to play basketball. "It's not Tom's writing. Look." He passed the bag around. "Dad got it from the Coroner. He said they didn't need it anymore. Dad says it's not Tom's writing either. He hasn't shown it to Mom—he says it'll just upset her more."

I had only seen it from across the room at the Inquest. It was a clear plastic bag with three small pieces of paper in it. Written in ink on the scraps of paper were five letters in cursive, which together spelled "Loser." The letter "L" was a big loopy capital, followed on the same scrap by a small "o." The middle scrap only had one letter, a small "s." The last scrap had two small letters, connected in cursive: "e" and "r." L-o-s-e-r. None of the scraps had anything on the reverse sides.

"Look," Richard said. "The 's' doesn't hang down from its connection with the top of the 'o'. It begins on the imaginary base line. Very, very weird."

"I know," I agreed.

"These letters were never one word," Richard said. "Somebody tried to make it look like one word, but it wasn't."

32.
CAR ON THE BLUFF

The next morning, I rode my bike downtown toward Mr. Fedder's Shoe Repair Shop, my brown leather dress shoes hanging from my handlebars by their laces. As I rode east on Train Park Avenue, I saw the taillights of the mobsters' Lincoln Continental. It was turning off the Avenue onto the foot of Castle Bluff, beginning to wind its way up the steep switchbacks toward the top. I was stunned. The only thing at the top of that Bluff, other than the woods and the edge of the cliff two hundred feet above the river, was P.J.'s house. He lived there instead of the original parish rectory because a deceased parishioner had donated it to the parish "on condition that it be used as a rectory for the Pastor of Immaculate Conception Parish." Although the parish continued to maintain the original brick rectory downtown for the Associate Pastor, P.J. apparently preferred to live in relative isolation at the top of the bluff.

Why were the mobsters going to see P.J.? I rode my bike to the foot of Castle Bluff Drive as fast as it could go, turned up the steep hill, and ditched the bike alongside the crazily irregular steps of an old liquor store perched on the base of the hill. I ran up the steps, darted along the store's white stucco side wall next to the road, and then started running up the steep hill.

I was gasping for breath by the first switchback, forcing me to a fast walk. Puffing hard, I started running again, ascending the next incline as fast as I could, dragging myself up the hill. It was exhausting. My legs were tired, my head lolled, and I couldn't begin to catch my breath. Halfway up the hill, I had to stop. I thought I might die right there if I tried to go any further. I wanted to fall down. Completely gassed, I resisted the very powerful need to quit, and instead walked a short distance, sagging in every fiber and breathing mightily. I prayed that they would not drive back down the hill, because there was nothing I could do to get out of the road. I continued to stumble uphill, panting.

I was so out of breath that all I could do was walk, but I walked as fast as I could, sucking air and blowing out hard as I went. Two more switchbacks, then the steep uphill lane curved south as it neared the top, and I could see P.J.'s house, set in a tiny clearing on the top of the bluff. I had never been up there before.

It was an old frame bungalow, painted white with dark green, almost black, trim. The gables sported gingerbread eave decorations. A large screened window opened eastward toward the woods, which bordered the top edge of the cliff. A one-car garage had been added onto the north end of the house decades ago. Its roof sagged, but a new garage door had been installed facing the bluff.

I approached the north side of the old garage, red in the face, pouring sweat, and blowing hard. The garage door was closed, and the mobster's car was parked in front of it. No one was visible. I continued along the driveway as it leveled out into the small yard; a thin strip of woods bordered the road on my left and hid the edge of the bluff. The woods on my right were close, running along the edge of the road before opening out for the garage, then continuing close up against the back of the garage and the house. I moved into the narrow walkway behind the garage, trying to catch my breath, my ears on high alert. I could hear the irregular hum of voices coming through a screened window that opened against the woods at the back of the house. I could smell the stink of Dapper Man's cigarette from inside.

Breathing deeply and trying to keep my panting as quiet as possible, I moved closer, and was immediately enveloped by an enormous spider web. I felt the strong, sticky tendrils on my face and ears, my hair and neck. I hated spiders almost as much as Tom hated bats. I gasped, but didn't yell, dancing around, fighting it off my face and neck, and picturing a monstrous spider capable of spinning that gigantic web crawling up my back. I could see in my mind a muscular black spider crab-walking up my spine toward my neck. Desperately, I pressed up against the house next to the open window and flattened my back on the boards, trying to squash it.

Immediately, something large and black floated in front of my face, nearly causing me to scream. I ducked quickly, snapping sideways from the waist almost to the ground. When I came back up, it was still there, a menacing lookout wasp hovering near my eyes, watching me. I raised my hand in slow motion, intending to shoo it away gently, then saw that my head was two feet below a large and very active wasp nest built onto the house cornice. The surface of the hive was covered with wasps, all of which were busy doing whatever it was that wasps do so intently, which was lucky for me, because I was far too close to it. I quickly ducked again, then backed off several feet. I had been in terror since the moment I arrived.

"Alright, I'll see what I can do." It was P.J.'s voice. I couldn't hear the mobsters very well. They just sounded like "Rumble, rumble."

The next thing I could make out was louder: "Father, we'll leave it up to you, then." That was Dapper Man.

Then P.J. again: "It sounds like there's a lot of money to be made."

"I guarantee it," Dapper Man said. "And good luck managing the gambling operation."

"Thank you," P.J. said. "It'll be like taking candy from a baby, huh?"

"That's right, Father," I heard Dapper Man say. "There's a sucker born every minute, eh?"

My eyes popped nearly out of their sockets. *Gambling operation! What the hell!? I must have misunderstood, but I know I didn't—he said it clear as a bell.*

I waited against the back of the house, my ears attuned to every sound. Two car doors slammed, and then I heard their tires on the gravel. The hum of their engine died away down the hill. I had to get out of there—and fast.

33.
THE OAK

I ran back down Castle Bluff, leaving the road to take shortcuts down the steep slopes between switchbacks, sliding on my rear end and occasionally on my back, until I reached the bottom. Retrieving my bike at the bottom of the hill, I blasted around the corner, nearly running headlong into the front grill of a lumber truck barreling directly toward me at thirty-five miles per hour. I swerved just past its front fender as the driver, his face contorted with shock and then anger, blasted the horn at me. I headed a short block east toward the river, then turned south on River Road, along the riverside foot of Castle Bluff, pedaling as hard as I could go. I stopped abruptly at the far end of Castle Bluff, panting as I looked around wildly for a place to stash my bike. Eschewing the long draping kudzu and grape vines, I dropped my bike to the ground behind a large wild privet bush, then located the ancient overgrown stone stairs which I knew ran up the gradual southern slope on the trailing end of the bluff.

The stairs were not used anymore. The woods had reclaimed them. They were completely invisible from the road. Even the two stone pillars, which served as an entryway into what was then a park on the bluff top, were visible only by moving a dense curtain of vine. Engraved in stone, now half-covered with trumpet vine, were the words, "Dedicated to the People of Mayfly for Clean and Wholesome Recreation."

The steps were vestiges of a day when women wore hoop skirts and carried parasols, promenading down River Road on Sunday afternoons, before climbing to the top of the bluff to enjoy the magnificent view. Now, they were irregularly spaced, running past elderberry bushes and autumn olive, which cascaded eastward toward the river from the base of the bluff, prospering in the morning sun. Some of the old steps listed sideways, tributes to the power of roots and erosion. Others were completely missing, either buried or fallen.

As I bounded up the stairs, heading generally northward toward the top, I approached nearer to the east side of the bluff. It was wooded, not quite vertical, and covered with magnificent trees. I passed through the under-story, unconsciously identifying the inhabitants by familiar leaf and bark: dogwood, redbud, and white ash, the occasional hackberry, mulberry, locust, box elder, and basswood.

Three stories below the top of the stairs and off to the right was a huge multiflora rose, taller than a man, whose powerful arching canes hung partially over the ancient steps. It had also spread out aggressively northward, away from the steps and along the underside of the cliff top. Its proliferating foliage was covered with an abundance of long, powerful, needle-sharp thorns. Just below the overhanging limestone ledge at the top of the bluff, and just beyond the enormous rose, hidden from all eyes, and visible only in my memory, was a narrow footpath used solely by deer and coyotes and smaller creatures traveling upriver in complete seclusion. Except....

Along all that length of wooded limestone face hundreds of yards long was a single thin fissure, a small cut forty feet north of the sentinel rose—a fissure that ran like a jagged knifepoint back into the bluff—a fissure large enough for an agile person to use as an entrance down to the path—if the path still existed—a fissure to which I now headed, running north through the woods along the top of Castle Bluff as fast as my legs would carry me. Dropping to my knees, still panting, both hands braced on the north lip of the fissure opening, I turned sideways and slid down the weathered limestone layers, relying on my memory, praying that the path had not eroded away. An agonizing second later, my feet landed squarely on a narrow path that ran along the edge of the abyss.

I turned and strode upriver as fast as I could, immersed in the smells of the shade: the ferns, the humus, rotting leaves. My sudden appearance had silenced the birds—there were no sounds but my footsteps crunching on the path. No humans had walked there in years. I climbed over fallen limbs and stepped around large rocks that had been arrested by tree trunks on their descent toward the great river. Ferns clung to the limestone, thriving in the shade. A bright orange sulfur shelf mushroom, so large it would take a pickup truck to bring it home, blossomed from a rotting tree trunk.

The hidden path was a comfortable walk, so long as I was careful to lean away from the abyss and into the cliffside, and the multiflora sentinel rosebush guaranteed perfect privacy and isolation from all but the birds and animals. I continued along its length, caressing the cool limestone with my fingertips at the narrow places, until I calculated that I was under P.J.'s house. Trying not to look down, I turned my head eastward toward the river, visually selecting the few tree trunks within reach of the path, and sighted up each one, gauging my ability to climb one of them high enough to see his house. Rejecting a thorny locust out of hand, I chose a hackberry with multiple lower branches, then made my leap of faith (*Jesus, Mary and Joseph!*) into its only accessible limb. Catching a firm hold, I hooked a leg over it, then resumed breathing and began climbing. I was forced to use some uncomfortably small branches, but I tested each one carefully before forsaking the prior limb, until I was finally able to look out over the top of the bluff.

The perch was uncomfortable, but I could see the white house peeking between the foliage of the woods. I looked around, resting in a high crotch where my narrow perch jutted out from the trunk. A number of larger trees covered the side of the bluff just below his yard, all of them growing out sideways toward the river before turning vertical in their search for sunlight. There were huge walnuts, Southern maples a hundred feet tall, and red oaks even taller, all their energy directed upward, so that no lower limbs sprouted from the gigantic trunks of the great trees for forty feet above their anchors into the cliffside.

I scampered back down, swinging and jumping from a higher limb onto the path, then continued running the narrow track upriver until I arrived opposite my goal: an enormous red oak with a massive trunk, a hundred twenty-five feet tall, straight as a post, growing vertically out of the bluff from its foundation fifty feet below me. Past the top of the bluff, its crown reared and spread. Its unseen taproot, long as the tree was tall, penetrated to the heart of the bluff, drinking its substance, seeking through rock and earth nearly as far down as the river. Its exposed surface roots, gnarled as an ancient human hand, held intact in its possessive grasp a vast rock shelf, which it would not permit time, weather, and gravity to shear away. The tree was a specimen, a granddaddy, a pinnacle tree, impossible to climb without technical gear.

Except that....

Leaning over against that colossal tree, sticking far out into midair from the bluff side, and wedged solidly against an oak limb as big around as my waist, was a fallen southern maple, a specimen tree in its own right. Maples are shallow-rooted trees, and even this giant had been uprooted just below the path, leaving a large crater in the face of the cliff where its root ball had been. Its trunk formed a perfect ramp ninety feet long which angled up into the middle section of the granddaddy oak.

Grabbing a grapevine in case I slipped, I skirted the root ball, walking along the rim of the large crater in the bluff side, then finally climbing onto the huge trunk of the fallen maple. I looked down to River Road and the Mississippi River far below the suspended maple, praying that my added weight was not the straw that would break the camel's back. A fall from there would be broken only by whatever trees I might crash into on the way down, and if the southern maple fell with me, I would be crushed like a fly. But the trunk pathway was broad and free of obstruction and invited me onward.

"Jesus, son of David, have mercy on me," I whispered, simultaneously alleviating my fear and earning five hundred days reprieve from the fires of Purgatory, which apparently I would inhabit for some time. Then, strengthened and encouraged—*I even feel lighter!*—I abandoned the grapevine and scampered up the trunk on all fours, out over the abyss, until I was gratefully received into the arms of the giant oak.

The interior architecture of the colossal tree was even more magnificent than the outside. I had arrived just halfway up the height of the tree, and its limbs were imposing. I needed both arms to pull myself up from one level to the next along the center trunk, the north side of which was covered with gray-green algae. Limb by gnarly limb, I climbed toward the crest of Castle Bluff.

Nearly a century prior, when the crown of the tree had first reached the top of the bluff and suddenly found itself showered in afternoon and evening sunlight, the infusion of additional energy had caused it to explode into a massive canopy a hundred feet wide, exuberantly sending stout limbs out in all directions to feed its foliage. Selecting one after another, I climbed upward until I had an unobstructed view of P.J.'s house. Choices of location were abundant. I was certain he would never see me ensconced in the dark, multi-layered green canopy. A perfect overlook. *Overlook Oak.*

My arms and legs were scratched and red, and my body was tired, sore, and filthy, but I was ecstatic. I had seen everything I needed for the present. Now, I had to get back to the stone foundation right away to tell the others. On the way down, I discovered a faster path through the limbs, further out from the trunk, which allowed me to grab smaller branches and, when necessary, jump down onto larger ones. It was slightly more unnerving, though, as I extended further out over the abyss. I was relieved when I reached the Southern Maple ramp. Retracing my steps, I ran silently along the cool dirt path under the ledge, climbed up the rounded limestone shelves on the interior of the narrow entry gash, checked for witnesses, pulled myself out, and ran for the ancient stairs. I descended in a gallop, landing on the trickier ones with two feet and stabilizing myself with overhanging branches before moving on.

I was the first one to arrive at the rock foundation. Tired as I was, I couldn't sit down. *Where are they? If they knew what I had to report, they'd be here right now!* As I paced around, looking at my watch, I spied a small marigold patch growing inside the foundation wall. I vaulted over the wall and picked three flowers and a handful of stems and leaves. Crushing them in my hand, I took them back outside the foundation, where I plunked myself down on the wall and began rubbing them onto my scratches, cleaning and cooling them instantly.

"Listen, you guys," I said, standing in front of Richard and Toby when they arrived, "I've got some really important news—I saw the mobsters drive up the hill to P.J.'s Rectory." It was rewarding to see that

Richard and Toby were appropriately shocked—their eyes startled, their mouths hung open in disbelief.

"What do they want with P.J.?" Toby asked.

I told them how I had run up the hill and hid behind the house, and reported everything I had heard.

"*We'll leave it up to you*"? Toby repeated. "What in the world is Fr. Reiser doing with those criminals? And why would he want to help them?"

"Money," I said. "There's money to be made."

"And '*good luck managing the gambling operation*'? Toby repeated. "What are they talking about? What gambling operation? What in the world is he up to that we don't know about?"

"A lot," I said. "We still don't know if he killed Tom and why he was going through his pockets."

"And whatever he was looking for," Toby said, "the mobsters were still looking for it when they came back to the motel the other night, and they knew to look for it in Tom's closet."

"Weird," Richard said. "What are they all looking for?"

"I don't know how we're ever gonna find out," Toby said.

"We need to find out where P.J. came from and how long he's been here," Richard said.

"He's been here eighteen years," Toby said. "They asked him at the Inquest. But I don't know where he came from."

"He came from St. Louis," I said. "My Mom told me. I think we're gonna have to spy on P.J., But that's the best part—I found a new meeting place for us. It's a huge tree that looks right into his front yard."

"Nah," Richard said. "He'll see us—we'll get caught."

"No," I said. "It's perfectly safe—wait 'til you see it. We can come and go without anyone seeing us, and he'll never know we're there." The two of them looked dubious.

"Come on," I said. "It's an excellent spot—I'll show you."

"I can't go right now," Richard said. "I'm late—I gotta go see Mr. Whalen about delivering handbills for his one-cent sale. How about tomorrow?"

34.
SHOWING RICHARD AND TOBY

The next afternoon, Richard, Toby and I rode our bikes the short distance down River Road underneath Castle Bluff, then hid them behind one of the many kudzu curtains which hung as a solid blanket at the base of the bluff. Dropping down into the slight roadside ditch, we parted a few tendrils on the side of the curtain, slipped behind the vine screen and deposited the bikes, then exited carefully at our point of entry, leaving the hanging green wall completely undisturbed.

"This way," I said, reveling in my role as Fearless Leader, and bounding up the ancient stairs with them in my wake. As we neared the top, I stopped and pointed at the enormous multiflora rose. Its huge arms, covered with thousands of very long, very strong, and very sharp thorns, spread out in long, arching canes toward us and down the bluff.

"It's right past here," I said.

"No way," Richard said. "We couldn't get through there if our lives depended on it."

"I know," I said. "That's the beauty of it."

"Is that what happened to you?" Toby asked.

"No, guys, there's a way around. I'll show you." And I took off again. In a flash, I bolted into the trees on the top of the bluff, then paused and waited. As soon as they reached the top step, I was off through the woods to the knife-like fissure in the bluff face.

"Come on down, guys; it's easy," I said, disappearing down the limestone shelving to the path. It took a little while, but soon, they were both behind me.

"Keen," Richard said. "Where does it go?"

"I'll show you," I said, my exhilaration increasing by the second. "Come on!" A real pro now, I ran the path like it was my front sidewalk, waiting as they hesitated on the trickier parts, their eyes fixed on their steps in concentration. Finally, I stopped.

"There it is," I said. They both looked up.

"Holy smokes!" Toby said. "Is that it?"

"That may be the biggest tree I've ever seen," Richard said. "What is it?"

"A red oak," I said. "You can tell it's red because the tips of the leaves are pointy. Also, the trunk has gray patterns running down the sides that look like ski runs. And that huge tree leaning against it is a southern maple. For some reason, they do well on the side of the bluff," I finished.

"And you expect us to walk out from the edge of the cliff on that thing?" Richard asked, agog.

"Yep. I've done it, and it's actually really safe. But I need to tell you guys that we're right below P.J.'s front yard right now, and even though he'll never see us, he might be able to hear us, so I think we always need to whisper when we're up here. And I don't mean just keep our voices low, because that makes a rumble which carries a long way, I mean we really need to whisper," I whispered, "or make hand signals, like this," I whispered again, giving them the "come follow me" beckoning-wave-of-the-arm. Richard sent me back the "AOK."

"He's hard of hearing," Richard said. "He won't wear a hearing aid, but you can tell he's deaf as a post."

"Good," I said. I turned, and this time, I jumped down directly onto the root ball, grabbing the grapevine as I landed, then climbed up the maze of projecting and crisscrossing roots, grabbed another grapevine, and leapt down onto the trunk that projected away from the cliff face, then waited. Toby followed, using the vines as a safety line, then Richard. When we were all assembled on the base of the southern maple, I turned and scampered up the wide ramp, walking like a baboon, using both my hands and feet on the trunk as I headed up the incline and out over the abyss. I stopped and turned to see how Toby and Richard were doing. They were moving along gamely, but more slowly.

"I hope this tree holds," Toby stage-whispered.

"Don't worry," I whispered back. You should see the size of the limb it's resting on."

Minutes later, we were all safely ensconced in the giant arms of the oak. We stood on the limb and looked at the interior of the tree.

"I see what you mean," Toby whispered, looking at the enormous limb that supported the maple tree. "This limb is bigger than most trees."

"Magnificent," Richard whispered. "I wonder how old this tree is and how it managed to hang here on the side of the bluff all this time."

"I'm guessing a hundred fifty years or older," I whispered, "maybe even two hundred. And look down—it's actually holding the bluff together."

"Oh my God!" Toby breathed. Richard and Toby both lowered slowly to their knees as they looked down into the abyss below us.

"Actually," I whispered, "maybe it's better not to look down. If it makes you feel any better, oak trees have huge tap roots. Some people claim the tap root is as long as the trunk of the tree. If that's true, this tree's tap root must go practically down to the river, so it's really anchored in here strong."

"Yeah, well, what about that fallen tree we climbed up here on?" Toby whispered back, apparently unconvinced.

"That's a maple tree," I whispered. "They have shallow roots. That's why it got blown down." Toby just gave me the raised eyebrows "you-better-be-right" look, but didn't say anything more.

"We need to get up to where we can see P.J.'s house. I'll show you where," I whispered, tightrope-walking away from the trunk, so I could use the smaller branches to make my ascent. Toby and Richard followed. When we were thirty-five feet above our starting point, we could see through the foliage that we were level with P.J.'s front yard. I kept ascending until I was above his roof line, then found a perch where I looked down at his entire property from deep inside the dense canopy. Richard and Toby climbed up behind me, each on a separate limb.

"This is a good overlook," I whispered. "We can see everything from here, and there's no way he will ever see us. But we gotta be quiet. Some of his windows are open."

"This is a good one, too," Richard whispered.

"Yeah, so is this," Toby said, moving back into the trunk. "And look," he whispered, moving up to the next limb, "from here, you can see it all from closer in to the trunk."

We stood on different limbs and watched. P.J.'s place was quiet. Soon we were sitting or straddling our respective limbs, and then lying down facing the house as we waited. Nothing. Suddenly we heard a car motor growing louder as it approached, and then gravel crunching.

P.J.'s Chrysler came into view around the curve leading up toward his garage. He pulled into the garage and walked into the house carrying a shopping bag. Moments later, the garage door closed automatically.

"I wonder if he has a housekeeper," Toby whispered.

"No," I whispered back. "My dad says he did when he first came here, an old woman named Mrs. Orba, who lived downriver near the cement plant, but she finally got too arthritic to do any work. Her granddaughter kept it for a while, but then she moved to St. Louis, and he hasn't had anybody since. He's the only one there."

"So I think this'll make a great meeting place," I whispered. "It's super private, and we can also watch P.J. from here."

"We're gonna need to build a platform if we're gonna spend much time here," Richard whispered. "Nothing fancy, just a place where we can sit down."

"We can't do any hammering up here, though," I whispered.

"We'll have to use rope," Toby whispered. "We can drill holes in the boards before we bring them up here, then tie them together. We'll have to use a brace and bit, though, since we don't have electricity."

"I know where there are some boards," I whispered. "The bridge keeper's shack is being rebuilt. They've torn down the old wooden one and are building the new one out of concrete block. The old boards are just sitting in a pile under the bridge. Let's ask the bridge keeper if we can have a few of them. I know him."

"How are we gonna get that stuff up here?" Richard whispered. "It'll be a lot to carry."

"Let's float 'em down the river," I whispered, "drill 'em first at the bridge keeper's shack so we can tie them together, then pull them out right below here."

"And then what?" Toby whispered. "We still gotta get 'em up here. We're gonna need a pulley with at least two hundred feet of rope."

"We could get someone to drive them up P.J.'s driveway in a truck when he's not at home," Richard suggested.

"Or else we'll have to carry them up the steps one at a time," I whispered.

"And I don't know anybody with a truck that we could ask," Richard whispered.

We looked at Toby, who just shook his head. "Me either," he whispered.

"We can carry them up one at a time," I whispered. "My brothers will help. I'll talk to Mr. Dindia about the boards."

"Who?" Toby asked.

"The bridge keeper," I whispered. "And if he says it's okay, John and Michael and I will float the boards down the river and stack them. And we can bring a brace and bit, so we can drill them before we put them in the water. Once I see the boards, I'll work up a plan for the platform. Is it okay to bring John and Michael up to speed?" I whispered.

"Okay by me," Toby whispered, "but make 'em take the oath first—we all did."

"Fine by me," Richard whispered.

35.
GUNFIGHT

I couldn't broach the subject right away with John and Michael, since most of the family was present for all the Saturday afternoon and evening activities.

As I lay in bed that night, I returned to one of my more familiar musings: The Gunfight at Immaculate Conception School. The well-known scenario formed immediately in my mind: a ne'er-do-well gunslinger, dressed all in black except for a red neckerchief, black hat pulled down low to shade his eyes from the glare of the noonday sun (or, in this instance, the fluorescent tubes buzzing overhead), showing up unannounced and uninvited in our classroom.... I heard the quick intake of breath from thirty-two boys and girls as I turned toward the doorway and watched him advance to the center of the room, a big iron dangling next to each hip. Even the fresh, young, and lovely Sr. Mary Carmé, absolutely my favorite nun, was frightened.

"This is yer lucky day, whippersnappers," he drawled, reaching down and tying the drawstring around his right thigh, "'cause ah'm givin' y'all a *chance*. If one a' y'all is quicker'n me, ah'll let *all* y'all live. And if not, well, ah'd say it's been nice knowin' ya, but the fact is, ah'm not gonna miss y'all much," he said, stopping to spit tobacco juice into the green painted metal wastebasket next to Sister Carmé's desk, and then wiping his mouth with the back of his arm. "So, who's it gonna be?" he asked, grinning, but not looking very amused. Thirty-one pairs of eyes turned to look at me. Sr. Mary Carmé was pleading silently. (With him? Please don't kill us all?) (With me? Please save us all?) (With God? Please help Jamie? Please keep us all safe?) I couldn't tell. But regardless, I knew what I had to do.

I looked over at Marva Lynn. Her eyes were riveted on me, and she looked scared. She was breathing quickly. I watched each inhalation push softly against the thin white cotton material on either side of her clasped hands. She was beseeching me to save her—yes, *beseeching* me. Passing briefly over her charms—I had no time in the current crisis to linger on the mysteries of those soft curves which were only hinted at under her blouse—I looked away. Of course, I would save her if I could, and if not, then I would die trying. But my soul yearned for a deeper connection. These could be the last moments of my life.

My eyes sought out Mary Ann. Her lovely eyes were wide, her lashes a row of exclamation points, her cheeks pink with alarm. I had never seen her afraid. For me? For herself? For all her classmates? Almost accidentally, I took in the attractions of her breasts, and felt myself rising to dangerous territory as I yearned in delicious detail for the chance to soothe her. I wanted to hold her and comfort her.

Was that a Mortal Sin? I couldn't even be bothered with that right now—now, there was work to do. This was a matter of life and death—and not just mine, that of all my classmates, and even Sr. Mary Carmé—*Greater love than this hath no man*.... And anyway, the gunslinger made me do it. I could worry about all that later.

I was suddenly angry. What right did this gunslinger have to come into our classroom and threaten to kill Mary Ann, to kill all of us? I needed somehow to let her know, to tell her not to worry, not to give up hope, that I would try the hardest I could, even though I was not a professional gunfighter. I turned back to the gunslinger.

"So it's you, is it?" he said, sneering at me, and pulling my attention back from Mary Ann. "Ah see ya don't have a shootin' iron on ya. Here, I'll loan you one a' mine. Ah don't think ah'll be missin' it fer very long," he added, chuckling as he handed it to me, handle first.

It was a beautiful weapon, the steel so black it was almost blue, well-oiled, the weapon of a man who knew how to use it. I took it and hefted it, sighted down the barrel, spun the cylinder slowly, checking that each chamber was occupied, then held it up next to my ear, listening to the measured clicks as it continued to rotate, and finally looked back at him. Our eyes locked, and I saw it—just the tiniest shadow of doubt creeping into his glare. *Good.* I never once took my eyes off him as I backed down the center aisle until I passed the last desk. *I need room to operate.* Because as soon as I had hefted the gun, a plan had formed in my mind, a plan to teach this outlaw a lesson. The odds were heavily against me, but at least I had a fighting chance.

"Lord, preserve him!" Sr. Mary Carmé ejaculated as she rushed over to the side windows. "Students, move over next to the walls—boys on that side, girls over here. Quickly!" There was a sudden rush and the sound of feet sliding and tripping and desks being pushed askew, as the center of the room was vacated. "Get down, all of you!" she said. Grabbing the big rosary at her waist, she began, "I believe in God, the Father Almighty, Creator of Heaven and Earth..." and a simultaneous murmur arose as thirty-one other voices joined in praying, somehow, anyhow, for a miracle, for my victory. Their lives depended on it.

My classmates' voices faded into the background as I continued to stare directly into the gunslinger's eyes. Now they were mere slits. I knew he was fast. I knew he was a killer. I watched his fingers twitching above his black leather holster.

"You ready?" he asked. I just nodded and watched. He didn't waste time. His hand moved like lightning. Too fast. I knew I could never get my piece up and aimed before he pulled the trigger. Luckily, I had a plan—although a desperate one. As his steel cleared leather, I dove off to my right, rolling low and fast-rolling as his deadly weapon exploded deafeningly, echoing off the floors and ceiling and blackboards, and blowing a hole in the plaster right where my chest had been. Rolling and then aiming, I came up onto my knees in one quick motion, my left arm crooked at the elbow, my forearm held horizontal in front of my face as a brace, bracing the length of the marauder's own gun as I looked straight down the barrel and through the sights at his shocked face, his mouth now open in surprise, and pulled the trigger. It was surprisingly easy. A single shot penetrated his chest to his evil heart, knocking him back against the blackboard and obliterating our homework assignment. He slumped to the floor.

What happened next was always a bit of a blur. Stunned silence. The smell of burnt gunpowder. Then, explosive cheering as I walked up the aisle, through the tendrils of gray-blue gun smoke hanging in the air, and laid the smoking gun on Sr. Carmé's desk. And Mary Ann, with both her arms around my neck, and Sr. Carmé, not only allowing this obvious breach of decorum, but actually encouraging it—was smiling. Apparently, she thought that I was entitled to a reward.

"I can't believe you beat him," Mary Ann said, and her breath was sweet as fresh-mown hay.

"Well, I knew he was faster 'n me," I said, humbly. "Since I'm not a professional, I had to duck first. Maybe not really fair," I admitted modestly, "but it's all I could think of at the time," I said with a shrug.

"You're wonderful," she said, looking at me dreamily and sighing, and in all honesty, I couldn't disagree.

36.
JOHN AND MICHAEL IN

There was no opportunity to bring John and Michael up to speed on Sunday morning, either, but my brothers could tell that something big was up. On Sunday afternoon, the three Fletcher "Big Boys" went to the basketball court at the school parking lot and sat on the steps away from everyone else. Although we brought a basketball, we refused all invitations to join the game. I knew it was going to take some time to bring them up to speed. We all took the oath together. I had already told them some things, but there was a lot they didn't know.

So I started from the beginning, going over everything we knew, some of which they had already heard and some of which they hadn't, about the last time Toby saw Tom, about finding Tom's body, and seeing P.J. talking to him and going through his pockets, and Ray Lee Po pointing and grunting at him, and about the Inquest and all the things they didn't know and didn't seem to care to know, and what we heard the coroner say about Tom, and meeting Ms. Mame, and the things Ms. Mame told us about her dream, and about that horrible night in the graveyard. And they listened, wide-eyed, and asked questions.

I told them about Richard spying on the mobsters at the library, and how they lied to the librarian and acted like they were Civil War history buffs, but they were really looking for an article about the wreck of the *Flying Eagle*.

Then I told them about the mobsters moving out of the River's Rest right after Tom's death, and then claiming they lost something in their room, and coming back and mistaking Toby for Tom, and Prince going nuts on Mr. Muscle, and his threatening to shoot Prince.

"I'll bet that Mr. Muscle guy had a gun on him," John said. "Prince could probably smell it."

That made sense to me. Prince probably didn't have fond memories of Mr. Milchard's gun. Adults tell you that dogs can't remember things, but that's just plain stupid. Prince remembers things really well—better than most adults I know.

"A gun!" Michael said. "Who are these guys, anyway?"

So I told them what we overheard them saying from the basement, and about their looking in the linen closet, and what they found there, and wiping the mirror off before they put it back, and the names they called Tom.

"Wiped it off!" John said. "Why? These are real criminals."

"I agree," I said, "and Fr. Reiser is helping them."

"What are you talking about?" Michael said.

I told them about seeing the mobsters at the Rectory and what I overheard them saying.

"That's impossible!" Michael said. "Why would he be helping them? And what kind of gambling operation is he managing?"

"I don't know," I said. "I only know what I heard, but we decided we had to keep an eye on him and find out."

"He better watch out, or he's gonna go to hell!" Michael said. "I never did like the way he says the Prayer to St. Michael—you can tell he's only doing it 'cause he has to." I agreed.

I told them about our decision to spy on P.J., which they heartily approved, and how we needed their help.

"But how are you gonna keep an eye on him?" John asked. "He lives up on that hill, and there's only one road up there. You're gonna get caught. It's a wonder you haven't been caught already. And if he killed Tom, he might kill you, too."

Then I told them all about the great tree I had found and what a perfect site it was and how we were gonna build a platform up in it and spy on him to our hearts' content with no risk of being caught.

"Seriously?" from John.

"Really?" from Michael.

"Really. But we need some help. We're gonna get eight boards from the bridge keeper's old cottage that they just demolished. I've already asked Mr. Dindia, and he said we could have them because they were just gonna sit there and rot until the next flood takes them away. They tossed them in a pile on the riverbank just below the bridge. And I told him we were gonna drill holes in them so we could tie them together and asked if we could do it there, and he said he didn't see why not, that we wouldn't be in anybody's way and nobody could even see us down there except him. He said just come and take them anytime we wanted. So I thanked him, and that's where we are now. And I need you guys to help us."

"Help you do what?" John asked.

"Drill them and tie them together and float them down the river and then carry them up the old, abandoned stairs at the tail end of the bluff," I said.

"I'll help," Michael said.

"Me too," John said, "but maybe we should take a look at this first, so we know how to plan it." For someone with no apparent ability for abstract thought, John nonetheless had an innate practical sense.

"Good idea," I said, "but we don't have time tonight. We'll have to drill and float the boards tomorrow morning, then Friday is that Spiritual Retreat for Boys entering the Seventh Grade, so Saturday morning is the first chance we'll have to move them up the bluff."

"Let's count on it," John said.

"Yeah! This sounds like fun," Michael said.

37.
TRANSPORTING MATERIEL

The next morning, John, Michael, and I biked north out River Road to the bridge control shack, said "Hi" to Mr. Dindia, and then picked our way down the hill toward the pile of boards on the riverbank. We had brought a canvas bag with Dad's brace and bit, two claw hammers, and my trusty pocketknife. We had chosen a one-inch drill bit, so it would be easy to thread our rope through the holes.

Michael carried the canvas tool bag as we approached the boards, which were lying in a haphazard pile. They were stout, full-thickness two-by-twelves, each ten feet long, which had served as the floor joists for the old bridge control structure. We extracted our claw hammers so we could pull the nails from them, before we drilled them and stacked them next to the water for their trip downstream. John and I stood on opposite ends of the first board and lifted. It was heavy. An explosion of compressed air burst from under the board as we raised it, causing us to leap backward. It sounded like a hose being uncoupled from a giant highway department air compressor, the kind you tow behind a truck. In place of the board, a sturdy, mottled brown-gray snake, head raised and spread wide like a cobra, reared up a full foot above its coiled body, displaying an ugly upturned hog-like nose. There was no question about its message. We had disturbed its hideout under the boards.

"What in the world is that?" John asked. You could tell he didn't read much.

"It looks like a cobra," Michael said. "I didn't know there were any cobras around here."

"It's not," I said. "It's a hognose adder, but it's not poisonous to humans anyway. It just does that to scare people off."

"Works pretty well," John said.

"It has other names, too," I said. "Puff adder, spreadhead. Let's just pick another board and leave him alone."

We moved to another end of the pile. Michael picked up a scrap of two-by-four and banged it on the pile several times before we started pulling boards.

"There may be more of them," he explained. "That should get rid of them."

"Yeah, or just make them mad," John said, suddenly an expert in snake psychology.

"Let's get eight," I said, but after we had our eight, they looked so puny sitting there beside the Mississippi, that we thought we ought to get an extra, "just in case."

"Better get it while it's here," Michael said.

We stacked them next to the water, then pulled out the brace, inserted the bit, and began drilling.

"I think we need two holes in each end," I said, "so we can stitch them together into a platform without them turning sideways or flipping over."

We took turns drilling the thirty-six holes, using the wood stack as our workbench. This also helped make the holes uniform, since, as we finished drilling each board, we were simultaneously marking the location of the hole on the board beneath it. When we got down to the last two boards, John and Michael uncoiled the rope and started looping it through one hole on each board.

"We can tie all of them together like a kite tail," John said, "but we better also have a couple rope lines so we can pull them while we swim. Because we're not gonna be able to swim holding these huge boards."

"Why don't we just sit on them and float them down the river?" Michael asked.

"We can try it," I said, "but I don't think it will work. The boards are too thin. We would need something much thicker, like a tree trunk, to provide enough flotation for us to be able to sit on it without sinking. And even then, most of the trunk would be underwater."

"I'm gonna see," Michael said, taking off his shoes and pulling two boards into the water, then stepping on them and pinning them to the bottom. "Yeah, I see what you mean," he said.

When we had finished stringing the rope through the boards, we made a loop on each end of the rope to slip over our wrists, and Michael and I waded into the water as John pushed the boards in. Several feet away from the bank, the bottom dropped away, and we were suddenly dunked in surprisingly cold water. When we resurfaced, we were floating downstream in the current, spluttering, with only our heads above the water.

"John, hurry on down and pick out a good landing spot and stand there so we'll know what to aim at," I shouted. A big muskrat, alarmed by our sudden apparition and raised voices, scurried for cover in the underbrush as we floated past. I knew that there were huge black eels living in the river, as well as every species of snake, including the perpetually angry northern water snake, as well as venomous swamp rattlers, and copperheads, all of whom were superb swimmers. Richard insisted there were no cottonmouths this far north, but I didn't know if that was true.

There were no alligators this far north, but there were alligator snapping turtles, huge prehistoric vestiges of the dinosaur era, still sporting a row of large spikes down their backs. Adult males weighed over a hundred seventy-five pounds, and there were tales of some as large as four hundred pounds. Their bite was extremely powerful and could easily take off a toe, or even half of my foot.

Something nipped at my bare toes, and I yelped and jerked my foot away. I looked frantically down into the murky water but could see nothing. Suddenly, it nipped my other foot. I jerked it away quickly. It was back almost immediately, just toying with my foot, tasting it, testing it with little nips.

We were floating over one of the deepest holes in this part of the river, caused by scouring on the river bottom, which occurred just downstream from the piers of the railroad bridge. Sixty-five feet deep. The biggest catfish in the Mississippi lived in these deep holes. I had seen a ninety-eight-pounder that completely filled the trunk of a '62 Chevy Impala. Its mouth was broader than my shoulders.

But the thing that terrorized me the most in the murky waters was the image of the billy gar, a plentiful species in the Mississippi. Over 100 million years old, it had a long, bony snout that could grow up to twice the length of its body, outfitted with rows of razor-sharp teeth. The billy gar is the apex predator in the river, known not only for the razor sharpness of its teeth, but also for its size—big ones grow to weigh more than a hundred pounds—and to make matters worse, they can swim as fast as thirty-five miles per hour.

"Are fish biting your feet?" I asked Michael.

"Yeah," he said. "Wonder what they are."

"No idea," I said. "I'm just glad they're not snapping turtles," I said, helpfully.

"Oh, no!" Michael said, apparently not much comforted by this. "How much farther?"

"I'm not sure," I said, looking around. The current had swept us out toward the middle of the river. "But we need to get back in, closer to the shore. We're way too far out. We're in the channel."

The channel was marked for barge traffic with huge hollow steel navigation buoys, anchored to the river bottom with stout aircraft cables, red elongated upright missiles for the east side, and short and squat green can buoys for the west boundary. The current had pushed us towards the middle of the river, hundreds of yards east of the nearest green buoy. As I assessed our location from my vantage point inches above the surface of the water, I saw that we were approaching the Mayfly harbor, and were zipping past it very quickly, with no possibility of stopping there even if we had wanted to. Even more alarming, however, was the appearance of the front end of an enormous towboat heaving into sight around the bend in the river north of us, bearing downstream under thousands of diesel-driven horsepower. Assisted by the weight and speed of the current, it pushed ahead of it five rows of three coal barges each, each trio cabled side to side, and each row cabled end to end. The barges had been loaded to maximum capacity. Their enormous steel holds sank to a uniform depth of nine feet below the dark surface of the big river. Their steel tops had been removed and stacked, displaying mountains of coal easily visible above the barges. The captain probably hadn't even seen us, mere specks on the surface of the water, and probably never would. He was making excellent time.

"And there's a barge coming," I said. "Let go of the boards—we're gonna have to swim for it. I see John—let's aim for him."

We slipped the rope loops around our wrists and started swimming for the shore downstream from the harbor. I became immediately aware that the current, which had seemed so lazy as we floated along with it, was now carrying us quickly past the point where we could make the shore. The boards were heavy and unwieldy. Both of us swam as hard and fast as we could, but barely made any progress. We just kept moving downriver with the powerful current, and we were still far out in the channel. In fact, it looked like we were moving further and further from the shore.

"Come on!" Michael yelled, and we both renewed our sprint towards the riverbank. After several minutes of swimming all out, we could feel the boards straightening out behind us as we labored, creating a more streamlined load. We were near exhaustion as we floated past John, standing far away from us on the shore.

"Get out of the channel!" John shouted. I looked upriver at the barge bearing down on us. It was much closer. From our vantage point at water level, the big steel prows looked enormous, pushing a white wave in front of them.

"He's right," I told Michael. "Let go. We have to swim for our lives."

Looking upriver, I could see a jon boat cutting through the wake of the barge and swinging wide around it, passing it on the Missouri side. Its bow was up in the air, and I could just make out the husky form of a commercial fisherman sitting on the stern seat, turned sideways while he held the tiller of the outboard motor. He flew past the barge, presumably headed for the Mayfly harbor. It was a long boat, all-aluminum, the gunwales low to the water, the stern and transom walls high. As he approached Michael and me, he swerved over toward us, then slowed and stopped about thirty feet from us, letting the motor run in neutral.

"What in *hell* are you boys doin' out here?" he yelled. "Don't you see there's a barge comin'?"

"We know," I yelled back. "We're tryin' to get out of his way."

He turned and goosed the throttle, then circled around, coming close to us with his bow pointed upriver, letting the motor idle. He moved up from the stern to the center of the boat and stood up.

"Here, boys, git in the boat; hurry up; we gotta git outta here. What are these boards?" he said.

"We're using them to build a treehouse," Michael said.

"Gimme them ropes, then," he said, "and git in the boat."

Michael handed over his end, and the fisherman took the wrist loop and wound it around a cleat on the gunwale, then held out a beefy arm. "Grab my wrist, not my hand," he told Michael. He and Michael grabbed each other's wrists while I treaded water, and the man hauled him over the low side gunwale, landing him in the bottom like a big fish. I was next. I handed him my loop of rope, which he wound around the cleat, and then grabbed his huge wrist. His hand circled mine easily, and he hauled me out in one fluid motion, landing me in a puddle on the aluminum bottom. Rainbow-colored liquid floated on top of the puddle, and I could smell gasoline. I looked around as he walked back to the stern. The bow was filled with round, collapsible fish nets partially covered with rust or mud, an old cooler, and some rope. Next to him in the stern was a gas can, a toolbox, and a pair of work gloves. Everything was marked with Mississippi River mud.

"Thank you so much, mister," I said. "We were floating these down the river, and we tried to stay near the shore, but the current took us out too far."

"Hold on, boys," he said, sitting down and grabbing the tiller, then accelerated, hurrying to move us out of the path of the three lead barges. The boat labored at first, until the heavy boards broke inertia and lined up behind us. We held our breath, staring at the huge barges as we passed close by the front of the steel behemoths, then turned to see if our towed tail would clear them. Once safely past their starboard side, he maneuvered over the bow wake created by the deep draft of the fully loaded barges, and we watched the boards rise one by one over the wake and then disappear on the far side. "Whar' you tryin' to take these boards?" he asked.

"That's our brother on the shore there, waiting for us," I said, pointing back upriver.

"Okay," he said, and advanced the throttle, heading toward John and our designated landing, the boards strung alongside and behind us. As we neared the riverbank, he put the motor in neutral and stood up, taking in the topography of the shore, then sat down and increased the throttle, easing off about fifty feet out, then ran the bow right up onto the riverbank.

"Wow!" I said. "That was amazing. Thank you so much, Mister..."

"Just call me Gomer," he said. "Now looky here, boys, ya almost died out there just now. Ah'm not gonna lecture ya, 'cause I used to be young and stupid once, too, and it warn't that long ago. But you boys need ta know this. This ain't Bear Crick...and it ain't the Salt. It ain't even that big muddy Mazzura. This here is the god-damn Mississippi River. It'll spit ya out dead if ya don't respect it. That water looks calm on top—but it ain't. It keeps on movin'—it never stops—it never even slows down—and it's powerful—stronger than any man that ever lived. And there's all kinda things goin' on underneath that ya cain't see—things ya don't even wanna know. And them barges out there, they put out a wake like a whirlwind—only sideways—and ya cain't never get out of it—it'll bounce ya right off'n the bottom of the river. You boys could be layin' there right now—down on the bottom with yer eyes and yer mouths wide open, and nobody even could find ya' 'til yer bodies swelled up so much you floated up to the top agin—long about St. Looey—or maybe even Cayro. You're damn lucky to be standin' here right now, and ya oughtta be down on yer knees, thankin' the good Lord for sendin' me along just in time to help ya. So just promise me ya won't go swimmin' in here again, at least not near the channel."

"Yessir," both Michael and I said. John just nodded.

"I'm Jamie Fletcher," I said, offering my hand, "and these are my brothers, Michael and John," I said, pointing, while they shook hands.

"Nice to meet you, sir," the boys said.

"Mister Gomer," I said, "if we can ever help you in any way, please let us know, because we'll do anything we can to help you," I said. "And please, *please* don't tell our parents about this," I added.

"Don't worry, boys. As I told ya, I was young once, and ah'm lucky ta be alive, too. And if my parents knew some of the things ah done, ah wouldn't be." We faced the river, watching the towboat push the big barges past us as he talked. We were all silent, each in his own thoughts. Finally, he waded into the river, took the ropes off the cleat, and tossed them to us. Then we helped him push his boat back off the riverbank, and he climbed in, and we stood there waving as he continued back upstream toward the harbor. He turned once and raised his arm in a wave, and I thought I could see him looking at us and shaking his head, now hundreds of yards off, but after that, he never looked back.

We took the ropes off the boards and stacked them in the weeds at the edge of the river in low piles three high until Saturday morning, when we intended to carry them up the bluff.

38.
THE RETREAT

At 7:50 a.m. Friday, I walked up the church steps in my school clothes, rosary tucked securely into my pocket, and pulled the brass handle on the enormous, polished oak door. I stepped into the darkened vestibule smelling of incense and wax, familiar as my bedroom since my earliest childhood. Looking around at my classmates, I gravitated toward Toby and Richard, who were milling around in the back of the church with the other boys in our class, all wondering what this was all about and how long it was going to take.

Just then, Fr. Reiser came out of the sacristy door into the sanctuary, walked over to the pulpit, and told us to come up and sit in the first two pews on the left side of the aisle, right in front of the podium. It was five minutes 'til eight. Richard, Toby and I hurried up the side aisle so we wouldn't have to sit in the front pew and were quick enough to lock in second-row places on the side aisle.

P.J., officious as ever, then left the pulpit and knelt on the bottom stair of the altar with his back to us. He began by buzzing through the customary Catholic trio of rote prayers, an Our Father, a Hail Mary, and a Glory Be, traditionally relied on to imbue any activity with a gloss of religion, then advanced to the podium. "Be seated," he said, in a tone that brooked no argument. We did. The stout, curved seat of the oaken pew accommodated my own seat quite nicely, as the three of us leaned forward in unison and raised the long, padded kneeler so we could stretch our legs.

"You're probably wondering what this is all about," P.J. began, "and you should be." He sounded menacing. *What did he mean by that?*

"Today, we're going to do the most important thing in your life—we're going to teach you how to save your immortal soul," he announced. He had our attention now. We were old enough to know that going to Heaven was not a slam dunk for sinners like us. He paused.

"The path to Heaven is hard, and the gate is narrow," he exploded. "And the alternative is unimaginable hell!" he thundered. He stopped and looked at us one by one, taking his time, and assessing us. "Hell...is for all eternity," he said, emphatically. "For...all...eternity," he repeated slowly, drawing out the words to allow us time to think about them. He paused and waited to let that sink in.

"Just how long is eternity?" he asked, finally. "If you are burning in hell, how long do you have to burn?" He waited, eyebrows raised expectantly, looking from one to the other of us.

Finally, someone cracked under the strain. "Forever," a voice said. It was timorous, almost inaudible.

"What?" he thundered.

"Forever," a chorus of cowed voices supplied hurriedly.

"That's right," he said, looking around smugly and nodding, apparently pleased at the prospect of our burning in Hell forever. "That's right. Forever." He looked from one to the other of us in silence while that sank in.

"Has anyone here ever been burned?" he demanded suddenly. We all raised our hands. "Did it hurt?" Everyone nodded, some more emphatically than others, each remembering his own experience. My nerve endings shuddered all the way down to my toes as I recalled closing my hand around a red-hot cast iron skillet. I had my hand bandaged for two weeks after that, and Mom had to rub some stinking yellow ointment on it every day.

"Burning is the most terrible pain there is," he said, "even if you only burn a tiny part of your body." No one disagreed.

"Imagine what it must be like to be burned all over—everywhere," he said. We imagined it. There were no jokes, just sober expressions.

"Now, close your eyes and examine your conscience:

>Have you ever taken the Lord's name in vain?
>
>Have you ever missed Mass on a Sunday or a Holy Day? This is a Mortal Sin which will damn you to Hell for all eternity.
>
>Have you ever failed to pay attention during Mass?
>
>Have you failed to go to Confession and Holy Communion during the Easter season? This is also a Mortal Sin.
>
>Have you ever made a sacrilegious Communion—gone to Communion while you were in Mortal Sin?
>
>Have you ever fought or been angry or hurt anyone?
>
>Have you ever lied?
>
>Have you ever had impure thoughts or committed an impure act, alone or with others, or wanted to? All sins against purity are Mortal Sins—they will damn you to Hell unless they are confessed and forgiven before you die.
>
>Have you ever been disrespectful to either of your parents? Or disobeyed them, or thought you knew better than they did? Or done something that you knew they would not want you to do if they knew about it?

Have you ever stolen anything? Taken cookies without permission?

Have you ever cheated? Even in a game?

Have you ever wanted something that belonged to someone else?

"Alright, everyone get up. Form a single line in the center aisle." We all looked at him, confused.

"Now!" he boomed. "Are you all deaf? Center aisle. All of you. Single line. Face the altar," he said, ejecting the directions in crisp staccato like a drill sergeant. There was a churchy rumble of kneelers being quickly raised, then feet and bodies in motion as we complied. We watched apprehensively as he walked over to the altar, picked up a book of matches, then stooped to lift a huge brass candleholder as tall as he was, and move it to the top of the three steps that led from the pews up into the sanctuary. He lit the candle and stood behind it at the top of the steps.

"Now, boys," he said, "I want you to close your eyes and imagine that this is the Day of Judgment, and you are coming before God Almighty with all your sins, and you are waiting for God to pronounce judgment on you, a *just* judgment, what you really deserve, for all those times you have gone against God's law, in all the ways that you do. Yes...you do. I know that you do, and I know what you do. And bear in mind that God doesn't take excuses, that it will be a waste of time to try to explain away your sins, or say it's not really your fault, or you couldn't help it, or you didn't realize it was wrong, or blame somebody else—because God knows. You won't be able to fool him with your excuses like you do your parents.

"And while you're thinking about what you really deserve," he said. "I'm going to give you just a little glimpse of Hell. You will come up here, one at a time, and hold your finger in this flame, for a count of three seconds. Just your finger." Our eyes were wide now—no one was looking around.

"First, you!" he said.

Daniel Miller came up, eyes huge, and tentatively held his finger out toward the flame, but it got stuck *en route*—he couldn't move it any farther. P.J. grabbed his wrist and pulled it over the flame, then started counting, "One thousand one, one thousand...."

His mouth wide open in a silent howl, Daniel jerked his hand away, his face a mask of shock, and then began licking his finger.

"How would you like to feel that all over your body?" P.J. asked. Daniel just shook his head, tears in his eyes.

"Go to your seat," P.J. said. "Next!" he intoned.

Jeff Lampton walked up slowly, looking left and right as if he might make a run for it, then finally put his finger out, stepped forward, and began counting quickly, even before it touched the flame, "One thousand one, one thousand two, one thousand three," then jerked his hand away.

"I don't believe that was a full three seconds, Mr. Lampton," P.J. said. "Do you think you're going to be able to trick God by counting fast? Remember, the counting won't matter. The flames of Hell don't stop after three seconds, or ever—they are for all eternity."

Next, John Gilbert walked forward, then stuck his finger out and began counting as quickly as Jeff had. This strategy became the norm for the other twelve. Surprisingly, P.J. didn't require any of us to do it over, more slowly, counting actual seconds, but I don't think it was out of pity or charity—he just looked to me like he was bored with the whole affair.

Summer of '63

When my turn came, I looked past the candle flame at P.J. His face looked like Satan. I stuck out my left forefinger and counted the actual seconds. By the time I got to 'two,' it burned horribly. The pain seared my brain. It turned into hatred there, while all my nerve endings screamed, not only on my finger, but on every surface of my body. I stared at him, willing it to continue. "Three," I said, turning away. I had been in Hell, and I had been burned. My finger still burned—like Hell. I walked back to my seat, seething, wanting to send him back to Hell where he belonged. *Where's The Archangel when you need him? If he tries this on Michael next year, I bet that jerk doesn't walk out of here on his own power.*

When the entire class had experienced his personally sponsored little taste of Hell, P.J. continued.

"You've just experienced the tiniest part of Hell, and it's something I want you to remember." *Oh, great, Hell on earth, courtesy of the Pompous Jerk. Jesus would be proud.* "But Hell is much more terrible than that little burn on your finger." *He should know.* "In Hell, you are thrown totally into the fire, the hottest fire there ever was, hotter than any fire you have ever seen, hotter than the hottest bonfire, hotter than the furnaces that melt iron, a white-hot fire. A fire so hot that a little candle is cool by comparison. And it doesn't just burn a tiny little part of you—oh, no—you are thrown into the fire completely. It burns you all over, every part of you, your most tender and sensitive and painful places. And it doesn't stop after three quick seconds. It goes on, and on, and on...and on. Forever. For all eternity. And eternity is a long...long...long time," he said, drawing the words out lovingly for emphasis. "Eternity never ends. Your burning will never stop." I looked at my classmates. Every one of us was very sad. Cricket Quinn was crying.

"How long is eternity? Picture a rock in outer space, a huge rock, a gigantic rock, a monstrous rock. And this enormous rock is bigger than the entire City of Mayfly. Bigger than the State of Missouri. Bigger than the entire Rocky Mountains. Bigger even than the United States of America. In fact, it's as big as the entire world. And this rock is made from the hardest material in the world. It is solid granite. If you hit it with a hammer as hard as you could, it wouldn't even dent it.

"And every year, a weak little baby bird, a sparrow, flies over to this enormous rock and lands on it, and this baby bird looks down at the rock it's standing on, and it pecks at it. Just one time, just a little test peck, to see what it's made of. And with that one peck, that baby bird discovers that the rock is not food, it's too hard, and he knows he can't eat it, so he flies away.

"And one year later, to the day, another little baby bird flies over to this enormous, this incredibly hard rock, and he does the exact same thing, just one soft little exploratory peck, and then flies away. And every year after that, just once a year, one little baby bird flies over to that rock and pecks it one time, a gentle peck, then flies away.

"And eternity is so long, that someday all these tiny little pecks, one soft little peck each year, by one weak little baby bird, will make that enormous granite rock, which is as big as our entire world, crumble, little by little, until there's nothing left of it except sand, and then finally each grain of sand will be pecked by tiny pecks, once each year, until every single grain of sand has become dust. And that will take a very long time—an unimaginably long time. And you are burning in white hot flame all of that time—all over you. And when that finally happens, and that rock is crumbled to dust, eternity will just be beginning." *Jesus Christ! My Jesus, mercy! Oh, God, forgive me, who am unworthy of your love!*

"And if you are burning in white-hot fire all of that time, with no hope of ever getting out, or the fire cooling, or the pain stopping, you will wish you had never been born. You will spend thousands of years, millions of years, millions...of millions of years, wishing you had never been born."

I was frozen in place, contemplating the unmitigated horror of it. There was no sound, no movement. Finally, I was able to look around. No one was napping. He had our undivided attention. The weight of our guilt covered us like six feet of earth. Our nerve ends were alive with anticipation of the pain to come.

"Now, boys," he said, "you are getting old enough to be tempted by the devil to commit sins of impurity. And sins of impurity are Mortal Sins—all of them. Impure thoughts are as sinful as impure deeds. Impure acts by yourself are as sinful as impure acts with another person. And they are all Mortal Sins. And if you die in the state of Mortal Sin, without going to Confession, you go straight to Hell. For all eternity."

He paused to let us absorb that, but I already knew it. I paid attention during religion class at school, and I received multiple admonitions at home, but I had never focused on it like I did at that moment. I was suddenly angry at my non-Catholic friends whose sole worry was being liquified in a nuclear annihilation. *Buncha sissies.*

"So, how do you save your soul?" he asked. "How do you deal with temptations against purity?" In spite of myself, I was all ears—we all were—he was gonna tell us the magic, the silver bullet.

"You do it with prayer," he said. "You ask God, in the words of His Only Begotten Son, to give you strength when you need it, strength to resist the attractive lures that Satan dangles in front of you, *to damn you to Hell.* You use the words of our Lord Jesus, who took the body of a man, and was subject to all the temptations which men are subject to, who was himself tempted. You pray in his words, 'Father, if it is possible, let this cup pass from me, yet not my will, but Thine be done.' Because remember, my children, that God will not allow you to be tempted beyond your strength, and so, if you fail, if you fall into sin, it will not be because the temptation was too hard for you to resist—it will be because you didn't want to resist it—because you wanted to reject God. So today, I'm going to give you a special prayer, a prayer that will help you in times of temptations against purity. Come here, Mr. Miller, and pass them out."

I knew what it was even before I saw it, but I didn't want anyone to know that I was intimately familiar with the "special prayer" to help with sins against purity. I had said it many times, hundreds of times, both to give me strength to avoid sin, and also in contrition for not having avoided it.

As Daniel Miller handed me a copy of the prayer strip, I noticed that this one was different from mine. It looked like the older version, before P.J. had gotten around to typing it. This version was handwritten, in cursive. It was a single line. As I read it, I jerked involuntarily, staring at the big loopy capital "L," which began the prayer: "Lord, be merciful to me, a sinner." I was riveted, gaping at what I saw. Stunned, I folded the strip in half, then in half again, and put it in my shirt pocket. I continued to see the "L" in front of me, like an after-image, as Fr. Reiser continued.

"Imagine for a moment that you have a sin which you commit regularly, a Mortal Sin. And you go to Confession and confess this sin. And you have a firm purpose of amendment. And you make a good Act of Contrition. And on your way home, before you have an opportunity to again commit this Mortal Sin which you are in the habit of committing, you get hit by a car and killed. You are the luckiest man in creation! Lucky! Because being killed was a blessing to you. But you say, 'Father, how can that be? I lost my life! I was young, and I had so many years ahead of me to live!' And I say, because you went straight to Heaven, instead of Hell for all eternity. Do not weep for your loss of life on this earth—rejoice because you have gained everlasting life! Killing you was the greatest blessing that you could have possibly received. The Lord truly does work in mysterious ways. Blessed be the name of the Lord."

Toby and Richard sat as if they had been turned to stone. None of us so much as twitched. We refused to look at each other—we were afraid to. *Was he insane? Is that what happened to Tom? Was Tom actually killed—murdered—and was that why? Is that what happened to the Dalton boy, too? And if we kept confessing the same Mortal Sin, would he wait until we had just been to Confession and then kill us, too?*

That night, as I knelt on the floor during family prayers, and later as I offered up my second rosary of the evening for the Poor Souls in Purgatory, I was especially fervent during the prayer customarily said after each decade of the rosary:

"My Jesus, forgive us our sins, save us from the fires of
Hell, and lead all souls to Heaven, especially those most
in need of your mercy." *Like me!*

I lay in bed, unable to sleep. Everything was confusing. What really happened to Tom? Did Fr. Reiser kill him so he could go to Heaven? I couldn't stop thinking about how angry he was when I found him talking to Tom's dead body, Tom lying there with his blood and brains splattered on the sidewalk next to him: "I warned you," he had said. "I warned you," over and over. Of what? What did he mean by that? And why was he searching his pockets? And what were those mobsters looking for? And how in the name of God was P.J. connected to the mobsters? And why did he claim there was another footprint next to Tom's body? And was there really? And what did Ray Lee Po see?

Finally, I slept. I had the most horrible nightmare of my life, the first of many. I had closed the bedroom door and tied a rope from my bed to the doorknob so it couldn't be opened. A hideous creature with a huge head, shaggy fur on his limbs, and red eyes jerked the door open with a tremendous roar, yanking my bed halfway across the room. He advanced into the room toward me, and I watched in horror as his head turned into a ball of fire. "Jesus, help me," I cried out loud, waking up. I was shaking. It was first light before I was able to sleep again.

The next morning, I asked Dad about the Dalton boy.

"John Dalton," he said. "Why do you ask?"

"The Coroner mentioned him at the Inquest," I said.

"Well, he was a young man in our parish who committed suicide several years ago, He was about sixteen at the time. He was a nice young man—he used to help around the church."

"How did he do it?" I asked.

"Kill himself?" Dad asked. I nodded. "He jumped off Lover's Leap," he said. "No way he could have lived—it's two hundred feet straight down. They found him at the bottom."

39.
CONSTRUCTION

Toby, Richard, John, Michael, and I met back at the stone foundation on Saturday morning, right after John had paid his weekly bill at the Courier-Post. We had also stopped at Haydon Hardware and bought two hundred additional feet of half-inch nylon rope from Mr. Sauer—seven cents a foot—since we knew we'd never be able to climb the tree while carrying the boards. I had oiled up the old pulley that hung unused in our shed and stashed it inside the duffel, together with the coil of rope, a collapsible pruning saw, and my pocketknife.

Since the project was clandestine, we decided to first move all of the boards across the narrow strip of riverbank to the foot of the ancient stairs and hide them behind the vines, before carrying them to the top of the bluff.

"They're heavy," I said. "I think it will take two of us to carry them—one person can rest on each trip."

"We need to make sure there are no cars coming along River Road before we start," Toby said.

"Not that heavy," The Archangel said, hoisting one over his shoulder and running for the hanging kudzu drape. "I can take one." The rest of us watched him, startled. Richard and I looked at each other and shrugged, then bent down, grabbed opposite ends of a board, and ran after Michael. John and Toby took another and followed as fast as they could. Once we had all the boards stashed behind the vine wall, we checked again for witnesses, then started up the ancient stairs, Richard and I in the lead, then John and Toby.

It took some practice, timing our jumps on the irregular steps so we weren't jerking the boards out of one another's hands, but we got the hang of it, using lots of "Ready? Now!" and "Here I go!" verbal cues.

"S'cuse me, girls," we heard The Archangel say, as he ran past us, holding his own board over his head, leaping from step to step and across the voids like an exultant ape-man. The rest of us paused, panting, to look on in disbelief, then resumed laboring up the stairs, our eyes down, intent on our footing. We dropped our boards gratefully at the top of the stairs, then started back down for the next load. The trip down was much easier. After Michael had made two trips, we sent him across the top, carrying boards to the edge of the fissure, while the rest of us made our final trip up the stairs. When we arrived at the fissure with the last boards, Michael slipped down onto the hidden path, and we passed the boards down to him.

Now that we were near the top and approaching the Rectory land on the hidden path, we reminded one another not to talk. Hand signals were preferred, but whispers were acceptable; lowered voices created rumbles and were not allowed. I had brought a bag of acorns, which I split up among the five of us, so that we could quietly bean one another with an acorn to get attention. As the morning progressed, however, we found that a simple "psssst!" was quicker and just as effective. I was disappointed—another of my great ideas was unappreciated.

Before hauling the boards up into the tree, we had to find at least two strong limbs, relatively level and even with each other, that afforded us a view of the Rectory property. The giant oak had begun its life in stiff competition with other trees, causing it to grow perfectly vertical, with no energy wasted on lower limbs, receiving its ration of nourishing sunlight only from straight above. Once it had crested the top of the bluff, however, and begun rising above its competition, the sunlight had poured onto it from sunup to sundown, resulting in an explosive growth of the limbs forming its canopy, not only up, but in all directions. If its trunk was huge, its canopy was more than a match for it. It was completely enveloped in abundant leafy green foliage. The possibilities of a choice location for our treehouse were plentiful in its vast expanse.

I took the duffel, slung it over my shoulder, and started up the long maple ramp, followed close behind by the others. I left the duffel near the junction of the fallen maple with the great supporting limb of the granddaddy oak, while we looked for a good location for our observation platform. It took the five of us nearly an hour of exploration, climbing with critical eyes around the sections of the tree that rose above the bluff and projected westward above the Rectory. We each chose our favorite spot and marked it with a brown strip of cloth, and then all of us toured each site together, hanging out in the surrounding branches and whispering about the advantages and disadvantages of each. Toby's location was the clear winner—a superb view of the Rectory from three nearly level limbs, close enough together to allow the ends of the boards to overlap them, which would provide some safety during the construction phase. Situated almost directly above the hidden path, it would allow us to haul supplies up and down with a minimum of difficulty. Looking at the perfect limbs, I had the strong religious conviction that God had, as part of His divine plan over a century ago, grown these limbs solely to allow his Mayfly boys to bring retribution to sinners—one sinner in particular. *The Lord does indeed work in mysterious ways—blessed be the name of the Lord!*

Joseph Welch

I had been working on the treehouse design in my mind, and I had a plan. "Boys," I whispered, after beaning several of them to get their attention, "I have an idea of how we can build this without nails. Let's start with just six of the boards and stitch them together."

"What do you mean?" Toby whispered.

"We'll pass the rope from the bottom of one board up through one of the holes, then across the width of the top, then down through the other hole to the bottom, then across to the bottom of the next board, and up through a hole to the top, across the width of the top and down through to the bottom again, and so on to the next board. That should keep them all level, with a row of rope stitches across the top on each end of the boards, and give it a little bit of sway, sort of like a wooden hammock," I whispered. "Let's start with just six boards, 'cause I have an idea for the other three."

"First, we need a strong limb above the platform to tie off our pulley," John said. Michael pointed while John climbed up above us. "Here?" he whispered.

"Looks good to me," I whispered, looking at Richard and Toby, who both nodded.

I retrieved the coil of rope, fished out my pocketknife, cut off a length of rope, and handed it to Michael, who stuffed it into his pocket. Next, he put the rope loop around his neck and climbed up to John. Together, they tied off the pulley, then threaded the long rope through it, and sent one of the ends down to the hidden path. Their work completed at that level, John and Michael then picked their way back down the fallen maple ramp to the hidden path to send up the boards.

As the first board came up, I cut two more lengths of rope to fix the first board to the limbs. "This is the most dangerous part," I whispered to Toby and Richard, "if the board we're sitting on would

285

slip off one of the limbs while we're climbing around building the platform. So I'm gonna tie the first board to the limbs on each end, and then we'll always work from that board out, facing west, during the building, okay?"

"Good idea," Richard agreed.

As we stitched, we continued anchoring the ends to the tree limbs, and when we had five of our platform boards stitched together and knotted tight, we also anchored the entire platform to the tree limbs at all four corners. We had three boards left. Toby and Richard traded places with John and Michael so they could get in on the actual construction, too.

"Let's build a backrest," I whispered. "This platform leans a bit back toward the trunk, and that would make it safer."

"And more comfortable," Michael whispered.

"And keep us from dropping things," John whispered, "because anything we drop is gone."

Michael and I looked at him and nodded. "Good idea," The Archangel opined.

We stood one of our three remaining boards up on its long edge and stitched it in, tying it to one of the platform stitches in front with two half-hitches, and tying it to limbs behind the backrest on each side, then added one more board, also on its edge, which we stitched in on top of the first, tying it the same way. When we finished, we had a very sturdy and comfortable backrest two feet tall. Richard and Toby sent up the last board and then joined us on the platform.

"What shall we do with the last board?" Toby asked in a whisper.

"We don't need the backrest to be any taller," John whispered. "How about building an observation shelf in front of the platform so we can kneel up and put our elbows on it while we watch?"

Joseph Welch

That guy may not have been equipped for abstract thought, but he sure had a practical genius—we all just looked at him, then raced to grab the extra board and pass it to the front. We were able to balance it on two of the three limbs, about thirty inches higher than the platform, and overhanging the front of the platform by several inches. It looked great—I cut ropes while the others tied it in tightly on both ends. It was super comfortable to lean on.

Finally, we sat back on our very strong and roomy platform, our backs on the backrest, our legs stretched out in front of us, and looked down at the Rectory property.

"This place is keen!" Toby whispered.

"We can see everything from here," Michael whispered, awestruck. "It would be fun to shoot at stuff from up here."

"Yeah," John whispered, "a BB gun would be great."

"But it would make too much noise," Toby whispered.

'Hmmm, a slingshot wouldn't, though," Richard whispered. "I've seen a big hunting slingshot in the front window at PD Liquor on the way to the library. It has a forearm brace and everything. I'll find out how much it is, and maybe we can pool our money."

"Yeah," Toby whispered, "and maybe we can buy a big carton of BBs, too—they're the best." He was quiet for a moment, lost in thought. "'The Cliffhangers,'" Toby whispered. "That should be our name—the five of us." And it stuck—even though we were the only ones who called ourselves that. It made us feel good every time we said it.

"I think we should call this 'Overlook Oak,'" I whispered. "Is that okay with everyone?"

"Oakey dokey," Richard whispered, slowly. We all looked at him; he was grinning. *Oh, I get it.*

"And that can be 'Hidden Path,'" Michael whispered, pointing straight down.

"And the fallen ramp tree should be 'Tree Ramp,'" John whispered.

"I'm gonna bring the notebook up here," Richard whispered. "And I'll bring a couple of waterproof ammo boxes so we can keep stuff up here."

"Good," I said, "then I'll bring my binoculars."

"And I'll bring our M-80s," Toby whispered, "The ammo boxes will keep 'em dry. I'm always worried Mom and Dad will find them."

"I'll bring a net we can use to haul stuff up and down in," Michael whispered.

"And I'll bring the oil can," I whispered. "We can't let the pulley squeak. And a candle, too. Toby, can you get your hands on a lighter or some matches?"

"Good idea," John whispered. "But we'll have to keep our rope hauled up onto the platform. I don't think anyone else uses Hidden Path, but that rope would be a dead giveaway to anyone walking along there."

"Good idea," I whispered. "And listen, Cliffhangers, we'll have to remind each other every time we meet here to...WHISPER," I said, emphasizing the word by whispering it slowly and loudly.

40.
FIRST FRIDAY

It was the afternoon of June 6. We were setting the table for supper.

"Michael," Mom said, "John and Jamie are serving early Mass, but all of you older boys should be at Mass tomorrow; it's the first Friday of the month. You can go to early Mass and come home and have your breakfast and get your work started by 7:30. If you work straight through, you'll be finished by 9:00 a.m. and have the entire day ahead of you."

Michael looked like he had just found a bug in his mashed potatoes. I looked at her, nonplussed, as I folded the napkins. *Why is she talking about going to Mass on a Friday in June? It's not a Holy Day of Obligation.*

"What's so special about Friday?" Michael asked, after a pause. I was glad he asked, because I had no idea either, but I didn't want to seem like the stupid one.

"It's First Friday, dear," Mom said.

"First Friday of what?" Michael asked.

"Of the month, darling," Mom said. "It's a chance for you boys to start your First Friday Devotions." *Oh, no! Another devotion?* I didn't like the sound of that. I was feeling devotioned out. I waited, hoping Michael would press for details, but dreading it just the same. Finally, John couldn't stand the tension.

"What's that?" John asked.

"The Sacred Heart Devotions," Mom said. "Haven't they taught you about the Devotions to the Sacred Heart of Jesus at school?"

The only thing I knew about The Sacred Heart of Jesus was the large gilt-framed picture of Jesus, which hung on the wall of our living room. A famous painting, it depicted a Caucasian Jesus with a nicely coifed beard, gazing out of the frame with patient, knowing eyes. His left hand held open his outer robe to reveal an idealized red heart displayed in the center of his chest, situated on top of a snow-white undergarment and unencumbered with connecting arteries. The heart was encircled by a crown of thorns, and small flames rose from its top. A small wooden cross stood above the flames. Jesus' eyes followed you wherever you went in the room—if you turned around in the doorway as you left, you could see Him still watching you.

"Sacred Heart Devotions are very important," Mom said, "because of the promises that Jesus made to St. Mary Margaret."

"What promises?" I asked, feeling it safe to join in the discussion now that even the Knight of the Altar had displayed total ignorance on the subject.

"There are a number of them," Mom said, "but the most important one is the Twelfth Promise. Jesus promised that if you go to Mass and receive Communion on nine consecutive First Fridays, you will be able to go to Confession before you die."

What?! Now, she had my attention. "Really?" I asked in a tone of feigned boredom, as if going to Confession right before you died qualified as an interesting bit of trivia, although an unnecessary event for me.

"I have some literature on it," she said, leaving the room.

She returned with a four-page color brochure. John's hands were in the dishwater, and Michael was unwrapping another stick of butter, so I took it and started reading. It turned out that the painting in our living room, which I had gazed at since before I could walk, and which was displayed in most other Catholic homes as well, including Toby's, was the symbol of an ancient devotion to the Sacred Heart of Jesus which had been practiced by saints and promoted by popes for two hundred years.

In 1763, a French nun named Sr. Margaret Mary Alacoque had visions in which Jesus asked the Church to honor His Most Sacred Heart by receiving Holy Communion for nine consecutive First Fridays of the month. In the visions, Jesus made twelve promises to those who venerated His Sacred Heart, including a promise to "bless every place in which an image of my heart is exposed and honored."

I devoured the brochure, reading the Twelve Promises, looking hungrily for the silver bullet. There it was, number twelve:

> I promise you in the excessive mercy of my Heart that my all-powerful love will grant to all those who receive Holy Communion on the First Fridays in nine consecutive months the grace of final perseverance; they shall not die in my disgrace, nor without receiving their sacraments. My divine heart shall be their safe refuge in this last moment.

Hallelujah! A guarantee! And by Jesus Himself! Straight from the ... er, straight from the Savior's mouth! (Sorry, Lord, that was completely inadvertent.) This is just what I need! Hell, yes, I'm going to Heaven! I'm going to Mass every First Friday for the next nine months—I just hope I can survive long enough to get across the finish line! By 7:00 a.m. on the first Friday next February, I'll be safe forever—for all eternity—no matter what!

Summer of '63

I was ecstatic during after-dinner basketball with Michael and John—completely untouchable in 3-Man-21. My court creativity flourished. I alternately drove the lane for layups and pulled up short for jump shots— I could pop the net blindfolded, and from anywhere on the court. And my corner shot—I could literally close my eyes and hit it—and I did, showing off and narrating to my brothers: "Watch this, boys, eyes closed." It was so great—it really made them mad!

But lying in bed after the fireworks and my second Rosary of the evening, I was too excited to sleep, and I started thinking. *This is too good to be true—there must be a catch.* After John's breathing indicated that he was asleep, I got up and took the brochure to the bathroom. I started to read the fine print. First, these promises are dependent on the "Enthronement of the Sacred Heart" in your home. *Got that one covered—it's enthroned on the living room wall—that's as "enthroned" as you can get in this house—better even than the tribute shelf to the Knight of the Altar.* I continued reading the brochure. You must receive Holy Communion "with the intention of honoring Christ's Sacred Heart." *Okay, I can manage that. Check.*

But then I read, "If you are not in the State of Grace, and thus unable to receive, you will also need to go to Confession." *Uh-oh. On Friday morning, I will have last been to Confession on the prior Saturday afternoon—almost a full week before each First Friday! How in the world am I gonna make it for a full week without having a single impure thought? I usually can't make it past the funny paper on Sunday morning—Prince Valiant's wife, Valeta, is so beautiful— long, dark hair, low neckline, and body-hugging bodice—if I were the cartoonist, I would never get anything done!—Lord, be merciful to me, a sinner!—it was absolutely physically and spiritually impossible to look at her without having impure thoughts.*

I was supposed to stay away from "the occasions of sin," but since the Sunday morning funny paper was one of those occasions, there was no way that was going to happen. Even Blondie was really hot, and Lois was attractively round in the right places—it caused a great deal of wonder and speculation. And I don't even wanna mention Brenda Starr. Only Nancy failed to move me.

So what was I to do? I had to figure out a way that a sinner like me could cash in on this First Friday promise. The only way I could think of to make this work was to go to Confession immediately before Mass on each first Friday morning. And even though Confessions were not scheduled then, any priest would hear my Confession, if I asked him, no problem—even P.J.—but, he'd know it was me for sure, and he'd know I'd be confessing the same sin over and over and over, and one of those mornings I just might not make it home alive! Plus, I was starting to have a real problem confessing anything to that jerk. *No dogs in Heaven, my ass! Prince and I will be looking over the side, laughing at him down below—for all eternity.*

I wondered whether Tom knew about the Sacred Heart Devotions and whether he had made the First Fridays before P.J. killed him. He might have actually known about it and cashed in—after all, he did get to go to Confession right before he died.

41.
FIGURING TOM

The next day, the Three Musketeers were ensconced in the treehouse on a beautiful afternoon in early June. The weather was perfect.

"What did the grapevine say to the Overlook Oak?" Richard whispered, looking across at Toby and me.

"No idea. What?" Toby whispered.

"I am the vine; you are the branches," Richard whispered back. This triggered simultaneous whispered I-can't-believe-you-said-that groans from Toby and me. Richard shrugged.

"Okay, then, if you don't like my jokes, let's work on the investigation," Richard whispered, opening one of the ammo boxes and extracting the case notebook along with a Bic pen.

"Alright," I whispered. "I keep wondering why Tom did what he did, or even if he did do what he did."

"I know," Toby whispered. "I don't think he did."

"Did what?" Richard whispered.

"You know, what he did—or didn't," Toby whispered back.

"But let's look at it anyway," Richard said. "Because the Inquest verdict was suicide. That's what we need to disprove if we wanna get Tom to Heaven. We've got to prove it wasn't suicide, or we can't get him moved to hallowed ground."

"Right," I whispered, "and I hate to say this, but if it was suicide, it wouldn't make any difference if he's buried in hallowed ground or not."

"You mean," Toby whispered, "because if it was suicide, he's already in Hell," looking first angry and then completely devastated as he envisioned Tom in Hell.

"Not necessarily," Richard said. "Even if it was suicide, he likely repented on the way down."

"We can never prove that," I said. "But we can certainly hope it."

"Or he wouldn't go to hell if he was out of his mind," Richard continued, "even temporarily."

We were silent, all of us trying to think of any evidence at all that Tom was out of his mind, or had ever been out of his mind, or any indication that he had been upset or confused. As much as I wanted it to be true, I couldn't think of anything.

"I'm drawing a blank here, I'm afraid," I said.

"Me, too," Richard agreed.

"Or if he didn't know suicide is a sin, then he couldn't commit that sin," Richard continued.

No way that could have been. Every Catholic knew suicide was not only a sin, but a Mortal Sin, the ultimate turning your back on God, the intentional throwing away of the life God gave you. Impossible that Tom didn't know that—he was thinking of becoming a priest, for God's sake.

"Toby, I gotta ask you something, but you need to promise you won't get mad," I said.

"What?"

"You know, I thought Tom was the greatest, and I don't really care, but it's important now, and I have to know how to think about this. I have to know the truth, because it affects our investigation. So you promise you won't get mad?" I said.

"Okay, what?" Toby said, forgetting to whisper.

"Shhhhh," Richard reminded us.

"Okay, what?" Toby whispered.

"Was Tom funny?" I whispered.

"What do you mean, 'funny'?" Toby whispered.

"I mean, did he like girls?"

Toby looked like I'd slapped him. He was quiet for a minute, but then he looked away, and I could tell he was trying to remember. "I think so—I think he liked girls pretty much." He paused. "Actually, I don't know. But he sure liked to look at pictures of them without their clothes on. So I'm pretty sure he did. He was older than me—he didn't talk to me much about it. But I don't care if he did or not—he was a great older brother!"

"Yeah, he was a great guy!" I said hurriedly, forgetting to whisper.

Richard nodded. "Sure was," he said. "but my notes say that the suicide verdict was because they thought Tom was queer, and because he was queer, he thought of himself as a loser, so let's look at just those two things. Why would they think he was queer?"

"They just said he was queer because he hung around the bandstand at Central Park, and there were restrooms below the bandstand," I said.

"He only hung out there because it was quiet at night," Toby whispered. "It was a place where he could be by himself and just think. And it was comfortable. And there weren't near as many mosquitoes up there as there were on the lawn benches. And anyway, that was just for a little while, before he started going up in the bell tower. After he started using the tower and had his own key made, he never went back to the bandstand. He used to sit up in that tower for hours, just thinking. He showed it to me—it was a really cool place—but he didn't invite us up there with him—it was just his private place. There weren't even any mosquitoes up that high—the only thing he didn't like about it was a few spiders and bats—and the pigeons, too, of course, but they didn't come out at night unless someone scared them outta their roost. He could smoke and drink up there, and nobody would bother him. He used to sit on the railing and let his legs dangle over the side and watch people and cars go by below."

"Ever see him with any other men?" Richard asked.

Toby shook his head. "Never," he whispered. "And I woulda remembered."

"Me either," Richard said, "and I never heard anybody talkin' about him bein' queer."

"P.J. is guilty of something," I said. "He was yelling at him right there on the ground, right after he died, and it was his writing on the note in Tom's pocket, and he acted really weird at the Inquest and also at the funeral—he wouldn't even look at Mr. and Mrs. Piper. I wonder if Tom committed suicide because P.J. had been molesting him, and he just couldn't take it anymore. Look what happened to the Dalton boy. He jumped off Lover's Leap, supposedly, which is right next door to P.J.'s rectory. Maybe it was the same thing. Maybe it was the only way he could get P.J. to leave him alone," I added.

"But Tom didn't act like he had that kind of problem," Richard said. "Because Tom didn't act like I think you would act if someone was molesting you. Because I think that really *would* make you moody and depressed."

"Well, he'd be ashamed of it—he wouldn't want us to know he had been letting P.J. do things to him—whatever he was doing to him. Just like if he was queer, he certainly wouldn't tell us," I said. Toby looked at me—he was getting mad. "Not that I think he was—I don't," I added quickly. "But if he was, he probably woulda been disgusted by what he was doing. And he probably woulda been depressed."

"Yeah," Richard said. "They also said he was depressed because he didn't have any friends."

"Yeah, but that's bullshit, too—he had us," I whispered. "*We* were his friends."

"Yeah," Toby said, "and we *knew* him. He didn't seem depressed."

"That's my point," I said. "He wasn't sad, and he wasn't depressed, and he wasn't moody, and none of us ever saw him with strange men, and I don't think there's any way that he was queer."

"No," Toby said, "he didn't have any real big secrets. Well, a few from Mom and Dad, I guess, but not from us. And the main one he had from Mom and Dad was just hiding Playboys from them! And booze and cigarettes, of course," he added.

"Yeah, that's right," I said. "And he did seem like he was happy."

"Yeah," Richard said, "he looked you in the eye, he wasn't shifty—he didn't seem like a pervert."

"And he didn't think of himself as a loser," Toby said. "He thought of himself as an average guy, and he knew that he was a nice guy, and he was happy about that."

"Just the way we thought of him, too," Richard said.

"He also had a really nice car, and he was proud of it," I said. The other two nodded. "Would you kill yourself if you had a car like that?" The other two shook their heads.

"What about his not liking Crazy Carly?" Richard asked. "She's pretty pretty." I thought so, too. "And she's a girl."

"She sure is!" I said, mentally reviewing her pert little breasts and her other qualifications. *Oh, shit! Lord, be merciful to me, a sinner.*

"Maybe he wanted a nice girl," Toby whispered. "He said she was really nasty. He said she talked really nasty and acted like a slut, and I think he wanted it to be something really special, but it wasn't—it was just nasty." *Oh, God— what did that mean? Why can't that ever happen to me? Lord, be merciful to me, a sinner.*

"And maybe he was trying not to get involved with a girl anyway until he figured out whether he wanted to be a priest," Toby continued.

"What about Ray Lee Po?" I asked. "Did Tom know Ray Lee Po?"

"Yeah," Toby said. "He was always speaking to Ray Lee Po."

"What do you mean, 'speaking to him'?" I asked, astonished. "Talking with him?"

"No, he just said 'Hi, Ray' whenever he saw him. Or he just waved at him and smiled. He felt sorry for him because he didn't have any family or friends. That was all."

"But Ray Lee Po couldn't talk, could he?" I asked. "Did he ever say 'hi' back to Tom?"

"Nah," Toby said. "The funny thing was, Ray didn't like anybody saying 'hi' to him—it just made him mad. Heck, he didn't even like anybody looking at him. But Tom kept doing it because he thought maybe someday he would."

"But he never did?" I asked, thinking I knew the answer.

"Not as far as I know," Toby said.

"Okay," Richard said, "none of us who knew him thinks he killed himself. Let's look at the possibility that someone else killed him. Whether he was queer or not—and we don't think he was—but whether he was or wasn't, why would anyone want to kill him?"

"You mean, why would P.J. want to kill him?" I said. "Because we all know where that note came from."

"But why would P.J. want to kill him?" Richard asked.

"He thought he was doing him a favor," I said.

"What do you mean?" Toby asked.

"You heard him at the retreat," I said. "It was disgusting. What if Tom was having trouble with sins against purity, and I think it's highly likely he was, whether he was queer or not, because, number one, he was a guy, and number two, he had a collection of Playboys." Neither of them said anything. "Plus, he had that note in his pocket, or part of it anyway—that prayer that P.J. hands out for help with sins of impurity."

"You think he'd kill him because of a sin he committed?" Toby asked, incredulous.

"Just hear me out, okay? So what if Tom had this problem, and he was trying to change, and he went to Confession and confessed it, and what if P.J. knew it was Tom, and he had confessed the same sins before, maybe many times before, over and over, but he couldn't stop committing the same sin, and maybe he even told P.J. that no matter what he did, he couldn't change, and P.J. knew it, knew he couldn't stop committing this sin, and he also knew he was in the State of Grace right then, right after he had been to Confession, and he saw his chance, so he decided to send him to Heaven."

"By killing him?" Richard asked, still incredulous.

"Yeah," I said, "by killing him. You heard him at the retreat. He even talked about it. He said getting killed in the State of Grace is lucky—it makes you the luckiest man in creation. He said it was the greatest blessing you could ever receive. And that jerk's just crazy enough to do it. My mom is like that. She's always telling us about St.

Louis' mother, who told him, 'I would rather see you dead at my feet than see you commit a Mortal Sin.' She thinks that's something to be proud of. He's the same way."

"Or maybe P.J. had been molesting him for years, every time he called Tom to come over and help out," Richard whispered. "And maybe Tom had enough of it, and told P.J. to leave him alone, but he wouldn't, and maybe Tom threatened to tell someone, like the bishop."

"Or maybe P.J. was just afraid he'd tell someone what he had been doing to him, so he killed him. He just pushed him off the bell tower. He probably pushed the Dalton boy off Lovers Leap, too," Toby whispered.

"Yeah, that would explain what P.J. was so mad about when I first saw him leaning over Tom's body, saying 'I warned you' over and over," I said.

"Yeah, and going through his pockets," Toby said. "He's probably the one who put the 'Loser' note in Tom's pocket, to make it look like he had committed suicide."

"But do you really think P.J. would kill him?" Richard asked.

"Hell, yes, I do—he either killed him because he was molesting him, or he killed him because he thought he was doing Tom a favor," I said.

"Also," Toby asked, "how come he was searching Tom's pockets? He didn't mention anything about it at the Inquest."

"Holy cow!" I whispered. "We gotta be careful about spying on him—if he killed Tom, he'll kill us, too." *Not to mention the danger of letting him catch me in the State of Grace after confessing the same sins over and over—maybe I need to stop confessing all of my sins—but that would mean making a bad Confession, which is itself a Mortal Sin. Oh,*

God—if he killed me after Confession, thinking he was sending me to Heaven, but it was a bad Confession, I would go straight to Hell.

"How will we ever find out for sure if P.J. killed him?" Richard whispered. "Tom can't tell us, and John Dalton can't tell us what happened to him either."

"Tom's St. Thomas medal is lost," Toby said, suddenly excited. "We haven't been able to find it since he died. I wonder if P.J. has it."

"St. Thomas Aquinas?" I asked.

"No, St. Thomas the Apostle," Toby answered.

"What's it look like?" Richard asked.

"Just St. Thomas' head. He has a beard, plus a spear in one hand and a book in the other. It's silver, on a silver chain. Well, really steel, but silver-colored."

For a fleeting moment, I pictured P.J. taking it off over Tom's head each time he took his clothes off, before he did whatever he did to him.

"Oh, God," I said, "we need to search the rectory."

"You're nuts," Toby said, "he'll kill us for sure if he finds us in his house."

"Look," Richard said. We know some of the times when he will definitely be gone. Daily Mass, for instance; Sunday Mass. Saturday Confessions."

"You guys are serious!" Toby said.

"We can't do it on Saturday—I'll be at Confession, too," I said.

"And we'll all be at Mass on Sunday," Toby said.

"I may not be able to do it during daily Mass either," I said. "Mom volunteers me to serve early Mass a month at a time during the summer. We're already serving for June. And even if I wasn't serving

Daily Mass, it's always during our morning work time. You guys'll have to do it on your own."

"Looks like daily Mass is our only chance," Richard said. "Just Toby and me. But the very first thing we need to do is plan a quick getaway route—we can't get caught running across the top of the bluff or down the road while he's driving up—and he'll be sure to know me, even from the back."

42.
AT THE HOP

"Come on," Catherine Camp said, reaching out with both hands and drawing me away from the pack of boys milling uncomfortably around the edge of the gym floor. "Let's dance."

It was the first time I had been old enough to attend the annual Summer CYO Sock Hop, which was a big event. I was pretty spiffy in my brown leather dress shoes, brown sport coat and white shirt, topped off by a paisley necktie selected for me by the clerk at Yates & Hagan. When I asked him if he thought it was too loud, he told me with a knowing wink that a "fella should look a little roosterish," so I deferred to his judgment, tucking that little bit of sartorial wisdom away in my "Suave Man of the World" file.

I couldn't dance a lick, but apparently that didn't make any difference—Catherine couldn't either. But she was very athletic, and she just hopped up and down. In retrospect, I'm sure that we both looked completely ridiculous—me even more so, because I didn't have the charms that turned her hopping into a riot of bobbling pubescent loveliness—but that didn't matter either, because at least it got me out onto the dance floor.

I saw Mary Ann talking animatedly with a group of girls. Two of the girls faced toward the floor, serving as lookouts, and keeping the rest of them fully informed about developments, especially which boys were walking around loose and who was dancing with whom.

When the song ended, I told Catherine 'thanks' and walked off the floor, visions of sugar plums still dancing in my head, attempting to locate the punch bowl, and absent-mindedly fielding adolescent macho remarks from my peers. As I staggered around the room, my eyes took in the loveliness of Mary Ann, still surrounded by the gaggle, and I found myself wondering how I could extract her without making a fool of myself. *Why are they always together? If they broke up their huddle and walked across the floor by themselves, they'd all have dance invitations before they got to the other side. Well, at least Mary Ann would.*

Well, hell! I didn't really want to dance, but I did want to spend some time with Mary Ann, preferably just looking at her—but I could also talk to her some, too, if she could think of something we could talk about. I never knew what to say when I was around her. *I guess I'm gonna have to go over there.*

It was worse than I thought. As I started across the floor toward the group surrounding Mary Ann, my approach was immediately noticed by both Lisa and Denise. Their faces became animated as their hands gestured inside the circle for attention. They were obviously informing the group of some breaking news—of what? Then six faces turned toward me in unison—only Mary Ann's didn't. I lumbered up to the group like Frankenstein trying out his feet for the first time, not knowing where they were taking me. Fortunately, apparently because they sensed that I was just going to bump into them otherwise, the circle opened by some sort of hive intelligence, clearing a path straight to Mary Ann, who raised her head and looked at me with calm, wide gray eyes.

"Hi, ladies," I managed, penetrating the outer border of her *entourage* and trying for suave, which elicited lots of giggles and sideways glances, as heads turned slightly away. Finally, Jill broke the silence. "Hi, Jamie, whatcha doin'?" she asked, all mischievous, while a half dozen girls either sipped nervously at their punch or giggled or bit their lower lips.

"Oh, just hangin' around. Hi, Mary Ann," I said, as nonchalantly as I could manage, just as the sweet string sound of violins began a new song. "Would you like to dance?" I asked, reaching out for her hand and riding the building waves of music into what promised to be a slow dance. I pulled her away from her *coterie*, exiting the circle of eager onlookers out onto the dance floor, then pulled her in close to me. I looked into her eyes just as Etta James' sultry voice began "At Last." Unable to break the gaze, I was drawn in slow motion into those pools. The world went dumb and muffled, and other awareness fell off like dried leaves around my feet. *Oh, hell,* I groaned, from that deep place without thought, *I'm in Heaven.*

Somehow we started moving with the music, and I came back to earth, to the dance floor, to Mary Ann in my arms. I will always remember that first dance. Her scent permeated my brain—perfume mingled with something else, something fresh and wholesome and delightful—I think it was straw, perhaps. Her breath was gentle and warm, and calm. Her hand was small in mine, her back unbearably soft. I had never been that kinda drunk until that moment, as I looked at her, inhaling her, feeling her skin. My mind was transported, but my body was fully alert, responding to her. And her eyes...and then I bumped into her—*Whoops! Excuse me—oh, God. Oh, God—does she know what that is? What must she think of me?*

But her eyes were wide and calm and revealing, and I was lost in them, too lost to worry, absolutely mesmerized, senseless. She smiled, and I saw her pretty lips part, framing her front teeth, and the shy pink tip of her tongue peeking from behind them. *Oh, God! Lord, be merciful to me, a sinner. God grant me chastity, but not now.*

"How have you been, Jamie Fletcher?" she asked, bringing me back from God knows where. "I haven't seen you in a while. Are you playing any basketball this summer?"

"Yes," I answered stupidly, trying to normalize my breath, my voice, trying not to pant. "I've been practicing a lot." And then, without thinking, I just blurted it out—I don't know why I did it—I was absolutely compelled right then to tell her my deepest secret: "I'm going to be the best basketball player in the history of Mayfly," I panted. *There, I said it.* I waited, scared, shocked by what I had just revealed, watching her eyes, her face, to see how she would take it—to see if she believed me, to see if she thought I could do it.

Her mouth fell halfway open. Her eyes searched mine. She leaned in toward me, as if to tell me a secret—or ask me for one.

"How do you know?" she whispered, serious now, pleading for the truth. "How can you be so sure?"

"I have a plan," I said. "And Toby is gonna help me." Well, I assumed he would—I hadn't actually asked him, but he had always helped me before. Admittedly, my plan was fairly basic—I intended to just practice and practice, but *really hard*, until I was the best, until everyone else agreed I was, too. Because I absolutely knew I could be the best if I only tried hard enough. But at least it was a plan.

Just then I felt a tap on my shoulder and turned to find Lucas Crane standing there.

"Mind if I cut in?" he asked.

Mind? Hell, yes, I mind. Get outta here, you jerk. "Be my guest," I said, pulling away from Mary Ann. I don't really know why I let him; I guess…just because…that's what gentlemen do. Besides, what was I gonna do? Tell him, *"No—go to hell, Lucas—I'm dancing with my girlfriend here."* But what would Mary Ann think about that? I didn't even know if she *was* my girlfriend. I knew I wanted her to be, but I hadn't really asked her. I didn't even know if she wanted me to be her boyfriend. I might just be a "regular" kind of friend. Plus, it wasn't like we ever actually did anything together. I didn't even know how to ride a horse, much less own one, and she didn't play basketball, so what did we have to talk about? School? *Yuck!* I had that in common with thirty-one other kids in my class. School was a total bore.

Seething, I ambled over to the punch bowl, and watched Richard out on the floor, dancing energetically with Catherine. Toby was with Kate Privet, a cute and wild girl who loved to party. I watched her pretty sister Maggie coming down the steps from the school into the gym. Supposedly, people went to the stairwell to kiss, and I wondered briefly who she had been kissing up on the stairs. *Lucky guy!* When I looked back at Mary Ann, she and Lucas Crane were still dancing together. He was so much bigger than she was—all I could see was Lucas' back—but it looked like he was laughing. *What were they talking about? Had she just told him my secret? Are they laughing at me? Oh, God!* I was furious. Suddenly, I couldn't bear to stay any longer, to have the song end and Lucas see me standing at the punch bowl, alone. I turned away, hurt and angry, no—mad as hell—and walked out the door. *She didn't have to dance with him. She could have said "no."* Toby came out a few minutes later, and we headed down to the River's Rest so we could sit in the basement and smoke cigarettes. We even stopped by the hospital across the street from the motel and bought a pack of Marlboros from the vending machine in the basement for forty-five cents.

"Toby," I said after we had both lit up in the basement, "I need to tell you something, and I need to ask a favor."

"Sure, what is it?" he said, squinting to keep the smoke out of his eyes.

"I want to be the best basketball player in Mayfly—in the history of Mayfly," I said. "And I want to win the Mayfly Future Famer Trophy for starters."

Toby was quiet for a moment, thinking about it. "That would be keen," he said, finally, "I think you've got a shot at it, too. You might be able to do it."

That was exciting—Toby thought I could do it. I was elated. "Thanks, man, but I need you to practice with me. I need lots of shooting practice, and I need someone to rebound for me. And I need someone to run plays with—someone on my team. Since you're the postman and I'm the point guard, you're my most important teammate. We can do a lot together that I can't do on my own."

"Yeah, okay, that sounds good," Toby said slowly, "you know I've always helped you whenever you wanted to practice."

"I know, but we'll have to practice regularly," I said. "Like every day."

"Fine by me," Toby said. "Just let me know when."

That night, as I lay in bed and began my second Rosary of the evening, I was hopeful. I had told John and Michael about winning the Future Famer Trophy, and I had told Toby. They were the people who knew me best and knew my game the best, and none of them told me I was full of it—they all thought it was possible.

I had also told Mary Ann, but I'm not sure what she thought. Had she told that asshole Lucas Crane? Were they laughing at me? *How would she know, anyway? She doesn't know my game. Plus, she's just a girl!*

Summer of '63

I didn't want to think about it. *I don't know why sock hops are such a big deal—they sure as hell aren't all they're cracked up to be. Buncha bullshit. I got bigger things on my mind.*

I really did have other fish to fry. I had to find out if P.J. killed Tom, and what he was doing with those mobsters, and I had to get a whole lot better in basketball if I were going to win the Future Famer Trophy so I wouldn't become a laughingstock, and I had to figure out a way to save my immortal soul, and the sooner the better. Because right then, at that very minute, if the devil came and offered me a way to get rid of Lucas Crane, I might have been a goner.

43.
MR. HEDGES

I was looking through a Rawlings Sporting Goods circular when my eyes were arrested by an advertisement for the Mississippi Hills Basketball Camp, to be held June 24 through 29 on the Mayfly Junior College campus.

> Boys! Do you dream of becoming a *great* basketball player? This is your chance to become the player you've always wanted to be—the player your teammates count on when the game is on the line! Elevate your game! Master the advanced basketball skills that will take you from good to excellent!
>
> Each registrant will receive individual shot analysis. You will increase your shooting percentage and learn new defensive, ball-handling, and passing techniques, including powerful strategies like the "pick-and-roll" and the "give-and-go." Our Player Development Plan will also allow you to *continue improving—even after the end of camp*! Two-week intensive basketball training camp. Boys: Ages 14-18.

The founders were all talented basketball players and coaches whose names I was familiar with—these people were my heroes. This was exactly what I needed, but I was still too young.

"Dad, I need to go to this camp," I said, handing him the catalog. He looked at it, then frowned.

"You're too young," he said. "You're only twelve."

"But I can't wait."

"What's the hurry?"

"I want to win the Mayfly Future Famer Trophy."

"Why can't you practice here with your brothers?" he asked. So then I had to tell him about Lucky.

"And he's *really* good," I said.

"I imagine Mr. Hedges would help you if you asked him," Dad said. "He has his own court."

"How can *he* help?" I asked. Mr. Hedges was an older guy in our parish. As far as I knew, he was just some old man I saw going up to Communion on Sunday.

"Mr. Hedges was a great basketball player when he was young. Played point guard at Notre Dame—started varsity as a sophomore. Held the record for most assists in a season. Great shooter, too—shot 56% from the field. He was famous for a while. Could've played professional basketball—he was that good."

"Why didn't he?"

"He ruptured his Achilles tendon. Ended his career. I'll introduce you to him if you'd like."

"Do you think he'll help me?"

"I know he can, but I don't know if he will—you'll just have to ask him," Dad said.

That evening, Dad took me over to Mr. Hedges' house and introduced me. Mr. Hedges was about six feet tall, and muscular. He had some streaks of gray in his hair, which was cut in a butch. He shook my hand.

"So you want to become a great basketball player?" he asked.

"Yes, sir."

"You want to be good, or you want to be great?" he asked, his eyes searching my face.

"I want to be great," I said, without hesitation.

"Why?" he asked.

I just looked at him, my face blank, as I wondered why I wanted to be great. No one had ever asked me that. He waited. Finally, I just started talking, not even knowing what I was going to say.

"It's hard to describe," I said. "I love the feeling I get when I'm playing basketball. I feel...creative. I feel like I'm dancing. I feel like I can make stuff up, stuff that surprises even me, and surprises other people, too—and it works! Sometimes, when I'm playing, I almost feel like I can fly. And I love being able to hit, especially when somebody is guarding me, and he thinks he has me covered. I love being able to just pop up and hit it when his arm is in the air, and his hand is in my face and he's trying to block my shot. I love looking one way and passing the other. I love seeing the net pop up above the rim when I hit one perfectly, dead center, and it doesn't even touch the rim on the way through. And I love the sound that it makes. I just love knowing what I can do. And I like knowing I'm good, and I kinda like it when other people know it, too," I said, smiling. "I like it when the varsity players choose me first. And I really, really want to win the Future Famer Trophy—actually, I have to, because I told my brothers I would," I added, finally running out of words and reasons.

He just looked at me, appraising me silently. Finally, he said, "Okay. I know what you mean. You may be just what I'm looking for."

What?! I was confused. I looked at Dad—he looked even more so.

"For years," Mr. Hedges continued, "I've wanted to coach a young man who has it in him to become great. Not just good—great. And I can help you become great—I mean *really* great. But you know," he said, "even though I can show you things and help you with specific aspects of your game, ultimately it will depend on you. There are no magic bullets. It's gonna take hard work, diligent work, every single day. And if I get the impression that you're not working hard enough, not trying hard enough, not paying attention to what I'm teaching you, that I want it more than you do, then you're not worth my time, and I won't coach you. Do you understand that?"

I nodded. I understood him perfectly. "Yes, sir."

"Good. And you'll need someone to practice with—someone who is on your same team."

That could only be one person. "Toby," I said.

"Okay," he said. "Talk to him. I work from six a.m. to two-thirty p.m. Bring him over tomorrow afternoon at three and we'll get started." He looked over at Dad. "Okay, if we work from three to five-thirty Monday through Friday?" he asked.

Dad looked shocked. "Really?" he asked. "I mean, sure," he said. "Are you sure you want to give it that much time?"

"That's what it's gonna take," he said. He turned to me. "And you each need to bring a basketball," he said.

The next afternoon, Toby and I dribbled our basketballs over to Mr. Hedges' house. John was on his paper route and Michael and Richard were on duty in Overlook Oak. I had brought my good basketball, and Toby had inherited Tom's, which was hardly used. I dribbled as I went, using my left hand two-thirds of the time, and looking elsewhere as I dribbled, *a la* Bob Cousy. I even fired off some passes when I had an accommodating wall to return the favor.

When we got to Mr. Hedges' house, I introduced Toby, and Mr. Hedges took us out to his court behind the house. He lived on a hill, but a portion of the backyard had been cut out of the hill to make a level spot for a large concrete basketball court, surrounded by a retaining wall on the high side and a tall cyclone fence on the other three sides. It had a regulation rim and backboard, and he had even painted the lane and the free throw line—on our dirt court at home, the "free throw line" was imaginary—a spot opposite the outside edge of our brick patio.

"Let's take a look at your shots, boys," he said. "Both of you step up to the line and shoot some free throws. Ten apiece. Keep track out loud, so I can hear you."

"One for one," I called out.

"O for one," Toby said.

"One for two." And so on.

He rebounded while we shot, passing the balls back to us on one bounce each, just the way the referee does in a game. I hit five and Toby hit three.

"Okay, boys, listen up," he said when we had finished. "You need to go through the same routine every single time you come up to the line. You don't take one dribble one time and eleven dribbles the next. You take three dribbles—every time. Three and only three. That's enough to give you the feel of the ball. When you take too many, it affects your confidence. You don't want to be standing there at the line asking yourself, 'Should I shoot now or dribble a little more?' Three dribbles, that's it, then you catch the ball and line the seams up across your fingertips, and you inhale. You do the seams automatically, in a fraction of a second. Then you look at the rim as you blow the air out, the whole rim, the circle, and you picture putting enough arch on it that you can drop the ball through that circle without touching either side, so it doesn't have to bounce off the back of the rim to drop through. You do that for one full second, while you exhale, and then, as you finish exhaling, you shoot. Got it? Now, put the balls down. Close your eyes and do it. I'll walk you through it again, without the ball."

He talked us through it with our eyes closed.

"Again." We did it again, as he coached us through it.

"Concentrate," he said. "Visualize it. Picture it while I'm talking. Again." He talked us through it five times.

"Now do it without my talking. Slowly. Perfectly." We did.

"Visualize it perfectly. Take your time. Again."

We did it by ourselves, five times.

"Alright," he said. "Let's look at your feet. Shoulder width, toes pointing forward at a comfortable angle. You might want to point your toes out a little, but only the tiniest angle out, mainly just forward. Move your right foot ever so slightly further forward, say two inches further forward than your left foot. So it's comfortable, so you're balanced. Now, bend your knees into a half squat. Feet still comfortable? Are you balanced? Toes on your shooting foot just slightly forward. Come up. Do it again. Now come up."

"Now," he said, "do the whole thing, eyes closed, without the ball. Ready? Three dribbles, breathe in as you catch the ball. Seams. Exhale, entire rim, arch to drop through the center of the hole, finish your exhale, shoot. Good. Again."

He walked us through, verbally, again.

"Okay," he said, "Listen up, boys, this is the most important thing I will ever tell you. Visualizing the rim is important—extremely important. *You must do it every single time you shoot*, no matter what type of shot you are shooting, even a layup. *This is a secret.* This is powerful stuff. But even though I've told you the secret, I can't make you *learn* it—that is entirely up to you. You will have to train yourself to do it *every single shot* you take—you will have to focus. It takes brain power. It takes effort. It takes study, and memorization. It takes *work*. Learn it in your mind and your body and in your bones. You boys will have to work on this *every day, every single shot*. If you can't learn this, I can't coach you."

We just looked at him, then nodded slowly.

"Ready? Again." And he talked us through it again, and again, and again.

"Okay, pick up your basketballs," he said.

We did.

"Wait. Hold it," he said. "Let's look at how you're holding the ball." He corrected our hand placement. "Each time you pick the ball up after your third dribble, and you place the seams, you place your hands just like this. So when you 'seam' the ball, you also check your grip."

"Your elbow should be mostly underneath the ball, just slightly to the outside, so it's comfortable, not pinched into your chest and not too far out to the side. That will give you strength and control. And when you push the ball up, the 'V' between your thumb and forefinger should go up right in front of your right eyebrow, not your nose. Like this," he said, "and this," demonstrating in slow motion. "Now, you do it. Show me. Again. And again. Ten times. In slow motion. Memorize that."

"Now, boys, do you think you can do all of that without my talking you through it?" he asked.

"Yes, sir," we both said.

"Okay, we'll find out. Give me thirty free throws each. Count them out loud, so I can hear you. Take your time and make them perfect—*in your mind.* Use your technique. *Visualization is everything.* You'll owe me one pushup for every one you miss."

I hit eighteen. Toby hit thirteen.

"Pretty good, boys," he said, "for your first time. Always use the method—you'll get better and better. Now, do your pushups, on your fingertips, backs flat—and they don't count unless your chest brushes the ground each time. Supine position, count them together, out loud. Ready? Go." We did.

Next, we worked on our follow-through, and the importance of getting a nice wrist break to add backspin to the ball. Then we shot thirty more, slowly, focusing, using the method from beginning to end.

"Boys, if your grip is correct, and your elbow is under the ball, and you're passing your shooting hand in front of your right eyebrow, if you're doing all those things correctly, and you're still off to the side, that is a simple matter of toe placement. If you're off to the left, your right foot is too far forward. If you're off to the right, it's too far back. Both of you, move your right foot forward—feel your body turn to the left? Now move it back—feel your body turn back to the right? It's simple geometry."

Next, we worked on defense, starting with defensive position, a half-squat, which he made us hold while he talked. It was murder on the thighs. He taught us to slide laterally, always picturing beating the dribbler to a spot we chose, so he would have to pick up his dribble. Finally, he had one of us take the ball and try to drive past the defender, whose job it was to make the dribbler pick up his dribble without fouling him. We kept score, one point for each successful drive, and one point for each time the drive was stopped without committing a foul. Our goal was to have more points for the defense than the offense.

Both Toby and I were exhausted as we walked home.

"Well, how did it go?" Dad asked during dinner.

"It was amazing," I said, and described what we had worked on, including all the time we spent on visualization. "I never knew there was so much to it. I thought you just shot the ball."

I was pretty dragged out after dinner, feeling like I could hardly hold on for prayer time. As soon as we went outside after chores, however, I managed to rally, demonstrating my newfound basketball techniques to John and Michael. It was a powerful feeling, coaching, wanting to impart knowledge, wanting to help my brothers learn what I had learned. Teaching them was almost as much fun as learning it myself.

I was exhausted by bedtime. I started my extra rosary, but fell asleep mid-Hail Mary, early in the first decade. I woke up horror-struck sometime later. *Holy Mary, Mother of God.* Alarmed, I shook my head and started the Hail Mary over from the beginning. Moments later, I caught myself coming back from sleep again. I sat up in bed and continued through the first decade, then woke to find myself slumped against the wall. Finally, I got quietly out of bed and paced the room barefoot. It was the only way I could stay awake long enough to give the Poor Souls their due, and I certainly owed it to the sorry bastards, since it was obvious that they were holding up their end of the bargain.

44.
FR. JIM

June 10. John and I were continuing to get up early every morning to serve 6:30 Mass.

As we finished pulling our starched white cotton surplices over our heads, we hurried through the narrow passage that ran behind the altar and connected the servers' robing room with the sacristy. High overhead, the stained-glass window depicted the Holy Ghost descending in the form of a dove, incidentally casting red, blue and gold shadows on the walls below. As we emerged into the incense-permeated sacristy, we screeched to a halt in front of a stranger in a black cassock, who looked at us with a bemused expression. He was of average height with longish sandy hair, blue eyes and a very boyish face.

"Hi, boys. I'm Fr. Curran, but you can call me Fr. Jim," he said, extending his right hand.

"Hi, Father," we said, relieved by his friendliness, then introduced ourselves and shook hands with him.

"I'm the new Associate Pastor here," he said. "Monsignor Reiser let me take the early Mass, since I like to get an early start." *I'll bet. That was certainly big of the lazy jerk.*

"He told me you boys were sort of last-minute, but he said you'd show up," he continued, with a twinkle in his eye. "I'm sort of last-minute myself, so we ought to get along fine. Now, if you boys will fill the cruets and light the candles, we can get started, and then you boys can get on with your day."

"Yes, Father," we said, hopping to it.

"Ready," we answered minutes later, coming back into the sacristy and following Fr. Jim to the three *prie dieux,* where we knelt and said the Prayer Before Mass.

I spent most of the Mass watching Fr. Jim and wondering if this was my opportunity to talk to a relative stranger about my little problem, including my plan to fulfill my First Friday devotions. I was certainly desperate enough. I had a solution in mind, but I needed a priest who would agree to act as my co-conspirator. P.J. was out of the question—I hated his guts for a bunch of reasons. First, because he thought he was so superior, while I thought he was just a big jerk; and, second, I couldn't trust any person who thought that dogs couldn't go to Heaven, no matter how good they were—any fool knew better than that, and if P.J. didn't, then he wasn't just any fool—he was an extreme case. Third, fourth, fifth, and sixth, I suspected him of having murdered Tom, and maybe he was also a child molester, plus I knew he was in league with the mobsters, and I thought there was a good possibility that he would try to kill me, too, for any of a number of reasons, either because I was on to him or maybe even to save my immortal soul, so basically I just didn't trust him as far as I could throw him.

By the time we got to the Agnus Dei, I had decided that this was my chance, perhaps my only chance, the miracle I needed. I decided to risk it. Fr. Jim might be an angel of mercy, sent to me by God. *The Lord works in mysterious ways.*

After Mass, John and I were taking off our robes when I suddenly blurted out, "Oh, right!" while snapping my fingers, as if I had just remembered something. John looked at me quizzically.

"Don't wait for me," I told him. "I'll be home in a few minutes. I want to ask Father something." John stared at me inquiringly, but I just stared back at him blankly. He shrugged.

"Okay," he said. "See you later," and he was gone.

I ran back through the corridor to the sacristy. Fr. Jim was alone. "Father," I asked, "can I talk to you for a minute? I mean," I said, remembering my brilliant idea to ensure that our conversation was covered by the Seal of the Confessional, "can you hear my Confession?"

"Sure," he said. "What's on your mind?" Done. Our talk could never be divulged, even if he were tortured.

"Father," I began, "do you know about the First Fridays?" I asked.

"Sure," he said, "why? Are you making the First Fridays?"

"I think so," I said. "I'd like to. But I have a problem. I'm not sure I can make nine in a row."

"Afraid you'll oversleep?" he asked, deadpan, but I swear I thought I saw just the hint of a twinkle in his eye. "Want me to call you?" he offered, helpfully.

"No, it's not that," I said. "It's just that Confession is such a long time before Friday, and I'm afraid I might not always be able to go to Holy Communion."

"Oh, you mean, you might forget to fast after midnight," he said.

"No, that's not exactly the problem," I said, uncomfortable at having to spell it out for him.

"Oh," he said. "I see. Well. Couldn't you just behave?" he asked, actually smiling.

"I try to, Father, I really do, but I'm not always able to," I said.

"I know what you mean," he said, laughing. "That devil is a tricky one, isn't he?" I just nodded ruefully.

"I'll tell you what," he said. "I'll hear your Confession every First Friday before Mass, just in case," he said. "That way, you can just plan to be here, and you'll be able to keep the First Fridays."

"Thank you, Father," I said. *Thank you, thank you, thank you! This man is a prince! And thank you, God, for sending him to us and for sending me this means of salvation!*

"But you need to do something for me, too," he said.

"Okay," I said, "what?"

"You'll need to serve early Mass every First Friday," he said. "Do we have a deal?"

"Yes, sir!" After all, I was going to be up anyway. "I mean, yes, Father! Thank you!" Then a thought occurred to me. "But what if Fr. Reiser has the early Mass that day?" I asked.

"Don't worry," he said. "I'll ask for it now, and we'll put them all on the Mass calendar."

"Thank you!" I said again.

"That's what I'm here for," he said.

I ran almost all the way home, laughing hysterically, until I was so out of breath I had to stop and walk.

"Where were you?" John asked.

"I'm going to make the First Fridays," I said, "and I'm going to serve Mass on each First Friday."

"You're nuts," said the Knight of the Altar. I wasn't surprised. I was always more spiritually oriented than he was, even though that wasn't saying much. He was a great concrete thinker, but he seemed to have an aversion to some of the metaphysical stuff. I never gave up hope for him, though, always trying to encourage him to elevate his ruminations from the physical world to things of a higher realm, even though trying to talk to him about those things was invariably an exercise in patience.

"No, it's okay," I said. "And he said I could go to Confession before Mass each First Friday."

"Really?" he said, surprised. I could see the concept of Eternal Salvation dawning in his disused brain—at least he could think that far. I saw his face screw up with the effort of abstract thought, and then watched him come to some sort of resolution. *This should be good.*

"I think I'll just wait 'til Saturday afternoon," he said. Either he didn't have my problems, or he didn't give them much thought. I looked at his eyes for some spark of a clue—nothing—maybe he didn't have one either.

After chores, I took the morning shift in Overlook Oak. It was a spectacular morning in June. The birds, who had quieted as I climbed up to my post, gradually resumed ignoring me, swooping through the limbs of the great oak tree, and calling to one another in their many voices. I identified robins and crows, titmice and cardinals, nuthatches, and several species of woodpeckers, including the gigantic, prehistoric-looking pileated.

I could hear a radio playing through the open window of the rectory. About 10:00 a.m., the garage door suddenly opened. Moments later, P.J. came outside, got into his car, and drove away. Since I didn't know how long he would be gone, I resisted the temptation to go inside his house. However, I reasoned that as long as I stayed outside, I should hear his car start to labor up the steep road in time to make it safely back to the fissure before he reached the top. Excited, I ran back down the Tree Ramp and along Hidden Path to the fissure, then scampered through the woods across the top of the bluff. I paused and listened before I walked out of the woods into his yard, then crept over to the front of his house. My ears on high alert, I stopped and looked out toward the edge of the bluff and Overlook Oak, trying to envision the quick getaway route we needed before we could risk going inside.

Nothing obvious occurred to me. Somewhat deflated, and feeling the heebie-jeebies about his returning any moment, I hurried silently back across the yard and into the woods, returning to my post in the treehouse. P.J. returned before noon.

That afternoon, Toby and I dribbled our basketballs all the way over to Mr. Hedges' house, using only our left hands, per instructions from Mr. Hedges. At irregular intervals, either of us would yell "Ball," and we would pass our basketballs to one another simultaneously. I bounce-passed to him the first time, and he bounce-passed the next time, so that our balls wouldn't collide midair, and after that, we alternated. The goal was to pass the ball to one another right on target, which meant immediately in front of the recipient's chest.

I wondered what else Mr. Hedges could possibly teach us. I had cut out the Mississippi Hills Basketball Camp advertisement and put it in my pocket to show him.

"Can you teach us the 'pick-and-roll' and the 'give-and-go'?" I asked when we arrived at his court.

"Sure can," he said, "and I will. But you're not ready for that yet. Today we'll work on zone defense, but first we're going to review your free throw method. So let's get you warmed up. Here's a couple of jump ropes. Give me sixty seconds. Then you boys can shoot around for a couple of minutes, then we'll shoot thirty apiece."

Several minutes later, we toed the line and began our thirty. He talked us through the first five, then left us on our own. After our pushups, we worked on zone defense. He taught us to keep our hands up always, sliding laterally as the ball moved around the perimeter. He brought out a box of bean bags which he held in his left arm, reaching in with his right hand and tossing them to various parts of the court, and teaching us which zone we should cover, depending on the location of the "ball."

Afterwards, we shot another thirty free throws and did our pushups, then moved on to dribbling drills, pivoting with our dribble as we traced the lines on the court.

"Too high, Toby," he said. "Bring the ball down. Just because you're tall doesn't mean you can't dribble. You can dribble as well as anybody else—you just need to learn how to do it and then practice it. Don't dribble the ball that far out in front of you unless you're racing from one end of the court to the other. Keep the ball close beside you, in front of your hip bone, where your hand naturally rests when you lean forward. That way, you can defend the ball with your body. You can pull it back in a hurry, even behind you if you need to, where the defense has to foul you to reach the ball. And when he gets too close to you, it's easier to drive past him, because all you have to do is put your left foot beside his left foot, and he's beat—you can dribble by him with your right hand, and there's nothing he can do about it," demonstrating with his body next to Toby.

"Or if you're dribbling with your left hand, and he gets too close, all you have to do is put your right foot next to his right foot, and he's beat—you can dribble right past him with your left hand. Try it. Toby, you dribble. Jamie, you get in defensive position—now get too close to him. Slow motion—watch his foot. Do it, Toby."

He had each of us use each hand, driving past the other in slow motion.

"Okay, now you're going to run the length of the court, using only your left hand, then cross over to your right hand as you turn, cross over to your left again, then return the length of the court using just your left hand."

We did.

"That was one. I need ten," he said.

Ten minutes later, we stood on the end line nearest the house, huffing and puffing.

"Now we're going to do the same thing again, but this time as fast as you can go without losing the ball. Fast means you're going to have to push the ball out in front of you. You lose the ball, you owe me ten, on your fingertips. Jamie, you're a point guard—you'll owe me twenty. On the end line, both of you. Ready? Go!"

I was way out in front of Toby, but to my surprise, he only lost the ball three times in ten trips. I lost it once, and I was mad and embarrassed about it.

"Pretty good, gentlemen, pretty good. Now, I'm going to show you boys something, and it's going to surprise you. This is a professional ball player's secret," he said, extracting a tin of Vaseline from his pocket. "Dip your fingers in here—get a big wad. Now, rub it into your hands. Wipe the excess off on the lip of the jar here," he said, handing it over. "Then we'll just let it soak in while you do your pushups. Supine position, count them out loud. Perfect form. Chest touches the ground, or you'll do two extra for every time it doesn't. I'm watching. Go."

When we got up we had grit stuck to our hands. He tossed us a faded towel. "Now rub that gunk off, all of it. Get in between your fingers." He waited while we cleaned our hands off.

"Shake," he said. We did. "Still too much. Clean 'em off completely. Rub them. Get all that gunk off—100%." We did.

"Now, pick up a ball." We did.

"Feels good, right? Vaseline gives you a better touch on the ball—it seals the moisture in. It plumps up your skin. It makes your fingerprints fatter. Plumping up your fingerprints makes you a better ball handler, a better passer, a better shooter. Each of you needs to ask your mom for a couple of old oven mitts. Every night right before you go to bed you put Vaseline on your hands and just let it soak in overnight. Tape the mitts around your wrists so you won't ruin your bedclothes. And wash your ball off before you come over here. Make sure it's completely dry before you let it touch the ground."

"Okay, let's dribble again, the length of the court, doing crossover dribbles the entire way."

And on and on it went. Finally, we shot thirty more before he let us go, talking us through only the first one.

"Okay, boys, tomorrow we work on man-to-man defense. Each day we'll review everything we've worked on so far, so as we go on, it will become more difficult to fit it all in, but I have faith in you boys, that you want to learn and that you will hustle from one drill to the next while you're here. Okay, your pushups. Hit it. Out loud."

"Thank you, Mr. Hedges," we said as we left. Our wrists were sore, and we were tired all the way down to our fingertips.

That night, as I lay in bed with a couple of old oven mitts taped on, right after my rosary for the benefit of the Poor Souls, it occurred to me fleetingly that Mr. Hedges might contribute to my salvation in more ways than one. *The Lord truly does work in mysterious ways.* And then I was asleep.

45.
RICHARD'S THEORY

"I gotta tell you guys some stuff," Richard whispered the next afternoon as he stepped onto the treehouse floor from its primary access limb. His eyes were gleaming with excitement.

"What is it?" It was obvious that he was about to burst. Toby and I just looked at each other.

"Guys," Richard said, "remember that article about the sinking of the *Flying Eagle* that those two mobsters looked up in the library? And they lied to the librarian and told her they were looking for some Civil War history? And we didn't know what was so special about the *Flying Eagle*? And I thought they were after some kind of treasure?"

"Yeah," Toby and I said.

"Well, I've been doing some research, and I found out some stuff about the *Flying Eagle*, and maybe more important, what was going on at the time."

"What do you mean?" I asked.

"I think it may have been carrying stolen Confederate gold."

"What!?" Toby asked, a little too loudly.

"Shhh. Listen to this," Richard said. "The '*Flying Eagle*' exploded on April 15, 1865. That was the very end of the Civil War. The formal surrender agreement was signed six days before that, when General

Grant defeated Robert E. Lee in the Battle of Appomattox Courthouse. But the writing was already on the wall before that time."

"One week before the battle, so two weeks before the explosion," Richard said, raising two fingers as he continued, "General Robert E. Lee sent an emergency message to Jefferson Davis, the Confederate President. It was hand-delivered to him during a church service in Richmond, Virginia, the Confederate capital. In the message, Robert E. Lee told President Jefferson Davis that Richmond was going to fall and that he needed to get out immediately. On that very night, Jefferson Davis left Richmond by train with two private railroad cars. He and his family rode in one. The other car contained the entire Confederate treasury, which Union officials claimed amounted to between *eleven and thirteen million dollars in gold and silver bullion and coins*—although the Confederates later tried to claim it was only worth half a million dollars.

"But either way," Richard resumed, "it was a fortune in gold and silver. And what they also took with them, which is not disputed by anyone, was an *additional $450,000 in gold* owned by the Richmond banks, which was entrusted to President Jefferson Davis to keep safe for them, since they knew the Yankees were coming. But when Jefferson Davis was arrested by Union troops a month later, all that gold and silver was gone—vanished into thin air—according to official U.S. Government accounts."

We stood looking at him, excited by the story, but not at all sure what this had to do with P.J. or Tom or the mobsters.

Finally, Toby asked him. "So what does that have to do with today, with Tom and us?"

"Maybe nothing," Richard said, "but some historians claim that a large portion of that gold ended up in Memphis, which was controlled by the Union at the time, as was the entire Mississippi River. And a whole string of circumstances indicates that may have been true. For one thing, several Memphis families went suddenly from rags to riches, which, at the end of the Civil War, in the South, is a miracle in itself. And Gen. Robert E. Lee's own *aide de camp*, a Lt. Benjamin Henry, showed up at his family farm outside Memphis on April 10, six days after the treasure train left Richmond, with two other Confederate officers. They picked up some clothes, and vanished, and were never heard from again, according to the deathbed statement of Lt. Henry's nephew. Also, two of Jefferson Davis' cabinet ministers confirmed that a certain rumor about that gold was true, and one of those was a statement made on his deathbed."

"What rumor?" I asked.

"That the treasure was loaded on board a riverboat heading north from Memphis on the night of April 11."

We both stared at Richard, wondering how he could have possibly learned these things and also wondering what that meant for Tom and us and Fr. Reiser and the mobsters—he was way ahead of us.

"But what makes you think it was the *Flying Eagle*?" Toby asked.

"Several things. One, the *Flying Eagle* left Memphis on the night of April 11, 1865, carrying one hundred seventy soldiers, all of whom disembarked at St. Louis on April 13, everyone on board except the crew and three other men described as Union officers. I think those 'Union officers' were actually Lt. Benjamin Henry and his two men.

"And instead of turning around at St. Louis and heading back south, where every other boat on the Mississippi was headed, because there was big money to be made—the federal government was paying boat captains by the head to haul soldiers back up north, including men who had been in Confederate POW camps. But instead of heading south and getting in on the bonanza, the *Flying Eagle* continued upriver, supposedly with no cargo, and only a skeleton crew, against the current, during a spring flood. It made a wood stop at 10:00 p.m. on April 14 at Cottonwood Point, and then continued north for less than two hours, then blew itself to smithereens just after midnight, supposedly killing everyone on board. The bodies of the crew were ultimately found, but the Union officers were never found.

"And guess what Lt. Henry's military background was?" Richard asked.

"Demolition?" Toby suggested.

"Close. Torpedo warfare against Union shipping. Oh, I forgot to mention: a favorite technique of Confederate saboteurs along the Mississippi in those days was to insert explosives inside the firewood used as fuel on the riverboats, and then load it on board during wood stops. Those three men probably helped load the wood and then told the captain they had family in the area and would be getting off, maybe even made arrangements to be picked up again on the way downriver, knowing that would never happen."

"Holy cow, man, you've done your homework on this," I said.

"You sound like a history nut, Richard," Toby said.

"And there are several really interesting facts about the wreck of the *Flying Eagle*," Richard continued. "First, to this day, the wreck has never been found. It sank just below the railroad bridge in really deep water. The current scours out the river bottom around the bridge pier, because the water has to accelerate as it's squeezed into a smaller area going around the pier. Well, part of the acceleration is down into the riverbed, so over time, the current digs a deep hole on the downstream side of a bridge pier. You can see the same phenomenon if you wade around a pier in a shallow river. So that makes it very difficult to salvage: deep water and fast current.

"Second, the cause of the explosion was never determined. The only thing we know about it is the boat had just made a wood stop. It exploded with enough force to kill the entire crew. The explosion was really loud, and the boat was completely engulfed in flames immediately."

"Also, the fact that the bodies of the three supposed 'Union officers' were never found. And I haven't been able to find their names listed anywhere—I don't think they were known, and they weren't listed as passengers on the ship's log. There was nothing in the Mayfly Courier-Post, and there were so many deaths at the time, and so many missing: soldiers on both sides, civilians, eighty thousand slaves dead, so apparently no one was able to narrow down who those officers were."

"Talking about treasure is great," Toby said, "and I'm interested in it, but we've got other problems, too—we've gotta figure out what happened to Tom, because nobody else is gonna do it."

Richard and I quickly agreed.

"But it may all be connected," Richard said.

"Maybe so," I agreed, "but I can't imagine how."

That night, I lay in bed amazed and confused. I could easily imagine that the mobsters were looking for the *Flying Eagle* treasure left by Confederate river pirates disguised as Yankee officers, but what I couldn't figure out was why Tom had died and what P.J. was looking for in his pockets—or what the mobsters were looking for either. Also, I wanted to help Toby figure out what happened to his brother, and I wanted to help Tom get to Heaven as soon as he could, but I also had chores to do every day, and right then I owed the Poor Souls in Purgatory an entire rosary before I went to sleep, and I needed to spend some serious time practicing basketball—the Poor Souls couldn't do it all on their own.

46.
THE VISITOR

"I think I hear him," Toby said the following afternoon, craning his neck over the side of the treehouse in Overlook Oak and checking the Hidden Path. Sure enough, Richard was heading toward Tree Ramp, and he was carrying something in his hand. He passed by the ramp, however, and motioned for us to let down the net, which we did. We watched as he placed an item in the net and wrapped the rope around it twice before giving it a jerk, our signal to start pulling. The object in the net was incredibly light. As we pulled, we watched from above as Richard ran up Tree Ramp, standing upright. We had all grown much more surefooted and confident in our ability to run Tree Ramp, nearly oblivious by now to the abyss which yawned a hundred-fifty feet below it.

"I got it," Richard whispered, as he climbed out onto the main limb leading to the treehouse.

"Shhh," Toby said. "There's somebody in there with him."

"Who?" Richard asked. "There's no other cars here."

"No idea," Toby said.

"Some kid," I said. "We don't know who it is. He just came out of the woods, knocked on the door, and walked right in. He's obviously been here before."

Joseph Welch

We all knelt there and watched, our elbows resting on the front shelf, passing the binoculars back and forth between us, looking at the backs of their heads through the window. They were sitting close together.

"So what do you have?" I asked Richard.

"Look at this beauty," Richard said, untying the rope which surrounded the net and extracting a big, industrial-looking slingshot. It was seriously heavy-duty, complete with a black handle indented with finger grips and a brace that rested on your forearm. Instead of rubber bands, it had huge rubber tubes, a quarter of an inch thick in diameter.

Toby whispered a whistle.

"A hunting slingshot," I breathed, admiringly. "Where did you get it?"

"PD Liquor," Richard said, "the one I saw in the window. $2.45 plus 14¢ tax, and 99¢ for 500 BBs in a cardboard cylinder. You should see all the cool knives they have in there, even long banana knives for 99¢."

"That's where we bought Dad's beer for Father's Day," I said.

"What do you mean?" Richard said. "You can't buy beer—you have to be twenty-one."

"Really?" I said. "I didn't know that. It must be okay if you're buying it for your dad. We just walked in and said we needed a case of beer and he asked what we were gonna do with it and we told him it was for Dad for Father's Day, so he just went and got one. Cost $2.21 with tax."

"Anyway," Richard said, "I've been thinking about using the slingshot up here when there's nobody at the rectory."

"Good idea," Toby said. "Bet we could launch an M-80 to the middle of the river with that thing."

"Yeah," I said, "and the fuse will keep burning, even under water. But we better not. Lots of people will hear it, including P.J. No sense giving ourselves away."

"Oh, forgot to mention," Toby said, "I brought my dad's old zippo lighter and a can of lighter fluid, and also a candle, in case we ever need it. And I brought a couple of punks, too. I put 'em in the ammo box with the M-80s. "If you guys want, we can borrow a rowboat some day and take them over to one of the islands and shoot them off there. We'll be out of Missouri and nobody will care."

"He's leaving," I said, grabbing the binoculars and peering through them at a little kid with curly blonde hair wearing glasses who had just exited the front door. I passed the binoculars to Toby.

"I've seen that kid before," Toby said, "but I'm not sure where. He's a chubby little dork. Real girly. He's got a candy bar, too," he said, passing the glasses to Richard. "Geez! Have you ever seen a more clueless lookin' little dunce? I wonder if he knows his way home."

"Oh, that's Sidney Armani," Richard said, peering through the glasses. "He lives with his mom on a farm just south of here. He's three years younger than us."

"There's somethin' funny goin' on there," I said. "What is that kid doing there and why is P.J. giving him a candy bar? He's not cutting his grass, or washing his car, or painting his house, or doing any work at all that I can see."

"Yeah, weird," Toby said.

"Listen, you guys," Richard said, "we have lots of issues on our list that we haven't investigated yet. We need to spend more time on this. Can you guys stay late?"

Toby and I looked at each other. Both of us felt strangely guilty, even though we hadn't been trying to keep our basketball coaching a secret from Richard—we just hadn't had the right opportunity to go into it. Because basketball wasn't actually very important to Richard, even though he was a decent player. There were just lots of other things he would rather do, like go to the library.

I hadn't told anyone else about my goal to win the Future Famer trophy. Well, okay, my brothers, and my dad, and Mary Ann Ventura, but even she didn't know about all the extra coaching I was getting from Mr. Hedges. I had wanted it to be a secret, to surprise people, and Toby was okay with that. The way he was going, he was gonna surprise some people, too. But Richard was a good friend, a close friend, a person I could count on, a confidant. We were both going to tell him anyway; we just hadn't done it yet. The entire thing was so fluid, we didn't even know what to tell him.

"Toby and I have an appointment to play basketball," I said, then told him about Mr. Hedges and how my goal was to win the Future Famer trophy.

"We've been meaning to tell you anyway," I said, "but we've all been busy doing other things. This is just our third day with Mr. Hedges." I didn't make him swear to keep it a secret, but I did say, "But please don't tell anyone, okay? We want it to be a surprise." Richard was fine with that—it wasn't a big deal to him.

"Great, no problem," he said. "I need to spend some time at the library anyway. I'm trying to find out what I can about my people."

I didn't know what he meant by "my people."

"Like what?" Toby asked—I don't think he did, either.

"Like anything," Richard said. "I don't know anything about them. You guys have family photos and diplomas and stuff on your walls, and albums filled with snapshots and even some furniture from your great-grandparents. I don't. I don't have anything like that. I've got one picture of my dad in his army uniform and I've got his medals and my mom's high school graduation picture and a picture of their wedding and that's it—nothing about my ancestors. I don't have any family heirlooms or even family history, except what my Mom and Aunt can remember—and they don't know much.

"My great-grandparents were slaves. There are no old family photos, nothing. We have a family Bible with their names in it and their dates of birth and wedding dates, and their children's names, and that's it. I don't even know where they lived, or what they did or what they liked to do, and I thought I'd go through the census records and see what I can find out. Because basically the only thing I have that proves they were ever even alive is me.

"And I want to feel like they were real, like they actually lived. I want to know where they spent their time and what they did. I want to feel some sort of connection with them. I want to be able to look at something, anything, and say, 'My great-granddaddy was here—he was actually here.'"

Toby and I were silent, thinking.

"Is there anything we can help with?" Toby asked, finally. "I'll help you with anything I can. You help us all the time."

"Yeah, you're really great on research," I said, "but what can we do to help you?"

"I can't think of anything right now," Richard said, "but if I do, I'll let you know."

"Why don't you head on over to the library and work there?" I said. "Toby and I can cover here, and Michael and John are on duty later, so we'll still get to basketball practice on time."

"Okay, good idea—will do," Richard said. "You guys are good friends. Thank you."

"We need to go see Ms. Mame," I said after Richard left, "and see if she can help him at all."

"I was just thinking the same thing," Toby said.

Before mid-afternoon, the treehouse in Overlook Oak was graced by the attendance of the Knight of the Altar and The Archangel. Toby and I filled them in quickly, and then left for basketball practice.

Practice was good. My shot was starting to groove rapidly. I was now hitting in the low 70 percents regularly, and Toby lagged just a hair behind, sometimes even beating me, which was unheard of prior to Mr. Hedges. After our daily fast-twitch rope-jumping warmup and shooting, we did ten minutes of intensive dribbling drills. He ran alongside us during the drills, and every time we let the ball get too far away from us his arm snaked out and knocked it away.

"Keep the ball in close to you, close to your hip bone."

Next, we worked on man-to-man defense, digging and sliding, trying to beat the dribbler to a spot, keeping score, offense *versus* defense. Then he used the bean bags to simulate passing the ball around the floor while he taught us to sink away from our invisible man, in towards the lane, when the ball was on the other side of the floor.

He taught us to set screens, dribbling the ball himself while Toby guarded him and I came up alongside Toby to set a screen for the dribbler. Then we switched places, so each of us got to practice setting a screen, and also how to get past a screen that had been set on us. He showed us how to use a screen twice in quick succession to "wrong foot" a defender who went behind it, rubbing the defender off on the screen to create open space to shoot or drive to the basket.

Summer of '63

"If you can bring two more players tomorrow," he said, "we can work on how to switch when someone sets a screen on you." *Michael and John.*

47.
RICHARD HAILED

"What's she like?" Richard asked the following afternoon.

"Different," I said, "but nice."

Toby and I had talked Richard into coming with us to visit Ms. Mame, ostensibly so we could talk to her about what had happened in the graveyard the night of Tom's funeral, but also because we wanted to see if she could tell Richard anything about his ancestors. I had been to her apartment above Little Africa by myself to ask if we could drop by, and also to tell her a little bit about Richard. As we approached Little Africa in the late morning heat, there was only one bleary-eyed man in a sleeveless white undershirt on lookout duty, squatting on the sidewalk with his back braced against the brick front of the building.

"Morning," I said, as I passed him and turned into the doorway. He nodded back to me suspiciously, his eyes moving to Toby and then to Richard as they stepped across the threshold into the open doorway. We moved across the wooden plank floor, inhaling the scent of dance wax and wood and beer as four dark heads at the bar swiveled to look curiously at us. The bartender looked up and nodded as I waved at him, then resumed polishing the bar with a cloth. His head jerked up suddenly and he paused his polishing as Richard moved into the halo of light cast by the overhead fixture.

"Hey, boy!" he said, "aren't you young Washin'ton?"

"Yessir," Richard said. The bartender nodded.

"Y'all better go on upstairs," he said, pointing. "Ms. Mame's been waitin' on you. Y'all know the way," he said, nodding toward Toby and me.

"Yessir," I said.

"Thank you, sir," Toby and Richard said together, and followed me to the end of the long room and up the set of wooden stairs. I paused at the top and waited for Toby and Richard to catch up. We could hear humming and muttering, accompanied by a dry rattling sound from the other side of the door, which stopped as soon as I knocked.

"It's Jamie Fletcher, Ms. Mame," I called through the door, "with Toby Piper and Richard Washington."

"Come in, boys," she said, her voice musical.

A strong, sweet odor assailed my nostrils as I opened the door. Sunlight streamed in a broad swath of light through the single open window behind Ms. Mame, illuminating dust particles swimming in the foggy air. Ms. Mame was seated at the table facing away from us and dealing cards onto the tabletop, but as we entered the room, she slid her chair back and turned to face us.

A white cotton turban wrapped around her head and tied in the front. Her dress was a dark blue African print splashed with large white fields that were encircled with viny tendrils surrounding a single brown serpent. Her dress bared most of both shoulders, and I saw for the first time a series of bright white dots, outlined with shiny black circles, running from her shoulders in graceful arcs down toward her chest, where the pattern disappeared under the material of her dress.

She wore an ornate necklace, fine strands of white coral twigs strung in multiple tiers, with tiny amber beads decorating the coral tips. Her earrings, fashioned of the same coral and amber, dangled several inches below their mountings on large ornate silver posts.

This was the third time I had seen Ms. Mame, and I was again struck by the beauty of her face, her high cheekbones, taut skin, and dark eyes. She smiled graciously at us.

I saw a movement on the table and turned to see a live snake, small and mottled brown, moving across the table. Pharoah watched it out of one eye from the back of a chair, his head tilted sideways.

"Well, good mo'nin', boys," she said. "Ah been wonderin' when ah maht see y'all again, and I see you brought a frien'. So you're young Washin'ton," she said, turning toward Richard and holding her hands out. He took them in both of his, while she gazed calmly into his face.

"Ah knew yo' people," she said. "Ah knew yo' great-grandpappy, Elijah. Used to come in here alla time after Janey passed. He was a god-fearin' man, though. Wouldn't have no truck wid no women—an' he could have. Lived to be 93." She let go of his hands and turned to Toby.

"And Toby," she said, coming to stand right in front of him, "did you watch yo' brotha's grave? At midnight?"

"Yes, ma'am," Toby managed, looking at her, his adam's apple stuck halfway up his throat.

"Well, what did you see?" she asked. Toby described seeing the man at Tom's grave by the light of the lightning strike.

"And you sho' he not yo' brotha?" she asked. I had the feeling she knew, but she just wanted to make sure Toby knew, too.

"Positive," Toby said.

"Ah knew it," she said. "Ah tol' you, didn't I? Did you see who it was?"

"No, ma'am—I didn't know him," Toby said, "and he was leaving."

"Good," Ms. Mame said. "That Papa Legba. You don' wanna mess wid him when he be talkin' to Bonye. Ah seen him again, Toby," she said, looking at him meaningfully.

"Who?" Toby asked, confused.

"Yo' brotha. In a dream. He be waitin.'"

"Waiting for what, ma'am?" Toby asked, alarmed, pleading.

"Don't know," she said. "No way *ah* can tell. Might be waitin' fo' you. But ah *can* tell you one thing—fo' sho'—he don't be waitin' in no hellfahr."

Toby's mouth and eyes flew open. "Are you sure?" he asked, reaching out to her with both hands. "How can you be sure?" he asked, taking both her hands in his, pleading with her. "Are you absolutely sure?"

"Yes, young man, ah is *absolutely* sure."

None of us were prepared for what happened next. There was a sound, an unearthly sound, a sound I had never heard before, and I didn't know what it meant or even where it came from, halfway between a cry and a moan, and Toby fell onto his knees, still holding her hands, and sobbing. Actually sobbing.

"Thank you, thank you, Ms. Mame," he said, crying, "oh, thank you," letting go of her hands, his shoulders shuddering and his back heaving as he continued to sob, hands on his thighs, his tears falling onto the dusty floor in front of his knees.

"There, there, chil'; it's alright; you love yo brotha, ah understand; it's alright now, Ms. Mame said, her voice musical, stroking his hair until he quieted. I glanced at Richard, who was looking at me. We nodded to each other, and stepped forward together, took Toby under the arms, and helped him up. He sniffed, then wiped his eyes. Oddly enough, Richard and I were not embarrassed for him at all—we all felt enormous relief to know that our friend was not condemned to Hell; Toby's relief was completely understandable—we all felt it.

"Ms. Mame," he said when he was again in control, "I know you can't tell me what he's waitin' for, but is there anything I can do...we can do, to help him?"

"Ah'm sorry," she said, "ah don' know nothin' 'bout that, but ah kin guess, is all. Ah might be right, and ah might not be. Ah might not even see the whole dream, or part of it might be buried, but ah saw him in a dream. He be in a boat," she said, nodding at Toby, "a rowboat, and the boat be tied to da sho', and he be jes' sittin' there all by hisself, waitin' fo' somebody, and the riva jes' be flowin' right on pass him, and it seem lak he jes' be waitin' fo' somebody to untie da boat so he can float on down da riva."

She paused, while the three of us stared at her, waiting. "And ah think he be waitin' on somebody to do somethin' fo' him, and mebbe that be prove he din't kill hisself, and mebbe ah'm wrong, no way to know, but that's what ah think."

The three of us looked at each other in silent resolve. Richard also had tears in his eyes.

"Thank you, Ms. Mame," I said, finally, tears in my eyes, too, when it seemed there was nothing else to say. "We're trying as hard as we can."

"Ah know you are, boys," she said. "Ah know you are. Good luck to you boys. Let me know if ah can help you."

"Oh, Ms. Mame," Toby said, "you've helped us more than you know."

"Oh, ah think ah know. Ah got *reg lar* eyes, too," she said, smiling. "And Richard Washin'ton," she said, turning to Richard, "I saw yo' great-grandpappy, Elijah."

"You told me that," Richard said. "I never knew him."

"No, ah mean ah saw him in a dream—a new dream. He be holdin' a Bahble. And he open it, jes' the cover, and he showed it to me. And there was writin' on it."

"What kind of writing?" Richard asked, but I could tell he was skeptical.

"Messy writin'; like it be done with a piece o' charcoal. The letters wasn't straight." Richard suddenly looked interested.

"But ah could read what it say," Ms. Mame continued.

"What did it say?" Richard asked, suddenly very interested.

"It said, 'You see yo' truth when the groun' be open fo' you.'"

Richard just stared at her, trying to comprehend what that meant. "You'll see your truth..." he repeated....

"'When the groun' be open fo' you,'" she finished for him.

Richard was still, silent, his eyes fixed on her, but his focus was far away, off in the distance, searching back in the years, trying to carve out a slice from the infinite reach of time, looking for the great-grandfather he had never known, nor even seen a picture of.

"But what does it mean?" he asked, finally.

"Ah don't know *what* it mean, boy, but I bet you fi'n to fahnd out," Ms. Mame said.

"I'm not sure what she was telling me," Richard said as we walked home, "when the ground is opened. Does she mean my grave? Do I have to wait 'til I die to see whatever it is—the truth? I'm not sure I want to see it that bad. Besides, aren't we all gonna see the truth when we die?"

"Richard," I said, "I'm really sorry, but I have no idea what she meant by that."

"I'm not sure she did either," Toby said. The three of us continued walking in silence, trying to deal with one more puzzle.

48.
TURTLE ISLAND

It was Sunday morning, the air was fresh, the day gravid with possibility, and the horizons endless. We three Musketeers were delirious with the vastness of boyhood freedom on the Mississippi River. Flushed with excitement, I felt like I could see most of the way to New Orleans.

"Let me row for a while," Toby said.

"In a minute; let me get past the next buoy, then you can have it," I said. It had taken some time for me to learn to row straight. Now I was focused on synchronizing my left arm with my right, both the angle of the oar and the length of the stroke. I was concentrating on the dip marks which showed on the face of the water as it ran out behind the stern, and trying my best to make them symmetrical.

We had all been to early Mass and were now free as larks, uncaged in time and space. The sky was a clear blue, and the sun reflected off the surface of the water, beating down on us, gathering strength as it headed toward noon. Fortunately, all of us had worn straw hats, because we knew the sun on the river was relentless. We were in a battered dark green aluminum jon boat with no motor. Toby had borrowed it from a friend of his father, who had offered to loan it to "the Piper boys" back when Tom was alive. The oars were old but functional, and the oarlocks had been replaced and were sturdy and reliable.

Our plan was to row north from the Mayfly harbor to the railroad bridge, and then "ship oars" and float downriver as far as Cottonwood Point, seeing where the current would take us. We had also brought some supplies: the zippo lighter, the big slingshot, and four M-80s. We intended to launch a couple of bombs into the stratosphere and also to find out if it were true that the fuses would continue to burn underwater.

Before we began our experimental dead float, however, we were distracted by a long sandy beach which beckoned to us from Turtle Island, a mile and a half upriver from the railroad bridge. It seemed to extend an invitation personally to us.

"Hey, guys," Richard said from the stern, "wanna check out that island first?"

I paused and turned around to eyeball the island. "Is the pope Catholic?" I asked.

"Does a bear shit in the woods?" Toby inquired from the bow. General snickering ensued—although the joke was old, the freedom to say the word "shit" out loud struck all of us as a celebration appropriate to the moment.

"Toby, can you take us up there?" I asked, standing up and relinquishing the oars to him.

After a few slipped strokes and some slight erasing of my upstream progress, Toby turned us upriver again, angling slightly east toward the island, leaning and pulling with long strokes, and learning to use his back instead of his arms. I sat in the bow, watching the small matching whirlpools caused by the oars as they slid past us into our wake. The surface of the water was glassy except when an occasional light breeze rippled it into a stippled pattern. Fish jumped around us occasionally, disturbing the reflective sheen, as Toby continued to labor, and the island grew nearer and nearer.

Finally, Toby cut across the current and headed straight in toward the beach.

"My turn," Richard said.

"Oh, let me land 'er; you can row on the way back," Toby said. When we were fifty feet out, I moved to the back and sat in the stern with Richard, which raised the bow just slightly. We took off our shoes and socks as Toby powered the boat onto the beach, then leaped off, elated, embracing the cushy warm sand with our toes.

"Gimme a hand here," Toby yelled, and we turned back to pull the boat further up onto the island, so the wake from a passing towboat wouldn't lift the boat back into the river while we were off exploring, leaving us stranded on the island.

We walked along the margin where the river lapped at the sand, pointing out the tracks left by turtles as they exited the water. The space between their footprints was punctuated by the unique endless "S" pattern made by dragging their tails in the sand, swinging it from side to side as they lumbered, left foot, right foot, left foot, up onto the beach.

Collectively drawn into the mystery of the island, we headed off, more or less together, a model of barely controlled chaos. Incense wafted off the heated leaves of millions of baby willows which grew head-high and provided thick green cover to a portion of the island, interspersed irregularly by tens of thousands of tiny cottonwoods.

Trekking through the dense young growth, we emerged suddenly upon the shore of an interior island lake, a vestige from the last flood, which remained after the river level receded several months ago. Scattered around its edges were the remnants of mussels which the great birds, with footprints larger than our own, had harvested from the shallow water. Skeletons of several large carp and billy gar lay on the bank, picked clean, their heads intact but desiccated, among scatterings of fish scales and bones. We resumed our trek toward the interior of the mile-long island, passing through a border of vines and poison ivy that edged the old-growth wetland forest. Filled with wonder, we penetrated to the interior of the island, dominated by vast cottonwoods whose canopy was so dense that virtually no vegetation grew beneath them. Here the sand was almost white.

"Look!" Toby whispered, pointing at a large western fox snake as it slithered into a rotted old stump.

"Wouldn't it be neat to stay here for a few days overnight?" Richard asked. "Maybe next summer we could plan a campout here. Stay a week, bring food and water, some fishing poles. We could catch our bait here."

"Yeah," Toby said, enthusiastically.

"Oh, yeah," I said, dreamily. "Maybe we won't be so busy next summer."

"Yeah, and some sun hats. And mosquito repellant," Richard said.

"And a tent in case it rains," Toby said. "We can build a shelter with those willow trees to keep outta the sun during the day. We'll need a hatchet."

"And some twine," I said.

"And the BB gun, and the slingshot and lots of BBs," Toby said.

"I hate to say it, boys, but we should probably get back," Richard said. "We still have to float down to Cottonwood Point, then row all the way back upriver."

"Wait! We forgot to check out the M-80s," I said as we shoved off. "Let's try one with the slingshot."

Richard, who was sitting amidships because he was rowing that leg, got to hold the slingshot, since he was the one who had bought it. He slipped his left arm into the brace and grabbed the leather pouch with his right hand. I fished out an M-80 and the zippo lighter and handed them to Toby, who loaded the M-80 into the projectile pouch. When Richard had his fingers safely on the sides of the pouch and the slingshot pulled back in cocked position with the green fuse sticking straight up, Toby lit the fuse and the two of us jumped back as far as we could. Richard waited for a long second to make sure the fuse was well lit, then launched the explosive up into the blue sky high above the island. Breathless, we watched the dramatically smoking projectile trace up one side of a parabolic curve and then begin its descent toward the trees, where it exploded with an earth-shaking "BOOM!" Hundreds of birds lifted simultaneously from the island canopy, followed by a dozen great blue herons in slow motion, together with a handful of huge snowy egrets. Two seconds later, a fainter echo returned from the Illinois bluffs eleven miles away.

"Wow! They work!" Toby said.

"Since we've already scared everything away, let's see if the fuses actually burn underwater," Richard said. "Want to try another one?"

"Sure," Toby and I both said. I handed another one to Richard.

"I'm just gonna toss this one in the water as soon as the fuse is lit," Richard said. I nodded.

Once again, Toby lit the fuse and we moved away as far as the interior of the boat would allow. Richard just stared at it for a second.

"Throw it!" I said.

"Get rid of it!" Toby yelled.

Finally, Richard threw it into the water towards the shore. Nothing happened. Two seconds went by while we waited, then it exploded with a muffled "boom!" Sand and water showered down on us.

"Man!" I said. "It's really true!"

"Yeah, we got our money's worth on these!" Richard said.

"Thanks, Tom!" Toby said, looking up.

"Yeah, Tom, that was really great of you. Thanks!" I agreed.

49.
THE FLOAT

"I'm not sure exactly where we should start our float from," Richard said, "but I think we can assume the *Flying Eagle* was in the channel when it exploded, so I say we just start underneath the bridge in the center of the channel and float downstream and see where that leads us. We can use the red and green navigation lights on the bridge as the east and west boundaries of the channel and just estimate where we think the center is." Toby and I just looked at each other and shrugged. I didn't mention that it hadn't even occurred to me to wonder, and I doubt that it had to Toby, either.

"Sounds good to me," I said, after a pause sufficient in my mind to have allowed me to weigh the various alternative and competing strategies. *Whatever they were.*

We arrived at the railroad bridge, and Richard maneuvered us to what he considered to be the center of the channel span.

"I think we should start right about here," he said, shipping his oars and rubbing his hands.

Floating downstream was uneventful compared with the trip up, but by this point it was a relief to just let the current take us without having to row. We were all getting blisters, and our "soft hands" ball-handling protocol was working against Toby and me.

"We shoulda brought some water," I said.

"Yeah, and some sandwiches, too," Toby said.

"No lie," Richard agreed. "At least now all we have to do is float."

River Road ran alongside us at the foot of the bluffs as we floated south, circling lazily through small eddies caused by irregularities on the riverbed below us. A man fishing from the jetty gave us his version of the fisherman's stylized wave as we floated past the Mayfly harbor. Twenty minutes later, we had passed Castle Bluff and were in front of Lovers Leap, craning our necks up at the anvil rock which jutted out two hundred feet above us.

"I told my parents about P.J. searching Tom's pockets when I first got there, before he even knew I was there," I said, as we floated out from under the rock looming overhead. "Mom said he was probably checking to make sure Tom had a rosary in his pocket. 'He's such a spiritual man,'" I said, mimicking her voice, then miming making myself vomit.

South of the anvil rock, beneath the Riverside Cemetery bluff, we floated alongside a massive section of earth which had slid out of the side of the bluff and now rested squarely on River Road. The bluffs continued their leveling process day after day, year after year, moving down relentlessly toward the great river. The landslide was devoid of miscellaneous rocks, mud and scree—it was a single thirty-foot-tall clump of earth with a group of large trees still standing in it, vertical and undisturbed. It would take a small army with large equipment to reopen River Road, and it would not happen soon, since River Road carried almost no traffic—most people used the State Highway which ran behind the bluffs.

Thirty minutes later we could see Cottonwood Point jutting out from the Missouri shore directly downstream from us. It was a long gravel bar. Several large dead trees had been deposited on it during previous floods. One massive cottonwood extended from its enormous root ball on the gravel bar out into the river. Smaller limbs projected into the river, both above and below the surface, trapping logs, sticks, branches, leaves, and other detritus, including a large red buoy.

The current took us right up to the edge of the bar, then began to sweep us along its length. It was so swift that Richard had to pull hard on the oars to beach the boat. Even then, we couldn't make it stay. Toby jumped out as Richard bumped the bow into the gravel. I threw a rope to him and moved to the back of the boat, raising the bow slightly, and Toby pulled us in several feet. Then Richard and I got out and helped pull it further up onto the gravel.

"We're just east of that bayou where we did our reptile viewing for biology," Richard said, pointing inland to a landscape dominated by mature draping willows and cypress, as well as numerous leafless trees, many hung with strings of moss.

"I wonder what the depth is like in front of this bar," Toby said, walking to the edge and stepping into the water. He immediately vanished from sight. By the time his red hair reappeared, he had been swept twenty feet downstream. The bank was so steep that Richard and I had to help him fight his way back onto the bar, dripping and sputtering.

On the upriver edge of the bar, however, near the junction where the gravel bar extended out into the channel from the earthen riverbank, was a long stretch of shallow water. It rotated slowly in front of a small estuary that separated the gravel bar from the riverbank and fed the bayou with water.

50.
MEETING SIDNEY

"We've still got two M-80s left," Toby said. "Let's shoot 'em off down here, where we can't get in any trouble. People will just think it's the cement plant, dynamiting the hill. Okay if I try the slingshot this time, Richard?"

Minutes later, Toby had arced one into the sky over the river, and the deep, resounding "BOOM!" thundered across the water. We were still awed by the initial shock when the echo returned to us, drawn out and muffled. A minute later, I matched his trajectory with our final explosive.

"Stop it! Stop it! This is private property!" We half-turned to see a chubby young boy with glasses and blonde curly hair running directly toward us out of the center of the swamp. He was carrying a long, straight stick and appeared to have materialized from the bayou. The three of us stood there gaping, stunned that anyone would run through that snake-infested bayou—it seemed impossible. And there was something oddly familiar about him.

"Look!" Toby said, "it's that dorky little kid."

"What kid?" Richard asked.

"The one who goes to visit P.J. up in the rectory," I said.

"Hey!" I said, as the kid ran up to us. "We didn't know anybody was around here. We were just shooting off some fireworks. We came here in that boat," I said, pointing.

"I know you," he said. "You're in Sixth Grade at Immaculate Conception. Well, Seventh now, I guess—if you passed," he corrected himself.

"Right," I said. "Pretty good, kid. I'm Jamie Fletcher. This is Richard Washington and Toby Piper. We're all in the same class, and we all passed. Who are you?"

"I'm Sidney," he said. "Sidney Armani. I live here, right on the other side of the bayou."

"Oh. Sorry, Sidney. So this is your land?" I asked.

"Yeah…well, my mom's. She's at work. Her grandma left her the place when she died, but it had a big mortgage on it, and Mom wants to keep the place, so she's gotta work to pay off the mortgage. She says it's our home."

"What grade are you in?" I asked.

"Going into Fourth."

"Got any brothers or sisters?" Toby asked.

"No, just me. Well, my mom and me."

"What do you do with this land?" I asked. "You can't farm it, can you?"

"Nah, we got some acreage on the other side of the bayou that's cropland, but it floods some years—depends on how high the water gets and what time of year. This bar here is just worthless, except there's a company that wants to mine gravel off it."

"Gravel!" Richard said. "Well, there's plenty of that here. Are you gonna let 'em do it?"

"I dunno. My mom's still thinking about it," he said.

"Hey, Sidney!" I said, suddenly inspired with an idea. "This would be a really great place to play pirates—do you ever play pirates down here?"

"Nah," he said, "I got nobody to play it with."

"We like to play pirates," I said. "We could dig for treasure down here, maybe even pitch a tent and make a pirate camp. Wouldn't that be great, guys?" I asked, looking at Richard and Toby, both of whom, for just a fraction of a second, looked as if I had just lost my mind.

To my relief, Richard was quick on the uptake. "Oh, sure," he said enthusiastically, nodding.

"Yeah, that would be cool," Toby chimed in.

Sidney was still looking at me, probably picturing playing pirates with new friends, but uncertain whether he was included in our scenario.

"Okay if we play pirates down here?" I asked Sidney.

"Could I play, too?" he asked. *Poor kid—it's his place.*

"For sure!" we all said.

"We'll all have to have real pirate names," I said. "And we'll need shovels to dig for treasure. Got any shovels down here?" I asked, turning back to Sidney, "and maybe a pick?"

"Yeah," he said, "we got a buncha stuff in the barn. I can get 'em."

"What do you use that stick for, Sidney?" Toby asked.

"Oh, this?" he said, apparently forgetting he was carrying it, "this is my snake stick." *Good idea!*

Before we left that afternoon, we had set our first pirate treasure hunt for two days later at 10:00 a.m.

We all agreed to bring red bandanas. "And bring anything else piratey you can find," I said. "It'll be lots more fun if we look like real pirates. Oh, and we all need to think up a good pirate name for ourselves."

In the meantime, Sidney would help us get ready to dig for pirate treasure by bringing a pick and some shovels across the bayou and out to the sandbar.

"How did you make it through that bayou?" Toby asked Sidney. "Is there a path through there?"

"Yep, but nobody knows it 'cept me."

"Hey, Sidney," I said, "we gotta shove off. We have to row all the way back upriver before dinner. Sorry we shot off those M-80s—we didn't know there was anyone around here. Tell your Mom we're sorry, okay?"

"It's alright," Sidney said. "No harm done. I'll see you guys in two days, okay?" he said, almost desperate to confirm that we were serious, as we got into the boat and shoved off into the current.

"Poor guy," Toby said, "doesn't have anybody to play with."

"Yeah," Richard said, "seemed like a nice enough kid."

"Yeah, but what's he doing with P.J.?" Toby asked.

"You mean, what's P.J. doing to him?" I corrected.

"Guys, if we ride our bikes straight down River Road, we can get here really fast," I said, "which is gonna be important if we work it hard, and we're gonna have to work it hard every single day to have even a ghost of a chance to find that treasure before the mobsters do."

"Yeah, but River Road is blocked, remember?" Richard said. "Part of the bluff fell out and slid down on it—we'll pass by it again on the way upriver. And the only other route is fourteen miles each way because you have to go out to the highway and head south to the county road, and then come back toward the river. And there'll be traffic."

"I bet we can get through on River Road," Toby said. "I'll ride my bike down there tomorrow morning and see if there's a way through. If not, one of us will just have to walk down there and tell him it's too far away."

"Yeah, and there goes the treasure," I said. "We *better* find a way through. I'll go with you."

51.
TOOLS OF THE TRADE

The next day, Toby and I were on afternoon rectory watch duty from noon to 2:30, when Richard and brother John were scheduled to take over, so Toby and I could go on to basketball practice with Mr. Hedges.

I also had early Mass altar boy duties and then morning chores, so late morning was our only opportunity to check out River Road. Toby got up early and finished his work at the River's Rest so we could both go down River Road in the late morning. At 10:00 a.m. we headed toward the foot of Castle Bluff on our bikes. Five minutes later we were at the site of the landslide. As we approached it, we were impressed by its size—it completely blocked the road. The east side of the enormous clump of earth barely overhung the sheer fifteen-foot drop to the railroad tracks which cut into the foot of the bluff just above the river. The earth mountain loomed threateningly over us as we neared it, the top of the mound still covered with trees and vines which were largely undisturbed, a few large vines trailing up the bluff toward where they had been torn off. We stopped, dismounted, and walked around. The sides were precipitous.

"No way to climb it, that's for sure," Toby said. "And we can't get down to the railroad tracks from here unless we climb down some ropes, and we'd have to leave our bikes up here, and we'd still have to climb back up on the other side."

We walked to the bluff side of the clump and craned our necks. We could easily see the huge divot in the bluff which the clump had vacated. It was a rounded limestone bowl, the back of the bowl glistening with clear running water. Several large vines with amputated ends hung into the bowl from adjoining trees.

We examined the terrain. If we could climb up the bluff about thirty feet, we could step across the small crease where the clump rested against the side of the bluff. But no one could climb that bluff, except with a rope tied from above. And what about our bikes?

"Wonder where that water is coming from?" I asked.

"Yeah, and where it's going," Toby said.

We peeked into the dark seam where the clump jammed up against the bluff but couldn't see past the curtain of kudzu and grapevine that hung to the edge of the road. We slipped into the seam as far back as the vine curtain, which we parted, revealing a passageway about two feet wide that we could walk into. It was short, five feet tall, before the overhanging side of the dirt clump touched the bluff above our heads.

Leaving our bikes, we made our way deeper into the tunnel, stooping as we explored our way through, moving vines aside and kicking rocks into the roadside ditch which carried the hill water away. It smelled of damp earth overlaid with the fecund scents of woods and bluff: weeds and vines, ferns and mushrooms and earthworms. Even Toby could make it through.

"This is dynamite!" Toby said. "I think we can take our bikes through here."

"And completely invisible," I said.

"Hope there are no bats in here...yow!" Toby exploded, gyrating around in the confined space. "Ah! Ah! Ah!"

"What is it?" I asked, alarmed.

"Spider!" he croaked, jerking his head and arms around in the confined space. "Huge—it's on me!" he said, dancing, stooped over, shaking his head and slapping all over his body with both hands. "Watch out!" he said, turning and trying to run past me. I had no choice but to turn around and run ahead of him until we were out in the light again, where I inspected him all over. No spider that I could see.

"It was a wolf spider," he said, "as big as my hand. I didn't see him in time."

"Sorry, man," I said, "I didn't see him. He's gone now." I didn't like spiders either, but I was nowhere near as hysterical about them as Toby was. He probably got it from his mother—they made her absolutely catatonic. So did any kind of bug—even birds. It looked like it ran in the family.

When Toby had collected himself, we tried again. It was quicker this time, with the path somewhat cleared. We left the overhanging vines in place to hide the entrance. We exited at the south end and found ourselves in sight of the bayou.

"Let's get Sidney to show us the way through the bayou to Cottonwood Point," Toby said.

"Good idea. And we can show him how to get through the tunnel to town," I said. "But we're the only people who have been through here. Let's make him promise to keep it a secret, okay?"

"Fine by me," Toby said. "It'll be handy for him to know about this."

We headed back upriver to Overlook Oak. When we got there, all was quiet on the western front. The garage door was closed, and there was no sign of life. We couldn't tell if P.J.'s big Chrysler was parked inside or not. Before long, however, we heard voices coming from the rectory. Toby and I looked at each other, surprised and questioning, and I grabbed the ammo box which held the binoculars. A strong breeze blew the living room window curtains in, and we could see inside, just for a moment. Two people were sitting on the living room couch with their backs to the window. Even though I was still extracting the binoculars, I easily recognized P.J.'s bald head surrounded by his ridiculously erect oiled curls.

Just then we heard a shuffling noise below and saw Richard coming up Hidden Path. He was carrying a white plastic five-gallon bucket with a green lid. We gave him the "double shush" sign and he motioned for the net. Toby let it down quietly while I trained the binoculars on the window, waiting for a stronger breeze. As soon as Richard had secured the bucket in the cargo net, he headed back down the path to The Ramp. He was stepping onto the platform by the time Toby landed the package.

"Shhhh! He's right in front of the window and he's got somebody in there with him," I said, passing the binoculars to Richard from my kneeling position on the platform, my elbows resting on the raised shelf which ran the width of the platform in front of us.

"Who is it?" Richard asked. "There's no other cars here."

"We don't know," Toby said, "We can't see his face."

Richard knelt next to me and held the binoculars up to his eyes, peering down into the large window in the front of the house. Finally, a breeze moved the curtains, and he could see P.J.'s head projecting above the back of a blue sofa. He was sitting very close to what appeared to be a young boy on the couch, although it was difficult to see the other person, because P.J.'s left arm was draped behind him on the back of the couch. P.J.'s right arm was not visible, but his right shoulder was moving.

"What's he doing?" Richard asked.

"Guess," I said. "What's it look like?" Richard passed the binoculars to Toby.

"They're getting up," Toby said.

A few minutes later, the front screen door opened, and a chubby young boy emerged, blonde curls gleaming in the sun. He was eating a popsicle.

"Oh, no!" I said. "It's that same kid—Sidney."

"Lemme see," Richard said. I passed the glasses down the row.

"Weird," Toby said. "You don't sit that close with your yard boy. I didn't think P.J. sat that close with anybody. Let's get inside there and see what we can see. He never locks his door when he leaves."

"Want to go tomorrow morning?" Toby asked Richard.

"Sure, if the coast is clear," Richard said.

"It might not be," I said. "There's a new Associate Pastor taking some of the early Masses," I told them what I knew about Fr. Jim. "That makes it more dangerous. We need to figure out what we're doing for a quick getaway before you go inside."

"Just how do you propose to do that?" Richard asked.

"I don't know yet—we'll have to think about it," I said.

"I have something that might help us," Richard said, reaching out for the five-gallon bucket and freeing it from the net.

"What is it?" Toby whispered.

"Shhh! I'll show you," Richard whispered back.

He sat with his legs wrapped around the bucket and began rotating it while he freed the lid. Toby and I knelt beside him, our anticipation high. Richard always had the best surprises. Finally, he pulled the top off, revealing a bucket filled with straw and containing a red bowl-shaped device. A pair of headphones was nestled around a post which rose from the center of the bowl. Richard pulled them out. They were connected to the bowl with wire.

"What in the world is that?" Toby asked, his whisper reflecting his incredulity. Even as he said it, I had a glimmer of recognition—I had seen something like this on the back of a comic book.

"The Big Ear," Richard whispered back proudly. "It's an electronic listening device—you point this post toward whatever you want to listen in on, and it amplifies the sound through the headphones to your ears. Let me get it set up and I'll show you."

He fished into the bucket and came up with a small tripod. Shaking the straw off it, he set it up on our front shelf, then mounted the disk and aimed it at the rectory's living room window. He put the earphones on, then made some directional adjustments with the disk, kneeling behind it and squinting, like he was sighting down the barrel of a rifle.

"Here," he whispered, finally, "listen to this," handing the earphones to Toby. Toby tried them on, then his eyes popped wide open.

"I can hear KHMO," he said, "he's listening to the noon farm market report."

"Shhh! Let me try," I said, holding out my hand.

"In a minute," Toby said. Finally, he relinquished the headphones. "I heard him flush the toilet," he whispered, his face registering his amazement.

I tried on the headphones. The first thing I heard was an advertisement for Wright's Furniture Store, interrupted by a cough. I could also hear running water and dishes being handled.

"This is great!" I said. "We can tell everything he's doing, and we don't have to risk going down there to listen."

"Except we still gotta go inside and see what we can see," Toby said.

As I drifted off to sleep that night following my second rosary of the evening, my hands encased in old oven mitts taped at the wrist, I realized that Sidney would be old enough to become an altar boy during the coming school year, just like my little brother, Mark.

I was never cute, but that didn't particularly bother me. I didn't want to be cute—I wanted to be handsome—it sounded much more manly. But the verdict was still out on that question. I was just little and had brown hair and brown eyes. Period. That was about it. But my little brother Mark was something else—all the girls thought he was cute, and maybe P.J. did, too—there was no way to be sure. It looked like P.J. had singled Sidney out for "special treatment" already, and he was the same age as my brother Mark. I had to get P.J. put away before he had a chance to ruin somebody else's life. I couldn't bear to think of my brother committing suicide. *And you better start thinking about Hell yourself, you pervert, because I hear it lasts a really long time.*

52.
GETAWAY PLANS

"We're going in," Toby announced, as he joined Richard and me up in the overlook.

"What do you mean?" I asked. "Going in where?"

"Into the rectory—Michael found a quick getaway off the top of the bluff."

"Where is it?" I asked.

"If you keep going down Hidden Path past The Ramp, there's another tree that overhangs P.J.'s front yard. It has a huge grapevine growing from the edge of the bluff up into the tree—it's as big around as my wrist. We named it 'Venerable Vine.' It comes up out of the ground and splits into two trunks, like a wishbone. We sawed through the base of it so all you have to do is reach your arms out as you run off the edge of the bluff and close them around each side of the wishbone—it takes you way out into space, and you can just put your feet on the bottom and ride it like a swing. There are two exposed white rocks close to the edge of the bluff that point right at it, so you can hit it at a dead run if you need to. You just make sure you run across the top of the two rocks, like tagging first base, then second base, then you can just jump off the cliff—the vine is right in front of you.

"You're gonna love it. You can either ride it back to the top of the bluff or just get off in the tree and tie it up and swing back later whenever the coast is clear. We left a coil of honeysuckle vine tied around the trunk that you can use to anchor the grapevine if you want to stay in the tree for a while. We'll show you sometime when we know for sure that he's gone."

Shortly before 1:00 p.m., we heard a familiar car motor laboring up the hill. As we waited, the mobsters' black Lincoln swung into view around the last curve, Mr. Muscle driving, as usual. He pulled up in front of the garage and opened the door for Dapper Man, who emerged in a cloud of smoke and tossed his cigarette into the grass, where it lay smoking. As they approached the front door, the screen door opened, and we saw P.J. shake their hands as they entered.

"They look like best friends," I said.

"Quick! Get the big ear out!" Toby said, as Richard pried off the bucket lid and hurriedly set up the tripod, mounted the dish and set up the headphones.

"Mrs. Armani—they're talking about Sidney's mom," Richard whispered. "They're telling P.J. about it. He said that sounds pretty good!"

"They must be paying him to swing the deal," I said.

"Now they're talking about P.J.'s gambling machine," Richard said.

"Let me listen for a while," Toby said. Richard handed him the headphones. "There must be something wrong with one of the gambling machines," Toby whispered. "Dapper Man said he'll be glad to take a look at it, and P.J. said he'll call him."

Shortly thereafter, the Mobsters got into their car and drove back down the hill.

"Why in the world is P.J. involved with those crooks?" Toby asked.

"Because he's on the take," I said. "He's corrupt. They're paying him for local advice, and they're in some gambling racket together."

"We gotta talk to Sidney's mom," Richard said. "If they get to her first, it's all over. They're gonna offer her money, and it sounds like she needs it. Let's talk to Sidney tomorrow morning. We're gonna have to let him know what they're after. He's our best eyes and ears at Cottonwood Point." And although none of us said it, we were all worried about whatever was going on between him and P.J.

That afternoon, Toby and I were back at Coach Hedges' house for extended practice. By this point in the summer, our games were not even recognizable, solely because of the tremendous skills development program which he had designed for us. We were shooting a hundred highly focused jump shots per day, calling them out loud, and reporting our totals to Coach. Our shooting had improved enormously, thanks to our internalizing his method. Coach Hedges had even changed my release point so I could shoot over taller players without getting blocked. These days, when I played H.O.R.S.E with Michael and John, they insisted I had to put C.H.I.M.P.A.N.Z.E.E. on each of them with double "provin's", and they only had to put H.O.R.S.E. on me, with a single "provin," and I was still winning most of the games. There was no doubt, though, that both of them were also getting better with all the practice and, especially, with their intense focus on beating me, which actually happened once in a blue moon.

Coach Hedges had taught Toby a gorgeous hook shot, with both his right and his left hands, arcing his arm out gracefully and rolling the ball off his fingertips, something which was unheard of in Mayfly. In fact, other than a high school kid named Leo Howarth, Toby and Mr. Hedges were the only players I had ever known who could hook with either hand. Toby had been given his own drill: fifty hook shots per day with each hand, reporting his scores to Coach Hedges. Between that and our free throws and jump shots and passing and dribbling drills, Toby was starting to look impressive. I didn't know anyone who could hit better than he could—except me, of course, and a couple times he even beat me, which both of us considered a minor miracle.

Although I was a good shot and getting better, I was still small, and taller players were able to block my shot if they were quick enough. To counter that disability, Coach Hedges had not only changed my release point by moving it higher, but had also taught me a lightning-quick release, which was mainly a matter of good balance and footwork. The final stratagem for the short shooter, however, was the quick step-back. He taught me to step backwards before shooting, and then completely arrest my backwards momentum, gathering all my weight over my feet, perfectly balanced, with no sideways drift, as I launched into my jumper. First, we practiced the footwork without the ball, miming the ballhandling as I leapt back and then jumped, pushing my weight squarely up. Next, he taught me how to do it off the dribble, first only one dribble, then two, then three. Later we would spend an entire afternoon working on my step-back shot after driving to my left. Like everything else he taught me, it was progressing nicely, a combination of superb coaching and lots of focused practice.

I made sure to keep my bargain with the Poor Souls every night, especially since they were keeping up their end of the bargain in spades. There was no doubt in my mind that those poor bastards knew how to get things done—they were sort of like the Jesuits.

53.
PIRATES

The next morning, after serving early Mass and doing our mandatory morning work session, The Cliffhangers traveled to our respective spy assignments. John and Michael took Overlook Oak duty while the Three Musketeers rode our bikes down River Road, walked them through the landslide tunnel (checking Toby all the way for spiders), and resumed our ride south. We found Sidney waiting by the road to guide us through the bayou.

"Gotta come in the house first," he said. "Mom wants to meet you. She's hardly ever home—she works two jobs, but she has the day off. She's a secretary at the cement plant during the day and at night she manages the A & W in town."

Sidney swung the screen door wide and walked inside, calling, "Mom, they're here." A large oval rag rug, woven in shades of rose and blue, lay in the center of the room. It was surrounded by scuffed white pine floorboards, aged a rich patina from the sunlight which poured through the windows as the curtains shifted in the occasional breeze. A wooden two-by-four railing outlined a narrow stairway which rose from the far corner up to Sidney's bedroom under the eaves. Rectangular squares of carpet in various patterns were tacked onto the treads. A smaller throw rug led through a doorway into the kitchen, where Mrs. Armani appeared, drying her hands on her apron.

"Hello, boys," she said. I was struck by how pretty she was. I don't usually have much interest in girls who are older than about sixteen, but Mrs. Armani was an exception. She had to be really old, like in her mid-twenties, but she didn't look it. She had beautiful dark hair that curled above her shoulders, huge brown eyes and high cheekbones.

Sidney introduced us, and Mrs. Armani shook all our hands, told us she was happy to meet us, and warned us to watch out for the snakes.

"They're everywhere down here," she said. "Most of them won't bother you, but once in a while you meet a cranky one."

As we headed back outside, I noticed a framed black-and-white photograph hanging on the living room wall and paused to look at it. It showed an elderly woman with wire-rim glasses and a penetrating gaze, her white hair pulled up into a bun.

"That was my grandmother, Mary Orba," she said. "I remember her. She used to own this place. My dad was her only child, but both my parents died before her, so she left it to me. She lived to ninety-six." Richard stepped up closer and examined the picture with interest.

"Come on, guys, this way," Sidney said, leading us into the bayou along a marshy hillock before bending upriver, then reversing direction on a serpentine path back toward the road, before finally turning east again toward the gravel bar. The trip was nerve-wracking due to our proximity to cottonmouths, swamp rattlers, copperheads, northern water snakes, and black rat snakes, all of which had a well-earned reputation for touchy dispositions and a universal "bite-first-inquire-later-or-not-at-all" policy. Fortunately, most of our close encounters showed us only the tail end of some legless thing slipping underwater.

When we left the marsh and ascended several feet onto the sand bar, we found a pick and several shovels which Sidney had hauled out onto the bar for our treasure hunt. They were heaped into a loose pile.

"Excellent!" I said, pulling a red polka-dotted handkerchief out of my pocket, "let's put on our pirate bandanas and have a pirate meeting, then we can start digging for treasure." Everyone garbed up. Sidney had made a wooden sword, which he retrieved from the tool pile. Toby donned a black eye patch made from construction paper and a rubber band, and Richard put on a big gold hooped earring. I felt underdressed.

"Okay, pirates," I said, "the first thing we need to do is choose our pirate names. If you don't have a pirate name, we'll be glad to give you one. My pirate name is 'Hawkeye'," I announced. Then, as an afterthought, "Aaargh!"

"I'm the Hook," Toby said. "Aaargh!"

"I'm Blackstone. Aaargh!" Richard said.

"I couldn't think of a pirate name," Sidney said. I looked at him.

"Ye be lookin' like Sharkbait to me," I said, using my best pirate intonation. "How be that fer ye?"

"Cool!" Sidney said. *Poor kid would have been happy if we had named him 'Fungus'.*

"Alright, pirates, let's go find the treasure chest. Aaargh!" Then, as an afterthought, "Who be carryin' the treasure map?"

We all just looked at each other stupidly.

"Forgot the map?" I roared. "You scurvy buncha landlubbers! How can we find the treasure without the map?" I asked, hands on my hips, glaring from one to the other. "Are ye just feelin' lucky, are ye?"

"I have an idea," Richard said.

"Well, spit it out, Blackstone," I said. "Where shall we be diggin' fer treasure? What be your plan?" drawing it out with my best pirate inflection.

"Methinks me divinin' rod will lead us to it," Blackstone Richard growled, picking up a forked branch from the gravel. He held it out in front of him and advanced across the sandbar toward the water. Oddly enough, it led him to the exact spot where the current had borne us on our exploratory float downriver from the railroad bridge. *Coincidence? Methinks not.* He stopped just short of the water's edge and made a big show of his "divinin' rod" pulling him this way and that, until it finally leapt clear out of his hands and hit the ground. He bent and picked up a sturdy piece of driftwood several feet long, and shoved it into the sand so it stood upright. Retrieving his divining rod, he then did an about-face and traipsed across the sandbar to the original dirt riverbank and walked along it. Still holding the divining rod out in front of him, he squinted upriver. I looked over his shoulder as he calculated.

Using his planted driftwood like a gunsight for his long view of several miles, he moved around until it bisected the middle span of the railroad bridge where the *Flying Eagle* had exploded. Suddenly, the divining rod was pulled directly toward the ground, and Richard drew a large 'X' on the gravel bar where it joined the dirt riverbank.

"Methinks the treasure be buried right here," he said, in his best pirate brogue. "'X' marks the spot."

"Aye," Toby the Hook roared, "We be diggin' right there, then, mates! Let's fall to it!" he growled, running to the tool pile and returning with the shovels and a pick.

"Aye, aye!" I said. "And an extra measure of gold fer him that finds it first."

"Aye, aye, sir," Sharkbait Sidney parroted.

"Oh, and by the bye, Sharkbait," I said, as I thrust my own spade into the gravelly sand, "thanks fer bringin' the treasure-diggin' tools. This be much faster than diggin' with our hands."

"Aye, so put yer backs into it, lads," Blackstone Richard exhorted us.

We fell to, huffing and puffing, standing next to each other four abreast and facing the bayou, as we threw shovelful after shovelful of sand into a pile on the riverbank. Thirty minutes later, we stopped to rest, leaning on our shovels. We had dug a trench six feet long and eight inches deep. There was no shade and we were hot and sweaty—no sign of any treasure yet.

"Well, mates," I said, real piratey, "see any signs of a wrecked riverboat?"

"No, nothin' I can tell," Toby the Hook said.

"What do you mean, 'riverboat'?" Sharkbait Sidney asked.

"We think the pirate treasure be hidden in a wrecked riverboat," I told him.

"Aye—and it likely be buried a long way down," Blackstone Richard said: "She was three stories tall when she blew up and went down to Davey Jones' locker, so I make it eight feet each, maybe twenty-four feet tall, but who knows how much of 'er be blown away in the explosion and burnt up in the fire."

"If she be sittin' on the bottom in thirty-five feet of water, the very closest she could be is nine feet under," Blackstone Richard said, his pirate brogue fading as he continued his calculations, "plus the height of this bar, say roughly five feet, so twelve or fourteen feet under the ground. If she burned down to half her height after the explosion, she would be twenty-four feet below ground. And if she burned to the waterline, which she would have unless she sank before she could burn all the way down, she could be over thirty feet deep."

Toby the Hook and I looked at Blackstone in disbelief, our jaws dropping open in dismay. Sharkbait Sidney just stared at him, looking confused.

"So what be we doin' here?" Toby the Hook asked. "Even pirates can't dig that far. Plus, this bar is huge. We don't even know for sure we be startin' in the right place."

"Aye, true enough," Blackstone Richard said. "All this be speculation. We have no idea if the wreck even be here, and we don't know if she dragged along the bottom when she came down the river or no. But the newspaper article said she *sank*—in fifty-five foot of water. She could have floated downriver, submerged but not sunk to the bottom, like ye've seen big trees do. Maybe she was still partially buoyant because of trapped air pockets on board, maybe in boilers or even barrels locked in the hold, but not buoyant enough to float on top of the water, and then she got caught on something, like the huge root system of a big cottonwood that was already stuck here.

"But I think we can assume she was completely underneath the surface because she was reported to have *sunk*. Plus, if she was only partially submerged, she would have been seen by another boat the next day. But we have no idea how far under the surface she might be—if she be here a'tall. Odds are, she's all the way at the bottom and there wasn't much left after the explosion and fire—so, odds are, she's really, really deep," Blackstone finished, tapping the side of his nose knowingly, in piratical fashion.

"Too bad we don't have a full crew to help us dig," I said.

"Wait, you guys," said Sharkbait Sidney. "You're not playing, are you? You're talking about something real. Is there really a treasure?"

We all just looked at him. Finally, I said, "Yes, Sharkbait, we think it's real—a real riverboat that sank. And there may even be a real treasure, but we don't know if there was a treasure, or if it's really here or not. We do know that the men from the gravel company think it's real—and they think it's here—that's why they want to rent this sandbar, not to mine gravel—that's just their cover story."

"How do you know all this?" Sharkbait Sidney asked.

"You have to swear before we can tell you," Toby the Hook said.

"Okay, I swear," he said.

"No, I mean really swear," said Toby the Hook. "Like this. Repeat after me: 'I swear by the trees and earth and stone,' he said, then paused and waited until Sharkbait Sidney repeated, mimicking Toby the Hook's touching of the earth while he parroted the lines all the way to the end.

"And if I ever do, I'll walk around blind," he finished, squinting his eyes hard shut in imitation of Toby the Hook.

So, when we could see that Sharkbait Sidney understood the gravity of the situation, we sat down on the edge of the shallow trench and gave him the Reader's Digest Condensed version. His eyes were huge throughout the narrative, but what could you expect? He was just a little kid—he was bound to be clueless. His mouth looked like a fish out of water as it alternated between gaping open and snapping shut again.

"A real treasure," he said, awestruck. "Mom wouldn't have to worry about the mortgage payments anymore."

"Yeah, but remember, Sharkbait," Toby the Hook told him meaningfully, "you can't tell your mom about it until we find it. This is our secret, and we trusted you, and you swore. You can't tell *anyone* about it. And if you break your oath you're gonna go blind." Sharkbait Sidney just nodded, eyes wide as saucers.

"And, anyway, we've got to find it before they do," Richard said, "and I don't see how we can dig deep enough and fast enough to find it before they start."

Sharkbait Sidney looked alarmed. "Come on, guys," he said, "are we men or are we mice? We're pirates—this isn't hard for us. Let's dig some more."

The three of us looked at each other, wondering what kind of monster we had just created, then shrugged and picked up our shovels.

"Put your backs into it, mateys!" he yelled in his high, shrill voice, throwing shovels full of gravel out of the pit. Two hours later we were exhausted, thirsty, and hungry. Our trench was now almost four feet deep—we had to stand in it to continue shoveling, and it was becoming more difficult to throw the sand and gravel up out of the trench. Soon we would have to dig a ramp on one end to carry out the buckets of sand.

"Do you guys have a wheelbarrow?" Blackstone Richard asked.

"Yeah, want me to go get it?" Sharkbait Sidney offered.

"Not now—we have to quit—we can't be late to basketball practice," I announced. Toby the Hook looked relieved. "Maybe we can alternate digging days—I'll talk to Michael and John and see if they're up for it."

"We need to cover our ditch," Blackstone Richard said. "It's a dead giveaway."

"We can use willow trees," Sharkbait Sidney volunteered. "There's a million of them in the bayou. I'll bring our machete and cut some of them and just lay them across the top of the ditch. We can keep the tools down in the ditch."

"Great idea, Sharkbait," Toby the Hook growled. Sharkbait beamed. "Now, can you show us how to get out of here without getting snakebit?"

"Sure," he said, "follow me." He grabbed his snake stick and we fell into line behind him. It was hard to keep up—not only did Sharkbait know every single step on the safe path through the bayou, but he was way quicker and more agile than he looked. He stopped suddenly, causing The Three Musketeers to bump into one another like the Three Stooges.

"Swamp rattler," he announced. "It's right in our way." We looked around him and saw a small camouflaged rattlesnake in front of him. We heard the vibrating hum from the rattle as the snake coiled. Sharkbait held his stick out toward the snake, which waited several seconds and then struck. As it did, Sharkbait swept the stick sideways, catching the body of the snake in mid-strike, halfway between its head and its tail, and tossed it into the water. The Three Musketeers looked at each other with raised eyebrows. *Impressive. This little kid is way faster than he looks.*

"The trick is to keep far enough away from them to use your stick," he said. "Of course, to do that you have to see them first."

"Sharkbait, can you cut each of us a snake stick to keep down here while you're cutting the willow trees?" I asked.

"No problem, Hawkeye," he said.

"Aaargh!" I replied, real piratey. "Thanks, Matey," I growled.

54.
THE WATER TABLE

When we arrived back at Cottonwood Point the next day, we found Sharkbait waiting on the landward side of the bayou to guide us through to the sandbar. He handed each of us our own snake stick for the trek through the swamp. They were willow, long and light, and each had a forked end, perfect for pinning a snake behind the head, if only we were quick enough to do it.

As we emerged from the bayou, we were gratified to see the willow trees laying haphazardly across our trench, disguising it. As we pulled them off, however, we saw our tools lying in four inches of water, rust blooming on the metal where it met the surface of the water—the bottom of our ditch was inundated.

"Oh, man!" Blackstone Richard said, "Of course! We're below the water level—I should have thought of that. We're never gonna be able to dig it out, even if we can find it. Unless it's buried in the top four or five feet of this bar, that is."

"What're you talking about?" Toby the Hook said. "There must be a way—how do they think they're gonna to do it?"

"Hard to say. Those guys may not have thought this far, either," Blackstone Richard said, "based on their research skills at the library. But if they have thought about it, they have to be prepared, once they find it, to bring in a pile driver and drive big steel panels into the riverbed in a circle around it, and then pump the water out of the middle—it's called a coffer dam. And they'll probably have to do it from a barge, because they won't be able to get close enough on solid land. Plus it'll cost 'em a fortune."

"So, then, how are *we* ever gonna do it?" I asked.

"We can't, unless it's lying within four feet or so of the top of this sandbar, which is pretty unlikely, at least according to our theory, since we think the wreck is what created this sandbar, and that means it's on the river bottom."

"Could we just dive down there and see if we can see it?" Toby the Hook asked.

"No. Out of the question," Blackstone Richard said, firmly. "We'd probably die—it's not worth any of our lives. We all saw how strong the current is here the first time Toby...er, I mean, Hook, jumped in here. Also, you can't see anything in this water, and if there's something on the bottom that we could feel, the odds of our getting caught up in it are super high. We already know the current is too strong to swim out of any root balls or any other entanglement."

"So our only hope is finding it close to the surface," I said.

"Yeah, and that's a long shot," Blackstone Richard said. "Very long."

"But we'll never know unless we try," said Toby the Hook. "I'm game—are you guys?"

"Yeah, but if it's near the surface, maybe we don't have to dig the entire sand bar up. Maybe we can just drive a pipe or a steel rod into the ground and see if we hit anything," I opined.

"I've got a five-foot soil probe," Sharkbait Sidney volunteered. "It has a sharp point and handles on the top and you can either work it into the ground with the handles or use a mall and drive it in." The three of us just looked at him. I didn't know about the others, but I had never even heard of a "soil probe."

"Great," I said, "Pirates'll use anything they can—let's give it a try."

Sharkbait Sidney vanished through the bayou with his snake stick at a run, returning five minutes later carrying a long steel spike with a "T" top, and lugging an eight-pound sledgehammer on his shoulder.

"Great," Blackstone Richard said. "Let's see how it works."

Sharkbait handed the probe over. "Here you go, Blackstone," he growled, in a pretty fair imitation of a pirate, albeit one with a high voice.

"Thanks, Sharkbait," Blackstone Richard replied, then stuck it in the ground. He used the handles, working the shaft back and forth laboriously as he inched it deeper into the sand and gravel. "Whenever we hit something solid, we'll have to use the shovels to find out what it is," he said.

"We're going to have to make a grid, so we'll know where we've already tried," I said. "Tomorrow I'll bring a ball of kite string. How far apart do you think we should try it?"

"Probably every foot, if we want to be thorough," Blackstone Richard answered.

"Every foot! That's a lot of holes!" I paced the sandbar while the others watched, using my best "Mother-May-I" giant steps to approximate a yard. "About ninety-feet wide by two hundred-thirty feet long," I announced. "I need to do some math," I said, looking around for a patch of sand without gravel. I walked over to the edge of the water, where the river had obligingly deposited a border of clean sand several feet wide along the edge of the bar. Grabbing a twig, I bent and started multiplying while the others stood over my shoulder and checked my work.

"Twenty-thousand seven hundred square feet, times maybe 75%, since it isn't really a rectangle, still makes over fifteen thousand probes, plus we have to dig holes wherever we run into anything. If we average fifteen minutes per probe, that is still over three thousand eight hundred hours. If all four of us dug nonstop for two hours per day, seven days per week, that would take over sixteen months, including all winter and all through the school year, without even time off for Christmas or Thanksgiving or Easter, and that doesn't even include the time it will take to dig down and investigate every time we hit something. Sounds like a job for Superman."

"Yeah," Toby the Hook said, "if we were Superman, we could just use our x-ray vision and find out exactly where it is. Maybe we should just try it every yard, instead of every foot."

"Hmmm," Richard mused. "X-ray vision would be handy."

"Even if we only drilled every yard, it would still take all four of us almost two months," I said, "and that's if we can each work two hours each day, seven days a week, even when it's raining, with no time off for Sundays or picnics or anything else."

"I wonder how long we have," Blackstone Richard said. "Say, Sharkbait, do you think your Mom is gonna let the gravel company mine this sand bar?"

"Yeah," he answered. "She's gonna—she already decided. She needs the money for the mortgage. She says it's the answer to her prayers. They're gonna pay her a hundred dollars per month, plus twenty percent of the profit on whatever gravel they can sell. She's leasing it to them for a year, and they have the option to renew it for two more years. It starts July 1st."

"July 1st!" the three of us echoed.

"Has she already signed the lease?" Richard asked, obviously alarmed.

"Not yet," Sidney said, "she's gonna talk to Fr. Reiser first."

"Fr. Reiser!" I said. "What does he have to do with it?"

"He's been helping Mom," Sidney said.

Sure he has.

55.
THE KEY

"I know," Toby said the next morning, agreeing with me on our lack of progress in proving that Tom hadn't committed suicide. The Three Musketeers were walking through the landslide tunnel on South River Road *en route* to Cottonwood Point. "We've gotta do something different. We're no closer to figuring out what happened to Tom than when we started."

"Oh, I think we've made some progress," Richard said. "We're pretty sure he didn't commit suicide."

"Yeah, but to get him moved to hallowed ground, we've gotta prove it," Toby said.

"I still think P.J. did it," I said.

"But why would P.J. want to kill him?" Richard asked. "We've talked about this before, and it just doesn't make sense."

"I've been thinking about this," I said. "Maybe Tom was gonna tell the bishop that P.J. had been molesting him," I said.

"But we don't even know if that was true," Richard said.

"Yeah, but look," I said. "Number one, the Dalton boy committed suicide by jumping off Lover's Leap, which is practically in P.J.'s front yard. Or maybe P.J. killed him, too. Maybe he pushed him off the cliff and Tom off the bell tower. Maybe that's the way he does it."

"But why?" Richard asked.

"Same reason—he'd been molesting him. But when the Dalton kid went to the seminary, P.J. got scared—or maybe the Dalton kid told him he wanted to make a clean break with him. Maybe he told him he was gonna tell the bishop."

"There's no way we'll be able to prove any of that now," Richard said.

"I know, but it's a pattern," I said. "We know what he's doing right now. He only uses one boy at a time. First the Dalton kid, then Tom, and now Sidney. Want to ask him?"

"No, I don't think we should," Richard said. "If P.J. really is molesting him, he'll be embarrassed about it. And if he's not, he'll be embarrassed that we asked him."

"Or maybe Tom found out that P.J. was working with the mobsters," I said.

"How could he know that?" Richard asked.

"He might've heard them talking to him on the phone," I said. "They always call him 'Father.' And you gotta admit that P.J. started acting really weird after Tom died. Plus, I caught him red-handed going through Tom's pockets, and we know for a fact that the mobsters were also looking for something and they thought Tom took it—we heard them talking about it. And we know that Tom was spying on them from the linen closet."

"I think the mobsters killed him," Toby said.

"I think that's more likely than P.J. killing him," Richard agreed.

"But even if they did," I said, "P.J. must've known about it. He was part of it—he still is. That also explains why he's acting so weird. And searching his pockets? He was looking for the same thing the mobsters were."

"I wonder what everybody's looking for," Richard said. "Have you looked in all the places Tom might have hidden things?"

"Every place I can think of," Toby said.

"I think we oughtta take a look in the bell tower," Richard said.

"How can we?" Toby asked. "I can't find the key."

"Do you know what it looks like?" Richard asked.

"Yeah, I've seen it. It's an old-fashioned skeleton key."

"Maybe he keeps it at the church," I said.

"I doubt it," Richard said. "Even if he did at one time, I bet he doesn't keep it there any more since Tom died. I think it'll be at the rectory."

"Let's ask Sidney when we get there," I said. "He might know."

We arrived at the Armani house. Sidney was waiting to guide us through the swamp. Once we were on the gravel bar and taking turns with the probe, I broached the subject.

"Hey, Sharkbait," I said, "you know Tom's brother died when he fell off the bell tower at church, right?"

"Yeah," Sidney said, "I heard that."

"We're trying to figure out what happened to him. It's really important, because at the Inquest they said he committed suicide, but we knew him really well and we know he never would have done that. But he can't get to Heaven unless he's buried in hallowed ground, and he can't be buried in hallowed ground unless we can prove he didn't commit suicide."

We watched Sidney's mouth open in slow realization as he mulled it over. His face was the picture of dismay. He looked at Toby sympathetically.

"We think maybe the mobsters pushed him off," Toby said, "because he found out what they were up to. We know they were looking for something they thought he took. And we need to go up in the bell tower to look around, but we're afraid Fr. Reiser won't let us. We need to borrow his key for a little while without him knowing it—you think you can help with that?"

"Why me?" he asked.

Good question. "We think he's got it at his home," I said. "And we've been watching his house because the mobsters have been there several times and we were trying to find out what they were up to, and we saw you visiting him."

Sidney looked surprised. He was quiet for a moment, while we held our collective breath. We certainly couldn't afford to have him tell P.J. that we had been watching his house.

"Okay," he said, "if I can, but I don't wanna get caught."

"We'll put it right back," I say, "as soon as we use it. Do you know where he keeps his keys?"

"Maybe. I know where he keeps a lot of them."

"Can you show me?" Toby asked. "It would mean a lot to me. And before we go inside, I'll show you a quick escape route so if we hear him driving up the hill, we can get away before he even gets to the top," Toby said.

"Okay," Sidney said, "as long as it's safe."

"Hey, guys," Toby said as the three of us rode home, "I've been thinking about it, and I don't think it's really safe for him to swing out on that grapevine the way we do. He's a chubby little kid, and I'm not sure he'll be able to hold his weight. If he fell, it would kill him for sure."

"Do you wanna look for another escape plan?" I asked.

"No, but I have an idea to make it safer. There's a real sturdy black net in the basement of the motel. It's a shipping net that my dad used to cover loads in the back of his truck, but he's not hauling anything anymore. I think I can tie it between the two wishbone sides of the Venerable Vine, and Sidney could just jump into the net, like it was a basket, and stay there as long as he needed to—he could even sleep in it. And nobody'll see it, because it'll be hidden by all the vegetation at the edge of the woods, just like Venerable Vine. So, if you take the walkie-talkie to early Mass and tell me the coast is clear, I can tie the net up before we go into the rectory. It shouldn't take long."

Sounded like a good idea to Richard and me.

"Okay," I said. "I'll call and let you know if he's saying the early Mass and, if so, you can have a half-hour to work on the net."

"Okay, we'll be ready," Richard said.

"Yeah," Toby said. "We'll bring a walkie-talkie with us and be at the fissure by 6:30."

"Okay," I said, "but keep the volume turned down to one, so he can't hear the static in case Fr. Jim is saying the early Mass and P.J. is still at home."

Toby and I had been working on two-man plays during our weekday sessions with Coach Hedges: the pick-and-roll and the give-and-go. He was relentless in his insistence on good footwork as well as the quality of our fakes. That afternoon, he also introduced us to a panoply of no-look passes into the post. I had two pre-set target locations, both triggered by audible signals. The beauty was that the words never had to be repeated—we could yell anything, and all the words meant the same thing. If Toby yelled, he was headed toward the blocks down low, and I could fire a no-look pass to the lower block on the ball side of the lane. If I yelled, I would hit Toby seven feet above the floor, halfway between the free throw line and the basket. "No-look" passes required focused peripheral vision. Coach showed me how to lead Toby by just one foot, so that when he caught the ball, he was in motion toward the basket instead of standing still. This allowed him an immediate transition into a layup or a hook, depending on where his defensive man was. Alternatively, he could stop abruptly and shoot a short jumper.

If I started driving down one side of the lane, while Toby was on the other side, he would match my path in mirror image, running down the other side, and parallel with me—and I tossed him quick alley-oops. If I drove the lane while Toby was on my side, he would step out onto the base line, taking his man with him, and then curve back around behind me for a quick pass over my shoulder or an arcing alley-oop. For the next week, we worked these combinations over and over, both sides of the basket, always no-look passes while I dribbled toward the corner or the hoop, until both of us were expecting it at any moment.

"Throw that ball hard and fast," Coach Hedges said, "that's the only advantage you have against the defense when you are passing the ball into the lane."

"Kodak!" I yelled, and zipped Toby the ball, high in the air and hard, as he faded down my side of the lane toward the basket.

"Lunch!" Toby yelled, and I zipped him the ball, high in the air and hard, but down low on the blocks close to the bucket. Toby worked on snatching it out of the air with his big, bony hands, always catching the hard ones with eight fingers on the back side of the ball, basket-catch style, like Willie Mays.

"No, like this," Coach Hedges said, dribbling down the lane and firing a pass at Toby off the dribble which was so fast it nearly went supersonic. Toby caught it one foot closer to the basket than his head.

He was so shocked that he went immediately into a graceful left hook which whispered into the net, the strings silently absorbing the backspin as it passed through.

Sometimes, though, I just drove into the corner and took the shot myself. I was famous for that shot. I loved the corner—it was a low percentage shot for most players, probably because it was hard to gauge perspective with only the edge of the backboard and the rim to look at—but I was really good at it. For some reason, I always thought it was easy to swish that long shot—the distance was fixed—it was always the same, a known commodity. From that corner, I could picture the rim with my eyes closed. Sometimes I just glanced at the rim and then closed my eyes and shot the ball. I could actually hit it without looking.

56.
THE HEIST

The next morning, I brought a duffel bag to early Mass and hid it in the bottom of the dark cassock closet in the altar boys' robing room. In the duffel bag was the walkie-talkie unit shared by John and me, with the switch in the "OFF" position.

"Morning, Father," I said, dutifully, donning my starched and blousy white surplice, and not meeting his eyes, as P.J. entered through the side door. As soon as he disappeared down the curved hallway that ran behind the altar to the sacristy, I retrieved the unit, took it outside onto the small concrete landing, switched it to "ON," then pushed the "Transmit" button.

"Oak, this is Base. Come in please, Oak, over," I said.

"*Crackle, crackle,*" then "Base, this is Oak, over," Richard said.

"Oak, are you in position? Over," I said.

"Roger that," Oak replied. "Over."

"It is safe to proceed, Oak," I said. "I say again, it is now safe to proceed. Over."

"Roger that, Base. In motion. Over," I heard.

"Over and out," I said, switching the device to "off," and holding it under my surplice as I reentered the robing room and stashed it in the duffel, then ran along the passageway behind the altar to the sacristy. Plunking myself down on the *prie dieu*, I joined John and P.J.

for the Prayer Before Mass, trying with some difficulty to keep my expression reverent.

Back on Castle Bluff, Richard and Toby sprang into action, running across the top of the bluff. Toby carried a black bundle of netting, and Richard had a length of quarter-inch gray nylon rope and a knife. Just as they approached the rectory, they heard a motor laboring up the driveway.

Trapped like rats! They each started running, but in different directions. Toby ducked into the woods, dropped the netting on the edge of the cliff top, tagged the two pointer stones at a full gallop, first base then second base, and leapt off the cliff, catching Venerable Vine in his arms as he swept out over River Road and the Mississippi, two hundred feet below. Richard ran behind the garage and waited, his heart hammering, wondering how he would ever get out of there without P.J. seeing him. He would not be hard to identify, even from the back.

As he watched, the Mayfly Dairy truck topped the rise. Richard held his breath as the truck stopped in front of the rectory door. The milk man got out, opened the rear door, and extracted a bottle of milk, then took it up to the door and left it on the corner of the porch. He got into the truck, backed into a two-point turn, then drove down the hill. Richard breathed a sigh of relief as he came out of hiding and hurried past the rectory to the two stones marking the location of Venerable Vine. Toby swung back to the cliff top from his perch in the Safe Tree, and the two of them completed the installation of the safety net, then crept quickly back to the fissure and the Hidden Path. By the time P.J. returned from saying early Mass, they were comfortably ensconced in the shady boughs of Overlook Oak, listening to the birds' morning calls and watching the squirrels running the limbs of the neighboring trees.

With the escape vine now modified for Sidney, we planned for Toby and Sidney to go inside the rectory on Saturday afternoon while I was at Confession. Confessions were from 5:30 to 6:30 p.m. If P.J. was on confessions duty instead of Fr. Jim, that meant he couldn't be back on top of Castle Bluff until shortly after 6:30 at the earliest.

On Saturday afternoon, I got to church early, intending to be the first in line. Toby, the Rover walkie-talkie strapped over his shoulder, waited at the fissure with Sidney. Meanwhile, Richard was perched in Overlook Oak with the Oak walkie-talkie and the Big Ear trained down the driveway, listening for engine noise.

As we had expected, P.J. was on Confession duty. I duly recited my usual litany, said my Act of Contrition, then left the church, hustled down the side passageway between the church and the school, and radioed my report to Rover and Oak.

"Roger that, Base," Toby replied. He and Sidney lit out across the top of Castle Bluff through the woods toward the rectory.

The first thing they did, however, before entering the rectory, was to test-drive the quick-escape route. Toby showed Sidney how to sprint toward a rock formation that stood up in the yard, use it to locate the two white limestone pointer rocks, and race off the edge of the cliff into the net cradle. In the event of an emergency, the plan was for Sidney to evacuate first, swinging all the way out once and then back to allow Toby to join him in the basket, then the two of them could swing out and tie up to the Safe Tree to wait until the coast was clear.

"All you gotta do," Toby told him, "is run off the edge. As long as you hit these two rocks with your feet when you run into the woods, just like tagging first base and second base, you'll run right into the net. You can't miss it. Try it—I'll show you—like this," and he ran over the rocks and off the cliff into the net, which swung out over the abyss. The speed of his long trajectory slowed as he approached the trunk of a tall hackberry, where he reached out and grabbed an inch-thick honeysuckle vine which had been wound around the trunk twice, leaving a large loop hanging in Toby's path. Grasping it, he arrested his progress.

"Look," he called, "I can tie up here if I want, but right now I don't." He let go of the loop and swung back to the top of the bluff.

"Now, you try," he said. Sidney seemed dubious—multiple emotions played out over his face. He bit his cheek, then took a step back. Finally, his eyebrows drew closer together and his face tightened. Goaded into action by the fear of being branded a sissy, even at the possible cost of his life, he backed up across the lawn, his face screwed up determinedly, then ran across the pointer rocks, and launched himself desperately off the edge of the cliff into the net, swinging out high over River Road, which looked like the highway of a miniature train set far below.

"Perfect," Toby said, as Sidney swung back to the top of the bluff, expelling his breath in a huge exhalation as he dismounted, leaving the base of Venerable Vine resting on the ground. "Try it one more time, but this time grab the loop on the safe tree and tie it around your grapevine."

Sidney walked to the edge and looked out at the large vine loop dangling from the hackberry. Then, without hesitation, he backed up halfway across the lawn and ran over the pointer stones again, leaping into the net and riding it out to the Safe Tree, where he tied up and then untied it and swung back.

After the second test evacuation, Sidney was pronounced competent. "Good," Toby said, "not that you'll need it, but if he does come home unexpectedly, at least you won't get caught."

Summer of '63

"Twenty minutes left," Richard called down from the treehouse, as the two would-be burglars proceeded to the rectory. "Going silent up here," he said, then put the Big Ear headphones back on.

Toby and Sidney pulled open the screen door and walked into the front hallway. They felt it as soon as they crossed the threshold—an ominous presence, silent and menacing, like somebody was still there, watching their every move, someone large and dark and angry. They quietly closed the screen door, eyes wide with alarm, hearts racing, ears attuned to the slightest sound, expecting to see P.J. come out of the bedroom with accusing red vertical eye slits.

Sidney whimpered. "Shhhh," Toby breathed, reaching out quickly and putting a hand on his shoulder.

They waited motionless for half a minute, listening for any sound of life. Finally, Toby tiptoed over to a double doorway on the right and peered into the living room. The blue couch sat silent and unoccupied under the bay window. He crept into the room, slowly and silently, and looked around. A large book lay open on the coffee table: "Art of the Vatican," he read aloud, then walked behind the table and started paging through it, pausing to peruse the partial nudes.

"In here," Sidney whispered urgently from the kitchen. Toby paged back to the "Ceiling of the Sistine Chapel," which was on display when he entered the room, then left to join Sidney in front of a kitchen cabinet. Sidney's face was white and his lower lip trembled. Toby was afraid he might start to cry.

"They're in here," Sidney whispered hurriedly, opening a top drawer and jumping back as if he had just seen a tarantula. Toby looked inside the drawer at the jumble of pens, notepads, and rubber bands. On one side of the drawer stretched a long, narrow Velveeta Cheese box. It was filled with keys. Toby pulled out the box, upended it quietly on the counter, and began sorting through them. Suddenly, he grabbed an old skeleton key.

"I think this is it," he said. He quickly checked the others, then put them back in the box and replaced the box in the drawer. He put the skeleton key in his pocket.

"Okay, let's go," Sidney said anxiously, heading for the front door. He was horrified to see Toby run down the hallway in the opposite direction, peeking into doorways as he went. Toby finally stopped at the end of the hall and put his head through the doorway into the bedroom.

"Come on! We need to get out of here!" Sidney called after him frantically, running out the door and holding it open. Toby withdrew his head from the bedroom doorway, quickly peeked into the bathroom, and finally ran down the hallway and out the door. Sidney closed it quietly behind him, and they both bolted for the fissure, where they parted. Sidney started for home.

"Okay, Base, we're clear," came Toby's voice minutes later over the walkie-talkie.

"Great," I said, "did you find the key?" It wasn't 6:30 yet, so there was no danger of P.J. listening in on our conversation—he was still in the confessional.

"I think so," said Toby. "I'll have to take it by the church and try it out."

"What about the St. Thomas medal?" I asked.

"Nah," Toby said, "I didn't have time—the kid was too scared. I'll look later when I take the key back. Do you know he even makes his bed?" Toby asked. "Can you believe that? If I lived by myself, I wouldn't bother to make my bed. For what? Oh, and guess what he and the kid were looking at?" Toby continued. "'Art of the Vatican.'"

"Art of the Vatican! What do you mean?" I asked.

"It's this huge book, and it was open right there on the coffee table in front of where they were sitting," Toby said. "I think he was turning the pages with his right hand—I think that's what we saw."

"Did you look through the book?" I asked.

"Yeah," Toby said. "Just old art. There were some nudes in it, but nothing very good—nothing as good as Playboy."

"Well," I said, "that's probably all that pervert has—he can't very well go into the liquor store and buy a Playboy, can he?"

57.
CARLY'S NEW FRIEND

"Guess who I just saw?" Toby whispered as he plunked himself down in the treehouse at Overlook Oak after his work shift, "Crazy Carly was in the mobsters' car."

"What?" I said.

"Yep," Toby said. "Mr. Muscle was driving, and she was in the front seat, scooted over right next to him, practically sitting in his lap, and he had his arm around her. Nobody was in the back seat. She acted like she didn't see me, but I think she did."

"Holy shit!" I expostulated. "You think they're going together?"

"It sure looked like it," Toby said. "And Mr. Muscle was smiling and having a good time, too."

"I bet he was," I said. I couldn't help but be a little bit jealous. *What did he have that I didn't, anyway?* Crazy Carly had never come on to me, no matter how often I had imagined it. *Lord, be merciful to me, a wannabe sinner—Just kidding, Lord! Well, not about the mercy—just the wannabe part—and I wish I really were kidding about that, but...well, you know.*

In addition to Sharkbait, all of the Cliffhangers would start taking turns drilling and digging, since John and Michael had agreed to help with the sand bar project. They were meeting Sharkbait for the first time at Cottonwood Point. Toby and I had loaned them our pirate bandanas and I had warned them that they needed to introduce themselves to Sharkbait with their pirate names. They were going to tell Sharkbait that they were there to help out, and that Blackstone, Hook, and Hawkeye were busy with some secret pirate treasure investigations. The fact that they knew Sharkbait's name as well as the names of the three of us would prove that they were who they claimed to be, and they were to tell Sharkbait that they had taken the secret oath also. It turned out that wasn't necessary.

"I know you guys," Sharkbait said. "But I didn't know your pirate names 'til just now." *Hard to put anything past that kid.*

Musketball Michael and Gunshot John were also carrying two walkie-talkies. We had decided to redeploy our four units because our operations had suddenly expanded, and our two most important locations had no telephone service. We kept one unit at home, although John and Michael had taken it with them to Cottonwood Point, since none of the Cliffhangers were home. The call sign for the home unit was "Base." They loaned the other unit to Sharkbait, who would report in as "Point." Toby also had a unit to keep with him, named "Rover," and he would communicate with Richard through regular channels when necessary, since they lived close together. We kept the fourth one in the waterproof bucket in the treehouse with the volume turned off except when someone was there to man it. It reported in as "Oak." When we were in the treehouse, we took the unit out and kept it on the front shelf, with the volume turned down to "1." This allowed us to still hear incoming calls, but the static was barely audible.

Richard was ensconced in the Mayfly Free Public Library, doing some research. He said he had an idea which might save us a lot of probing and digging, but he wasn't sure it would work. He said Toby had given him the idea when he mentioned Superman's x-ray vision.

"It's called a 'metal detector'," Richard said, when we saw him the next day. "When President James Garfield was shot in 1881, Alexander Graham Bell invented it in a hurry to try to save the president's life. They needed to find the bullet that was inside him, but it didn't work very well because it also detected the metal bedsprings underneath him, so it didn't save him—he died anyway. But they've improved it a lot since then."

"How can we get one?" Toby asked.

"The first problem is they cost about a hundred dollars. We might be able to build one, but it would take weeks to get all the parts and then we'd still have to build it and hope it works."

"Sounds like we need a hundred dollars," I said. "We don't have time to build one."

"Also," Richard said, "I couldn't find out how deep it would detect metal, but the larger the piece of metal, the better it shows up, so things like the boilers, if they're still on board, may be detectable from a long distance."

"Yeah, but where are we gonna get a hundred dollars?" Toby asked.

"I've got an idea," Richard said. "I walked by Laze-E-Daze yesterday to see if the mobsters were still staying there, and they had a 'Help Wanted' sign in the window, so I went in. And guess who else is working there? Crazy Carly. She lives there, too." We just looked at him, trying to digest this information. *Why would Crazy Carly have left the River's Rest just to work at the Laze-E-Daze?*

"Anyway," Richard continued, "I can make seventy-five cents an hour, which means in a month I'll have enough to buy a metal detector and pay the income taxes, too."

"Income taxes! Why do you have to pay income taxes?" Toby asked.

"The government makes you pay taxes when you earn money," Richard said. "They charge you 16% of your income as tax. So to save $100, you actually have to make $116, plus taxes for the State of Missouri."

"16%!" I said, stunned, "that's robbery! How much is the Missouri tax?"

"1% additional," Richard said.

"How much did your parents pay Crazy Carly at the River's Rest?" I asked Toby.

"Seventy-five cents an hour," he said.

Richard applied for the job and was hired, but for only four hours per day. Checkout time was noon, and he was on duty from 11:00 to 3:00 p.m., seven days per week. So now it would take thirty-eight days to make the $116. But that left The Cliffhangers short a man on our afternoon surveillance roster. Even worse, we needed to complete our sandbar probe before the lease started on July 1, and there was no way we were going to be able to finish it. Maybe the mobsters wouldn't be there on the first of the month—maybe they still had people to hire and permits to get and equipment to rent. Maybe they wouldn't even show up this summer.

We had staked out a line using sticks and kite string, but even drilling the holes a yard apart—which Richard thought was probably insufficient because we might just skip past any part of the wreck that projected upwards—we had not yet finished a single pass down the length of the bar, and we still had 29 more to go. At this point, we were relegated to merely hoping, relying on pure blind luck to strike something before the mobsters arrived and took over. Richard needed to work at least until his sixth weekly payday before he would have enough money to order the metal detector and pay the taxes he would owe, and we had no idea how long shipping would take. We figured we were at least two months away from being able to try it out—which basically meant the end of the summer—and we still didn't know if it would even work.

I hadn't seen Mary Ann Ventura all summer. I wished I could think up some reason I needed to contact her, but I couldn't think of a good excuse. I could just call her up, but I wouldn't know what to say to her or what to talk about. And I had no way to just bump into her, although the Knights of Columbus picnic was Saturday, and she might be there. I had mixed emotions about seeing her, though, because I didn't think I could stand it if she were walking around with Lucas Crane. They might even be holding hands by now. I needed something or someone to help me look like I was busy and interested at the picnic, besides just watching Mary Ann. I wracked my brain but couldn't come up with anything.

Coach Hedges had taught me the Hundred Layup drill to keep me busy while Toby was doing his Hundred Hooks drill. He had me starting with my back to the basket and rolling the ball out with a long finger-roll layup, which could even morph into a hook if necessary, then turning around and corralling the ball as it came back through the net and running the opposite direction with the other hand and the same options.

He had taught me how to "open the seam" when faced with a 2-1-2 zone defense, driving off to the side of the free throw line until the closest out-front defender shifted over toward me to "take" me, and then taking advantage of the split-second lag time before the far side out-front defender "covered up" the vacated spot, by which time I would have zipped the ball to Toby in the lane. Coach Hedges had drilled me on the importance of using a bounce pass into the lane as a safer option until it was automatic, and had taught me the necessity of both speed and deception in passing into the lane, including using my new no-look one-hand passes straight off the dribble.

In fact, of all the things I was trying to accomplish, the only thing that was going well was basketball. At this point I was the hottest player of my age in Mayfly, and Toby wasn't shabby either. Both of us could have played with the high school varsity, and if it weren't for their pride while picking teams on the playground, we would have been chosen before some of their lame teammates.

And as good as Lucas Crane was, I was pretty sure he wouldn't have a chance with me in a game of one-on-one, and guaranteed he wouldn't even be in the running if teamwork was factored in. I could hardly wait to play him again—I wanted to see the look on his face when I smoked him. There was no way Lucas Crane could keep me from scoring—I just had too many options, and I could hit on all of them.

But I was largely dissatisfied. As I lay in bed that night, reflecting, I realized that, in spite of everything we had done to investigate Tom's death, including finding out about P.J.'s involvement with the mobsters, we were actually no closer to finding out what happened to Tom. And in spite of all our efforts to find Richard's treasure, we had zip to show for it—zilch. It wasn't for lack of trying, though—we had certainly devoted ourselves to it—it just wasn't working out—none of it was.

Only basketball. And that was because I had made a bargain with the Poor Souls in Purgatory. Well, to be honest, my own effort was also a huge factor in my success, but I had put the same amount of effort into trying to find out who killed Tom and into trying to find Richard's treasure, and it hadn't gotten us anywhere. I was happy to be helping the Poor Souls with their problem, for sure, but I was beginning to feel like I had sold my soul to the Devil.

That's when it hit me. Why not ask the Poor Souls for help getting Tom buried in hallowed ground? Hell, he might even be one of them—probably was—there was a cost for ogling naked women in Playboy—even if you did make it to Confession moments before you died. But what did I have to offer? Yet another nightly rosary? I was having trouble staying awake for my second rosary as it was. And what about giving Richard some help with his search for connection with his forebears? I would have to talk to Richard and Toby about it, and I would have to lay bare the bargain that was making me such an outstanding player, a bargain I had hoped never to reveal to any living soul.

I slept fitfully that night, feeling selfish, like I was letting my friends down. I was hiding a secret which we had dire need of. Nothing else was working out for us. I got on the walkie-talkie and told Richard and Toby I had an idea and needed to talk to them about it as soon as possible. We agreed on 11:00 a.m. at Overlook Oak.

"Listen, you guys, we're desperate," I began. "I think we need to get the Poor Souls involved." Toby was staring at me like he didn't know what I was talking about.

"Whaddayamean?" he asked.

"The Poor Souls in Purgatory," I said. "They're as desperate as we are—probably even more so. They're burning every single second, waiting to get out."

"How does that help us?" Toby said. Richard looked at me appraisingly.

"They can get things done," I said. "They're incentivized. We need to offer them prayers for the relief of their suffering and tell them what we need, and they'll help us get it."

"Seriously?" Toby said.

"Yeah, they're really powerful," I said. I had decided not to tell them how things were working out on my basketball deal unless I absolutely had to.

"Like what kinda prayers?" Toby asked.

"Like a rosary, every day," I said.

"An entire rosary?" Toby said. "Couldn't we get it done for something that didn't take so long, like maybe three Hail Marys?"

"Nah, we don't wanna come off as cheapskates, especially on something this big. We could split it up. I could say the beginning part and the first decade, and you guys could each say two decades apiece. That wouldn't take too long."

"Okay, good idea," Richard said. "I'm game—count me in."

"Do you really think it'll work?" Toby asked.

"Definitely," I said. "I'm sorry we didn't think of this earlier."

"Okay, I'm in," Toby said.

"Okay," I said. "I'll tell them our promise and what we're asking them to do for us. But we have to all do it, every single day, either before we get out of bed in the morning or at night before we go to sleep. I don't want them to think we're welching on the deal," I said.

"What about the Mysteries?" Toby asked.

"Any Mystery will do. Just pick your own every day, whatever you want," I said. "Nothing says we all have to use the same set of Mysteries. Just make sure you say the prayers—that's the thing that matters. We definitely don't want a buncha pissed off Poor Souls after us."

58.
SERVING MORE MASSES

July 1st was fast approaching, and it was shaping up to be a pretty big day. First, the Mobsters' lease would officially begin, assuming they signed it and paid the first month's rent. Secondly, and maybe even more important, it would also be the first day that I could finally fulfill my summer's goal of sleeping in—and I intended to take full advantage, even though that meant that my chores for the day (weeding the garden) would be much harder because I wouldn't be able to do them in the cool of the morning. I had been looking forward to it for weeks and had already told John and Michael not to count on me for early weeding duties on July 1, since I would still be celebrating at "Miss White's Party." They had decided to join me in the sheer hedonistic luxury of sleeping late, despite the fact that we would all have to pay the fiddler later.

"Boys," Mom said to John and me at dinner on June 26, "Mrs. Lampton called today. Her family is going on vacation for the first two weeks in July and her boys were scheduled to serve early Mass. She wanted to know if you boys would mind doing it for them. I told her it was a privilege to serve Our Lord in the Blessed Sacrament and that you boys would be glad to do it."

Out of the corner of my eye, I saw John's head jerk back. We looked at each other, our eyes bulging. *Are you shitting me?*

"What?" said the Knight of the Altar, aloud.

Actually, we knew, of course, that it really was a privilege, but we thought we already had all the privilege we needed. She had no idea how much I had been looking forward to sleeping late—I got delirious just thinking about it. By the time we finished with our new round of early Masses, it would be midsummer, and I still wouldn't have slept in on a single morning.

Mom apparently interpreted our reaction as displeasure, because she added, "And look how much you boys have been getting done around here, and all your work finished before the heat of the day." She had a point there. By the time it started to really warm up, I was usually sprawled in deep shade in the treehouse, watching the birds and squirrels, and luxuriating in the updrafts that swept up the face of the bluff from the river as it warmed in the morning sun. Or else playing pirates down at Cottonwood Point. Well, it wasn't all play, of course—that part definitely involved work. But since we *really were* looking for *actual treasure*, it was exciting work. The problem was that we had so much more to do, and we didn't know if we would be able to continue once the mobsters came through on the lease.

"We all have to make sacrifices in life," Mom said. "Offer it up for the Poor Souls in Purgatory," she suggested, brightly. I just glared at her—I had already said a third of a rosary for the Poor Souls that morning, and I still had two full ones to go that night before I could go to sleep—I was burning the candle at both ends, so to speak.

59.
K.C. PICNIC

On Saturday morning, I headed over to Riverview Park for the annual Knights of Columbus picnic. Richard and I sat on a picnic table in the shade. Richard was telling me about working at Laze-E-Daze with Crazy Carly, who was apparently living with Mr. Muscle. Dapper Man was also staying there but in a separate room.

I quit talking as I watched Mary Ann Ventura walk across the lawn toward us, first, because I was under oath to keep the Tom investigation a secret and, secondly, because she looked so pretty I couldn't have kept talking anyway.

"Hi, fellas," she said, climbing up onto the table and sitting next to me.

"Hi," I said, and couldn't think of anything else to say. *You're so pretty? Let's go for a walk together?* "Richard and I were just talking about school," I said, finally. *Sheesh! What a square comment!*

"That's hard to believe, Jamie Fletcher," she said, looking at me mischievously. "I could believe that about Richard, but I've never thought you cared anything at all about school, other than a place to play basketball," she added, her head tilted coyly. *Maybe she really would* like to go for a walk.

"There's Miller," Richard said suddenly, breaking the silence. "I gotta see him about teaming up on our science project before somebody else does." He slid off the picnic table. "Nice to see you, Mary Ann. Later, Jamie," he said as he wandered off.

"He's so nice," Mary Ann said.

"I know," I said, "He's one of my best friends."

"Wanna go for a walk?" I asked. "I'll show you something really neat."

"Sure."

"Okay, see those two big pear trees down the hill?"

"Yes. Is that it?"

"No," I laughed. "That's just the beginning. Those are The Gates of Hercules. They mark the way to a secret spring that comes out of the ground."

"A secret spring?" she asked, intrigued. "Really?"

"Yep," I nodded knowingly.

"Who else knows about it?" she asked.

"No one except Toby and Richard and me," I said.

"What about Marva Lynn?" she asked.

"Nah. Come on, it's really keen—I'll show you."

We ran down the hill between The Gates of Hercules, which towered above us on both sides, and entered the woods directly behind them. I found the path down a long, gradually rounded slope, still covered in last year's leaves. Before we reached the bottom of the slope we changed course, heading off to our right until we reached the brow of a deep ravine which opened at our feet, revealing a tiny stream at the bottom. The ravine was precipitous, and the route down was so treacherous that I offered to help Mary Ann. *Oh, God. Lord, be merciful to me, a sinner.* It was noticeably cool and damp as we approached the bottom, sliding and falling from tree to tree among the lush ferns and mosses which grew out of the steep sides. Hidden by the walls of the ravine, we were deep inside a private exploration of an exotic new world.

When we reached the bottom, I straddled the tiny stream, facing a fissure in the side of the opposite cliff, and scooped hopefully at the layers of wet leaves, removing thick, heavy clumps and dropping them into the stream behind me. And there it was, the secret spring, a natural fountain of crystal-clear water bubbling up out of a tiny round hole in the rock at the base of the cliff, and I knelt low over it, my left foot planted on a small level rock next to the spring and my right foot braced against the nearly vertical wall I had just descended. I inhaled the sweet fecund smell of wet earth and fern spores and hanging green moss and last year's dead leaves, all hovering in the air in that wet gash in the earth, and I drank the sweet water as it fountained into my mouth, and then I helped Mary Ann drink it. She laughed as it bubbled over her face and her hair where it hung forward in front of her shoulders, a soft musical laugh that lingered there in the stillness and the silence broken only by the soft babble of the bubbling water, and I stared at her, transported, and the image of her kneeling and laughing as the cool clear water played over her has never left me.

We took turns drinking and looking around at the sides of the steep ravine, the beautiful mosses and lichens and ferns which had never seen the sun. After a while, I said, "Guess what? There's more." She just looked at me, incredulous. A bit of her was far away. Part of me was, also. "I'll help you back up," I said.

Getting back up the ravine proved much more difficult even than the descent, but in fifteen minutes we were again at the top. We chose a gradual slope to the bottom of the hill, then rejoined the stream where it meandered back and forth in a hip-deep channel carved out of the bedrock over thousands of years. Following a faint path along the bank, we crossed the stream on a wooden footbridge built decades earlier as a Young Explorer project, and then re-crossed it, and crossed it again, as we wandered through a deep valley covered in virgin forest.

A thrush exploded from the foliage at our feet, causing Mary Ann to grab my arm, and stunning me into stillness as she clutched me, until finally we both looked at each other and laughed. I couldn't speak for Mary Ann, but the event was far more moving than funny to me. I silently hoped that there would be more occasions when Mary Ann would cling to me for protection. I made a show of selecting a stick of the right length and heft. "Just in case," I explained. Mary Ann's eyes grew wide. *Now they looked green!*

A red fox started up from the undergrowth and stared at us, his whiskers twitching, then turned and slipped away silently into the underbrush. We looked at each other—her green eyes wide with wonder. Fortunately, I didn't have whiskers, because they would have been twitching, too.

We continued to follow the overgrown footpath until it vanished from sight. As we stood still and looked around, trying to discern a clue as to where the path led, we heard splashing. Taking Mary Ann's hand, I led her carefully to the top of a small black basalt waterfall, the rocks smoothed by the stream which had cascaded down them for eons into the gorge below. We peered across the gorge to a sheer limestone wall at the far end, which rose eighty feet until it met the sky. Its exposed surface was marked by the remnants of drilled dynamite tubes. Moving closer to the mouth of the waterfall, we could see laid out on the ground below us, between the base of the waterfall and the far limestone wall, a train track running from right to left.

"We slide down this waterfall," I said. Mary Ann looked at me in utter disbelief, eyebrows halfway to her hairline, mouth open, preparing to either laugh or cry, I couldn't tell which.

Finally, she closed her mouth and leaned in closer to me. "We do?" she asked earnestly, her eyes wide open, head nodding a question, trying to ascertain if I were serious. Her eyes suddenly had a hint of brown and, maybe...gray?

"Yes," I said.

She took my hand. "Are you sure?" she whispered earnestly.

"Yes."

"This isn't a joke?"

"No."

"Is it safe?" she asked.

"Completely," I said. "I've done it lots of times. The rocks are all smooth. Nothing to bruise yourself on." She thought for a moment.

"How do you do it?" she asked.

"I'll show you—just do what I do," I said. I walked over to a wide, smooth chute, straddled the rushing water with my feet placed wide on two higher dry rocks, then sat down between them and was immediately swooshed over the edge. "See?" I said, looking up at her from the train tracks fifteen feet below, next to the shallow pool at the base of the fall. "It's fun—try it."

Hesitantly, she copied my footsteps, then sat down and yelped as the current took her over the edge and down to the bottom, where I helped arrest her progress. She was breathless, but her cheeks were rosy and her eyes just glowed. Definitely blue-gray. *Did this girl have chameleon in her blood?*

"I've never done anything like that before," she said.

"I've never done it with a girl before," I said. She smiled.

"Thank you for showing me, Jamie Fletcher," she said.

60.
HIGH ADVENTURE

We were standing in a deep man-made cut in one of the river bluffs, upstream from Mayfly. The waterfall fell into a creek bed parallel to the train track, which curved into the arched stone mouth of a train tunnel.

"Through here," I said, advancing toward the mouth of the tunnel. We could see the gleaming steel tracks curving away into the darkness and then disappearing. The other end of the tunnel was not visible.

"What if a train comes?" she asked. "We can't even see the other end."

"Don't worry," I said. "We listen for trains before we go in. You put your ear on the track, like this," I said, demonstrating. "Plus, they have to go really slow through the tunnel because of the big curve on this side of it. Also, they always blow their whistle. We'll have plenty of warning. And look," I said, advancing to the mouth of the tunnel and pointing inside, "there are places in the tunnel where you can duck into crevices in the wall and be safe even if a train does come."

So we both listened, and then we ran to the mouth of the tunnel and saw the deep fissures in the natural rock walls where a body could stand until the train had passed, and then we held hands "just in case anyone trips," and ran alongside the creek into the tunnel, our hearts pounding as we ran like the wind, rounding the long smooth curve inside, until we finally saw with relief the daylight framed by the matching stone arch at the far tunnel mouth. Minutes later, we exited the tunnel into blinding light, and our vista changed from the stone arch surrounded by black walls into a bright blue sky dotted with fluffy white clouds. The gleaming steel tracks in front of us continued on, penetrating the center of a rusting steel railroad bridge, where they straightened and elongated like a study in perspective as they shot away across the river.

The railroad bridge was an ancient swing bridge. It had been built on cut stone piers laid by masons working in diving bells on the riverbed. It had withstood innumerable floods, as well as collisions from enormous floating trees, and even huge boats and barges. It was lower to the water than the newer highway bridge, and the long channel span revolved upon a gargantuan turnstile which opened the channel span so that large boats and barges could pass through.

Perched right in front of us, at the near end of the bridge, stood a small one-room shack with windows on all four sides. Inside the shack were the controls which operated the swing bridge, along with a single railroad employee, whose job was to open the bridge for large boat traffic on the river and to make sure that it was locked in place for trains using the bridge.

We walked up to the shack and opened the door, revealing a superb view of the tunnel, the bridge, and the river, both upstream and downstream. Inside was a large dark green steel control box covered with switches, dials, and red and green lighted buttons. Standing in front of a tall gray steel stool at the control box stood an old man wearing an engineer's cap and chewing the wet stump of a cigar.

"Hi, Mr. Dindia," I said.

"Hello, son," he replied. "Who's your friend?"

"This is Mary Ann Ventura, Mr. Dindia," I said.

"Pleased to meet you, Mr. Dindia," Mary Ann said.

"Very nice to meet you, too, young lady," Mr. Dindia said.

"Can we ride the bridge, Mr. Dindia?" I asked. He looked at the control board.

"I don't see why not," he said. "No trains due for a while."

"Thank you, Mr. Dindia!" I said, turning to leave and holding the door for Mary Ann.

"Thank you!" Mary Ann said, as we left. Mr. Dindia waved.

"This way," I said. "We have to get past here," hopping across the break in the tracks which separated solid ground from the turnstile section. "Hang on!" I said, grabbing the bridge railing which ran along the plank walkway next to the tracks, then waving to Mr. Dindia. There was a booming "clunk" as the bridge released from the Missouri shore and slowly began to rotate. The end on which we stood swung downstream, out into the air thirty feet above the river, apparently unsupported. I looked across the length of the span to the other end and saw it swinging northward against the backdrop of sky and the Illinois shoreline as our end moved in the opposite direction. Mary Ann held onto my arm with both of her hands as we swung effortlessly over the water.

The river below us was calm, reflecting the azure sky and the few puffs of floating white clouds. It looked like a painting I had seen in "Great Western Art" from our school library, its surface muted and smooth, except for the contrail of small ripples which furrowed out downstream from the stone bridge piers. A light honeysuckle scent permeated the warm air, and a few early cottonwood tufts floated over the river like tiny hot air balloons, bright white in the sun.

I leaned over to Mary Ann and said in a low voice, "We're on a carnival ride in Heaven."

She just looked at me, far away, lost in thought, then gazed out over the water, and smiled, and nodded, then chuckled and turned back to me and said, "I think you're right, Jamie Fletcher—and imagine you being here!" I felt my eyes startle and my mouth drop open. I was speechless. She was still smiling. Her eyes were, what, gray-green? *She's right, but how does she know?*

The bridge slowed to a crawl, and we heard and felt the heavy iron "clunk" run through the steel superstructure and echo off the far riverbank, as Mr. Dindia locked the turnstile span into its fully open position.

"Looks like we're gonna stay for a while," I said, sitting down on the edge of the plank walkway and dangling my legs over the side. Mary Ann did the same.

"Watcha gonna do for the rest of the summer?" she asked.

"Work on basketball," I said. Then a sudden inspiration hit me. "Wanna know something?" I asked, confidentially.

"Is it a secret?" she asked.

"Yeah, you'll have to promise not to tell anyone," I said.

"No one?"

"No one. You promise?"

"Okay, I promise."

"You'll have to take the oath," I said.

"What oath?" So I told her.

> "I swear by the trees and earth and stone,
> I swear by my skin and blood and bone,
> I swear not to tell by my head and behind,

If I ever do I'll walk around blind."

"That's a horrible oath!" she said.

"Only if you break it," I said. "If you keep it, it can't hurt you a bit."

"Alright," she said, exasperated, "but this better be something good."

"You have to put one hand on a tree or the earth or a stone first," I said. She looked at me like she couldn't believe that was really necessary.

"We're in the middle of the river, Jamie—there are no trees here, and the closest earth and stone are probably on the bottom of the river, and I don't think I want to go there—I don't even know how deep it is here."

"Deep," I said, "like fifty-five feet. But the bridge plank counts as a tree." She wrinkled her nose.

"Smarty pants," she said, but she put a hand on the plank walkway. "How does it go again?" she asked, looking up at me. I knelt beside her and helped her through it, one line at a time. Then I stood up and held out my hands and she took both of them while she raised herself, gracefully, without any help from me, but still holding my hands, and she stood in front of me, facing me, and looking at me expectantly.

"Okay," I said. "This is it: Remember when I told you I'm gonna be the best basketball player in Mayfly?" Her eyes grew wide, her lashes blooming, reaching out to me, encouraging me. She remembered my secret, nodding.

"Well," I said, staring at her, and feeling the need to tell her more, "I'm gonna win the Mayfly Future Famer Trophy." Her eyelids popped open—she looked incredulous, her lashes now standing at attention, little exclamation points surrounding her irises, which had gone, what, gray-blue? *She was impressed. Why stop here?* "And I'm gonna play for the St. Louis Hawks in the NBA."

Mary Ann closed her mouth and looked off, gazing far away. Her eyes had an unfocused look, like she was trying to see into the future. I wondered what she saw—was it the same thing I saw? Because I saw headlines: "Fletcher Named Future Famer"; "Fletcher to Play for Notre Dame"; "Fletcher Drafted by Hawks." I saw myself being carried off the court by adoring fans; I saw Mary Ann cheering excitedly; I saw myself holding a large trophy, sweaty and smiling, my hair mussed, flashbulbs popping around me. I saw myself famous, a star in the NBA with lots of money and driving a Cadillac, owning a big house and eating steak for dinner every night, and having whatever kind of cookies I wanted for dessert, as many as I wanted.

"Oh, Jamie, I hope so!" she said. I felt like I could float. I had told her my dream and she didn't laugh. She even hoped it would come true for me.

We sat back down and watched the river flow past the bridge in silence. Neither of us spoke. Finally, I asked, "What are you going to do the rest of this summer?"

"Ride my horse," she said.

"What's your horse's name?"

"Sugarloaf," she said, smiling at me.

Just then we heard the "clunk" as Mr. Dindia disengaged the lock, and we started the long journey back. Climbing back up the waterfall was out of the question, so we didn't return through the train tunnel on our way back to the picnic. Instead, we walked another way, heading north on River Road, then ascending an ancient, eroded gravel road which wound up the bluff on switchbacks through deep woods, past an old quarry where older kids parked on a flat rock platform overlooked by a portion of the bluff face, then on up to the top. We were quieter now. I felt a bit shy about having told her my big secret.

As I lay in bed that evening, I thought about Mary Ann and Sugarloaf. I didn't have a horse, and I didn't know how to ride one even if I did. I didn't know a thing about horses—they would probably bite me. How was I going to learn to ride? Would Mary Ann always have a horse? Where would we keep it?

I couldn't muse long, though, because the Poor Souls were burning all day and all night, too, and I had better get on with my second Rosary before I got too tired and just fell asleep. Fortunately, I had decided to say my fractional rosary during my morning chores because I doubted that I could stay awake for anything past one full rosary at a time, so I had already done that one for the day—John and Michael understood and had agreed to be quiet so I could say the prayers—but I still had a full one to go. I reached under my pillow for my Rosary. I couldn't put my oven mitts on until I was finished with the beads.

61.
FOILED ATTEMPTS

Crackle. Crackle. "Base, this is Rover; come in please, over."

It was almost 9:30 that Saturday evening. Toby and I had already talked once, so I was alarmed to hear him calling again. *Must be an emergency!*

"Rover, this is Base, over," I replied in a whisper from my room. "Give me a minute, over," I continued, then turned off the unit. I ran out the back door into the far end of our yard and leaned against the trunk of the old elm tree next to Prince's house. Prince came over eagerly, and I knelt down and patted him while I switched the unit back on.

"Okay, Rover, this is Base. What's up, over?" I asked.

"Base, we gotta get this thing back," Toby said. "I'm afraid he's gonna notice it's gone, and I think he'll know who took it, over."

"We can try for Monday morning," I said. "I'll be serving, over."

Crackle, crackle. "Base, this is Blackstone here with Rover. I think sooner is better. We have no way to predict when he might look for it again, over."

They were both obviously worried. Toby had already been to the church and checked the key; it opened the door from the vestibule to the bell tower alright. He had climbed the stairwell to the top and looked around in the tower briefly, but found nothing helpful. The tower was brick inside and out, and the interior was open to the elements. The window ledges were laid in wide white stone and the window arches were framed with decorative white stone roping two inches in diameter. There were no hiding places that he could see, and nothing of any interest—no Playboys and no bottles—only a few ground-out cigarette butts on the floor. A dead end.

We decided to return the key as early as possible. Our first opportunity was to use P.J.'s Sunday Mass schedule as "Guaranteed Safe Time" for the second burglary, which meant the next morning. This created a problem, however. Neither John nor I were scheduled to serve Sunday Mass, so I would be with the rest of the family the entire time. I wouldn't be able to bring the walkie-talkie to church with me in the duffel bag, and I certainly couldn't transmit during Mass, even if I could manage to smuggle a walkie-talkie in under my sport coat.

We decided that I would sneak out of the house as soon as Dad and Mom were asleep and hide the base unit in a huge evergreen bush right next to the passageway between the church and school. Then, when I went to Mass with the family in the morning, I could duck out under the pretense of using the restroom, grab the walkie-talkie on my way into the passageway, make my transmission from the tiny little-kids' playground between the back of the church and the school (away from the prying eyes of other parishioners hurrying into church at the last minute), replant the unit in the bush, and hopefully be back in church before the *Introibo ad altari dei*.

The plan was neat, but I grudgingly reflected on the cost. It required me to stay awake until Mom and Dad were asleep and again risk getting caught out of the house at night. That was bad enough, but it was relatively small potatoes in the big scheme of things. The worst part was that I would have to give up my customary pre-liturgy

Joseph Welch

scriptural study of the beautiful Susannah taking off her clothes and bathing in her garden with her "oil and washing balls," whatever they were. This passage never failed to transport me to heights of spiritual ecstasy not attained by reading other parts of Sacred Scripture. Since this was an emergency, however, sacrifices had to be made. *Greater love than this hath no man.* Perhaps I would have time for spiritual renewal by way of a private scriptural session in the bathroom after breakfast. *Lord, be merciful to me, a sinner.*

Even though the plan was beautiful, the implementation was problematic. Phase One of the plan went okay. I had prior experience sneaking out by this point, and practice makes perfect. I removed the screen before turning in, said my extra rosary while I waited, and was out and back in fifteen minutes, having kept to the alleys to avoid apprehension. The problems began the next morning.

Phase Two began perfectly. Mom thought I was coming down with the flu because I was pale and sweaty before Mass—an unanticipated benefit of my nervousness, that played well into my ruse for needing to go to the bathroom. Eight minutes before Mass was scheduled to start, I rose and excused myself, leaving the pew and ignoring Mom's questioning eyes. I had just seen that the celebrant was Fr. Jim and not P.J., and I had to warn Richard and Toby that P.J. was still in the rectory. And I had to get back quickly; otherwise, Dad would come looking for me to see if I was alright.

Quietly, I ducked out through one of the big front church doors just as it was closing on a last-minute parishioner, jumped down the front steps two at a time, dashed to the bush, and retrieved the unit. Just as I entered the narrow walkway between the church and school, walkie-talkie in hand, another figure darkened the opening onto the playground at the far end. The figure was accompanied by a fat, ancient dog on a leash. *Oh, God—Mrs. Buben and Buddy.*

It would have been impolite and perhaps threatening for me to enter the narrow tunnel while she was in it, and it would probably take that pair a full five minutes to traverse the passageway, at which point I would no doubt then be drawn into "polite conversation." I would be lucky to make it back in time for the sermon—actually, not lucky at all, because then I would have to go to a *second* Sunday Mass because I had missed some of the important parts.

Some parts of the Mass were so important that if you missed them, you hadn't really "attended Mass." The mandatory parts included the reading of the Epistles and the Gospel, and, of course, the moment of Consecration, when bread and wine were changed into the actual body and blood of Jesus through a miraculous process known as "transubstantiation."

And although I had never seen it in any of the Church-approved published Catechisms and had never specifically checked with a priest on this particular fact situation, I was pretty sure that missing a required critical part of the Mass so that I could make a walkie-talkie transmission in furtherance of a conspiracy to commit a repeat burglary at the pastor's house would not be considered an "excusable absence" by the One True Church. Cradle Catholics develop a sense for these things. *Lord, be merciful to me, a burglar.*

Since this was new territory for me, and since I really had to get back inside the church in a hurry, I prayed for inspiration. *Holy Ghost, be my guide,* I breathed, in heartfelt supplication. And, just as I prayed for inspiration, at that very moment, my prayer was answered—I knew what I had to do.

Holding the walkie-talkie out of sight inside my sport coat, I walked quickly back out to Broadway, turned left and dashed to the school steps, checking for traffic in both directions as I went. I then ducked behind the wall to the front steps, which shielded me from westbound traffic, while a large juniper shielded me from anything eastbound.

I pulled out the walkie-talkie and pressed the "Transmit" button. "Oak, this is Base. Come in, please, over," I said.

Crackle, crackle. "Roger, Base," Richard's whispered voice said, "this is Oak, over." I heard, as relief flooded over me.

"Oak, abandon the attempt! I repeat, abandon the attempt. Confirm. Over."

"Roger that. Abandoning attempt. Say again, abandoning attempt. Over." Richard's voice came through above the static.

"Gotta run, Oak. Base over and out," I said, hitting the "off" switch just as Mrs. Buben and Buddy emerged from the passage. I stashed the walkie-talkie in the prickly bush—I'd just have to pick it up later—and ran for the church door, speaking to Mrs. Buben as I passed her.

Since we were committed to returning the borrowed key as soon as possible, however, I went back to church at the start of the next Mass, walked into the vestibule at 8:02 a.m., and peeked through the swinging doors at the back of the church. *Fr. Jim again. Damn!* Same result at 10:00 a.m. *Damn! Damn!* Not only had I not been able to catch P.J. scheduled out of the rectory for a guaranteed "safe time," but also it was nearly noon and I still had not had my much-anticipated private scriptural session with Susannah, nor even so much as a passing frolic in delicious comic-strip color with Prince Valiant's comely bride, Valeta (both of which were customary Sunday morning "indulgences"—to coin a term—different concept entirely) *and all because P.J. would rather sit at home on his butt than do some of the priestly work that was his job. Sloth is one of the Seven Deadly Sins, you lazy jerk.* I would have to try again with the tried-and-true duffel-bag-in-the-cassock-closet ploy the next morning at early Mass. At least there was a silver lining to my continuing altar boy duties—this created more opportunity to verify P.J.'s whereabouts so I could give Toby and Richard some Guaranteed Safe Time to replace the key.

At this point, I decided I couldn't afford to waste any more daylight and needed to get my Hundred Layups in, then head south to meet Richard and Toby at Cottonwood Point and see if we could put in a day's work searching for the wreck. Richard was still at work at Laze-E-Daze, but I radioed Toby, who was game. I then radioed Sharkbait and told him we'd see him at 1:30.

"Have you taken the key back yet?" Sharkbait asked as he led us through the swamp.

"No, Sharkbait," Toby said. "He's been home all day—we tried at all three Masses. We'll try again tomorrow morning."

"Please," Sharkbait said, biting his lip, "I hope you can get it done."

"Me three," Toby said, looking at me.

62.
REPLACING THE ITEM

We set up the key return attempt for early the next morning. Richard agreed to be in Overlook Oak at 6:20 to man the Big Ear while Toby, armed with Rover, waited at the fissure. Then, once I knew who the celebrant was for early Mass, I could radio Rover and Oak and let them know.

I carried my duffel bag to early Mass via "Shank's Mares"—which is what my Grandmother called traveling by foot. While we were *en route*, I radioed Richard at Overlook station and verified that he was in the Overlook position and Toby was at the fissure.

"Call you back in a few minutes," I said. "Going silent. Over and out."

I walked up the high steps outside the back of the church that led to the altar boys' robing room and waited outside the door. John opened the door quietly and walked inside, looked around quickly, then turned and motioned me in.

I entered quickly and dumped the duffel bag in the bottom of the closet, then tossed a black cassock over it while John donned his cassock and surplice. I grabbed a cassock in my size and put it on, then moved to the starched white cotton surplice cabinet and selected something clean and starchy, and shrugged it over my head. John, meanwhile, left the room, ducking into the passageway behind the altar on his way to the priest's sacristy while I waited at the opening.

"Good morning, Fr. Reiser," I heard him say, clearly enunciating and speaking a bit too loudly.

That was my signal—the coast was clear at the rectory. I immediately retrieved the duffel and took it outside. I bent over and unzipped the bag to retrieve the walkie-talkie. As I straightened up with it in my hand, I was stunned by a very loud voice which thundered right next to my ear.

"What do you think you're doing?"

My blood froze. I was too shocked to speak. I turned and saw P.J. standing there, furious, glaring at me.

"I said what are you doing?" he repeated.

"I was checking the range on our walkie-talkie," I replied, and added, lamely, "to see if it would travel this far."

Then, on a sudden inspiration, I held down the "transmit" button, brought the walkie-talkie up to my mouth, and said, "Sorry, Fr. Reiser is here. I have to go now. Over and out," then immediately switched it off before Richard could answer me, and looked at P.J. with what I hoped was a contrite and obedient expression.

"Put that thing away," he said. "You're here to serve Mass, not play games."

"I wasn't playing," I mumbled as I turned away.

"What did you say?" he demanded.

"I said I thought I had time," I said.

"Don't dare backtalk me, boy. You thought wrong," he said. "Get in there and kneel down."

Joseph Welch

I put the walkie-talkie back in the duffel, then put it on top of the cabinet by the door while he stood there and watched me. Without looking at him, I proceeded down the passageway to the sacristy as he followed behind me. John met my eyes quickly as I entered, and we each knelt on a *prie dieu* and waited. P.J. made us wait, doing God-knows-what behind us. We didn't give him the satisfaction of turning around—after a little while, I closed my eyes and started breathing heavily, like I was so grateful for the break that I was taking a catnap. Finally, he knelt on his own *prie dieu* between us and blasted through the Prayer Before Mass, loudly and angrily, which prompted me to open my eyes and adopt an extremely earnest and prayerful expression while I said it slowly and deliberately, leaving him with the choice of kneeling there waiting for me to finish or getting up and leaving in the middle of the prayer. I could feel the heat radiating off him as he knelt there impotently, waiting until I wound it up, in the most moving display of spiritual transcendence I could manage. *How's it feel, jerk? Watch—I can act as pious as you can.*

I spent most of my time at Mass thinking up ways to make him mad. While I didn't have the nerve to repeat my trick of intentionally ignoring his stupid "that's enough" signal at the Washing of the Hands, I contented myself with imagining that I was pouring the water down the back of his neck instead. Extremely gratifying. If he had glanced up at my face he would have wondered what I found so enjoyable about the handwashing.

I also managed to move backward and forward on the balls of my feet, very slowly, while holding the book open as he tried to read the Epistles in Latin. Finally, he grabbed the sides of the book to hold it still, by which time he was enraged and probably dizzy. I gave him my puzzled look, brows furrowed, like I couldn't understand what was wrong with him, or maybe I was concerned about his health. "*I thought I was helping,*" my eyes said, obviously wounded.

When Mass ended, after the Prayers for the Conversion of Russia, I grabbed the duffel and was out the door like a shot. As soon as I was out of sight, I radioed Oak for a status report.

"Did you put it back?" I asked.

"Affirmative," Richard replied.

"What about the medal?" I asked.

"Negative. No sign of it. Important discovery for in-person only. Over."

"Okay," I said, surprised. "See you at the landslide tunnel, then. Over and out." I switched off.

Important news! I wondered what in the world that could be. I hoped they had found some proof of something: preferably murder, but any other crime would do. *How's that for backtalk, you pompous jerk?*

I hustled through my chores, weeding like an International Harvester-engineered nightmare. I was the gandy-dancingest John Henry of the tomato patch. Finally, our time in the trough ended. Twenty minutes to go before I could head south on River Road, and I couldn't stand to just stand around. I didn't want to get there early, though; I knew I didn't want to wait around either.

"Got time for a quick game of 3-Man-21?" I asked John and Michael. "I'll only shoot with my left hand, except for one basket with my right." I had to tell them that to keep them honest, because otherwise they would just overplay my left hand the entire game. So I just shot left hooks and layups until my last basket, and still finished in thirteen minutes: 21-9-6.

"So long, suckers," I said. "I got places to go and things to do," then grabbed my bike and headed to River Road. I still had to wait around at the landslide tunnel until Richard and Toby arrived.

"So, what's the news?" I asked, when the Musketeers were all present.

"Wait 'til we're all together—Sharkbait needs to hear this, too," Toby said.

We picked up our snake sticks where we had left them leaning against the trunk of a willow tree in Sidney's yard, then followed him through the bayou.

"So, what's the big news?" I asked, when we were all together on the gravel bar.

"He has a walkie-talkie," Toby said.

"What?" I asked.

"P.J. has a walkie-talkie," Toby said.

"Why would he have a walkie-talkie?" I asked.

"No idea," Toby said. "Maybe in case his phone goes out."

"If we're talking on our walkie-talkies, could he hear us on his?" I asked, looking at Richard.

"Sure," Richard said, "if he has the same frequency as ours and if it's tuned to our channel."

"Oh my God!" I said. "How can we know if he's on there?"

"No way to know, as long as he's quiet," Richard said. "He could be listening to us every day if he's on our frequency and discovered our channel."

"We don't know if he has or not, but just in case, we better switch channels," I said.

"And let's change the name of Oak," Richard said.

"To what?" Toby asked.

"How about 'Dirt,'" I suggested. "That's what we're trying to get on him, anyway."

"'Dirt?'" Toby asked, looking around. Sharkbait looked puzzled.

"We've already got 'Overlook Oak'" Richard said. "And I think we shouldn't use the walkie-talkies except in emergencies, and even then, we should talk in code," Richard said.

"Yeah," I said. "The Mobsters might have walkie-talkies, too. Let's change everything. So Overlook Oak can be 'Double O,'" I suggested.

"Good. And let's call watching the rectory 'Playing Tiddlywinks,'" Toby suggested.

"And the mobsters can be 'Cinderella'; Mr. Muscle can be 'Cinder' and Dapper Man can be 'Ella,'" Richard said.

"And the gravel bar can be 'The Projects,'" Toby said.

"Good one," I said. "P.J. can stay the same. He has no idea what that means."

"Although he tries to be P.J. pretty hard," Toby said.

"All day, every day," Richard said.

"What's 'P.J.'?" Sidney asked.

Toby looked at Richard, who gave him a quick, almost imperceptible shake of the head, then said quickly, "It's Fr. Reiser's initials. Phillip John Reiser."

"I didn't know that," Sharkbait said.

Toby and I nodded approvingly at Richard. We had called him Pompous Jerk for so long that we had forgotten his initials were actually "P.J."

"Have you taken the key back yet?" Sharkbait asked after a while.

"Yes," I answered. "Toby did it yesterday morning."

"Yeah, it went fine," Toby said.

"Good," Sharkbait said.

As the three of us emerged from the landslide tunnel on our way back to Mayfly, I asked Toby if he had looked for Tom's St. Thomas Medal while he was in the rectory.

"Yeah," Toby said, "I looked everywhere I could think of—even in his jewelry box—it wasn't there."

"Well," I said, "just because you couldn't find it doesn't mean he doesn't have it, does it? He might even carry it with him." The two of them just looked at me, faces blank. *Huh! I guess that hadn't occurred to either of them—am I the only one who sees through this jerk?*

63.
SNEAK PEEK

It was Tuesday, July 2. Sidney's mom had been worried sick because the mobsters had told her that July 1 was their starting date, but they hadn't signed the lease or paid her the first month's rent.

A light mist was burning off the river below a blue sky as Blackstone Richard, Toby the Hook, Sharkbait, and I were nearing Cottonwood Point on our winding trek through the swamp. Sharkbait was still the only one who knew the entire safe route, even though he had led the rest of us through it multiple times, but I was starting to feel comfortable on parts of the journey. We had all learned very quickly to keep our eyes peeled on the path, since the snake population was incredible—higher than any place I had ever seen—we saw multiple snakes every day. Each of us had had opportunities to use our snake sticks, but none of us were as quick or accurate with them as Sharkbait.

As we approached the gravel bar, we heard the unmistakable sound of a boat motor. Surprised, we stopped to listen, then Sharkbait quickly checked our surroundings and led us forward, until we stopped and knelt on the last wooded verge of the swamp. We saw a work-style jon boat approaching the sandbar.

"It's the mobsters," Toby said. "I'd recognize Dapper Man anywhere. He looks funny sitting in the boat in his hat and suit."

"Yeah, and that's Mr. Muscle with him," Richard said, "but I don't recognize the third guy."

"I do," Sidney said. "He's been by the house. That's the manager of the mining company."

"Has your mom signed the lease?" I asked.

"No, but she's going to. She thought they were going to start work yesterday," Sidney said.

"I think Toby and I need to stay out of sight," I said. "They know us from the motel, and they know Tom was spying on them, and they don't like us. They'll be suspicious if they see us."

"I need to stay out of sight, too," Richard said. "They see me every day at Laze-E-Daze."

"I'll go talk to them," Sharkbait said.

"Okay, but take off your pirate gear," I said. "Try to get rid of them before they find our tools."

"No problem," Sidney said. "They shouldn't be here before they sign the lease anyway."

He left the swamp as we watched the pilot gun the motor and then turn it off, allowing the boat to run up onto the sand bar.

"Hey!" Sidney yelled as he walked toward them, "This is private property!"

"Hey, kid," Dapper Man called, as the three of them stood up and stepped over the sides of the boat.

"Oh, it's you," Sidney said, as if he'd just recognized them. "What are you doing here?"

"Prospecting for gravel," Dapper Man said.

"But you haven't signed the lease," Sidney said. "And there was supposed to be a month's rent—a hundred dollars."

"Well, well," Dapper Man said, "you know an awful lot about this."

"I only know what my Mom told me," Sidney said. "She said there was no deal until you signed the lease, because you could change your mind any time you wanted, so I don't think it's fair to be prospecting here without signing the lease and paying her."

"Well, maybe we're not so sure we want to sign the lease," Mr. Muscle said.

"Exactly," Sidney said, "and that's why you shouldn't be here prospecting—you might not like what you find and decide not to. She said you're gambling, but she says she can't afford to gamble. So if you get to look around before you sign the lease, then you make her have to gamble instead of you. So my Mom could be taking a chance letting you in here to prospect before you agree to pay her."

"You think you're pretty smart, don't you?" Mr. Muscle said.

"Quiet, Rocko, I'll handle this," Dapper Man said.

"Well, I'm gonna be in Fourth Grade this year," he said, in his best attempt at endearing *naivete*.

"What's that string, kid? And those stakes?" the Manager asked, narrowing his eyes as he piped up for the first time.

"What?" Sidney asked.

"Over there," the Manager said, as all three heads swiveled in the direction he pointed. The three of us held our collective breath from where we crouched back in the swamp.

"Oh," Sidney said, kicking at the gravel at his feet, "I was trying to measure how much land Mom is leasing."

"Why?" Dapper Man asked, flashing Sidney a fake smile.

"So I could see if the price was fair," Sidney answered.

"How much land is it?" Dapper Man asked.

"I never finished figuring it out," Sidney answered. "I have to divide it into so many little sections because of its irregular shape, and it takes a lot of time for just one person. Mom won't walk through the swamp because of all the poisonous snakes."

"Snakes!" Mr. Muscle erupted, his mouth open.

"Sure," Sidney said. "That's a swamp—snakes love the place."

"Do they ever come out here?" Mr. Muscle asked.

"Yeah, sure, all the time, but not near as many as there are in the swamp. That place is lousy with 'em. You can't hardly take a step in there without walkin' on one."

"How do *you* get through it, then?" the Manager asked, suspiciously.

"Snakes don't bother me, even the poisonous ones—I used to play with 'em when I was a kid. Plus I know the safe path. I keep my eyes peeled, though, and hit 'em with a stick if they look like they're gonna strike me. Even the really big ones don't like gettin' hit with a stick. They can be pretty fast, though," he said, "and sometimes they'll have a mate with them that you don't see at first."

The three men were quiet, just staring at Sidney, probably reevaluating their assumption that he was just a chubby little kid—we could see them exchanging glances. I could tell just what they were thinking. *Growing up in a swamp on the banks of the Mississippi River probably makes a boy fairly handy with a stick.*

"Come on, boys, we need to get that lease signed," Dapper Man said. "I don't want to wait another month. We'll be back soon, young man," he said, turning to Sidney.

"Okay, I'll help you push off," Sidney said, as the men climbed into the boat, and the Manager started the motor. "See you later, then," he called, standing on the shore and waving at them, like the lonely little kid he had been when we found him. He stood there until they were almost at the Mayfly Harbor, then walked into the swamp.

"I heard the Manager call me 'that little shitass,' when they were driving back upriver," he told us, chuckling, as he rejoined us on the edge of the swamp. "Moron has no idea how far voices carry across the water. Plus, he was yelling over the boat motor," he continued, breaking out into a laugh. I realized that was the first time I had ever seen him laugh—he always seemed so serious, like he was worried about something. I'm not sure why it happened, but while we stood there and watched him laughing, we all started laughing, too. And it just kept going as we looked from one to the other.

Finally, Toby said, "I think we need to move our tools into the swamp, though."

"Yeah," I agreed. "What about our string and stakes? They're sort of a giveaway."

"I think they're okay where they are," Richard said. "That was a great explanation. How did you ever think that up, Sharkbait, about the string?" Richard asked.

"Yeah, that was a really great lie!" Toby said, admiringly.

"Hawkeye gave me the idea," he said, looking at me. "The first day we met, when you were calculating the area of the sandbar. I've been thinking about how I might go about it."

Blackstone Richard just laughed. "I see you have," he said. "That was a great answer."

"Yeah," I said. "You'd make a good poker player."

"Yeah, especially Liar's Poker," Toby said.

64.
THE VISITORS

That afternoon, Toby and I dribbled over to Coach Hedges' house for basketball clinic. We were still doing our daily shooting drills, and had raised our percentages dramatically under his tutelage, now that we understood the importance of balance, attention to detail, and focus. At this point, we had been working on rocker steps for a week. He had taught us to keep our weight low and evenly distributed, so that when we stepped out with one foot, we had the option of stepping back into a perfectly balanced position for a jump shot. He also showed us how to avoid traveling, which was one of the primary risks of the rocker step, but which could be eliminated by starting to dribble first, doing a rocker step while dribbling, and either shooting, passing off the dribble, or switching directions with a crossover dribble to the other hand.

Coach Hedges had no use for players who "showboated," but he taught us the situations where fancy moves, like dribbling between our legs or behind our back, or even passing the ball behind our back, served a legitimate function. Changing direction while dribbling could be done faster, with better deception and a lower risk of having the ball stolen during the crossover, if the dribble was passed from one hand to the other by bouncing it between our legs. Or, if we were being pursued down the floor by a faster defender on a runaway fast break, we could be assured of an unblocked layup by a quick slowdown before suddenly

Summer of '63

dribbling once behind our back to the other hand, simultaneously changing direction and laying it up on the other side of the basket. Both Toby and I practiced these moves hundreds of times, and with both hands. Finally, Coach Hedges had us put on masks so we couldn't even see the ball, which made us focus intensely on its whereabouts during the maneuver.

"I want you to remember this time, right now, this drill," he said, "when you're in a game situation. Your focus should be the same as it is right now. Close your eyes and memorize this. Walk it through in your mind, step by step. And I want you to do it again, slowly, five times before you go to sleep tonight."

And so it went, on and on. Toby and I continued to improve, to learn new skills, and to become basketball terrors, at least for our age, due to his superb coaching and our practice. He worked us every day until he wore us out, and we dragged home late every afternoon, continuing to perform our crossovers and left-handed dribbling as we went.

When John and Michael arrived home from Cliffhanger duty in Overlook Oak, I perked up right away—it was obvious they were bursting with news.

"You're not gonna believe what we just heard!" Michael said. "The mobsters were back at the rectory. John was listening with the Big Ear."

"Yeah," John chimed in, "after the two of them went inside, I heard Dapper Man say, 'Did you get her to agree?' and P.J. said, 'Yeah, she'll do whatever I recommend to her.'"

"And guess what!" Michael said. "They're paying P.J. to get Sidney's Mom to sign the lease!"

"What?" I said, "Are you sure?"

"Yep," John said. "I heard him say it. P.J. said, 'Do you have my commission?'" John said, his eyes bulging. "My commission!"

"Oh my God!" I said.

"I know," John said, "and Dapper Man said, 'You'll get it when she signs.'"

"Then P.J. said, 'Well, I hope you have it with you because she already signed. I have two copies right here.' Then they were quiet for a minute, and I could hear paper rustling, and then Dapper Man said, 'Well, it just so happens that I do,' and P.J. said, 'Alright, then, sign both these copies and take one of them down to her with her first month's rent, and I'll relieve you of a couple of those hundreds.'"

"And then Dapper Man said, 'Alright, there's one hundred, and two hundred' and P.J. said, 'Thank you,' and Dapper Man said, 'Thanks for your help. We're going down there right now.'"

"And they were talking about P.J.'s gambling operation again. Just as they were leaving, Dapper Man said, 'How's your gambling operation going?' and P.J. said, 'I think we're ready!'

"Then we saw all of them come out the front door and Dapper Man said, 'Thanks for your help, Father,' and P.J. said, 'It's a pleasure doing business with you,' and then the mobsters got in the car and drove down the hill."

"And right after they left," Michael said, "John gave me the headphones, and I heard P.J. say to the operator, '1723 South,' then he was quiet for a minute, then he said, 'Hello, it's Fr. Reiser. A couple of men from the mining company are on their way down to your place to give you a signed copy of the lease and a hundred dollars for the first month's rent.' Then he said, 'Happy to help. Send Sidney up sometime, will you? I'd like to see him.' Then he just said goodbye."

65.
FENCING THE BAR

The next day was Independence Day, and the Fletcher boys were excused from morning chores in honor of the holiday. John and I were home from early Mass by 7:30, ate breakfast, and made our beds. Then the Cliffhangers deployed for the day's duties. John and Michael headed to Overlook Oak. I biked down River Road to the landslide tunnel rendezvous with Richard and Toby. Toby had obviously come down early—he was standing next to his bike when Richard and I arrived together.

"Guess what I found?" Toby announced, pulling an envelope from his pocket and opening it hurriedly. He pulled out an article entitled "Lost Confederate Treasure," and held it up for our inspection. The first page showed a photo of a gold bar bearing a round stamp with the initials "C.S.A." As Richard skimmed the article, Toby pulled a second item out of the envelope. It was folded up like a map. The title was typed on a mailing label attached to the front: "*Patterns of Sedimentation Deposit on Mississippi River 1865 – Present.*"

"What is it?" I asked.

"A hydrology report," Richard said, handing me the treasure article and reaching for the second document. He unfolded it, kneeling on the road, and pored over it. "This is what they were looking for—look—Cottonwood Point is shown right here," he said, pointing. "This red line shows the bank in 1865, and the blue line shows the outline of the sandbar as it exists now. These curvy lines show river currents."

"Where'd you find them?" I asked Toby.

"They were stashed in the wood bin at the top of the back stairs. I think he was trying to get out of there fast and figured he'd get rid of the incriminating evidence and pick it up again later. I'm sure he had no idea they were going to kill him," Toby said.

"You need to put these in a safe place," Richard said, folding them up and handing them back to Toby, "someplace where the mobsters can't find them. This is evidence. But we also need to study them."

"Maybe we should keep them in Overlook Oak," I suggested.

"Good idea," Richard said. "We need to keep them dry, but that shouldn't be a problem."

The three of us headed to Sharkbait's. As we rode along River Road, we could see a towboat churning downriver in a rush, judging by the size of the white bow wave. It was pushing a single barge, a work platform with a crane perched on it, together with coils of rope and cables and rolls of chain link fencing.

"They drove down late yesterday afternoon and gave Mom the signed lease," Sharkbait said, passing out our snake sticks, "and paid the first month's rent. They were complaining about River Road being closed by the landslide and having to drive an extra seven miles each way on the State Highway. I went out and got all our tools and hid them back in the swamp. I thought they'd need me to guide them through to the sand bar, but they didn't want to go through the swamp. They said they would rather come and go by boat since the road is blocked."

We could hear the diesel thrum of the towboat growing louder as we made our way through the swamp. When we got near the sand bar, we left the swamp, turning upriver at the foot of the overlooking hill. We searched the area with our sticks, then stopped behind a small natural levee, dropped to our knees in the tall grass, and watched.

"We need to take off our pirate bandanas," Richard said, "and put them in our pockets." We did.

The towboat was heading in toward the sandbar, shoving the work platform in front of it. Besides the barge pilot, there were seven men on the work platform, including Dapper Man, Mr. Muscle and the manager. Within an hour, the men had tied the barge up to two big cottonwoods just upriver from the bar, using huge ropes three inches in diameter. Then they returned to the barge, grabbed two loops of steel cables, and started in our direction. We hit the ground quickly, staying low and still. They looped the cables around two large cypress trees and closed the loops with cleats, then a man on the work barge used a ratchet jack to tighten them, while the towboat pilot pushed the work barge tight against the bar.

"We need to get out of here," I said.

"This way," Sharkbait said. "We can watch them from higher up on the hill."

We returned along a path we had not yet seen, sticks in hand, until we left the foot of the hill on the verge of the swamp and started to climb the tail end of the upriver bluff. As we moved higher, walking across the face of the hill on a deer path through the woods, we had sporadic views of the men unloading rolls of chain link fence, and dropping them at regular intervals along the swamp side of the bar.

Sharkbait showed us to a comfortable seat on a fallen log halfway up the hill where we could sit quietly and watch the operation.

They drove posts in the corners, interspersed by T-stakes, then stretched the fence and affixed it to the stakes. They ran the fence all the way into the water at both ends. There was no gate. Finally, they posted two signs on the fence facing the swamp: "No Trespassing" and "Trespassers Will Be Prosecuted." They didn't fence the water side, but just drove two stakes up- and downriver from the work platform, then posted the same two signs on them, which we read as they lay on the bar prior to installation: "No Trespassing" and "Trespassers Will Be Prosecuted." They were still working when Toby and I had to go back to town for basketball clinic.

As we left, I looked around at our pirate crew and saw only slack faces and vacant stares.

"Now what?" Toby asked.

"I think our dig is over," I said.

Sharkbait said nothing.

"I need to think about this," Richard said.

When Toby and I left, Richard stayed with Sharkbait to watch.

66.
HEAVEN

The next day was July 5, the first of the nine First Fridays which I had committed to observing, in exchange for my guaranteed ticket to heaven: the promise of the Sacred Heart of Jesus that I would have a chance to go to Confession right before I died.

Fr. Jim had promised to say early Mass so I could go to Confession immediately prior—I certainly ought to be able to maintain a "state of grace" until I received Holy Communion thirty minutes later. I would just need to monitor my thoughts carefully until then and hope to God that there wouldn't be any pretty girls at early Mass, because the best intentions could be overcome in a second if I were taken by surprise and inadvertently had an impure thought before I realized it or could even stop myself. *Lord, be merciful to me, a sinner. Seriously, Lord. Please.*

That night, after my second rosary and donning the oven mitts, I tried to reason out any problems with my Big Plan to ride this First Friday promise of the Sacred Heart all the way into Heaven. Jesus promised that if I went to Holy Communion while in the "state of grace" on nine consecutive First Fridays, I would get two very valuable spiritual benefits: a Plenary Indulgence, and a chance to go to Confession before I died.

A Plenary Indulgence was the absolute gold standard of indulgences—it erased all the burning-in-purgatory time I had accumulated in a lifetime of sinning—up to that date, anyway. But, I reasoned, even a Plenary Indulgence might not be of much use to me. Sure, it satisfied all the purgatorial comeuppance I had stacked up to date, but that was assuming that I could even make it into Purgatory—first, I would have to avoid Hell!

Plus, an indulgence did nothing for my future sins, and at the rate I was accumulating them, the total length of my required personal purification by fire, even a week later, could be staggering. Plus, the indulgence did nothing to actually *forgive sins*, it only erased the punishment still owed for sins which had already been forgiven! Which didn't really sound much like forgiveness to me—it sounded like Somebody—not to mention any names—was holding a pretty serious grudge—but of course, God really does have a long memory, so maybe that just goes with the territory. Nothing I could do about that, anyway.

No, the big-ticket item in the entire First Friday Devotions strategy was the chance to go to Confession right before I died. And even that was not foolproof. What if I declined the opportunity? Because, truth be told, I have a "chance" to go to Confession every single weekday morning when I am serving Mass, but I don't do anything about it. If I asked Fr. Jim—or even that jerk P.J.—if he would hear my Confession, either one of them would surely say 'yes.'

Like, what if I didn't know I was gonna die? Sure, if I knew I was about to die and this was my last chance, I would certainly ask to go, but what if I didn't know? The Promises of the Sacred Heart of Jesus don't mention that you'll know you're about to die, in which case you'd certainly take advantage of your last chance. You might not know it was your last chance, so you might just casually pass on it, like I did every single morning.

Like maybe I had already been to Confession on Saturday afternoon, but P.J. was hearing confessions that day, and maybe I didn't know that was my last chance, 'cause I was gonna get hit by a truck and killed on the way home, but there were certain things I didn't want to mention to him, so I held back and didn't confess all my sins, but that made it a "bad Confession," which was another Mortal Sin, in addition to all my other sins, so when I died with that on my conscience, the "bad Confession" Mortal Sin alone would send me straight to Hell; do not pass 'go'; do not collect absolution.

Because unless I knew I was about to be killed, I wouldn't want to mention to P.J. that I helped Toby break into his house—twice—or that I hated his guts because he thought he was so much better than I was and treated me like dirt, and because he was cruel to Mary Ann when he told her she couldn't have her horse in Heaven, and because he was a liar who said that dogs couldn't go to Heaven, when anybody with half a brain knew they did—at least the good dogs, which was almost all of them. *If faith teaches us anything, it's that good dogs go to Heaven.*

Hell, I thought, *Heaven must be completely overrun with dogs by now.* I figured they were mostly all cloud-broken, or whatever it was in Heaven, and knew where to go to the bathroom, and after they went, it probably changed by some kinda miracle into something good and nice and maybe even beautiful, maybe just some kinda pixie-dust stuff that maybe went into the rain, and showered down on people, watering the earth like some kinda blessing, and made the trees grow and the flowers bloom and the crops flourish, and filled the ponds and lakes and ran into the rivers and made people smile and help each other and give more money to make the Pagan Babies little Catholics so they could have a chance to get indulgences and go to Confession so they could get to Heaven, too.

And unless I knew for sure that I was about to die, and that was my last chance, I also wouldn't tell P.J. about calling him names behind his back every chance I got—even though he deserved it—or about trying my darnedest to get him arrested for murder—not unless I absolutely couldn't help it.

No, it was clear I would have to be on the alert. Nothing was foolproof. I could only do the best I could do.

67.
FIRST FRIDAY

So, early the next morning, on Friday, July 5, I was up and at church early. I told John I was gonna get the cruets filled and the candles lit, so he didn't have to show up until 6:25 a.m. He didn't argue—he didn't even wonder what I was up to—he just thought I was paying tribute to his status as a Knight of the Altar. I ran all the way to church and up the steps into the sacristy. I wasn't sure Fr. Jim had remembered, and I didn't want to make P.J. suspicious, so I just put on my long black cassock and starched blousy white surplice over the top, like always, then headed quickly along the curved passageway behind the altar to the sacristy.

"Well, Jamie, I see you remembered it's First Friday," Fr. Jim said, a twinkle in his eye.

"Yes, Father," I said, suddenly embarrassed to be standing there with him face-to-face. I had only ever gone to Confession anonymously, at least in principle, because usually the priest and the penitent were in separate rooms with an opaque screen between them so the priest couldn't see my face and, theoretically at least, didn't know who I was, but Fr. Jim knew for sure who I was and was about to find out what kind of sins I committed and how often. I didn't know how to begin under these circumstances.

"Why don't you just kneel here on the *prie dieu* while I hear your Confession," he suggested. "I can't imagine that it will take very long," he said, smiling. So I did—I told him everything—everything I could think of, at least. I gave him my best estimate of how many impure thoughts I had every single day, and all the rest of it, and even told him I hated Fr. Reiser and called him names. He asked what names and, when I told him, he actually chuckled.

"Yeah, I can see that," he said. "Sometimes I do the same thing. Whoops! Don't tell anyone that—remember the seal of the confessional," he said, smiling, even though I think he was kidding, because I didn't think it worked that way.

When I had finished, he just said, "For your penance, say three Our Fathers and three Hail Marys and now make a good Act of Contrition."

"Oh my God, I am heartily sorry…" I began, while he murmured in a Latin undertone the prayer by which priests granted absolution to penitent sinners. Then I stood up, feeling like a new man.

If John had been awake when he stumbled into the sacristy five minutes later and plunked himself down on the *prie dieu* for the Prayer Before Mass, he might have noticed a faint golden luminescence hovering in a circle above my head. Apparently, it wasn't a permanent fixture, however.

Michael and John took the morning Cliffhanger watch at Overlook Oak. Richard, Toby, and I were to head south, meet up with Sharkbait, and spy on the mobsters searching for the *Flying Eagle*.

We got to Sharkbait's house in record time, picked up Sharkbait, and hiked up into the hills. The crane on the workboat was busy digging up sand and gravel and piling it on the south end of the bar.

"Shouldn't they be loading it onto a barge?" Toby asked.

"Yeah, unless they're going to process it right here," I said.

"I don't think they can process it in the same place they're mining it," Toby said. "They would need all sorts of huge equipment here. I don't think the sand bar is big enough for a processing plant."

"Yeah, and they'd still have to load it after it's processed," Richard said. "But I don't think they intend to process it at all."

"If they don't process it, and they don't load it, they can't sell it, can they?" Sharkbait asked. "And if they don't sell it, my Mom won't get any profit. Those cheaters! Those lying assholes!" he shouted. I marveled that a little kid was able to summon that level of vehemence.

"I'm afraid that's what they are, alright," Richard said, "but we already knew that—I wanna see if they can actually find the treasure."

68.
ALTAR BOYS CAMP

The much-anticipated Altar Boys Camp finally arrived. Eager as I was for a week of uninterrupted play, I worried about our surveillance project while four of The Cliffhangers were gone. John, Richard, Toby, and I were all going to the camp, leaving only Michael and Sharkbait back in town. Michael agreed to devote some time to surveilling P.J. from Double O, and Sharkbait would oversee the mobsters' progress at The Projects from our watch site on the hill.

I had never been to any kind of summer camp, but I had certainly heard tales about it. It was held every year at Camp Oko-Tipi, located high in the hills south of Mayfly. The entire area was wooded, and it was wild country: bluff tops and steep ravines made it challenging to walk to and from the cabins—even locating them could be tough. The cabins were spread out over hundreds of acres, connected only by deer paths to each other and to the lodge and swimming pool.

On Monday morning, Mom checked to make sure each of us had packed a sheet, pillowcase and blanket, a washcloth, toothbrush, and toothpaste, then loaded all four of us into Old Betsy, the family station wagon, along with our duffels. I had brought my rosary, so I could keep my promise to the Poor Souls. Toby and I also brought our basketballs, but had dispensed with the Vaseline, tape, and oven mitts. John and Richard carried baseball gloves—John's was suspended from "The Gunnar," which rested on his shoulder, our hickory Louisville

Slugger baseball bat, freshly retrieved from its station near the border of our property with the Greens.

Then we were off, excitement at fever pitch as we drove south on Highway 79, past Castle Bluff, then Lovers Leap, then the cemetery where Tom lay, past the swamp, through Ilasco and down almost to Saverton Dam. Finally, we drove between the stone gateposts to Camp Oko-Tipi and wended our way up an eroded gravel road, straddling the deep gulleys as Mom cowboyed Old Betsy uphill, until we arrived at a level grassy area next to a great weathered wooden lodge. Across the road from the lodge at a still higher elevation were two large grassy fields which had been carved out of the hill ages ago. The closest field was a baseball diamond. At the far end of the outfield was a steep terrace which led up to a higher field used for bonfires. Woods bordered the bonfire field on three sides.

We poured out of the vehicle and grabbed our gear. I kissed Mom goodbye, then bounded up the wide wooden steps, swung open an old dark green painted screen door which squealed on its hinges, then stepped into the lodge.

Dust motes swam languorously in the shafts of sunlight pouring through ages-old glass windowpanes, made translucent with grime and neglect. A primordial scent of warmed wood permeated the large main room. The pitched ceiling showed entire unsawn logs supporting the raftered structure on which the building was framed. An occasional fly wandered lazily through the air.

The main room of the lodge served as the dining room. It was set up with old wooden trestle tables and watched over by an ancient and only partially preserved buffalo head mounted on the wall. It was missing one eye and displayed a baseball cap perched jauntily on one of its antlers. Even without being able to enunciate it, my twelve-year-old brain recognized that it provided superb *ambience. Cool!*

The camp counselors stood around the room, talking while we registered. They were older boys who had served at Mass in their youths but were now in high school, having left their altar boy duties to the younger boys. We respected and admired them. We had witnessed their prowess on the football field and basketball court with awe—in fact, some of those moments would glitter in our memories forever. They were the heroes we cheered for and hoped to emulate someday.

And these guys were old enough to drink and drive—some of them had even been in wrecks! We heard and repeated the stories of their extracurricular exploits: adventures with girls and with beer, and their encounters with the police in the middle of the night—everything we heard that they said and did.

The oldest and most mature of the boys there, Mike Cannoli, was the Head Counselor. He was in charge of all camp functions—there were no adults. He sat at the end of one of the tables, and boys queued up in front of him as he took down names, grades, and phone numbers.

"You boys are in 'Shady Nook,'" he said. "Here's a map. Head up to your cabin, pick out a bunk, put your sheet and blanket on it and your luggage under it, then get back down here for lunch at noon sharp."

The four of us ran up the hill, briefly consulting the map at forks in the trail and noticing the names and locations of some of the other cabins.

Several minutes later we came to a small grassy clearing surrounding an ancient stone cabin. Old board shutters hung askew at the windows. The cabin had been built right up against a wooded hillside, so that the roof appeared invitingly accessible along the back side, if approached with some effort and ingenuity.

Summer of '63

We walked into a single rectangular room with a dusty wooden plank floor. Four sets of bunk beds occupied the four corners. Two old wooden dressers with peeling paint stood under open windows at each end of the room. One of them was obviously a favorite roost for a chipmunk or squirrel because the top was littered with fragments of nut shells. I opened a dresser drawer. Finding it empty, I decided to lay claim to it by tossing my socks and underwear in, but changed my mind when I saw the piles of little black pills accumulated in the corner. *Ewww...mouse turds.*

"I think I'll just live out of my suitcase," I announced.

Richard and Toby both wanted top bunks, which was no problem to John and me because we had slept in a bunk bed for years, the one that our youngest brothers, Stephen and Tim, now occupied. I spread the sheet over my bed, tucked it in, made nice hospital corners the way my Mom had taught me, then ran down the hill with the others, keeping to the narrow path and ducking under overhanging vines and branches which attempted to ensnare me.

Lunch was bread, cold cuts, pickles, potato chips, and iced tea. Mike Cannoli welcomed us, told us we were all on our "best behavior," that anybody who caused a problem would be sent home, and that we were to listen to our counselors and obey them. We clapped as he introduced the other counselors, calling off their names and telling us which counselor was assigned to which cabin, and the cabin occupants gathered around their counselor in small groups. Our counselor was Harry Tiller, a nice guy who was a good football player and owned his own car—a maroon '52 Ford with silver trim. The counselors would each sleep in their cabin with their group. *Reveille* was at six a.m., and breakfast was served from 6:15 to 7:00, when camp cleanup began, supervised by the counselors.

The counselors passed out the Camp Schedules to their cabin inmates. The first item was "Meetings in Cabin with Camp Counselor," so we walked as a unit up the steep path to our cabin for the big meeting, surrounding Harry Tiller like he was the Pied Piper, first following him, then skipping ahead, full of excitement and questions. At the meeting, Harry asked each of us how old we were, what grade we were in, and what we had been doing that summer. He told us that he was seventeen and a junior at Mayfly High and he played right guard and linebacker on the football team and this was his seventh year at Altar Boy Camp. He talked about keeping our cabin clean and making our beds every morning as part of the camp cleanup. He also told us that he was there to help us, and if anyone had any kind of a problem to tell him about it and he would do whatever he could.

"What's next on the Camp Schedule?" he asked. We looked.

"'Sports' until 2:30," John said, "then 'Swimming Pool' until 5:00."

"We better get down there, then," opined Harry Tiller.

"Sports" meant baseball to most of the kids there, and basketball to Toby and me and a few of the older boys who played on the high school team. Toby and I grabbed our balls and headed to the concrete courts, then started our shooting drills, after which Toby started in on his Hundred Hooks drill, ten at a time, while I did my Hundred Layups. We were interrupted by four of the counselors who had been sitting at a picnic table watching. They came sauntering over to us.

"Wanna play a game?" Josh Valley asked. Josh Valley was one of the best-liked and most colorful older boys. All the younger boys emulated him. He was also a total wild hare, as were the other kids in his family, but it suited them—most of them were so well-liked that they never got in trouble, even for things that other people would have caught hell for.

Summer of '63

Josh was tall and fast, a superb athlete with quick hands, a great jumper with excellent body control in the air—and he could dunk a basketball. He was the starting center on the high school team. The other three were Kerry Munzinger, a big strong kid who played starting forward, David Lager, who played the other forward, and the starting point guard, Spike Murphy, whom we called "Dog" because...actually, I'm not sure why we called him "Dog."

"I guess so," I said. "Okay, Toby?"

"Sure, why not?" Toby said.

We played three-on-three. Toby and I were on different teams. Each team had a guard, a forward, and a center. This worked out well since we always played man-to-man defense in playground ball. Toby, Kerry, and Dog were a team. I played with Josh and David.

"I'll take the little guy," Dog called to his teammates. Dog was a decent high school point guard. He intended, I guess, to teach "the kid" the rudiments of the game at the high school level—he had apparently decided that he wasn't gonna let me score. I took the ball, dribbled to the right, then suddenly planted my right foot and crossover-dribbled to my left. While he struggled to switch directions, I blew past him for a left-handed layup.

The next time I was out front with the ball, I did it again, except he was ready for it—he jumped out to my left to cut me off and force me to pick up my dribble—what he wasn't ready for was my immediately reverse-dribbling back through my legs to my right hand, then, while he was trying not to fall down, blowing past him for a right-handed layup. As I approached the basket, Toby sank off Valley to block my layup, so I arced a high pass over his head to Valley, who caught it *en route* to a dunk. Dunking was still illegal in high school games, but we allowed it on the playground. Most people couldn't do it anyway, and we loved to see anyone who could.

On the next play, I passed the ball to our forward, David, then set a good pick on his defender, which allowed him to drive toward the bucket, before pulling up in the lane for a short jumper.

I had the ball out front again. Dog was really buckling down, embarrassed by then, determined to stop me this time. He was playing textbook defense, staring fixedly at my belt line, knowing I couldn't fake with my waist. I did a crossover from my right to my left, which he tracked perfectly, sliding sideways and cutting me off, just before I crossed back between my legs to my right, which he also anticipated, sliding over, but losing a fraction of a second in the direction change, while I did a step-back and swished. Later I worked the same progression with the other hand, starting and finishing on the left side. My other two teammates just stood and watched. I think they were embarrassed for him.

Having made my point, next I devoted myself to passing to my teammates, working my moves before each pass, dribbling and driving, cutting toward the hoop, then executing bounce-passes, no-look passes and alley-oops, leaving my defender in my wake as often as possible, making him pay. Over the next thirty minutes, I was the second-most dominant player on the court, behind only Josh. And I had managed to save a few moves for a surprise later on.

A half-hour later we stopped to switch teams up, and Toby and I played together with Kerry, and then the show really began.

"Satchel!" I yelled, launching a supersonic pass seven feet off the court. It hurtled toward an imaginary circle located just basket-side of a floppy carrot-top which my periphery showed was moving down the lane. Toby's huge hands arrested it as he flowed toward the basket and, in a motion smooth as a wave, laid it in.

"Wormwood!" he yelled, a few minutes later, heading down toward the blocks, where a bounce-pass ricocheted off the court into his big hands. Back to the basket, he faked to his right, then reversed course and launched into a beautiful left hook, which rolled off his fingertips, spinning backward as it arched into the basket. *Swish!*

"Wormwood?" Josh said. "What the hell is that?"

"Secret code," I said, laughing.

I whispered to Toby that I was gonna yell "Satchel" again, then break into the corner and he could hit me there for my favorite shot, so we did. I passed to Toby from the left wing, then cut briefly toward the free throw line, stopped abruptly, and ran down and out to the corner, arriving squared up at the same time as Toby's pass. Right before I launched the shot, I saw Dog running out in a desperate attempt to block me. I just smiled and closed my eyes in an over-exaggerated squint.

"Look ma, no eyes," I called out, as I launched the shot. *Swish! I love that sound!*

Toby and I both played solid defense, sinking away toward the ball when "our man" wasn't in possession. I managed to steal the ball a couple of times during crossovers, using Coach Hedges' strategy of intercepting the ball as it came up off the bounce.

All in all, it was a great coming-out party for both Toby and me. I don't wanna say those older guys were agog, but, honestly…they were agog. If they had to buy new equipment every time they lost their jocks, they'd have all been broke. Toby and I were elated with our first time out in public since the Coach Hedges clinic began. Too bad Lucas Crane wasn't there, but there would be time for that.

A whistle blew from the lodge deck, and Mike Cannoli yelled through a megaphone: "Pool time boys—get your trunks and towels and be there in ten minutes."

69.
THE POOL

We didn't need a second invitation. We were super-hot from ninety minutes of intense basketball in the humid heat of the Mayfly summer—even the baseball players were overheated from standing around in the sun for the last hour and a half. We changed and were at the outdoor pool showers minutes later.

Camp Oko-Tipi had a large, spring-fed swimming pool. It was ice-cold on the hottest summer days, and life-threatening on the others. Huge cottonwood and willow trees overhung the pool and shaded much of it. You had to keep moving to survive in those waters.

To say the shower was cold was a rash understatement, but at least you could step away from it. The pool was positively freezing. It was impossible to walk into it slowly—the only way to endure the agony was to jump in.

"Line up here on the end of the pool. Everybody's gotta be able to swim the length of the pool or you can't go in the deep end," Mike announced, and we were off. Obviously, you couldn't participate in the diving if you weren't allowed in the deep end, and diving was about the only thing we did at the pool. As the swimmers began to pull themselves out on the deep end, they queued up on both sides of the diving board, and the diving began.

Summer of '63

We spent most of our time at the swimming pool learning new dives, staring in awe as the older boys executed the most difficult and daring dives, pushing the envelope against what was possible off a one-meter springboard. The counselors lined up the non-divers on the side of the pool and coached them to dive headfirst into the deep end. When they had overcome their natural aversion to plunging headfirst off the side, they were allowed to dive off the board. The neophytes executed cannonballs and can-openers and advanced to back dives. The intermediate divers did watermelons and jackknives and German jackknives. Some of them would ultimately progress to front and back flips, which was as far as most boys ever got—you had to have a death wish to advance beyond those. The older boys who were excellent divers, however, covered themselves in glory, soaking up our adolescent adulation as they performed one-and-a-halves and inwards and gainers. Several of the daredevil older boys who spent most of their time trying to push the envelope wore t-shirts to partially absorb the sting of the water smack.

I watched the great divers run through their panoply of dives. They spun so fast! There were only three boys there (only three boys in all of Mayfly, so far as I knew) who could do the most complex dives. They were all counselors at Altar Boys Camp. Two of them were brothers, Jim and Bob Cavendish, who were both short, tanned, and muscular, and the other was Josh Valley. We called them the "Big Three."

Those guys were men compared to us boys. They laughed with deep voices compared to our girly little squeaks, and they were as raucous as they wanted to be. They were endowed with the *accoutrements* of manhood—they even shaved! We still sported dinky dinkies with tight little scrota and only a handful of pubic hairs among us. Not these guys—looking at them moved me to prayer: "Dear God,"

I prayed fervently, "please make my penis grow really big, too, and if it's not too much to ask, make me have to shave at least once a week."

The Big Three put on a diving exhibition which we mere mortals could only admire, with no hope ever of being able to emulate them. The diving board thundered at their liftoffs and then stuttered in recovery as each of them leapt high into the air, then tucked into a perfect cannonball and spun. The rest of us were awed by their fearlessness and agility. The double-flip off a one-meter board was the epitome of athleticism—the apex of diving domination, and only the Big Three could pull it off. Not content with their current place at the pinnacle of the Mayfly Divers Hall of Fame, however, they spent most of the afternoon trying to do the unimaginable: a two-and-a-half! Over and over their faces and torsos smacked the water with the force of their fierce rotations, but no matter how high they vaulted off the board or how tightly they tucked or how fast they spun, they were never able to accomplish the final quarter-revolution. The rest of us were sympathetic but awestruck nonetheless. They also worked incessantly on a double gainer while the others stood around, admiring and critiquing.

"You almost made it that time!"

"You got one and three-quarters!"

And so that blissful and raucous summer afternoon in the wild hills south of Mayfly passed in a haze of glory and striving and accomplishment and fellowship with other altar boys, past and present. And, mercifully, I was unaware of what the future held.

Dinner was a boys' feast of hot dogs and baked beans, then playtime until dark, which allowed Toby and me to finish our Hundreds. Close to dusk, I noticed the counselors carrying wood to the fire pit in the high grassy field overlooking the baseball diamond.

Summer of '63

"Hey, Fletcher!" Josh Valley called. "Come over here and help carry some wood!"

"Come on," I said to Toby, pleased that he had singled me out. We both went over and helped haul wood up the hill to a large fire pit, on the uphill side of which was a long single wooden bench supported by steel posts staked into concrete footings.

When we finished hauling wood up the hill, Toby and I returned to our basketball drills. At dusk, I saw smoke issuing from the firepit and noticed that the counselors were all sitting on the bench. Shortly thereafter, Mike blew a whistle.

"Bonfire, boys—come on up!" he yelled. "Just sit on the ground."

"What about chiggers?" Richard asked.

"There aren't any," Mike replied. "It's been sprayed with DDT."

"Oh, good," Richard said, as we settled into the grass, "that stuff really works!"

70.
MY FIRST CAMPFIRE

The dusk deepened. Our eyes gradually opened wider, gathering in our surroundings. The campfire danced in the big stone firepit, casting shadows against the trees and flickering light across our faces as full dark settled over us.

"Kerry," Mike said in the silence, "better warn the boys about Bony Gus."

"Good idea," some of the other counselors chimed in, nodding, serious expressions on their faces.

"Well…okay," Kerry started, after a pause, like he hadn't even thought of this before and it was just one more chore he had to perform, "Bony Gus is in a grave up on the hilltop. The grave's been opened up, nobody knows who or why, but there's a really old coffin lid, and in the daytime, you can raise it up and look down into the grave, and you can actually see him lyin' there—well, just his bones, but it's definitely a man lyin' down there in his grave. But there's somethin' funny about him. And I don't mean 'ha-ha' funny either, I mean somethin' odd." Here he lowered his voice and looked around meaningfully. "He only has one arm," he announced in a really low voice that I could hardly hear—but I did hear it. "All his bones are there," he said; "you can see his skeleton—except…he only has one arm."

"Aww," someone said from the shadows where we sat, "is that true?"

"Swear to God," Kerry said. "We'll take you up there tomorrow and you can see him yourself." Then he sat back and folded his arms.

"We don't worry too much about him, boys," Bob Cavendish said after a pause. "He's left us pretty much alone for a while now." The rest of the counselors nodded.

"But stay together on the trails," Mike said. "You don't wanna be alone out there, especially after dark."

"Yeah," David Lager chimed in, "there was that one camper...."

"Oh yeah," Bob Cavendish said.

"Yeah, forgot about Johnnie," Dog said.

"I don't think these boys wanna hear about Johnnie, men," Mike said.

All went quiet as the counselors stared into the fire and we stared at them, waiting. The tension built. An owl hooted in the woods off to the left, and we looked around uneasily.

"What happened to him?" someone finally asked from the shadows.

"Who, Johnnie? What happened to him?" Bob repeated. "That's a good question." He looked at Mike. "Should I tell 'em?"

"Might as well," Mike said. "You've gone this far."

"Well," Bob said, "the thing is, nobody knows. He was never found. It happened several years ago. He went up the trail alone, that one, right over there."

We all swung our heads to stare at the edge of the woods. The black hole which marked the trail to our cabins was just visible in the dark mass of trees which shifted back and forth in the flickering campfire.

"That was the last anybody ever saw of him. Nobody knows what happened. We think Bony Gus got him," Bob said. "We still hope someday he'll come home."

"Yeah, but some people said they heard a scream," Josh Valley chimed in. "Actually, more like a howl than a scream. And some people say they can still hear him out here, some nights, and they say, "There's Howlin' Johnnie—nobody ever found him—and he's comin' back for justice."

"Yeah, but it mighta just been a bobcat," Jim Cavendish chimed in. "They can sound awful human when they scream. We can't be sure that's Howlin' Johnnie." *Just a bobcat! Holy shit! That's supposed to be comforting?*

71.
THE CABIN

"Alright, boys," Mike said. "Time to turn in. Tomorrow's gonna be a big day. Kneel down again and we'll say a quick Our Father, Hail Mary, and Glory Be." After which, he said, "Okay, boys. Off to your cabins. Stay on the trails and keep together. And keep a sharp eye out for Bony Gus. And if you hear a strange howl, don't worry about it—it's just Howlin' Johnnie."

"Aw, you're kiddin' us!" someone shouted.

"There is no Bony Gus!" someone else opined.

"The hell there isn't," he said. "Tomorrow, we'll take you up to his grave and show him to you. And if I were you, I'd just pray you don't see him before then."

We turned toward the dark mouth of the tunnel through the woods which marked the path to our cabin. Our disbelief faded and our eyes and ears sharpened as we left the campfire and entered the blackness. We stayed together, walking up the steep rutted and rooted trail to Shady Nook with Harry, who had the flashlight.

On the way up to our cabin I thought about Howlin' Johnnie and bobcats and Bony Gus, who couldn't possibly be real—except Kerry said they'd show him to us tomorrow—and I made sure to stay with the group and keep my eyes and ears pealed for the slightest sound or movement in the underbrush. I hurried along, wanting to reach the cabin as quickly as possible, picturing some insane skeletal monster with a gaping mouth and vacant eyes and one grasping bony arm exploding out of the woods just as I passed.

The cabin was black dark as we approached it. We stood aside, turning to watch behind us while Harry opened the door and flipped the light switch. It illuminated a single bare bulb hanging by a wire from the cabin ceiling. I looked up as I walked through the doorway. Shadows cast by the rafters divided the room into pools of dim light separated by bands of darkness. The day's heat was still trapped inside the room, and the air was still and dry.

"Alright, boys," Harry said. "You heard Mike. Tomorrow's a big day. Hang your clothes on the hooks, then hit the sheets. Lights out in three minutes."

'Hooks' was a generous term for the four rusty nails which had in ancient times been hammered into the wall next to each set of bunk beds—two nails per boy. We stripped to our underwear and jumped onto our bunks.

"Everybody ready?" Harry asked, advancing toward the light switch. Just as he reached out his hand, a scream of absolute terror split the night and ricocheted off the stark stone walls, and Toby shot out of his top bunk and landed head-and-arms-first on the plank floor.

"What the..." Harry started, as seven other boys leapt out of their beds onto the floor.

"Snake! Snake! Snake!" Toby screamed at the top of his lungs, crawling away along the plank floor, leaving wounded-animal tracks in the dust, his head twisted around and up, eyes fixed on the top bunk.

"A snake in your bed?" John called.

"No, above it," Toby gasped, "looking right at me." Cautiously, the group advanced toward the bed, all eyes searching the rafters above it.

"There it is!" Craventz yelled, "I'll get a stick," he said, as he headed to the door.

"Take the flashlight," Harry said, handing it to him, "and be careful what you pick up. These hills are full of copperheads and they all come out at night."

We watched the snake as we listened to the branches rustling outside. It was a huge black snake, six feet long, stretched along the top of the rafter. It didn't move. Finally, Craventz came in with a long, bent tree branch.

"I'll get it," he said.

"No, you don't," Harry said. "Give that thing to me." Craventz reluctantly surrendered his weapon. "Holy cow, that thing's big!" Harry said. Advancing with the stick, he tapped the snake once on the back. It reared up, mouth open, and followed the stick with its head, then turned back on itself and slithered along the rafter to a hole in the wall—and it was gone!

"Bet there's no mice in this room," Donnie Johnson said.

"Bet there are—that's what he's doing in here—hunting," Gary Miller replied.

"We gotta patch that hole," Toby said. "He might come back when we're all asleep."

"Okay, but not tonight," Harry said.

"Well, we gotta do something," Toby said. "Here, Jamie, see if you can stuff this in there," handing me his shoe. "I'll watch out."

I don't know why I did it—because it was Toby, I guess, and because he was more scared than I was, but I got up there and stuffed that shoe in so tight I was afraid Toby would have to go barefoot the rest of the week.

"Thanks," Toby said when I was finished. "But we still gotta move the bed. We might not hear him come back in." So all four of us moved that pair of bunk beds out to the center of the room. "You wanna sleep on top?" Toby asked me.

"Sure," I said. *That snake'll never come back in here—Toby scared the shit out of it.*

"Okay, boys, it's late—let's try it again," Harry said, and hit the light switch.

"Night."

"Night."

"Night."

"Night."

"Night."

"Night."

"Alright, alright, on three, everybody say good night and then *no more talking*," Harry said. "One, two, three."

A chorus of 'goodnights.'

I started to turn over, then was shocked to attention. *Oh, my God—the Poor Souls!* I fished my rosary out from my pillowcase and began with "The First Joyful Mystery, The Annunciation...." When I finished, I realized two things: one, my head was lying in a pool of sweat; and, two, no one else was asleep either. There was no heavy breathing—everyone else was lying awake in his own pool of sweat, probably picturing that snake and wondering what else we might be sharing the cabin with.

"Harry, it's too hot," I whispered.

"You're right," he answered in a low voice. "I was just thinking about going up on the roof. You can come, too, if you want."

"Can I?"

"Me, too?" A chorus of questions.

"Yeah, okay," Harry grumbled in resignation. "I've got some mosquito repellant. You all need to put it on. They'll pick you up by your ears and carry you away out here."

He turned the lights on and shared out the bottle. "Do your backs and your feet, too," he said. "Rub some on your palms and do your face and your ears and even your hair. And put some on your underpants, too. Lightly, three touches and no more or you'll go to hell," he said. We all made sure we got our money's worth.

"Put your shoes back on," he said. "You can take them off once you get to the roof."

"Do you think that snake is up there?" Toby asked.

"Nah, he's off hunting something," Harry said. "We'll beat on the roof when we go up there, and I guarantee anything that's up there will leave in a hurry."

And we did. We all stretched out on the gentle slope of the roof, heads up toward the peak. We had a decent patch of visible sky overhead, framed by the overhanging trees. To the south, Orion was making his nightly advance from east to west, and the Pleiades were visible high overhead, almost in the center of the dome of the heavens. The air was cool, pregnant with the nocturnal exhalations of the sleeping woods. An almost unbearable sweetness of honeysuckle enveloped us.

A coyote called distinctly from a nearby hill, and then, far away, another, and then, floating on the night air, the answering calls of multiple coyotes, announcing their presence to one another in singles and in groups. I was lost in thought, in awe of the majesty of this summer night on this hill.

And then I saw a flicker of light tremble across the black sky.

"Was that lightning?" Donnie Johnson asked.

"Looked like it," Craventz said. Then, in a moment, "There's another."

"I wonder if it's gonna rain," Gary Miller asked.

"I hope so," Harry said. "We need it. That might only be heat lightning, though."

I woke an hour later to a bright flash followed by thunder. Not a distant rumble—a boom. The sky was lighting up in earnest now. I waited for the next distinct lightning flash and then began counting seconds. Eight.

"Hey, Harry," I said, "that storm is a mile and a half away. Maybe we better get down." Additional peels of thunder confirmed my call. Harry and I woke the others as the storm front arrived—a big wind, cold, announcing serious storm energy. I looked up and saw a silver cloud front rolling across our patch of sky. We gathered our shoes and hurried back over the side of the roof just as the first large drops of rain splattered onto us and slapped against the roof. BOOM! *That one was for real!* We hurried into the cabin just as the full force of the gale arrived, forcing us to close the windows. We huddled together in the doorway on the lee side, watching with awe as the trees danced crazily. Electricity flashed continuously across the sky, highlighting the torrential sheets of horizontal rain and illuminating the woods in sudden colorless daylight.

BOOM! Lightning struck something on our hill, something very near. I wondered where the big black snake was now, what he was doing, if he was scared by the storm or completely unphased by it.

Then I wondered about the rabbits and squirrels and coyotes and deer. Were they frightened? They couldn't possibly be dry. Then I wondered about Prince and wished he were there with me, so I could pat him and reassure him. At least I knew he was snug and dry in his house, but he didn't like thunder.

In fifteen minutes, the worst of the storm had passed. We could still hear the thunder echoing in the valley as it crossed the Mississippi, and it was still raining, but we were dry and too tired to worry about non-human roommates, and it was finally cool enough to sleep.

72.
LANYARDS AND BONY GUS

The birds were deafening. Wrens, redwing blackbirds, sparrows, starlings, titmice, chickadees, nuthatches, and bluebirds trying to outshout one another in a riotous cacophony, accompanied by the distinctive summer song of the cardinals, but I could have willingly listened to all of that as I slept. No, it was the repetitive and obnoxious cawing of the crows that made me open my eyes. Golden light from the rising sun, filtered by the trees into dappling, poured through our cabin windows. Moments later, the jarring brassy clanging of Harry's Baby Ben alarm clock startled the rest of the sleepers into involuntary wakefulness.

Harry slapped the alarm off.

"Six a.m., boys, up and at 'em," he announced. Boys rose off the lower bunks and slid down from the tops. All of us stumbled out the door in our underwear to pee, spreading out like a just-released herd of cats and walking over to the edge of the woods. The grass was wet and the leaves sparkled on the trees as we stood and stared at them, posing in peeing mode in our stupor.

"Get some clothes on, boys," Harry said, as we returned to the cabin. "Let's see what's for breakfast."

The path was soaked and slippery, and there were new gulleys and muddy washes where the soil had run downhill and pooled against rocks and roots. As we blundered downhill, we came more fully awake. A slight breeze stirred the yellow and lavender wildflowers which speckled the undergrowth, and the air was cool and fresh. *Thank you, my Lord and God!* It was a glorious day to be alive.

As our path widened into the lodge clearing, we could smell bacon, and we eagerly opened the screen door to mounds of scrambled eggs and piles of bacon and toast and potatoes fried with onions and green peppers. We got in line, filled our plates, and hurried to our table.

When all the cabins had arrived, Mike announced that archery would be postponed until tomorrow because of the mud, which elicited groans from several quarters.

"But don't worry," he said, "we have a great substitute activity for you until the ground dries up. This morning you'll all be making lanyards." This change in the schedule was met with an even louder and more universal chorus of groans. I had never made a lanyard, so I was looking forward to it, but I tried not to let on.

"So go brush your teeth and go to the bathroom and get your cabins cleaned up and be back here in thirty minutes," he said.

Thirty minutes later the entire camp had returned to the lodge. Mike sat at the supplies table.

"Take two strands of any color you want," he said. "Two strands per person. And take one clip, then go back to your meal table."

Harry was already there waiting for us. When we were all assembled, he demonstrated how to weave the lanyard, and we began. I had a problem making my knots neat, but he showed me how to pull each one tight, and it started looking pretty good. The noise level in the room gradually increased until Mike blew the whistle.

"Listen up, girls," he said, "you gotta keep it down to a dull roar. Anybody making too much noise or causing any kind of trouble, your counselor will send you up here to me. I've got a stack of paper here and a pile of pencils and you can sit here with me and write a letter to your parents. I'm sure they're missing you. I'll help you with your spelling."

"What do we do when we're done?" Gary Miller asked.

"As soon as you're finished, you can do another one," Harry said. "Take an extra one home with you and give it to your kid sister. Or sell it to her for ten cents." Heads snapped up around the table, then looked back down with renewed interest. I noticed that the pace of assembly doubled at that moment.

Buzzy Donaldson, one of the older counselors and a really nice guy, came in and whispered to Mike. The two of them talked quietly for a minute, then Mike nodded.

"Okay, schoolgirls," Mike announced. "Buzz tells me it's dry enough to go outside. Remember Kerry promised to show you Bony Gus? Well, you're gonna get to go up and see him."

The room exploded in cheers, yays, and shouted questions. Mike held up his hand, then blew his whistle again, hard.

"We're not gonna go until all the supplies are put away and the room is cleaned up. QUIETLY! That means no talking—whispers only. If you can't control your noise, you won't get to go, and you'll just have to sit here 'til lunch. You understand me?" *Sheesh! Seems like he just gets madder all the time!*

Dozens of dispirited "yeahs" responded.

"And another thing, when I ask you a question, the answer is 'Yes, sir' or 'No, sir' or 'I'm too stupid to know, sir.' Do you understand me?"

"Yessir," we all said in unison.

"Alright, that's better. Now, you're going to follow your counselor up to see Bony Gus, one table at a time, five minutes apart, when I call your cabin. Take your lanyards with you. In the meantime, you will sit quietly and play cards. Anybody making too much noise will sit here for the duration. Am I understood?"

"Yes, sir," we all yelled, as our counselor passed out the playing cards.

Mike blew the whistle. "Cliffside," he called. Cheers as seven boys followed their counselor out the door, skipping and running and jumping. We turned back to the table as Harry dealt the cards.

"Cut," he said, sliding the deck over to John, who cut the deck and returned it.

"Poker," Harry announced. "Five card draw."

I could hardly concentrate on the game, but since we weren't playing for pennies or marbles, it didn't matter so much, except I only liked playing when I won. The deal moved to the left. Gary Miller took the deck, shuffled it, and passed it to Harry to cut.

"Same game," he announced, "but deuces are wild." The whistle blew again. I looked up hopefully.

"Sky High," Mike Cannoli announced. Disappointed, I returned to my cards, but couldn't keep my eyes off Mike, watching for any sign of movement toward his whistle, trying to imagine what Bony Gus would look like. Finally, the whistle blew again.

"Shady Nook," he called. *Yay!* We all tossed our cards into the center of the table and waited while Harry packed them back into the box, and we were off.

I ran ahead of Harry with the others, but had to wait for him at every fork in the trail. After ten minutes, I was winded from multiple dashes up the steep and muddy trail, interspersed by bouts of running back downhill to see if Harry and the other slowpokes were still on the same route. I had no idea what I would do if they had taken some detour. Finally, I decided to just stay with Harry. We soon caught up with the rest of our group waiting alongside the trail, since they had apparently worn themselves out sufficiently to plod along with us.

We walked down the side of a deep ravine and then up the steep trail of a neighboring hill until we emerged *en masse* onto the east end of a grassy knoll at the top. The Sky High group was arranged in a circle, bending over and looking at something as we approached.

"Okay, boys, let's get out of here, quietly; don't disturb him anymore," we heard David Lager tell his Sky High group. They turned and headed toward the path we had just emerged from. As they filed past us, they didn't acknowledge us or even seem to see us. Their eyes were wide and far off. Peter Treat looked grim; his teeth were set. John Brooks looked white. As we approached, I turned back to where they had been standing and saw a big old coffin lid lying on the ground, raised slightly above the surrounding earth. The hinges were rusty and there was mud on it. Some grass grew in the accumulated dirt. I had no idea what to expect, but I gathered around with the others.

"For God's sake, boys, be quiet," Harry whispered. "Gather around in a circle. Quickly, now, we don't have much time. I guarantee we don't wanna be standin' here with our thumbs up our asses if he wakes up."

I looked at Toby, who just looked back at me, eyes wide. John was staring intently at the coffin lid. Harry motioned impatiently for us to spread out evenly. When we were in position, he bent down and lifted the coffin lid. It creaked and he froze—we all jumped, staring at Harry, whose face was etched with alarm as he waited, motionless. We couldn't see into the grave yet—all eyes remained fixed on Harry, taking his cues—we were ready to cut and run in a heartbeat. After a few moments, he raised the lid higher. We leaned forward as one and then jumped back in unison. Several feet below us, lying there in the dirt, was a human skeleton.

I stared at it for several seconds. It was lying on its back and its skull still had teeth in it. It was smiling at us, but its eye sockets were empty. Its pelvis and legs looked like they could dance if they wanted to. Its ribcage was intact and hollow, and one arm was stretched along by its side, and I saw with horror that it was true—it only had one arm!

Then Harry did something that shocked me to my marrow. "Bony Gus," he called into the grave, "Are you okay?" My hair stood on end—*What the hell is he doing?—Is he trying to wake him up?* And then I almost jumped out of my skin when Bony Gus answered, in a deep echoey voice, slow and sepulchral, like it was coming from another world, "Who's got my arm?" and then, louder, and it vibrated like it was coming up a tunnel from the underworld, "Who took my arm?"

Our eyes were saucers, our mouths wide open, all our teeth on display. Harry raised his head—his face looked as scared as I felt. With his free hand, he raised his finger to his lips and shushed us—but he needn't have bothered. No one was going to so much as squeak—then he closed the coffin quickly and quietly. "Let's get out of here," he said. He didn't have to say it twice.

As we went down the hill, I guess we passed the next group coming up, but I don't remember it.

Lunch started out as a more subdued affair than the day before. A couple of the boys pretended they hadn't been scared.

"It's fake," Tim Goode said, "you know it is. They've got a walkie-talkie down there. Heck, I bet those bones aren't even real. They're probably made out of plaster." I just stared at him. *He's an idiot. I know what I saw and what I heard.*

Thoughts of Bony Gus gradually faded during the afternoon swim. Once again, the Big Three put on an exhibition, and the rest of us worked on lesser dives.

After dinner, we played basketball again. There were eight of us this time. Harry had joined us, along with Leo Howarth, the counselor from Breezy Point. They were football players and didn't start on the basketball team, but they were both good athletes. Leo Howarth even possessed a *bona fide* hook shot, maybe only the second player in Mayfly, besides Toby, who did. It was a beauty.

The basketball was again spectacular. Both Toby and I were being watched and appraised by the older boys. But even more than that, they had resolved to stop us. Toby and I took that personally and resolved to beat them as often as we could. The dinner whistle blew all too soon. Before we left the court, however, I decided to try out one of my new moves on Josh. Since I knew I would have numerous taller opponents trying to block my shot, I had invented a trick jump shot where I switched hands in mid-air, moving my left arm outside my torso a full foot toward my left and shooting with that hand from out on my side. This was the ideal time to see if it would work against a great jumper—and Josh Valley was a great jumper.

"Hey, Valley!" I said. "Try and block my shot." He turned instantly and gathered himself, determined to make me eat the ball. I dribbled a couple of times, nothing fancy, squared up to the basket, and jumped. He leapt up into the air, his arm fully four feet higher than the ball, descending on me, poised to smash my shot. I quickly pulled the ball away from under him, out to my left, beside his right ribs in a small arcing motion which ended with my left hand under the ball, then launched the shot. I was aware of his mouth open in shock as his head turned to follow the arc while he was still airborne. *Swish*. He landed and looked back at me, dumbfounded.

Summer of '63

"Thanks," I said. "I just wanted to see if that would work."

"Well, it worked, alright," he said, nodding but chagrined.

When we left the court, he was still looking at me kinda funny.

73.
SECOND CAMPFIRE

"Tell them about meeting the King of Siam," Dog said to Bob Cavendish as we sat around the fire in the deep dusk.

"Yeah," Mike said. "It'll be good to teach them all a little Siamese. They can show their parents how much they learned at camp."

"Okay," Bob said. "Well, boys, years ago when I was your age, my parents took me on a vacation with them to the Orient. And we visited Siam for several days, and it was really an amazing place. The buildings were all marble, and instead of sidewalks they had these Persian carpets on the ground everywhere you walked so your shoes wouldn't get dusty, and all the men had dark black beards and wore funny little painted slippers with turned-up toes on their feet and turbans on their heads with big jeweled clasps, and all the women were incredibly beautiful. None of them looked old and they all had really long black silky hair and tiny little feet with silk slippers, and big almond-shaped eyes, and they all wore a little white silk napkin on their faces, but it didn't really cover very much, and you could see they all just had beautiful teeth and their skin was flawless."

He paused as Josh got up and put another log on the fire.

"So how did you meet the king?" Arwain shouted behind me.

"Well, the first night we were there," Bob continued, "my parents made me go to bed early, but the place was so exciting I couldn't sleep, so I got up to look out the window, and it had a fancy carved wooden grill over it, and when I leaned against it, it opened in the middle, like a shutter. And you could step out of it onto the roof, so I did, and I walked over to the edge and saw a drainpipe, so I shimmied down it to the street, and just as my feet touched the carpet down there, two huge men with black beards and bare chests and scimitars grabbed me and picked me up under the arms and carried me into a building.

"I yelled and wrestled and kicked them and told them to let me go, but they just ignored me. They threw me into an empty room with no windows and no furniture except the carpet and locked the door and left. And I could hear them arguing through the door, but I couldn't understand a word they said because they were talking Siamese. But before long, they came back with a little fella with a black goatee, and he spoke English.

"'I am Vizier A. Solon,' he said. 'You will please to follow me.'

"'Where are you taking me?' I asked. 'I need to get back to my room. I'm supposed to be in bed.'

"'Quiet!' he said. 'You are obviously a spy. We are taking you to see the King.'

"'I said, 'Oh no, sir, I'm not a spy—I'm just a tourist,' and he said, 'Quiet! Or I'll have you whipped,' so I was quiet. And besides, I was kinda curious about seeing the King and all, and I decided I would just wait and explain it to him when I got there.

"We went down a long marble hallway covered with Persian rugs three deep—it was like walking on a mattress—and we passed lots of tall arched windows with little points at the top, until we got to a huge double door guarded by two enormous men with scimitars. The little guy spoke to them, and they opened the doors into a grand room, with lights and carpets and a golden throne at the end of it, and a red canopy over the throne that was set with gleaming gold stars. And there, sitting on the throne, was the King. Three women were dancing in front of him, and there was a group of musicians off to the side, and they all had black cloths tied over their eyes."

"Why, were they naked?" Gary Miller yelled.

"About half," Bob answered, "but I'll get to that later. Anyway, as we walked toward the throne, the king suddenly clapped his hands and the music stopped immediately, and the dancing girls scurried out a door off to the side like they were afraid of something, and the Vizier stopped and bowed, so I bowed, too, and he said in English: 'Oh great majesty, I bring to you the spy.'

"And I said, 'Just a minute! I'm not...' but I was interrupted because one of the bodyguards hit me so hard that I fell to my knees.

"'Do not speak!' the Vizier said, all mad now, 'unless the King commands it,' so I was quiet. The Vizier and the King talked in Siamese, and then I heard the King say, 'What do you have to say in your defense, spy? Speak, or I shall give you to my monkeys to play with.'"

Bob looked around at our faces, as we considered this. It was slowly dawning on me that this might not be as much fun as it sounded at first. *What do monkeys eat? Would they bite?*

"What did you tell him?" John yelled. He never did have any patience.

"I told him it was all a mistake, and I was just on vacation with my parents and I didn't want to go to bed because his country was so beautiful I couldn't sleep, and I just wanted to see more of it, so I climbed out the window of my room.

"The King said something to the Vizier, who turned to me and said in English, 'He thinks you are a liar and a spy,' and I looked up at the King with my mouth open. He looked at me like he was mad, and I thought I was gonna be monkey food for sure, but then he just started laughing, and he laughed so hard that everyone else started laughing, too, except me.

"Then he said, 'So you want to see more of my beautiful country, eh? And see it, you shall.' Then he turned to one of his slaves and said, 'Bring him a chair and set it here by me.' And he sat me down and then he clapped his hands again, two times, and the blindfolded musicians started playing again, and the three women came rushing back into the room trailing real long scarves behind them in a wavy cloud of silk, and their faces were uncovered, and I could see they were probably the three most beautiful women in the world, and their backs and legs and bellies were bare, and the rest of them was almost bare, because what they had on was so thin you could see right through it, and they were so beautiful and so graceful I wanted to stay there forever.

"Finally the music ended and the Vizier asked the King if he could teach me to do homage to the King in Siamese, and the King thought that was a great idea, so the Vizier taught me how to do it, and then the King said 'It is my wish that you spread the tale of your night with the King of Siam and of the King's mercy and hospitality, and that you teach the young people in your country how to do homage to the King of Siam, and whenever one of them comes to visit Siam, I will extend my hospitality to them as well.' That's what he told me.

"So would you all like to learn the homage, in case you ever get to Siam?" Bob asked.

"Yeah!" every one of us shouted, raising our arms.

"Okay," Bob said, "everybody kneel down." We did.

"Watch me and do what I do," he said. "There are three parts. The first part is like this," he said, kneeling with his arms up in the air, elbows bent, palms facing forward. We all mimicked him.

"Then you bend forward, halfway down, and extend your arms straight out, like this." We did the same.

"Okay, now the third part is you keep your arms out and you bend all the way down and touch your forehead to the ground." We did that.

"And now the words," he said. "We're gonna do it in Siamese. 'Oh wah,' which means 'long live.' Repeat after me," he said, his arms up, bent at the elbows, palms out: 'Oh wah.'"

"Oh wah," we chorused, mimicking his posture.

"Very good. Next," he said, bowing halfway down with his arms out, 'tah goo,' which means 'the King.' Say it after me as you bow down: 'Tah goo.'"

"Tah goo," we said, all of us bowing halfway down.

"Very good. 'Long live the King.' 'Oh wah tah goo,' he said, demonstrating.

"Oh wah," we said, then, "Tah goo," practicing the first two motions.

"Siam. Long live the King of Siam. 'Oh wah.' Then, 'Tah goo.' Then, 'Siam,'" he said, showing us the three postures of the homage.

"Oh wah. Tah goo. Siam," we all sang, bowing appropriately.

"Pretty good. Long live the King of Siam. Oh wah. Tah goo. Siam. Now let's practice a few times, slow and distinct. Stay with me," he said, then launched into it. We followed.

"Oh wah. Tah goo. Siam."

"Again," he said.

"Oh wah. Tah goo. Siam."

"Okay, I think you've got it. Now, when you do the homage, you do it loud, and you must do it seven times, faster and louder each time, so here we go. Ready?"

All around the campfire, boys moved in unison, yelling as they performed the heathen wave of homage to the King of Siam.

"Faster!" Bob urged.

"Oh wah. Tah goo. Siam. Oh wah. Tah goo. Siam. Oh wah. Tah goo. Siam."

"Oh, shit!" Jones yelled. The volume of the homage decreased noticeably, then grumbled to a stop.

"What's wrong?" someone asked.

"Aww, man," from somewhere else in the shadows. Then another. I heard someone slapping his forehead with the palm of his hand. The homage to the King of Siam petered out and muttering ensued as we all got to our feet, our mouths open in disbelief, looking sheepishly at each other.

We returned tired to our cabins, but not too tired to keep our eyes peeled for any sign of Bony Gus and our ears sharp for Howlin' Johnnie.

"I wish I woulda brought Prince," I whispered to Toby and Richard.

"No lie," Toby said. "Bet he'd love to get his teeth into some of those Bony Gus bones."

Nobody got into bed without checking the area thoroughly for snakes.

Later that night, after my rosary for the Poor Souls, I became aware that Toby wasn't asleep in the bunk below me.

"Wanna go out on the roof?" I whispered, leaning over the side of the top bunk. "It's too hot in here."

"Sure," he said.

"I'm coming, too," Richard whispered from the other bunk bed.

We grabbed our pillows and crept out the door, taking care to close it quietly behind us. We hadn't been on the roof long when I saw a light moving in the woods.

"Shhh!" I said. "Look!"

We were silent as the grave, wishing we had stayed in our bunks. Then we heard voices.

"It's a stove pipe that comes out the side of the hill. You just put your mouth up to it and you can hear what they're saying at the grave. I just said the same thing to each of them. 'Where is my arm?' 'Who took my arm?'" It was Dog.

The light was now flickering closer to the clearing, and I could see there were two boys. The other one was David Lager. They came to the end of the trail very close to our perch on the roof and then turned off the light.

"After you yell, I'll turn on the light for two seconds so you'll know where to run to, and then turn it off."

"Okay," Dog said. "Get ready, here I go."

We held our breath, trying to see in the darkness, but could only make out the dark form of David Lager standing almost directly below us. Suddenly we heard the screen door thrown open on its squeaky hinges and then slam and a shockingly wild, unearthly voice scared the Bejesus out of us, even though we knew who it was.

"Who's...got...my...arm?" it thundered in a stentorian voice, loud and angry. Screams and yells erupted from inside, and I heard a "thunk" and a "splat" from someone falling out of an upper bunk onto the floor.

Then a light appeared under the trees. In one full second, it was gone, and we heard the rustling and crashing of the retreating counselors as the light went on inside the cabin. I heard frightened voices.

"Where is he?"

"He's outside—I heard the door slam."

"Yeah, me too!"

Then we heard Harry say, "Where are the others?" We slid off the roof and walked around to the front door.

"Let's pretend like we didn't see them," Richard said.

"Good idea—mum's the word," Toby said.

"What happened?" Toby asked. "We were sleeping on the roof."

Everyone talked at once. By the time they finished telling us, Bony Gus had come inside the cabin and his bones shone in the dark, and he pointed around the room with his one remaining arm demanding who had taken his arm and telling them he was gonna kill them all, and Craventz jumped off the top bunk at him, but his feet got caught in the sheet and he fell on the floor instead, but Bony Gus was so shocked that he ran away. We just listened, looking at them in disbelief, which was not hard to do.

"He's gone, boys—he won't be back tonight," Harry said, "unless one of you has his arm. You don't have his arm, do you? Does anybody have his arm?" he asked, looking from one to the other with a straight face. We all looked back at him solemnly, shaking our heads.

"Alright, then, he's probably gone off to some other cabin. Let's get back to sleep."

"I'd hate to be the guy who tries that next year," Toby whispered as I climbed back up to my bunk.

"Why's that?" I asked.

"The Archangel will be here," Toby answered.

That night, as I lay there in my bed, too hot to sleep, I heard Howlin' Johnnie for the first time. It was an unearthly howl—part wildcat, part angry wolf, and part fingernails on a chalkboard. Unlike the night before, when other animals had answered the first coyote's call, nothing answered this howl. All other noises ceased, as if the other wild things were holding their breaths. Even the tree frogs and crickets had gone silent. It was quiet for several minutes before any other noises were heard, and even then it was only the insects.

74.
TARGET PRACTICE

After breakfast the next morning we split into two groups. Our group had archery first. As we left the dining room, we walked uphill towards the baseball field, where four colored bullseye targets had been set up in front of straw bales. Behind the targets rose the very steep terraced slope which separated the ball field from the fire pit.

We lined up in four rows while a counselor instructed us in the proper form for holding the bow, nocking the arrow, pulling the bowstring, aiming, and releasing. The counselor for our row was Dog, the high school starting guard who had tried to shut me down offensively and whom I had burned just about every way from Sunday. Although I was willing to let bygones be bygones and have a good chuckle about it, I could tell he wasn't. He acted like the two of us were not going to be best friends. The boy at the front of the line was allowed to shoot five arrows. When the first boy in each row had finished all five shots, the four of them ran to the targets and retrieved their arrows, then returned to the end of the line.

I could hardly wait for my turn—I considered myself close to a professional with the bow and arrow, due to my hours of practice, shooting at targets pinned against the bluff across the street on the high side of Ridgeline. Most of the boys were lucky if they even hit the hay bales. I thought I'd probably hit the target five times and maybe the bullseye three times. So it was a blow to my ego to have Dog tell me that my form was all wrong. Form wasn't very high on my list when I was shooting boxes on Ridgeline—my main focus was hitting the damn thing.

He wouldn't even let me shoot until I did things his way: holding the bow straight up, and so on. Now, I had seen a lotta Indian movies and that is where I got my form from and I had never yet seen an Indian who had to hold the bow like he was maybe gonna break for high tea right after that shot, or whatever. But I didn't have time to argue with him—I wanted to dispense with the preliminaries so I could start shooting. I could practically hear the gasps and spontaneous applause breaking out from the crowd, and from Dog as well: "Wow! You're just great at everything, aren't you?"

Finally, he thought I had sufficient instruction that I could try my practice shots. By that time I was so determined and impatient I was practically grinding my teeth. *Watch this—five bullseyes in a row*, I thought. *Bet it's never been done in the history of Oko-Tipi*. So he handed me my first arrow. It had apparently been left outside for an entire winter, because it was bent into a rainbow.

"I can't shoot this," I said.

"Why not?" he asked.

"It's bent," I said.

"You don't get to pick out your favorite arrow," he said. "It's only practice." So I nocked it into the bowstring and got ready to "let 'er fly," as we were fond of saying in our Ridgeline parlance.

"Wait, wait, wait," he said. "You'll never hit anything like that. You need to hold the bow straight up and down." So I did that and then pulled the bowstring back.

Summer of '63

"Wait, wait, wait," he said. "You need to pull it back right next to your ear, then hold it still for a second, then exhale and release it." So I did all that, too. My arrow departed on a long spiral trajectory which widened as it went. It flew high, passing closer to the adjoining target than to mine, and ended up stuck in the terrace behind the straw bales. Zero for one. I looked at him like "I told you so, moron," and was outraged to find him shaking his head, like I was a hopeless case.

"You need to keep practicing," he said.

The next one he handed me was missing two of the three flight feathers. As it left the bow, the back of the arrow started shimmying in a lopsided figure-eight pattern that became so pronounced I was afraid the feather end of the arrow would hit the target first. I needn't have worried—it dove to the ground about three-quarters of the way there. It didn't even have the grace to stick—it just plowed along the ground like a tennis ball in deep snow and petered out ten yards shy of the target.

The next arrow he handed me was missing half of the nock. I got to shoot it twice, though, because the first time I shot it, it just fell down right in front of me. All the kids in line behind me laughed, as well as half the kids in the lines on either side of ours. This amused Dog so much that he neglected to guard the arrows. Quickly, I seized a good-looking arrow, nocked it before he could say anything, drew the bow quickly, just the way I liked, and shot. Not a great shot, but at least I hit the straw bale.

By now, Dog had recovered. He handed me an arrow which was split down the middle, held together only by the metal tip on the point end and the plastic nock at the back.

"Thanks," I said, taking the arrow from him, examining it, and weighing it on my index finger. I turned toward the target, reared back and threw it like a spear with all my might. It hit the target, my best shot. Turning toward my brother John who was waiting his turn right behind me, I handed him the bow. "They got really shitty equipment here," I told him, loud enough so Dog could hear.

But he gave John all good arrows. All five of his shots stuck in the target—two of them were bullseyes.

That was just the practice round. The next two rounds were real. Dog kept score on a clipboard. First Place excused the winner from cleanup duty in the lodge for the rest of the week. A bullseye counted five points, and each wider concentric circle counted one less. Most of the boys didn't score at all. Dog let John pick his own arrows. He had three bullseyes and a total of sixteen points. Dog continued handing me rejects. I had no bullseyes and three points total. I wasn't even third. No one else had bullseyes. I didn't mind not winning, since John had won, but I would have been seriously pissed off about it if my brother hadn't won.

At mid-morning we traded places with the BB gun group. I was eager to shoot my way to redemption. We also had a different group of counselors on the BB gun range. The targets were much smaller, just a foot wide. We stood on a ridge in thigh-high prairie grass and shot across a small ravine toward the targets, which were mounted on boxes set on the next ridge top. Same basic drill, except we got twice as many shots—ten practice shots, and then two sets of ten rounds each, which would be scored.

As I raised my rifle to sight down the barrel, I heard a distinct "ting" and felt the barrel vibrate. *That's odd.* I looked around. Seeing nothing, I raised my rifle again. "Ping"—louder this time. Surprised and confused, I lowered my rifle and looked around again. Sixty feet away, Josh Valley was standing with his rifle at his side, shaking with laughter. This was too much.

Summer of '63

"Valley!" I yelled, flattered that he had singled me out again for some good-ol'-boy camaraderie, and without thinking, fired a return shot in his general vicinity, then quickly cocked and fired again. He ducked down in the grass, and the fight was on. A lifetime of warnings and prohibitions about ever getting involved in a BB gun fight? Gone in an instant. My certainty that I would never even consider doing anything so stupid? Vanished. None of that even crossed my mental threshold—in the excitement of that moment, such warnings never even existed. The possibility of injury was never considered—it just seemed like such excellent fun.

I saw Josh hiding behind a tree, so I squeezed off a shot into the bark—thunk!—just to let him know I knew he was there, then ducked down onto my knee in the tall grass and cocked my weapon. Cautiously, I raised my head. Pop! Right in my left eye!

I can't remember what happened next, only yelling and dropping my gun and putting my hands to my eye.

"You okay?" Josh called.

"Yeah, sure," I said, but I wasn't. Not even close.

I can't remember what happened with the BB gun contest. My left eye was swollen shut, and I couldn't see out of it, so I couldn't sight down the barrel anymore. I had a headache and my ears were ringing. I told Harry I had a headache and had to go lie down. There was a mirror covered with grime hanging from a nail in the wall of our cabin. I looked in the mirror the best I could using my right eye, but I couldn't see much. The BB had hit my eyelid, not my eyeball, and there was a red mark there and it stung. I lay down and passed out immediately. I slept through lunch.

I didn't feel any better when I woke up. I could hear everyone down at the pool and thought maybe the ice water would help it. Actually, I just didn't want to end my week at camp, especially so ignominiously—everyone else was still having fun and the week was only half over. I put my trunks on and went down the hill. The trek was difficult because I only had one eye, my depth perception was off, and something was wrong with my balance. I kept bumping into branches on my left side and tripping over tree roots.

When I got to the pool, I jumped right into the freezing water and swam underwater for a while, trying to ease the stinging in my eye. My eye was so swollen I couldn't open it, but I kept trying. After a while, the cold water had reduced the swelling somewhat and I was able to open my left eye—I couldn't see anything out of it—I was totally blind in that eye. Maybe it would get better. I kept swimming underwater and then testing it each time I surfaced to take a breath. I knew I had to do something, but I had no idea what.

75.
THE GAINER

"Hey, Josh!" I yelled, just like I was one of his buddies. "Teach me to do a gainer!"

He looked at me for a second. "It's easy," he said, finally. "You just go off the board as high as you can standing straight up, then throw your arms and head backwards as hard as you can, and you'll do it automatically."

I thought about it, practicing in my mind while I stood in line waiting my turn.

"Just don't stop," he added, as I stepped up onto the board. "When you throw your head back, just keep going over."

I gathered my gumption, what I could of it, and started my one-eyed run down the length of the board at a jog, gathering speed for the vault up, then leapt up high so I could come down at the very end of the board, springing up as hard and high as I could go, standing straight as an arrow, and...all my resolve deflated in an instant, and I dropped feet-first into the deep end.

I was angry at myself and embarrassed as I swam over to the side of the pool and pulled myself out. I wasn't embarrassed about chickening out in front of anyone my age, because none of them could do it either—none of them had ever even tried it—and none of them ever would. There was something about doing a back flip while running forward that seemed unnatural and, frankly, dangerous. But my demons were bigger than the rest of them. My need for acceptance by the older boys was paramount. And right now, my need to forget the fact that I couldn't see at all out of my left eye.

"What was that, a pencil?" Josh was walking over toward me. I don't think he knew I was blind in my left eye.

"Like this," he said, bending his knees then shooting up and throwing his head and arms backward. "But don't stop."

I practiced the motion while I stood in line, pictured myself vaulting high off the board, then throwing myself away—backwards—while I was moving forward in the air. When my turn came, I stepped up onto the board and stood for a few seconds, running through the entire sequence in my mind, then started my approach to the end of the board, where I launched upright, then threw myself backward as hard as I could. To my astonishment, I went all the way over, entering the water feet first. My legs were bent and slightly separated, but I had done it—my first gainer! And I was the only boy—not only in my class, but also in John's class—that had ever done it. I was elated.

"Not bad," Josh said. "Keep working on it and make it a little neater. Tuck tighter, and then straighten your legs and put your ankles together before you hit the water."

So I did. I did a dozen of them. I worked on my form. My muscles acquired the memory of the dive, and my body acquired location awareness as it rotated through the air, and my mind acquired confidence, and I acquired pride and swagger. By dinner time, the dive was mine. And it was good enough to show off with. Most of the older boys couldn't even do a sloppy gainer. Mine was sharp. I could join the older boys' diving exhibitions—I was one of only four people there, possibly in all of Mayfly, who could do a gainer.

Also, the cold water had reduced the swelling in my eyelid. The downside, however, was that now I knew I was completely blind in my left eye. I couldn't even see daylight—it was all black dark.

76.
TIME OUT

I didn't know what to do. When I told John I couldn't see, he said I needed to tell Harry.

"I don't want them to know I was in a BB gun fight, though," I said, "and I don't want to get Josh in trouble."

"Tell them you were running through the woods and got poked in the eye with a branch," John suggested, with that finely-honed Fletcher gift for fabrication. I didn't have any better idea, so I told Harry about getting poked in the eye with a branch.

"Oh, shit!" he said, "you can't see at all?"

"No," I said.

"You're gonna have to tell Mike Cannoli," he said. "We're gonna have to get you into town to see a doctor."

So I went into the little office room off to the side of the dining hall where Mike was seated behind a battered old desk.

"Mike," I said, "I was running through the woods and I got poked in the eye with a branch and now I can't see with my left eye."

"Okay, wait a minute," he said, coming over to my side of the desk, "when you say you can't see, you don't mean you can't see at all, do you?"

"Yes," I said.

"Alright," he said, leaning over me and covering my right eye, "you can see me, can't you?"

"No," I said, "I can't see you at all. All I can see is dark."

"Oh, wow—that's not good. Okay," he said, "I've gotta call your parents first and then we're going to the hospital." Mom and Dad met us at St. Elizabeth's hospital. I was admitted and put into a room on the second floor which I shared with an older man, Mr. Bell.

The doctor patched both my eyes to keep them still, since they move in tandem with one another. If my right eye was left uncovered, it would move every minute of the day, and my left eye would move along with it. He told me I had to stay completely motionless, or I would lose the sight in that eye permanently. I couldn't even turn over in bed or get up to go to the bathroom—I had to use a bedpan!

"We need to let it settle so I can look inside," he said. "Right now, it's filled with blood. I had a patient like this earlier this summer and he got up to go to the bathroom and lost his sight permanently," he told me. I didn't tell him I had done a dozen gainers after the injury.

That night, while my roommate lit up one cigarette after another, I debated whether it was worth the trouble of saying my rosary for the Poor Souls in Purgatory. For one thing, I didn't have my rosary with me. It was still under my pillow at Camp Oko-Tipi. And for another thing, I realized that no amount of help from the Poor Souls was going to win me the Future Famer trophy if I could only see out of one eye. But it wasn't their fault I got shot in the eye and they were suffering terribly regardless, so I buckled down and said the entire rosary, counting the Hail Marys on my fingers.

Afterwards, I still couldn't get to sleep. I knew the others would be at the bonfire by now. I felt like I was missing out. I wondered if anyone even missed me. Maybe Harry would bring the guys from our cabin into town tomorrow to see how I was doing. Maybe Josh would come by and say he was sorry he shot me in the eye. Maybe the high school basketball players would come up to see how I was. I wondered what they had for dinner, and suddenly realized that I was hungry. I fumbled with my call button. A few minutes later, a nurse arrived.

"Well," she said, "dinner time was over hours ago, but I'll see what I can do. What do you like?"

"Anything," I said, "I'm just hungry!"

"I'll see if you're allowed anything," she said. She came back a short time later. "Doctor doesn't want you chewing," she said. "You're supposed to eat through a straw. I'll see if I can get somebody to make you a milkshake."

I lay there and waited in the dark. It seemed like forever, while my roommate smoked two more cigarettes, but finally she brought me a milkshake.

"You lie still, now, while I crank up your bed," she said. I drank my milkshake. It was good, but I was hungry for more by the time the straw gurgled the remnants from the bottom of the glass. I rang again.

"I'm sorry, but that's all for tonight," she said. "Would you like a sip of water?"

Shortly thereafter, I had to pee, so I rang again. She brought me a tall square plastic bottle with a flip top and told me to call her when I was finished. It was so constricting that it was hard to relax. The ability to stand up and luxuriate in an unfettered pee seemed at that moment to be one of the greatest of freedoms.

The next three days were filled with liquid diets, complicated peeing, even more complicated bedpans, and waiting expectantly for visits from my friends. I didn't talk to my roommate much. I could hear his TV shows and smell his cigarettes, but I had never seen him.

Summer of '63

My parents came every day, Mom in the morning and Dad in the evening, but there wasn't much to talk about. I told them about running through the woods and getting stuck in the eye with the branch—by now, I had practiced it so often that I actually remembered doing it. There was no way I was going to tell them I had been in a BB gun fight. They would never let me forget how stupid I was, and I had already figured that one out.

"Your little brothers wanted me to say 'hello' to you," Mom said. "They hope you'll be well soon." *Yeah, I bet. They've probably already got my stuff divvied up in case I don't make it. Bet they're knocking each other over volunteering to do my chores, too.*

"Is anybody doing my chores?" I asked her, picturing myself with my eye patches, kneeling in a huge swath of the garden which they had left for me, as I felt around trying to differentiate weeds from green beans by touch.

"We're getting along just fine," she said. *Hmmmmm.*

Michael came in at noon of my first full day and gave me the Cliffhanger report from Double O. Basically, nothing going on, except for some visits from different church ladies, one in particular who kept showing up. Michael listened in with the Big Ear.

"I think Mrs. Werschman is sweet on him," he said. "You should have heard her. She brought him cookies and just kept hanging around, telling him how nice everything was in his house and she could come by and straighten things up if he wanted, no trouble at all. She even asked him if he wanted anything else before she left. 'I'll be going, then, unless there's anything else I can do for you,' he trilled, mimicking her in his best church-lady voice. As she was driving away, I heard him say, 'Just what I need! Jesus, save me!'"

Sharkbait showed up on the second day.

"I'm sorry, Jamie, I didn't know you were here! Does it hurt very much? When do you get your eye patches off? You're gonna be okay, aren't you?" I couldn't see him, but there was no question who my visitor was.

"Hi, Sharkbait."

"Oh! Guess what! They found it!"

"Who? Whaddayamean? Who found it? Found what?" The television was blaring on the other side of the room.

"The mobsters," he said. "They found it—the riverboat, buried in the sand bar. They're pulling pieces of it up with a big shovel. Then they spread the stuff out over the sandbar with the shovel and they look through it with rakes. So far, there's only a lot of timbers and a big ol' mangled rusty tank which must be the boiler. Some of the wood is painted with blue and white paint."

I was stunned. *Damn! They beat us to it!* They still hadn't found the gold, though, but I didn't know what difference that made to us—there was no way we were going to beat them to it at this point.

"Listen, Sidney," I whispered. "Come over here right next to me." I grabbed him by his upper arm and pulled him right over next to my face. "Is anybody else in here?" I whispered.

"Just the man in the other bed, and he's watching television," he whispered back.

"Okay, let me know right away if anybody else comes in, okay? You've been watching them, right?"

"I sure have. All day every day. They're down really deep. They're pulling up tons of water in the bucket."

"What time do they quit?"

"Four-thirty. They get back in the boat and leave."

"You have your walkie-talkie, right?"

"Yes."

"I want you to contact Michael. Try him at Double O, and if he's not there, try him at Base. Tell him what's going on. And tell him he needs to leave Double O and the two of you take turns watching the mobsters at The Projects. We need eyes on them all day long. Oh, and tell him to bring the binoculars with him. You have a bucket with a lid that you can keep them dry at your lookout and leave them overnight?" I asked.

"Yeah."

"Okay, bring it up to your lookout. And let me know if there's any news," I added.

I felt him nodding.

"Okay, thanks, Sharkbait, good luck."

Toby came by in the afternoon. I was glad to see him, but he seemed down.

"How're ya doing, man?" he asked.

"Okay," I replied. "I'm ready to get out of here, but the doctor says I have to stay at least one more day. What happened after I left camp?"

"Nothing, really. You didn't miss anything. It wasn't so great after you left."

I was glad to hear that.

77.
MRS. BUBEN AND BUDDY

The next morning, Toby came by early.

"Guess what?" he said. Without waiting for an answer, he launched into an account of his previous evening.

It was dusk as he walked home from the school playground basketball court. As he passed the narrow walkway between the church and the school, he heard a gasp and looked quickly down the passageway toward the source of the noise. Materializing out of the dark passage was an old woman whom he recognized. Mrs. Buben was holding a leash, on the far end of which ambled her aged companion, Buddy, a very short and very fat dog with cloudy eyes.

"'Oh, I'm sorry, young man,'" Toby said, mimicking Mrs. Buben's quavery voice, "'you startled me. I 'spect you're the younger boy, is that right?'"

"'Yes, ma'am,'" Toby answered.

"'I'm so sorry about your brother,'" he continued, getting more fully into character now. "'You look so much like him. I think about him every night when I go through here, every single time.'

"I didn't know what to say," Toby said. "I thought about Tom every time I passed by there, too, but I thought of his body lying crumpled and lifeless on the concrete."

I didn't know what to say either.

"'This place was awfully busy that night,'" he continued in Mrs. Buben's voice.

"'Pardon me?'" Toby said. "'What do you mean?'" he asked.

"'Just busy,'" she said. "'On my way down the street, I saw a young woman come out of the church in a hurry, then she went down the steps and just walked away, but she kept looking back at the church.'

"That certainly piqued my curiosity," Toby said. "'Do you remember what she looked like?'" he asked her.

"'Sure,' she said, 'I can see her right now. She had long and straight hair, very dark, and she was thin, but when she closed the door behind her I thought....' Her voice trailed off as she remembered, thinking.

"Thought what, Mrs. Buben?" Toby asked.

"'Well, I don't want to gossip,' she said, 'but I thought she was a little rounder than you'd think a thin girl would be, a young girl like she was, and I had the impression that maybe she was in the family way, like maybe she was in there praying about a baby, maybe about her baby, and she seemed upset.'

"Did you see the car she got into?" Toby had asked.

"'Oh, she didn't have a car. She was on foot. She walked down the street toward the hospital. I've often wondered if your brother had already fallen by then or if he was still up in the bell tower and maybe he saw her, too. Because I don't go down Hayden Street at night, and I don't remember even looking down there. I always have to watch for traffic when Buddy is crossing the street with me.

"'And that wasn't all,' she continued, and her eyes were far off, remembering that evening, 'because later, when I came back by here, it was already dark by then, but I saw a man coming down the steps at the back of the church with a bunch of bottles. At least I thought they were bottles.'

"Could you see who it was?" Toby asked her.

"'Not for sure—the streetlight was behind him, so I couldn't see his face at all. I assumed it was your priest, but I couldn't really see him. I figured he was just taking some empty bottles out.'"

I sat riveted, looking at Toby with my mouth partially open.

"'Or, no,'" he continued in Mrs. Buben's wandering, quavery voice, "'actually, that might have been another night and maybe I was just thinking about your brother at the time, I'm not sure now, but you have Communion wine in your church, I know, and it comes in bottles, so it's only natural to have to carry the empty bottles out—I didn't mean he was taking the wine home—no, I never thought that,'" Toby went on, shaking his head, his eyes large and knowing, "'and those bottles would have to be carried out regularly, wouldn't they?'"

He stopped only to draw a breath, then continued.

"'That might be the night I saw the two men come out that side door, I can't be sure anymore. No, I think maybe there were two men on my way out and one man with bottles on my way back, but as I say there was also the girl coming out the front on my way out, and of course, I have to keep a pretty close eye on Buddy—he doesn't see very well, you know. Or maybe one was your priest and I don't know who the other one would be. I don't think they were the ones carrying bottles out. And it was dark, and I was pretty far away. I can't remember now for sure if that was the night your brother died or not, but I always go back to that in my mind and wonder if he had already fallen and maybe was already lying there on the ground and maybe nobody knew it; none of the men knew it, and the young woman didn't, and I didn't, but it's all just jumbled now when I try to think about it.'"

Summer of '63

I sat there in my bed, dumbfounded, looking at Toby and trying to make sense of it all, but there was more.

Because then, standing there in the low gray light of dusk, Toby saw a faint silver gleam on her neck. He could clearly see a robed figure holding a spear—St. Michael? He couldn't make it out. No, not St. Michael The Archangel—the figure wasn't standing on the devil and he wasn't thrusting anyone into Hell with the spear—which is what St. Michael did. Then he saw the opened book in his other hand.

"'Nice medal,'" he said, pointing. "'Is that St. Thomas?'"

"'I guess so,' she said. '"I wouldn't know St. Thomas from Adam, but there's a prayer to St. Thomas on the back. Would you believe I found this in the gutter? It brings me luck.'"

78.
LOTS OF NEWS

On my third day in the hospital the doctor removed my bandages. The light was so bright I couldn't keep my eyes open.

He spent a long time peering into my left eye with some type of scope. I listened to him breathing in my face as he tried to crawl closer and closer, finally half-climbing onto me with his scope pushing into my face. His breath smelled like stale cigarette smoke. Finally, he sat back abruptly and sighed.

"I'm sorry, Mr. Fletcher," he said, "but it looks like the damage is permanent."

"What does that mean?" I asked.

"It means you'll never see out of your left eye again," he said. "The blindness is permanent."

I was stunned. *Blindness! Permanent!* The adrenaline jolt exploded behind my forehead and rebounded off my temples, lifting me nearly off my feet, as real as one of John's uppercuts. My mouth went slack in the aftermath, my face blank—I was incapable of comprehension. He had told me that was a possibility, but I had never really believed it. My mind had blithely filed it away as an extremely distant likelihood, theoretically possible because it was imaginable, but only that—a one in a million—not something that could actually happen.

I leaned back away from him and tried to focus. He must be mistaken. I closed my right eye and tried my left. *Nothing!* I tried it again, forcing my left eye to see. *Still nothing! Aw, shit!*

Shit! Shit! Shit! Shit! Shit!

"Mr. Fletcher?" he said. "Is there anything else I can do for you?"

My breath was coming so fast it seemed like I had been running. "Is there anything I can do?" I asked, my voice unnaturally high.

"No," he said, "it's a permanent injury. That must've been some branch—the mark it made is perfectly round."

I just looked at him out of my right eye. His face was unreadable. *Does he expect me to come clean?*

"Huh!" I said, like "Will wonders never cease!"

But wonders had ceased. The wonder of my amazing basketball career had ceased, and I hadn't even broken out yet—I was one of the few people in the world who knew how great I was. *Was. Like, in the past.* And I *knew* I was great—I was already a Legend In My Own Mind—and in the minds of a few of the high school players, too, I imagined. Now, I couldn't see half of the floor or half of the players. I couldn't look behind me to my left or even beside me to my left. I had no peripheral vision at all on that side.

And my shooting talent was gone—vanished in a second. Depth perception depended on stereoscopic vision, and I wouldn't be able to gauge distance worth a darn—ever again. I wondered if I would even be able to get a driver's license when I turned sixteen, since I wouldn't be able to look behind me on my left side for oncoming cars to change lanes or to pass a car in front of me.

But that was all off in the future. My basketball career was over *right now*, but I was the only one who knew it. Maybe I could compensate somehow. I stared around the room, measuring the outer limits of my peripheral vision. In order to see out in front of me, to the left of my nose, I had to hold my head turned toward that side, but *that reduced my peripheral vision on the right side exactly equal to the gain on my left!* I created a game situation in my mind, looking around the room at imaginary images of the other players, of my defenders, and realized I would not be able to see when one of them left their own man to double-team me. I was devastated.

"Can I borrow one of your cigarettes?" I asked Mr. Benz after the doctor left the room.

"Sure, kid," he said, "help yourself; I didn't know you smoked."

"Thanks!" I said, accepting his lighter and firing it up. *My parents don't, either.* Both Dad and Mom came in over the lunch hour. The doctor had called them and given them the bad news. They tried to be comforting, but nothing helped.

"Just count your blessings," Mom said. "You still have one good eye. You're still able to read and write and see people and watch a sunset, and look where you're going. Think of all the people who are completely blind and can't do any of those things. What any one of them would give to trade with you! You are actually very blessed."

She was right about all of those things, but that didn't help me with my shattered dream, with the thing that was more important to me than anything in the world. It didn't help me win the Mayfly Future Famer Trophy, or get a college basketball scholarship, or play in the NBA, or become rich and famous and admired. As she was leaving, I mentioned to her that I wouldn't be able to be any good at basketball.

"Basketball is not important," she said as she bent over to kiss me goodbye. "Besides, you'll find that when God closes a door, He opens a window. Offer it up for the Poor Souls in Purgatory."

Summer of '63

Late that afternoon, Coach Hedges came in to see me. "I talked to your Dad," he said. "Tough luck, kid. Can you see anything?"

"Not out of my left eye," I said. I told him I was afraid my basketball career was over. He told me not to give up hope completely, and that he would give it some thought. He wanted me to call him when I got out of the hospital.

On Saturday afternoon, the doctor said there was nothing else he could do for me and released me from the hospital. None of the counselors had come to see me, not even Josh or Harry. The doctor told me I might have headaches for a while, but there were no activity limitations. He also told me to wear the left eye patch most of the time, simply to protect the eye structure.

"Your eyes have built-in defenses," he said. "Your eyelids close to protect the eyeball whenever something comes toward it. You no longer have the ability to defend your left eye. Sorry, kid," he said. "Let me know if you have any problems."

Mom and Dad wouldn't let me leave the house until after the weekend, so Richard and Toby came over when they got back in town, and we went out to the end of the yard. John joined us and we sat down on the low wall. Prince jumped up on the wall and squeezed in next to me and rested his muzzle on my thigh, his brow furrowed, while he looked up at me expectantly.

"Really sorry, man," Toby said. "Can you see at all out of that eye?"

"No," I said, "and the doctor says I never will."

"I wish there was something we could do," Richard said.

"Thanks, guys," I said. "There is. Listen, I'm stuck here 'til Monday, at least, but we have an emergency." I told them everything I knew about the mobsters finding the wreck and how Michael and

Sidney had been watching them all day every day, and they needed help—and the sooner the better.

"Can you guys get with them on the walkie-talkies and set up schedules for watching both places? I'm not sure how long it'll be before I can join you—hopefully Monday. And remember to use the code: 'Double O,' 'Playing Tiddlywinks,' 'The Projects,' 'Cinder' and 'Ella.' Can you do it?" They all nodded.

"And whatever you do, don't tell The Archangel how I really lost my eye. Josh didn't mean to do it, and I don't want Michael out there looking for him. If he catches up to him, they'll send him to the penitentiary." Everyone saw the wisdom of that—they all nodded knowingly.

"And I don't think we should tell Sidney, either," Richard said. "This should stay just between us." We all agreed.

The walkie-talkie crackled next to me.

"Base, this is The Projects, come in please." It was Michael's voice. I grabbed for it and missed. *Shit!* No depth perception. I felt my way back to it, like a blind man—like a man with one eye. I picked it up and clicked 'Transmit.'

"Projects, this is Base, what is it? Over."

"Lots of excitement here. Letters appearing, over."

"Letters? What kind of letters? Over."

"Printed letters, blue trimmed in gold, looks like an 'e' from here, over."

"'E' as in 'elephant'? Over."

"Affirmative. A capital 'e' then a small 'a.' Over."

"Eagle," Richard said.

"Oh shit!" Toby said.

I just looked at them, disgusted. "Any sign of the items? Over."

A pause. Finally, "What items? Over."

"You know, the special items—the reason for your job. Over."

"Oh, those items, no, not that we can see from here. Over."

"I'm sure you'll see it, over."

"We'll keep watching. Over."

"Okay, thanks! Keep us updated, willya?" I said. "Over and out." I faced the others, holding my head left of center so I could see them all with my remaining right eye.

"Well, it looks like it's over," I said, then suddenly thought of something. "We gotta get somebody up to Double O with the Big Ear," I said. "Right now!"

"Why?" John asked.

"In case they call and tell him what they've found," I said.

"I'll do it," Toby said.

"Me, too," John said.

"I'm gonna check on something," Richard said.

"What?" I asked.

"Tell you later. It may be nothing and it may be important," Richard said, smiling and looking mysterious. "There's something else I need to tell you, though—I forgot to mention it last week. I saw Crazy Carly leaving the doctor's office where Mom works. When I told my mom I worked with her at the Laze-E-Daze, she said, 'Oh, really? Is she married?' I told her no, but she was going out with one of the customers there, and she said, 'Oh, that's interesting.' I didn't know what to think about that at the time, but I started watching Crazy Carly and I think she's pregnant."

We all just looked at him.

"What makes you think that?" I asked.

"Well, you know how thin she is," he said. "She doesn't have an ounce of fat on her body—not even baby fat, like some girls have."

"Yeah," Toby and I said, because we had both spent a lot of time memorizing every inch of her that we could see, plus every inch that we couldn't see but could imagine. *Lord, be merciful to me, a sinner.*

"Well, when she stretches up to reach something high, it looks to me like she's got a little curvy belly, which is awfully odd on her tight little body." We just nodded. "So I was starting to really watch her. And one day I walked into a room behind her when she was spreading a sheet out on the bed, and she was bending from the waist and leaning over the bed, and her blouse was untucked and hanging away from her stomach and I could see it for sure, a real round belly on that girl. And I swear she wasn't built like that before—I'd have noticed."

"You better watch out," I said, grinning. "You gon' get hung," giving him the hairy eyeball—just one of them now, but he caught it.

"Ah knows it," he mimed, eyes the size of saucers. "But I already *am* hung. And all the white chicks know it."

"Yeah, yeah," Toby and I both muttered.

We were all quiet for a minute, then Richard piped up again.

"And something else I've noticed, too," he said.

"What?" all three of us said. Prince looked up at him inquiringly.

"Well," he said, thoughtfully, "Crazy Carly doesn't act a bit crazy. She's actually a pretty level-headed girl." We just looked at him.

"I see you've been making quite a study," I said, finally.

"Are you fallin' in love now, Richard?" Toby asked.

"No," he answered, "but Tom described her as a total nymphomaniac, and you can't even believe what she sounds like in there with Mr. Muscle. She's got to be the hottest, sexiest bitch that ever took her clothes off."

"So?"

"Well," he continued, "she's never come off that way with me, not even in the slightest."

"Maybe you're not her type," John said.

"You mean maybe she doesn't like black guys?" Richard asked.

"No, not necessarily," John said. "There are a lot of white girls who think you're cute, but maybe you're just not her personal preference."

"Like Tom was her personal preference?" Richard asked.

"Yeah, it sure seemed like it," Toby said.

"And like Mr. Muscle is, too?" Richard asked.

"It sounds like it," John said.

"Well, but the thing is, they don't look anything alike, they're not built alike, they don't talk alike, they don't think alike, and they sure don't act alike," Richard said. "If Tom was her type and Mr. Muscle is her type, what on God's green earth do Tom and Mr. Muscle have in common?" he asked.

"A dick," Toby said. *Funny guy.*

"Exactly!" Richard said. "A dick—you'd think that girl was desperate for a dick. But for some odd reason, my dick won't do, even though I'd gladly share. What's up with that? Everybody who knows anything knows about the superiority of the black dick—it's been proven: 'Once you go black, you never go back,' right?"

"Yeah, right," I said, with as much derision as I could muster—I didn't know if it was true or not, and could only hope it wasn't.

"Get real," John said.

"Bullshit," Toby said.

Prince looked appraisingly at Richard—I could tell he didn't believe him either, but Prince had a lot of confidence going—he was pretty well hung himself.

"And I'd be glad to share this beauty with her if only she'd ask," Richard continued.

"Shhhh!" I interrupted him, holding a finger up for silence—since I'd heard all this before, "What's that squeaking sound?" Everyone stopped and looked around intently. After a couple of seconds, I said, "Oh, right, it's the whine of the teeny weenie."

John and Toby guffawed. Richard looked at me with an air of exaggerated patience. Prince gave a deep sigh.

"I just think it's odd, that's all," Richard said, ignoring my witty rejoinder. "Total nympho, nice intelligent girl—what's up with that?"

"That's why we call her 'Crazy Carly,' I guess," Toby said.

"And it's not because she's prejudiced, either—I can tell she really likes me," Richard added.

"He was at all times a dreamer, dwelling in realms of the unknown...," I said, quoting some Anonymous Sayer of Smart Stuff, whose name escaped me at the moment, although Richard probably knew who said it.

79.
PLAN B

Mom and Dad wouldn't let me play basketball yet—or even pick one up—and I wasn't allowed to go "climbing around in that treehouse" or "running around those hills." Instead, I had to spend some "quiet days at home." Unfortunately but predictably, weeding the garden and washing the dishes were sufficiently quiet activities that I could safely pursue them. I finally convinced them to let me go over and talk to Coach Hedges, but I had to promise not to even pick up a basketball. Toby and I went over at three p.m. on Saturday afternoon.

Toby was quiet on the walk over. I don't know if he thought we were wasting our time or just had no idea how this could work or was afraid that I was going to hear some very bad news. At least he agreed to go.

Mrs. Hedges was working in the flower garden in front when we arrived.

"Just head around back, boys; he's out on the court," she told us.

"Thank you, ma'am," we said, as we loped around the side of the house. We found Coach Hedges seated in a lawn chair under a tree, diagramming plays in a notebook.

"Hello, boys—long time no see," he said. "Have a seat." We did. "Still completely dark in your left eye?" he asked, looking at me.

"Yessir," I said.

"I assumed it would be," he said. "I've been giving this a lot of thought. We're just gonna have to play the cards the way they're dealt, and you boys are smart enough to know that this changes everything, especially for you, Jamie, but also for Toby. Jamie, I think it's safe to say that you won't get a college scholarship to play basketball, and you definitely won't be playing in the NBA."

"I figured that," I said, and I must have looked pretty dejected—I certainly felt that way.

"But that doesn't mean your basketball career is over," he said, standing up and walking over to the court and picking up a basketball. We followed him.

"What do you mean?" I asked. "I can't see half the court, and I don't have any depth perception. Plus, I'll never get close to the basket again in a game situation without some defender on my blind side stealing the ball from me. Hook shots on my left side are out of the question, except in a game of H.O.R.S.E."

"I know," he said, "it's a problem, a big problem, a serious problem for sure. But there are things you can still do. And you already have a terrific foundation, an incredible skillset that most players will never have—even the good ones. You can handle the ball by pure touch, and do a great job of it, too. You can still dribble with either hand, you can switch hands, and go between your legs and behind your back without looking. You can drive and shoot layups, and you can pass the ball really well—passing requires very little depth perception—most of them are just rockets. So we're gonna use Toby even more than we have in the past, and you already have the tools to use him and to help him, too."

Toby looked thoughtful. I was not convinced.

"Yeah," I said, "but I still won't be able to shoot."

Summer of '63

"I think you're wrong about that," he said. "I think you *will* be able to shoot, and shoot well, and even shoot a decent percentage if you're smart about taking your shots."

"What do you mean?" I asked, incredulous. I wanted to believe it, but I didn't see how it was possible. I wanted him to explain it to me, to convince me, to make me believe.

"You'll just have to shoot from known distances," he said, "from fixed points. From places that make you comfortable about your lack of depth perception."

I was puzzled. I couldn't think how that could possibly work. I envisioned the floor, taping "Xs" on it and practicing shooting from those spots, but the "Xs" wouldn't be there during games.

"You can shoot your layups, just the way you always have," he said. "The same with free throws. You stand in the exact same place time after time and you *feel* that shot, you feel it coming from your toes all the way up through your body to your fingers, and your release is the same every time. You can feel it; you could do it with your eyes closed and still hit a decent percentage. And the other one, for you, especially, since I think you love the shot," and I knew it even before he said it, "is your shot from the corner."

I stood up and just stared at him. Was this for real? I needed a basketball in my hands and I needed it now. But he wouldn't give it to me. He stood there holding it. He knew I was asking for it, that I wanted to touch it more than I'd ever wanted anything in my life. I wanted to see if it was true—if he was right. But he just let me ache. I held out my hands in the universal signal: pass me the ball. But he didn't.

"Your parents say you're not to touch a basketball," he said. "You'll have to talk to them first." I dropped my arms. So he knew.

"Go home and tell them," he said. "I'm ready when you boys are. I've created a whole new workout for you. We have just two weeks before the Mayfly Summer Tourney, and I want you boys ready for it. Don't even think about the Future Famer Trophy. You're not gonna win it, but that doesn't matter. The things that trophies can bring you are not part of your future anymore. But great basketball is still possible. And I want you boys to have it. You've earned it."

"Yes, sir!" we both said. Toby was as excited as I was.

"And one other thing before you leave," he said. "Actually, two other things. No, make that three. First, you two don't tell anyone the strategy about shooting from certain areas only. You need to promise me today that you will not disclose that to anyone, even if you two are playing on opposing teams. The only exception to that is your parents, Jamie, and tell them we have a pact not to tell another human being, okay? Do I have your word on that?"

We both agreed.

"Secondly, Jamie, I need you to start practicing scanning left and right. You're gonna have to learn to play holding your head a bit to the left and scanning back and forth frequently, so you can open up your vision of the court."

"I know," I said, "but when I look to the left, I lose part of my peripheral vision on the right," I said.

"Yes, I agree, I've been experimenting with it," he said, "but it's more important to see more of the left side of the court ahead than the farthest end of your right periphery. And scanning left and right will give you the entire thing for every circuit you make, so I still think it will increase your basketball capability to hold your head a few degrees left. It will be tiring at first, which is why I want you to start getting used to it as soon as possible."

"Okay," I said.

"Third, from now on out, your success or failure as a basketball player will depend on how well you communicate with one another. That means visually, by signs that only the two of you understand, as well as by words. We're going to be spending a lot of time on communication and timing."

As Toby and I walked home, the prohibition against my touching a basketball seemed outrageously oppressive. I had to talk to Mom and Dad as soon as possible.

"What a coach!" I said to Toby.

"No shit, man," he said. "*No shit!*"

When I got home, I told Mom and Dad that I needed to talk to them as soon as possible.

"Not now, dear," Mom said. "We can talk after dinner when your chores are finished." At dinner, the boys asked me what Coach Hedges had said.

"He said I can still play, and he has a new workout for me—designed for a player with one eye," I told them. "I don't know much about it, except that we need to start practicing as soon as possible." I saw Mom look over at Dad.

So after dinner, we went into their bedroom and I sat on the bed and gave them the entire report, that my trophy chance was gone, that my scholarship chances were ended, but I could still be a good player, and I wanted to try.

"Leave the room and let me talk to your mother," Dad said. "We'll call you back in a few minutes."

I waited nervously in my room until I was summoned again.

"Alright, young man," Dad said, "we're going to let you try, but you will still have to keep up your chores around the house, and if you want to go to college you will have to get a job when you're old enough," he said.

"Deal!" I said. *"Thank you!"* I ran out of the room and called Toby to tell him the good news, then I called Mr. Hedges and told him we would be there on Monday afternoon as usual.

I was so glad that I had continued my prayers for the Poor Souls ever since the injury, and not because I thought they could help me win the trophy anymore, but just because, after thinking about them for so long, I felt so sorry for them that I wanted to do whatever I could to help them escape the burning. And that night, after my second rosary of the evening, I even said an extra decade of Hail Marys for the relief of their suffering. It seemed to me that they were still working behind the scenes, in the mysterious way the Poor Souls had of getting things done here on earth.

As I turned over and went to sleep in the summer heat with our window wide open, something happened that confused me—I was certain I heard Howlin' Johnnie—miles away, but there was no mistaking what it was. I was surprised. I hadn't heard him since I had been home. *I wonder what that's all about? He must be coming back—he's a very long way from Oko-Tipi.*

80.
SNOOPING WITH URGENCY

The next two weeks were furiously busy. When it became obvious that I wasn't having any big head problems from playing basketball, my parents allowed me back into full activities.

Toby continued to help me with my basketball, but he was frustrated. "One of those bastards killed Tom," he said, "or maybe all of them. And we've got to prove it, and soon—how are we gonna do that?" he demanded.

"I know, Toby," I said, "I know, but we're doing everything we can think of. And we're making progress. We found out what they're up to, and we're the only ones alive who know it. And we know Tom found out what they were up to, also, and we know they caught him spying on them and killed him. And we know he took the article about Confederate gold and the Hydrology Report that connects them to the treasure. And we also know P.J. is helping them. I wonder if he went to confession about killing Tom."

"You're right," Toby said, "that is a lot of progress, but we've got to *prove it,* so we can get Tom into hallowed ground, so he can get to heaven, and so my Mom can rest easier. And also, I want to put those murderous bastards away—all of them."

I was completely in favor of that, but I couldn't think of any way to force the issue. All I knew to do was to watch and wait, hoping that the criminals would give themselves away.

We set up a schedule around our various work hours, with all of The Cliffhangers and Sharkbait alternating between Overlook Oak—"Double O," as we now called it— and The Projects in the hill above Cottonwood Point. We stuck to our new code words religiously to minimize the danger of being overheard by P.J. or even the mobsters.

The next morning after chores, Michael and I were reclining in Overlook Oak. Toby was still working at the River's Rest and Richard wasn't on Overlook duty until his Laze-E-Daze shift ended at three p.m. I was absent-mindedly watching a pair of mourning doves mating on the limb of a tree far below us and thinking about Mary Ann, wondering what she was doing right then and wishing I could bring her up to Overlook Oak with me. *Lord, be merciful to me, a sinner.* But it wasn't only that—I also just wanted to look at her face and talk to her and hear her voice. *Oh my God—it's happening again! Damn—I was only thinking of her face! Lord, be merciful to me, a sinner!*

Michael was lolling against the backstop, wearing the headphones. We had the Big Ear trained on the house. P.J. had left early but had come back with some groceries, and there was nothing interesting going on except for some rustling and footsteps. A bee buzzed lazily past our perch. The walkie-talkie lay between us on the front shelf, turned down low, when we suddenly heard a barely audible crackle. I grabbed it and put it to my ear, wrapping a towel around the unit to muffle any escaping sound.

"Double O, this is The Projects, come in, please." It was John's voice, on duty with Sharkbait down at Cottonwood Point.

"This is Double O, Projects—what's new?" I whispered. "Over."

"They're bringing up a bunch of stuff," John said. "They're way down deep—lotsa water pouring out of the bucket each time they bring it up, over."

"Can you tell what they're bringing up?" I asked. "Over."

"Hard to tell," he said. "it mostly looks like boards. Some are painted, over."

"What color? Over."

"Blue and white, and there's some letters, trying to read them. Over."

"What do they say? Over."

"Gimme a second. Looks like maybe a 'T' on one piece of wood and also a 'W' and 'I' together on another piece, over."

Twi! Michael and I looked at each other.

"Twin?" I said. "Twinkle?"

"Twilight?" Michael said.

The radio crackled again. "This is Sharkbait. I also think I see an 'S,' over."

An 'S'? We were all silent, puzzled.

"Are the letters capital or small?" I finally asked. "Over."

"Capital. All capital," John answered. "Over."

"Okay, thanks. Just keep us posted, okay?" I said. "And call if you figure that out. Over."

"Roger that, will do," John said. "Over."

Michael and I spent the next hour trying to figure out what the letters meant. No luck. I needed to see it written out on the floor in front of me. An hour later I radioed Toby and told him to ask Richard to bring some chalk when he came.

When Richard showed up with the chalk, we started working with the possibilities on the wooden plank floor. Most of the possibilities didn't sound very riverboatish, however. *Twine?* The "W" would almost certainly have to come before the "I," but the "T" could come before or after. Same with the "S." *Witness? Winters?* Or even from another word, because no matter which way I worked it, there was no "EA" in any of them. *Eager Twins? Early Winters?* But not *Flying Eagle*.

I radioed The Project again. John had left, but Sharkbait was still on duty.

"So are all those letters capital? Over."

"Yes, all capital, but the 'E' is bigger than the 'A' and the 'W' is by itself, but I think it's big, too, over."

"Okay, thanks, let me know if you see anything else. Over."

"10-4, over," Sharkbait said.

I began two words in chalk, mostly blank, on the floor, one under the other, the first starting with "Ea" and the second with "W," then wrote "T" and "I" and "S" off to the side. We all stared at them.

"East Wind!" Richard said, suddenly. "That sounds like the name of a riverboat. I'll find out if there was ever a riverboat with that name. I'm going to the library," he stage-whispered as he swung down from the supporting limbs to the suspended Tree Ramp, then ran away down Hidden Path, quick and soundless as a squirrel.

81.
REMNANTS

"Pssst!" I snapped alert, back from a dream where Gunnar Green was chasing me with a hatchet. *Is he in our bedroom?* The moon shone onto my brother John, sound asleep in his bed next to the window. I was dimly aware in the back of my skull that the complex summertime night song had been fractured. I sat up in bed, listening intently. A single cricket resumed singing. "Pssst!" There it was again. The cricketing ceased abruptly. The sound had come from the window. I crawled out of bed and crossed the room in my underwear. Toby was standing outside, bathed in the moonshine. His red hair was muted, dusky, and luminous, his face spectral, his features hidden in shadow.

"What are you doing here?" I asked, unhooking the window screen at the bottom and pushing it out.

"I gotta show you something," he said. I lifted the screen, freed the top from the metal hanger, and set it down on the ground beside the house, then stepped through the window onto the grass below. The air was sweet with the scent of the summer night. A light breeze, little more than a sigh, caressed my skin, teasing the tiny hairs and giving me goose bumps. I crossed my arms in front of me.

"What time is it?" I asked, yawning. The cricket resumed his love song, unnaturally loud in the silence of the night.

"One-thirty," he said. "I needed to tell you something and I couldn't wait."

"Obviously," I said, exhaling heavily. "What is it?"

"I found the note."

"What note? We already have the note," I said.

"The rest of the note," he said. "We only had a few pieces of it."

"What are you talking about?"

"I couldn't sleep, so I went downstairs to smoke a cigarette. So I'm sitting there in the basement, smoking, and I must've left the light on in Room 111 'cause there was light coming through a crack in the floor, so I went over to look at it and I could see something stuck in the crack and hanging down a little bit, so I pulled on it, and it was the rest of the note," he said, pulling a small roll of folded paper out of his pocket.

"The rest of what note?" I asked, taking the paper from him and unrolling it. I couldn't read it in the moonlight.

"Here," Toby said, pulling a zippo lighter out of his pocket and firing it up. He held it next to the paper while both of us examined it, our heads together in the dark, shadows flickering across our faces while the flame danced above the lighter.

"Not here," I said. "Let's go to the end of the yard where we can set this down and see better." Prince came out of his house, looking quizzically at us, and then began patrolling the perimeter, demarcated by the furthest reach of his chain. We sat on the small wall together and examined the items.

There were two pieces of paper: a tiny piece rolled up inside a longer one, both white strips, both written in cursive. The first one read "inn." Something to do with the motel? I knew that the door of each room had a framed copy of the Missouri Inn Keeper's law posted on it. I turned it aside and looked at the second paper, the larger one, in the flickering light. It was immediately recognizable. It said: "rd be merciful to me, a." It had been torn at both ends.

"It's missing some letters," I said.

"I know," Toby said. "Guess which ones."

"L and O," I said, slowly working my way from left to right. "Then 'Sinner.' But we have the 'I, N, N,' so it's just missing the 'S' and the 'E' and 'R.'"

"Right, and the 'L' and 'O,'" Toby reminded me.

My mouth flew open. I jumped up off the low wall. *Loser!* I bent down and read the paper again, then looked again at the smaller piece. "And they've been torn off the ends," I said. "Do you have the note from the Inquest?"

"No, but my Dad has it," he said. "I didn't want to wake them up, but I'll get it tomorrow."

"What floor was this stuck in—what room?"

"111, the one the mobsters rented."

"Oh my God!" I said, standing there stunned. "So they took this note, probably from Tom, and they used the letters to make it look like he committed suicide."

"I know," Toby said.

"Do you know what this means? It's the proof—the proof that Tom was murdered, and he was murdered by those mobsters. I wonder if P.J. knows about this. I wonder if he was in on it."

I noticed that the sole cricket had hushed. There was no traffic noise, either—in fact, there was no noise at all. All motion had ceased; every living thing held its breath. Then, in the absolute silence of that moment, deep in the sudden quiet of that night, I heard it again, floating over the hills, faint but distinct, clear as a bell, and I knew what it was as soon as I heard it—I knew for a fact that distant wail was Howlin' Johnnie.

Toby heard it, too, and he knew who it was. We both stood stock still, staring at each other. And suddenly I knew something else—I knew it wasn't because Bony Gus was after him—that was just a story. But Howlin' Johnnie was real—and he was coming back. And I knew why, standing there in my underwear and shivering in the summer night—I knew why he was coming—he was coming back for justice.

Prince looked back at us to see if we were alright. He didn't whimper, but I could tell he was worried.

"Good boy," I said, patting him. He stood and walked with us back toward the house as far as he could go, then stood there watching, a deep furrow on his brow.

82.
THE EDGES

When he finished his morning work hours at the River's Rest, Toby brought the three Inquest "Loser" scraps ("Lo" and "s" and "er") to Overlook Oak. We took the two remaining pieces that Toby had found in the floor crack (the "rd be merciful to me a" and the "inn") and we placed the three Inquest "Loser" scraps in their proper places before, between, and after them, so they spelled out "Lord be merciful to me, a sinner," lining them up on the front shelf of the treehouse. None of them mated at the junctures. Disappointed, we put them back in the dry bucket so they wouldn't blow away.

I puzzled over it all afternoon and evening. I had expected the edges to mate. It was the only thing that made sense, but it didn't make sense.

"Help me, Holy Ghost, Font of Wisdom, Teacher and Revealer," I whispered as I turned over after my rosary for the Poor Souls. Then, having left the problem with a higher power, I was asleep almost instantly.

And I dreamed. I was playing Scrabble around a huge table in a glitzy casino. Mary Ann was at the table, and she was smiling at me, encouraging me—she wanted me to win. The mobsters were there, too, and I knew they were trying to cheat, and I was watching them, trying to catch them cheating. Some of the Scrabble letter blocks were painted solid black, and if you could make a word using all black letters, you got an extra two hundred points. I looked up and saw Tom there, too, and he and Toby were talking to each other and laughing.

And the Scrabble *croupier* said, "Remember, this is a one-step game. You must play the letters you have drawn." I looked down at my letters and saw "Remember man that thou art dust and unto dust thou shalt return," and somehow I understood it, and as I was thinking about it, I caught the tail end of a quick motion on my left, and I looked down and noticed that some of my letters were missing, and I looked over the mobsters' shoulders and saw them coloring some letters with a black marker, and I said, "That's two steps. First, you chose your letters, and now you're changing them. Two steps are illegal."

And that's all I could remember when I woke up. But I could tell it was important—I lay in bed for ten minutes replaying it and obsessing about it with my eyes closed, trying to remember—I couldn't let it alone.

Two steps are illegal. First, you chose your letters, and then you changed them.

Then I thought about the "Loser" note. *So, first the mobsters chose letters that would spell "Loser," tearing them off the original prayer scrip— which they wouldn't have done unless Tom was already dead, and they wanted to make it look like suicide—and why would they bother at all— why did they care what had happened to Tom unless they had killed him? Why would they risk planting the "Loser" scraps in Tom's pocket if they hadn't killed him?*

I got up and let Prince off his chain, so he could sniff around in the cool morning. Breakfast, then chores. The ground was so dry we were driving spikes into the ground with hammers right next to the weeds to get them out by the root. I was eager to be off to Overlook Oak so I could look at the scraps again.

Summer of '63

I got there right after morning chores, untied the bucket and laid the two "crack-in-the-floor-floor-found" scraps out in front of me, then took the three Inquest scraps out and set them on our shelf before placing them in proper order in the line of prayer. That's when I saw it for the first time—something really weird: the tail end edge of the "Lo" piece perfectly matched the front-end edge of the "s" piece. I looked at the other end of the "s" piece, the tail end, and saw that it matched perfectly with the front edge of the "er" piece.

When I looked at them previously in the evidence bag, it hadn't seemed remarkable that their edges had matched—it seemed right and natural. And the only time I had seen them out of the bag was when we were lining them up in proper order, interspersed by the two "floor found" pieces, when none of the junctures lined up with one another. But when they were placed end-to-end by themselves, without the two "floor found" pieces, it was jarring, unnatural, non-continuous, obvious.

Because the edges of the three pieces that spelled "Loser" matched.

They didn't mate—they matched. Their edges were identical. Each void on one edge was opposite an identical void on the other. Each projection on one edge was opposite an identical projection on the other. Not an "innie" situated directly opposite an "outtie." Not a male fitting into a female. Not yin and yang.

They had tried to make it look like it had all been one single note, "Loser," that Tom had torn up in despair and disgust. First, they tore out the five letters that they needed, and then they held them together, the two end pieces facing into the center piece, and tore them again so that the edges would match, so it would look like they had come from one single note which Tom had torn up, instead of a hodgepodge of letters from a larger tract—and of course they had to get rid of the larger tract, too, so that nobody would ever piece it together. But they outsmarted themselves. The edges should've mated, not matched. A male should jut into a female. Oops! They leapt the wrong way. Their fathers obviously didn't give a damn about them or they would've had a special sign for their bedrooms: "Think Before You Act."

I showed Richard and Toby when they arrived.

"The problem is, without a confession, we'll never be able to prove it, but now at least we know how they did it," Richard said.

"Yeah, that plus P.J.'s big loopy 'L' which proves where the letters came from in the first place," Toby said. "There's something else I've been thinking about," Toby said. "After we talked about Crazy Carly being pregnant. What if it's Tom's?"

"What do you mean?" I asked, slow on the uptake.

"What if she's carryin' Tom's baby?" Toby said.

Richard and I were quiet.

"Oh, wow," I said. "I never thought about that."

"That would explain some things," Richard said.

"Like what?" Toby asked.

"Like why she's been coming on so strong to Mr. Muscle. Like why any white dick will do."

Toby and I just looked at him.

"Well, what if it is? What if it *is* Tom's baby?" I asked, finally.

"I'd just like to know, that's all," Toby said. "Richard, does your Mom have a key to the office?" he asked.

"The doctor's office? Yeah, I think so," he said.

"Think you can steal it from her?" Toby asked.

"Probably," Richard said, "but I don't have to—there's an easier way to check if she's pregnant."

"What?" Toby and I said together.

"Just look around her room at the Laze-E-Daze while she's in with Mr. Muscle," Richard said. "I can use the passkey."

"What will that tell us?" Toby asked.

"I don't know. Maybe she has some magazine articles or a note from the doctor or some prescriptions—we'll just have to see. We can always decide to break into the doctor's office later if we need to. It's way more dangerous, though."

We just looked at him. *Worth a try.* We nodded.

"Okay, I'll see what I can do," he said, "but don't hold your breath—I definitely don't wanna get caught."

83.
OOM-POW-WOW

"Wanna get a cold drink?" I asked, walking up to Mary Ann, who was perched on the edge of a picnic table at the Parish Picnic and engaged, as usual, with a group of her friends.

I had been looking forward to the event for weeks, partly because I always had a good time there, but mostly because I hoped to talk to Mary Ann some more, *alone*. Remembering my problem with separating her from her entourage at our last meeting, I had agonized over a solution and finally devised an opening line to extract her from the group—a sure winner. How could she refuse—who would not want a cold drink on a hot summer day in Mayfly?

"I just had one," she replied.

Yikes! What do I say now? I had been counting on her thinking along similar lines, expecting her to jump at the chance to leave her friends for more stimulating company. I stood there mute for a second, then I saw that she was smiling at me.

"No," I finally said, "I mean something fresh, like right out of the ground, a real drink, maybe even from a secret spring."

Her eyes opened wide, lit up, framed by soft lashes curling away in the sun. Now I was shocked—they were pale blue-green—different again.

"Sure!" she said, sliding off the table. I came close, ostensibly to help her down.

"Meet me behind the Gates of Hercules," I whispered. "I'll go around the curve in the road and then double back through the woods—you can just walk down the lawn and go behind the trees."

She nodded at me slowly. She had a faraway look in her mind, but she may have just been picturing the route to the Gates of Hercules.

"You know how to get there, right?" I whispered. She nodded quickly—she remembered.

"Okay," I whispered. "Give me five minutes."

"Okay," she said, her voice amplified for the benefit of the others, "see you later, Jamie."

I waved good-bye to the group and left, heading down the park road with purpose. As soon as I was out of sight around the long curve, I ducked down into the woods and started working my way back. As I neared our rendezvous point through the woods, I was dismayed to see eight girls coming down the hill in a rowdy group, running and tagging one another, and singing "Dominique," by The Singing Nun, which was big in Catholic girls' circles that year. This was definitely not what I was hoping for. When they got past the Gates and were behind the big pear trees, however, Mary Ann separated from them, called "Thanks!" and disappeared into the woods onto the path where I waited. The rest of the girls played around behind the trees for a while, occasionally popping out to the side to tag one another in view of people at the shelter, then finally calmed down and walked back up the long slope toward the road.

"They came along so no one would notice me going into the woods alone," she said. *Great. Virtually our entire class of girls are co-conspirators with Mary Ann and me. Sensible, though, but I was sure they would demand a full report as a quid pro quo.*

Mary Ann looked beautiful among the tree trunks. I took her hand and we ran down the wooded hill together, laughing. Even though it was mid-summer, there was nothing except occasional fallen trees to impede our progress—the canopy overhead was so dense that undergrowth was virtually nonexistent.

We headed for the spring, and, once again, I helped her descend the steep bank. The water was cool and fresh and pure.

"Wanna go out on the bridge?" I asked.

"I'd love to," she said. *A ringing endorsement.* We walked down the path together, me in front, her following closely. I stopped and pointed at a painted turtle, and again to show her some butterflies playing in a shaft of sunlight.

"Here's where the thrush's nest was," I said. "They're long gone."

"I hope they're okay," she said. I didn't mention the possibility that a snake had gotten all of them in the middle of the night.

"They probably raised their clutch and then moved on. Maybe they build a new nest for each family. This valley is probably full of thrush nests now—the chicks that they raised right here are probably building nests of their own." She smiled thoughtfully, pleased at the prospect. *Who says I don't know how to talk to girls?* But it wasn't something I had strategized—it wasn't forced—there was no planning or scheming or conniving. Being with Mary Ann made me think about things like that. *Sheesh! At least Toby and Richard can't hear me talking like this.*

We both heard rushing water at the same moment and looked at each other, listening intently, verifying that it registered on both of us, then ran toward the source. She put her hand on my arm as we approached the waterfall. But this time there was no fear. We were partners on our journey to the bridge.

Summer of '63

Once again, I slid down first, then caught Mary Ann in my arms at the end of the chute. She was so beautiful and happy. In the deep cut leading to the tunnel, her eyes shone a light gray, sparkling with soft amber jewels.

Once on solid ground, we both knelt and put our ears to the train track, then stood and approached the tunnel and listened again. Nothing.

"Ready?" I asked. She nodded. We grabbed hands and dashed into the maw of the tunnel, which curved away sharply into the darkness. Even though we were both veterans by now, it was still heart-stopping. We looked for deep recesses as we ran, crevices where we could shelter in case an enormous train engine should suddenly materialize in front or behind us. Even when the sharp curve opened out into the far end of the tunnel and daylight, we raced the gigantic phantom engine until we had exited and hopped off to the side of the tracks and safety.

I was relieved to see Mr. Dindia's profile outlined against the window on the river side of the shack, engineer's cap on his head, unlit cigar in his mouth. When we knocked, he didn't seem surprised to see us.

"Hi, Mr. Dindia," we both said.

"Hello, kids," he said. "I thought I might see you today."

"Can we ride the bridge, Mr. Dindia?" I asked.

"I don't see why not, kids," he said, looking at the control board. "You can go out there for a little while, anyway. No trains due for an hour and a half, but I'll have to bring you in long 'afore that. Got to have plenty of time to shut the train down if the bridge don't work."

"Thank you, Mr. Dindia!" we said, running for the bridge and jumping across the seam where the tracks joined to the shore. We both hung on to the railing and waved. Moments later we heard the loud machinery "thunk" and felt the accompanying steel shudder reverberate through our bodies, signifying the separation of the bridge from the shore, and we held on as the great span swung out in a long, graceful arc.

The surface of the water below us was so bright it almost hurt as we watched our shadows skim across it. We looked up, to the south and downriver, miles away to the lush green islands and the brown sand beaches beckoning in the lazy summer sun, then north, upriver and around the bend, as our vantage point continued to back away from the Missouri bluffs, opening the entire panoply of the great river to our sight.

The familiar river smell of fish and vegetation wafted up to mix with diesel and warm creosote, immersing us in scent as we stood leaning over the rail and gazing down into the water. The lack of rainfall had allowed much of the river sediment to settle out, and the water was clearer than I had ever seen it. We watched four large fish swimming lazily upstream, just below the surface in the slow low water current.

It was a spectacular day. The sky was deep summer blue, showing only a smattering of white cottony tufts which evaporated slowly as we watched them. Mary Ann's eyes were now a light blue, twin cornflowers framed by the soft curve of her feathery lashes. Her skin had been sun-kissed into a tawny brown. She squinted as a sudden breeze blew her hair into her eyes, causing her nose to wrinkle briefly. *My God she's pretty.* I thought I could smell oranges. And straw.

"Are you still practicing basketball?" she asked, gazing at me.

"Yes, every day, with Toby," I answered. "And it's helping. But I won't be able to win the trophy anymore." She looked sympathetic.

"I'm very sorry, Jamie," she said, "but that's okay." I was quiet for a moment.

"Are you still riding Sugarloaf?" I asked. She looked at me, surprised.

"You remembered her name. Yes, I ride her every day."

"With Lucas Crane?" I asked. A shadow crossed her face.

"No, I don't ride with Lucas Crane."

"Why not? He has a horse, doesn't he? I thought you liked him."

"He's not a gentleman," she said. I was quiet for a while, hoping she'd tell me more.

"Oom-pow-wow!" she said suddenly.

"What?" I said, not sure I had heard her correctly.

"Oom-pow-wow!" she said again.

"What's that mean? What are you talking about?" I asked, confused.

"Wanna have an oom-pow-wow?" she asked, suddenly aggressive, taking both my hands in hers, her eyes twinkling.

"What's an oom-pow-wow?" I asked, warily.

"Don't you know? It's simple. I ask you a question and you have to answer it and you have to tell the truth, then you ask me one and I have to tell the truth."

"Okay, sure," I said hesitantly, my eyes narrowing slightly, wanting to cooperate, but not at all sure what I was getting into.

"Okay. First, we put our right hands over our hearts," she said, demonstrating, and waiting for me to do the same. "Now we say the Oom-Pow-Wow Vow:

'Oom-pow-wow, oom-pow-wow, oom-pow-wow vow;

I vow to tell all in this oom-pow-wow now'."

So I said it.

"Okay," she said. "Since I called the oom-pow-wow, I get to ask the first question."

"Okay," I said, my sense of wariness growing, as I wondered where this was all headed.

"Who do you like?" she asked coyly, scrutinizing my face.

"Oh!" I said, startled. "Oh, I don't know," stalling for time. *This had gotten serious in a hurry.* "I like Toby, and I like Richard...."

"No, silly," she said, "I mean, what girl do you like?"

Stunned, I looked into her eyes. She was facing west. The color had changed back again. Now they were green. Her pupils were enormous. Time had stopped without my noticing. I don't know how long I gazed at her. I was not completely conscious—I had been charmed—I was floating in a dream—my dream—but it was her spell. Gradually I came back from that faraway place, and a few of my senses returned, just part way, but enough for me to realize that I was stupefied, that my mouth was gaping as I gazed at her. I had to force it closed, force it to work, and then my voice came out in a whisper.

"I like you."

"What?" she asked, giggling, her eyes merry.

"I like you," I said, louder, closer to normal this time. And I did. A lot. And then she smiled at me.

"I like you, too," she said. Then she leaned in closer and whispered, "I always have."

I could smell her fresh girl smell, her girl skin, clean and flawless, warmed by the summer sun. I wasn't sure what was happening. I leaned in, too, and saw her pretty nostrils flare, saw the pink tip of her tongue, and the fine long lashes on her closed eyelids.

"Boom!" *Is that inside me?*

Summer of '63

I was completely stunned by the reverberating iron "clunk" and the shudder that ran through the steel superstructure of the bridge, as our span began its long journey back to land. *No! Wait!* I had the sudden feeling that I had almost caught the loveliest creature, but I missed—it flew away. Ecstasy and irretrievable loss warred in my mind as we swung, weightless, at the end of the span, into the vast arc that returned us to the base of the bluff, to the curving parallel tracks which disappeared into the darkness behind the arched stone mouth of the tunnel, and to our former lives, now forever changed by the power of an oom-pow-wow.

Not until we reached the last stair up from River Road into the park and stepped into the sunlight was the spell lifted. We separated, and I offered to wait a few minutes while Mary Ann walked down the road first.

As I headed back through the festivities in a daze, I was stunned to see Dapper Man's hat over the top of the crowd. *What is he doing here?*

As I approached, I also picked out Mr. Muscle, his arm around Crazy Carly, at a booth manned by men of the parish. The front of the booth was a long board with red and black numbers painted on it—the back of the booth showed a spinning roulette wheel mounted vertically, which made loud clicking sounds as it spun. I approached as near as I dared, while trying to keep out of his sight, and saw P.J. approaching Dapper Man, who was standing off to the side of the booth, watching the wheel. I slipped behind the canvas back of the booth and listened.

"How's business, Father?" Dapper Man asked.

"Business is good—I think this is going to be a money maker," P.J. said.

"Roulette always is," Dapper Man said, laughing. "You know what they say, 'There's a sucker born every minute.'"

There was a pause, then I heard Dapper Man say, "So, the wheel's working okay then?"

"Appears to be working great," P.J. said. "Thanks for your help."

84.
MRS. WASHINGTON

School was due to start in three weeks. The summer had nearly exhausted itself. We had been in a long drought—the last significant rain we had was the storm we watched from the cabin at Camp Oko-Tipi. We were still carrying buckets of water to our young bushes and trees. There was no grass to cut—we could feel the prickly ends of the grass crunching under our bare feet. There was some vegetable picking to be done, which always went easier than the planting, plowing, and weeding, but even that was slim. Our entire world was dusty, except in the deep woods. Overlook Oak, however, was still shady and cool. Breezes drifted through the boughs on even the calmest of days.

Toby and I were approaching the end of our morning shift at Overlook Oak. We had not seen Richard since the previous day, so we stopped by the library on our way home. We found him seated at a microfilm reader in the basement, going through old newspaper accounts. A huge textbook lay open beside him.

"I don't have anything definite yet," he said, "but I'm still hoping."

Toby dug into his pocket and brought out the papers he had found in the floor crack and laid them out on the table, then took the three Inquest scraps and assembled them all in proper order. Next, I showed him how the three Inquest scraps had been held together and torn again, and how they matched instead of mated. Richard was aghast.

"But this changes everything," he said. "This is evidence. This should be enough to get Tom moved to hallowed ground. We need to reopen the Inquest or just talk to P.J. about it."

"Are you kidding?" I asked, horrified at the very thought. "For all we know, P.J. was in on it. If we talk to him, we might just end up dead. We gotta talk to someone else." They both looked at me.

"Yeah, there is that, alright," Richard said. "We need to think this over first."

By the time we went to basketball practice, Toby and I still hadn't heard anything more from Richard, so we stopped by his house on the way back from our session with Coach Hedges.

His Mom answered the door in flip-flops and a cotton summer dress.

"Hello, Mrs. Washington," we said, as soon as she came to the door. She was an attractive black woman with beautiful features, pleasingly plump, with straightened hair.

"Well, come in, boys," she said, leaning out onto the front porch and holding the screen door open. "Richard's not home yet, but he should be here any minute."

We stepped into the living room. It was small and neat, tidy except for an oval wicker laundry basket on the floor in front of the couch and a pile of folded clothes on the coffee table—we had obviously interrupted her.

"Have a seat, boys," she said. "Would you like some cookies?" Toby and I looked at each other and choked down our "Is the Pope Catholic?" rejoinder.

"Yes, ma'am," both of us said at the same time. "Please," we added.

"I'll be right back," she said, smiling. "'Don't nobody go nowhere,' as the man says."

Summer of '63

"What man, ma'am?" I asked as she went into the kitchen.

"Oh, it's just what the band leader says down at the Ding-A-Ling Club when they take a break. 'Don't nobody go nowhere.' Double negative. Both of 'em wrong, but ever'body knows what he means, so maybe two wrongs do make a right." We heard her opening cabinets and then the refrigerator door.

I thought about that but didn't really have an opinion because I couldn't put two wrongs together in sequence, except with P.J. or the mobsters, and there was no way I could make a right out of any of that.

Toby and I sat in chairs on either side of the couch. I loved Richard's living room. It was bright and airy—it even smelled nice, like flowers and fresh bread. Lace curtains moved in and out against the window screens in a faint breeze, causing filtered daylight to play across the cream-colored walls. A console television set stood in the middle of the wall opposite the couch. Above it hung a black-and-white portrait of President Kennedy in a simple black frame.

A painted bookcase was built into the wall, holding vinyl LPs and an old Bible which stood open to the title page. I walked over and looked at it. There were some handwritten notes on the page in large, heavy letters which had been penciled in two separate hands. The first entry read: "August 2, 1930 Janey Washington died 83." The next entry read: "February 16, 1937 Elijah Washington died 93." No dates of birth. I did the math—he would have been seventeen when the Civil War broke out in 1861 and twenty-two when he was made a free man.

The only other furniture in the room was a hi-fi record player cabinet. A Turkish rug, its once-vibrant colors muted by time, covered the floor, surrounded by a margin of polished hardwood.

Mrs. Washington came back through the kitchen door with a tray of cookies, a pitcher of milk, and three glasses, then bent forward and slid a pile of laundry off to the side of the coffee table with her elbow, as Toby and I jumped up to help her.

"Thanks, boys. You can see we don't stand on ceremony around here," she said as she began pouring milk into the glasses. Just then the screen door opened and Richard entered the room. His eyes bulged as he took in the situation—you'd think the poor guy didn't get cookies and milk before dinner every night.

"Hi, guys—glad I could make it," he said, laughing. "I was just gonna call you guys." My eyes popped wide in warning, but Mrs. Washington saw them, too, and smiled.

"It's okay, I told her where we were," Richard said. "I know it's a secret, but Mom won't tell anyone, and I wanted her to know where she could find me."

"Oh yeah?" I said, trying not to sound shocked that Richard could tell his Mom things like that. *You did what!?!*

"You're a good son," she said, nodding and smiling at him.

"Thanks," he said. "You're a pretty good Mom, too. There are some old boards down by the river with letters on them," he explained. "We've been trying to figure out if they spelled out the name of a riverboat."

Toby and I sat there stunned, looking at Richard. It wasn't that I minded Richard telling his Mom. I trusted Mrs. Washington, almost as much as I trusted Richard. It was just that I had never considered telling any of it to either of my parents, and I was pretty sure Toby hadn't either. I knew they wouldn't want me getting involved in anything those mobsters were involved in.

Toby and I operated on the theory that what our parents didn't know wouldn't hurt them—or us either—so they were pretty much on a need-to-know basis on nearly everything. After all, at least one of them thought that P.J. should be canonized shortly after his death, and I was pretty sure he was going straight to Hell, so right there you could tell we viewed things differently.

Plus, if I told them, I would also have to tell them about what Ms. Mame told us, and I didn't think Mom and Dad would exactly approve of my walking into any bar in Mayfly, much less Little Africa. Unfortunately, their impression of the merits of the place was probably colored by the bleary-eyed men in the dirty sleeveless undershirts squatting on the sidewalk out in front. Let's face it, they didn't look much like the people we went to church with. Mom and Dad probably didn't realize what a nice place it was inside, especially upstairs in Ms. Mame's apartment. And any way you looked at it, Ms. Mame was certainly unusual, and they probably would have held that against her, too, even though I knew she was not only very good but also very nice.

Richard turned back to Toby and me. "It *is* the *East Wind*," he said. "At least it was. It sank in 1872 trying to reach the Mayfly harbor. It was a flatboat carrying a load of cotton from Mississippi to Minneapolis. The captain claimed it hit a snag, but it sounds like it might have just come apart—the boat was ancient. It was never salvaged because the cargo was ruined and the cost of salvaging the boat exceeded its value. And nobody died, so it didn't make much of a splash. It just went to the bottom of the river."

Toby and I were speechless. So, the mobsters had the wrong boat. The *Flying Eagle* might still be down there.

"It's funny you boys playin' around down at Cottonwood Point," Mrs. Washington said. "Your great-grandaddy Elijah always said there was somethin' hid down there. This was durin' the Civil War—he was a slave and he lived on the farm right next to Cottonwood Point, and he used to go out at night—he wasn't s'posed to, but he did—'cause

Joseph Welch

he had a certain lady friend at the next farm over. She was a slave, too, and they would spend time together down there.

"But they had to be careful, 'cause there was a wood lot at Cottonwood Point, and the riverboats stopped there all times of the day and night and loaded up with firewood, so they couldn't get caught down at the beach.

"But your great-grandad found a place up in the hills, a little cave with a secret entrance, and they used to slip out at night and meet, and go in there and spend time together. And Janey would steal little stubs of candles for light, so there wouldn't be no wood smoke to give them away. And that girl turned out to be your great-grandmother, Janey Washington, and after they were freed, they got married, but they still stayed there and worked on the land—Elijah did—he worked outside—Janey was a house maid because she could cook and sew."

"But what was hidden down there?" Richard asked.

"Oh, that's right," she said. "Well, it was the night that boat blew up, the one that blew up at the railroad bridge. That boat stopped at Cottonwood Point right before it blew up, and loaded up with firewood. The *Flyin' Eagle*, I think it was called, and your great-grandaddy saw men carryin' boxes off the boat, heavy boxes, lots of 'em. And they put 'em in a wagon, and then the men loaded the wood onto the boat, and it left and it blew up an hour later—they heard it, in their cozy hideaway, and they ran down onto the beach and they could see it on fire way up the river by Mayfly.

"And your great-grandaddy never told anybody about that, because he was out late, and he didn't have permission, and he was with your great-gramma, and she didn't have permission either, and he didn't know what those men was carryin', but he figured it was somethin' bad, like smugglin' somethin' illegal, because otherwise they would have unloaded it in the harbor up at Mayfly where there was stevedores to help 'em and the roads were paved, so he was afraid to tell anybody about it—it was just a family secret." She was quiet for a minute, her eyes far away, remembering how she learned about the family secret.

"I don't s'pose there's another person alive who knows about it now, except me," she said, "and now you boys. I don't think he'll mind me tellin' it now, 'specially to his great-grandson."

The three of us just stared at her, mute, mouths open, nothing coming out. I was wondering if what those men were carrying off was all that Confederate gold and silver, and wondering whether it was still there. From the looks on their faces, Richard and Toby were thinking the same thing.

"What's wrong, boys? Don't you like the cookies?" she asked, worried, as she reached down and picked one up, then bit into it.

"Oh no, ma'am—I mean, yes, ma'am—they're delicious," I said, coming to. "I just need to get home to dinner. Thank you so much, Mrs. Washington."

"Me, too," Toby said. "Thank you for the cookies."

"You boys are so polite," she said. "I like that."

"Thank you, ma'am," Toby and I said together.

"Come on—I'll walk you up the hill," Richard said.

"What the hell!" Toby said as soon as we were out of earshot.

85.
THE STORM BREAKS

We still hadn't had any rain since the downpour at Oko-Tipi, and that rain had come so fast and hard that most of it had run off instead of soaking into the ground. The ground was cracked and dry. Only the big weeds were still flourishing—they had an uncanny ability to pull moisture out of the ground even when there wasn't any to be had. We had been forced to give up weeding by hand and were using a hoe, hammering it against the hard-packed ground. Even the moles and the earthworms had gone deep. Farmers were worried about losing their entire crops. We had been praying for rain for a month, both at home and at Mass. The ground was hard-packed and shrunken.

As we walked up the sidewalk toward Broadway, thunder rumbled through the valley, surprising us again. All three of us looked up reflexively—the sky overhead was absolutely clear. When we crossed the street at the corner, we were able to see above the overhanging tree canopy. Enormous purple-gray thunderheads were visible, billowing thousands of feet upward, stalking the southwest horizon like a predator horde—a huge burst of unconfined energy issuing up from the Gulf. We would be lucky if it didn't spawn tornadoes.

"Listen, guys, we gotta make this quick—this storm looks like it's for real," Toby said.

"I think you're right," Richard said. "Two things: first, the *Flying Eagle* may still be there."

"I know," I said. "I got that. But we don't know that for sure, and we don't know if the mobsters know that. I think all we can do is wait to see if they find it—if they don't, then we can look for it."

"Yeah," Richard said, "but the second thing is—and I'd bet money on this one—the *Flying Eagle* doesn't matter anymore—the gold was taken off the boat before it blew up. And we're the only ones who know it!"

"Oh my God!" Toby said. "You mean all this work was for nothing?"

"Not for nothing," Richard said. "It's got us to this point. We wouldn't know anything if we hadn't done all that work, plus all the spying."

"That's true," I said.

"Oh my God!" Toby said again. "That means Tom died for nothing—those bastards killed Tom for nothing!"

Richard and I just looked at him, nodding. He looked me in the eye, and he looked Richard in the eye, and Richard looked me in the eye, and nobody said anything.

Our reverie was interrupted by a huge lightning strike that created jagged shadows, even in the daylight. Seconds later came the BOOM!—followed by another rolling volley of thunder as it echoed through the valley.

"Ten seconds—that's two miles away, boys," Richard said. "If that storm's traveling at thirty miles per hour, we have four minutes to get home. Let's think this over and talk later."

"Okay, bye!" I said, turning and running up toward Broadway alongside Toby.

We didn't make it. The storm must've been moving sixty miles an hour, not thirty. We were half a block away from the River's Rest when a huge cold wind blew us sideways and broken limbs were tossed across the street in front of us as we ran. Then the rain started, enormous drops that hurt when they landed, and green light and black dark descended on us, and the heavens opened up and lashed out hail, just as we made the River's Rest canopy. The hail was deafening—it crashed onto roofs and cars, bounced and shattered as it hit the parking lot and knocked down limbs. We sheltered under the canopy in drenched awe as lightning flashed nearby. We heard an explosion, and then the thunder blew our ears out, shaking us to our bones. I stood transfixed, in utter terror.

Another flash of lightning and Toby was illuminated—a Toby I will never forget—standing there under the canopy, rainwater running down his face; his eyes squeezed tight shut and both fists clenched. He didn't even know I could see him, because he was sobbing, and I distinctly heard what he said, even over the force of the storm. Because he was howling: "I'm gonna kill them! I'm gonna kill them!" Howlin' Johnnie had nothin' on Toby.

The hail finally stopped, and I ran all the way home in the drenching rain.

We said our family prayers fervently by the light of the Blessed Candle, which Mom only lit to keep us safe during really bad storms, and afterward I lay in bed and said my second rosary for the Poor Souls.

The thunder and lightning continued into the night. The first weekend of the big CYO Summer Tourney was scheduled to start the next day, and I needed my rest. I lay there with my oven mitts taped on, tossing and turning. I knew God could strike me at any minute, and the thunder and lightning made me feel like He was definitely entertaining the idea.

I also knew for a fact that if I died right then, before I finished the nine First Fridays, and with approximately ninety Mortal Sins on my soul for each day since my last confession, I would go straight to everlasting Hell, and every inch of me would burn in fire for all eternity. It was not conducive to a good night's sleep. "Lord, be merciful to me, a sinner."

Then I remembered: if you can't go to Confession, you can at least say "a perfect Act of Contrition," and it is possible, not a sure thing, but only possible, that God, in His infinite mercy, would spare me the fires of Hell. At that point, I would have taken anything—I was positively grasping for any chance at salvation. "Oh my God, I am heartily sorry, for having offended Thee...," I prayed, "and I detest all my sins, because I dread the loss of Heaven and the pains of Hell...," and that Act of Contrition, as I lay there with my eyes wide open in the heart of the storm, was the most ardent of my young life.

I turned over and went right to sleep, trusting my fate to the God to whom I prayed.

86.
EARLY ROUNDS

It rained all night and into Friday morning, which was the first day of the big tournament. Mayfly Catholic had a reputation to uphold. We were seeded second out of sixteen teams. Our first game was against St. Bartholomew on Friday night. They were not anticipated to be much of a challenge, and they weren't.

The coach of our CYO team was a volunteer, a young man who had played high school basketball ten years prior, and who had stepped forward when no one else would. He had been a good player, but had no experience as a coach. I was wearing my eye patch, so it was easy for him to realize that I was not the same player he had coached the prior year. He was impressed with Lucas Crane, however (who wasn't?), and made him the point guard, while I was moved to forward on the left side. This gave me a decent view of most of the court, although I was awfully small for a forward. That meant that Toby would need to handle almost all of the rebounding duties.

I might as well have been sitting on the bench, however, since I never got to touch the basketball. I ran through our offense multiple times, my arm up in the air to signal when I was open, but it didn't matter. Our offense consisted of Lucas Crane bringing the ball down the floor, then driving to either side of the free throw line and shooting, while the rest of the team rebounded his misses. His shot was off, but we still won 66 to 27.

Toby had eighteen rebounds and twenty-two points, mostly on putbacks after Lucas Crane missed. Lucas shot so many times that he still managed to score twenty-eight points. I had two field goals, both on long rebounds that I was able to corral and then shoot follow-up layups. Lucas had one assist, when he passed the ball to Toby at the top of the key and then broke for the basket, expecting a return pass. Instead, Toby, who was feeling left out because Lucas never passed the ball to him, turned and hit a jumper. Richard also had four points.

After the game, Toby, Richard, and I got a ride to the motel, where Toby's mom fixed us bologna sandwiches on white bread with mayonnaise and potato chips, then left for the front desk.

"If they took the treasure off the boat before it blew up, it might still be hidden down there somewhere," Richard said.

"There are a lot of caves in those hills," I said.

"Tons of them," Richard said. "At the end of the last ice age, the river didn't just flow in front of those bluffs—entire rivers flowed right through them, too, when all the glaciers were melting. There's over two hundred miles of passages already mapped out, just in the small area immediately south of Mayfly and around Lover's Leap. And the caves around Cottonwood Point have never been mapped or even explored in any systematic way," Richard said, "but the rock is the same, and it's the same river, and I think it's safe to assume that there are hundreds of miles of unexplored caves there as well. It's a regular feature of limestone bluffs alongside a river."

Our next game was Saturday evening at 6:00 p.m. against St. Alphonse, which featured more of the same. We won 58 to 40. Even though Lucas Crane wasn't hitting, it didn't keep him from shooting—if anything, he actually shot *more*. He ended up with twenty points and no assists. Toby also got twenty points, mostly on putbacks, plus sixteen rebounds. I was two for three from the field, plus five assists, and I made a couple of free throws, for a total of six points.

The tournament would resume the following weekend, with the Semifinals on Friday and the Finals on Saturday night.

"We're going to have to search those caves," Toby said after the game.

"We don't have enough manpower—it'll take us a lifetime," Richard said. "Plus, if the gold was taken off, it was probably moved out by those men long ago. The only way it wouldn't have been would be if they were killed before they could get back to it. Even if it's still there, which is hard to believe, those caves get closed off with landslides after big rains. They change all the time. Whole passages get sealed off. We'll be lucky if we don't all get killed. Plus, people will figure out what we're up to, because we're basically going to have to spend our lives down there. Probably the reason no one has found it, if it was ever left there in the first place, is that the cave entrance was sealed up by a landslide, maybe even a century ago.

"Also, we'd have to abandon the Overlook Oak surveillance and The Projects," I said.

"We can't do that," Toby said. "The goal of this whole thing is to find out what happened to Tom so we can get him moved to hallowed ground, and we haven't done it yet, and summer's almost over."

Nobody argued.

87.
LIARS

It was late Tuesday evening, after Fletcher family prayers. John and I had wheedled permission from Mom and Dad to "spend the night with Toby because he misses his brother"—we hadn't mentioned where. Richard would be joining us, too.

After the 4th of July, every school kid begins to sense the end of summertime rushing in upon him like a runaway train, and we were all feeling pressure to get the goods on P.J. and the mobsters as soon as possible. The possibility that Tom would be denied entrance to Heaven was unthinkable. We knew if we didn't figure it out that summer, we never would. We had to get our proof on all of them in the next several weeks.

We hadn't seen the mobsters since the deluge. The rain had greened everything up. It washed the dust off the leaves and rejuvenated the grass. Iowa had received even more rain than Missouri, and the Mississippi River was at flood stage. Only a small fraction of the gravel bar was above water, but we had been watching the crew continuing to dig alongside the swollen current.

Unfortunately, however, Sharkbait had just radioed in a catastrophe—he had watched the gravel bar completely dissolve in front of his eyes. It had started with the water boiling along the edges, then the boiling moved in closer to the swamp, and in less than a minute the entire bar was gone. It happened so quickly that the men were unable to escape, although they were picked up by the workboat as they swept downstream in the flood. Their machinery was completely gone—sunk out of sight.

I hustled down on my bike as fast as I could go, while John, Toby and Richard stayed up in Double-O with the Big Ear trained on the rectory.

"Let me know right away if he gets a call from the mobsters," I told them.

The gravel bar was completely gone—Cottonwood Point was no longer a point—it was now a swirling bay that served as an inlet to the swamp.

Sharkbait and I were sitting on the fallen log that constituted our lookout post at The Project when I heard the motor on the mobsters' Lincoln Continental issuing from the draw between the bluffs. Sharkbait and I looked at each other, then looked back and waited for the car to appear. Within moments we could see it moving along the Armani driveway.

"Uh-oh," Sharkbait said, "Mom's at work—better go down and see what they want." Sliding off the perch, he grabbed his snake stick for the trip down the hill. I watched him zigzag quickly and silently down the deer path below me. The mobsters were already out of the car when Sharkbait emerged from the woods next to the porch.

"Can I help you?" I heard him say, pretending to be unaware of the disappearance of Cottonwood Point.

"We need to talk to your mom, kid—is she home?" Dapper Man said.

"No, she's at work," Sharkbait said, "but I can give her a message."

Dapper Man paused a moment. I could see him ruminating from fifty yards away. Apparently, he didn't like having to come the long way around by the State Highway, an extra fourteen miles round trip, because he decided to leave the message. "Okay, fine, just tell her we're not gonna be able to make the payment this month. We've had some unforeseen costs."

"Whaddayamean?" Sharkbait asked, his voice rising. "Why not?"

"We've had some extra start-up costs and we just can't make it this month. We'll have to catch it up later."

"What kinda start-up costs?" Sharkbait demanded. "She needs that money; she's been counting on it—she needs to make the mortgage payment."

"That's tough, kid," Dapper Man said, dismissively. "We just don't have it. You can't get blood from a turnip."

"Liar!" Sharkbait exploded. *Oh my God, Sharkbait! Careful! These guys might kill you!* I grabbed my snake stick and the walkie-talkie and started quickly down the path, but I wasn't nearly as fast as Sharkbait.

"Watch your mouth, boy," Mr. Muscle said. "You apologize to Mr. Napolitano."

"You're crooks—both of you! You're nothin' but lying crooks!" Sharkbait yelled. "You don't have any start-up costs—you're not even mining gravel! I know what you're up to—you're after the treasure!"

That stopped them both cold. *Oh, my! Sharkbait! What the hell!?* Mr. Muscle looked back at Dapper Man.

"What are you talking about, boy?" Dapper Man asked, smiling, like the very idea was ludicrous.

"You know what I'm talkin' about!" Sharkbait was still yelling. "The treasure—Confederate gold. You killed Tom because he was on to you. I'm gonna tell Fr. Reiser and then I'm gonna tell the police."

Mr. Muscle reached for him, but Sharkbait was ready for him—he played him like a poisonous snake—he leapt back out of reach. The snake stick moved through the air so fast I could hear it whistle—it whipped him right across the face. *Whip!* Then, immediately, without missing a beat, Sharkbait cracked him on the head, hard—I heard it hit his skull. *Crack!* Mr. Muscle stopped cold, stunned. I swear I heard it echo back from the other side of the river while he was still standing motionless.

"Why, you little bastard!" Mr. Muscle growled, "I'm gonna kill you!" He reached for him again, but Sharkbait was too quick. He leapt sideways, the stick already flying through the air. *Whip!* across his face, and *Crack!* hard, again, right on top of his head. Mr. Muscle was stopped in his tracks again. *This guy doesn't learn! Crack!* came the echo. Sharkbait didn't hang around—he lit out across the road toward the swamp. He looked like a bowling ball vanishing in the distance—his legs were moving so fast they were a blur. Mr. Muscle reached behind his back and pulled a pistol out of his waistband.

"No, you idiot," Dapper Man said, "we can't shoot him—it has to look like an accident, like the other boy."

But Sharkbait was gone—he had disappeared right in front of our eyes.

"Get him!" Dapper Man said.

"I'm not going in there," Mr. Muscle said.

Dapper Man hesitated. "Get in the car," he said. "He's going to the priest's place—we can get there before him."

"We have to take the long way, boss—the road is closed."

"I know that, you moron. Drive—fast!" Dapper Man said, slamming his own car door.

I crouched in the understory next to the driveway until after they passed me, the big motor roaring, the tires shooting gravel, then triggered the walkie-talkie.

Summer of '63

"Double-O! Double-O! Come in, please—this is The Projects, over. Double-O! Double-O! Come in, please—this is an emergency, over."

"This is Double-O." It was Richard's voice. "What's going on, over."

"What are you doing, Double-O, over."

"Playing tiddlywinks, over."

"Listen, Double-O—Sharkbait is on his way there, on foot, running. Cinder and Ella are chasing him in their car. They're gonna kill him if they catch him. He told them he knows they're after the item and he knows they killed Tom, and now he's on his way there to tell P.J. and we can't let that happen—P.J. will probably turn him over to them."

"What!?" I could just picture the three of them looking at each other in disbelief. I felt that way, too, but there was no time for that now. That horse had already left the barn.

"I'll explain later," I said. "Cinder already pulled a gun on him. Sharkbait hit him over the head with a stick—hard. Twice. I really think they'll kill him if they catch him. You gotta keep them from doing it."

"Okay, sure, but how?" Toby asked.

"They'll be driving up the hill in a few minutes—they had to go the long way around. Toby, you and Richard get ready with the big stuff—I mean the boomers. Get the zippo out and fueled. Gonna have to rain down on 'em fast and loud. Keep 'em distracted. Put the fear of the Lord in them. I'll see if I can get Prince there."

"Prince, hell!" It was John's voice. "Get The Archangel!"

"Affirmative," I said. "I'll radio him right now. Sharkbait will be coming up through the woods from the south side. I'm coming up

River Road right now on my bike, so I might be able to catch him, but, Richard, you need to hustle down to the base of Castle Bluff immediately and intercept him before he goes up to P.J.'s. Don't tell him P.J. is working with the mobsters, just tell him the mobsters are gonna be there waiting for him, over."

"10-4," Richard said, "headed there right now, over."

"Over and out," I said, mounting my bike and heading north, riding hell for leather alongside the river. The sun had already set behind the bluffs on my left, and the overhanging trees deepened the gloom. I came suddenly up against the landslide roadblock in the deep dusk and skidded to a halt, trying to ignore my horror at entering the black maw where the narrow tunnel passage led between the foot of the bluff and the giant clump of earth and trees blocking the road. I had never gone through the passage in the dark—it was seriously spooky even during the day. I stuck my head into the layer of huge overhanging tendrils and entered the narrow crack, imagining the army of predatory hunting spiders that was no doubt falling on my head and back, pushing my bike ahead of me like a ramrod as fast as I could, hoping that the sound of my crashing through the brush would scatter any nocturnal animals, including the snakes, before I got there. There was no way to avoid the overhanging poison ivy vines, however—I just swallowed my fear and revulsion and pressed forward.

Finally, I exited into the dusk and the open road. I jumped back on my bike and rode hard toward the Mayfly harbor lights. I could still see the outline of the bluff tops against the sky above me.

"Sharkbait!" I called as I rode. No response. Richard came running out at me as I reached the base of Castle Bluff.

"Have you seen him?" I asked.

"No, but I think I hear him," he answered. I stood still and listened. We could hear someone pushing through the underbrush above us. He must have had his own route to the rectory on top of the bluffs instead of up River Road. It sounded like he was in the woods that separated the cemetery from Lovers Leap. Within minutes, he would be on the top of Castle Bluff near the rectory.

Richard and I dashed up the old stairs at the tail end of Castle Bluff in the gloom, gaining more visibility as we ascended toward the fading sky, holding onto bushes and tree branches as we jumped from one stair to the next. As we reached the top, we both heard it at the same time. We froze and listened.

Graaawwp! Graaawwp! Graaawwp! It reached our ears in loud extended bursts. We stared at each other—I knew that sound—there was no other sound like it on Earth.

"Prince!" He was biting the tires of a car laboring up the steep hill on the back of Castle Bluff—some car that he didn't like the smell of. Then we heard the big Lincoln motor lumbering up the side of the bluff, navigating the sharp switchbacks, moving slowly enough to remain a target for one large and thoroughly pissed-off animal.

Then several things happened in quick succession.

The mobsters' black Lincoln turned out of the final curve onto the hilltop with Prince running alongside, growling and trying to take huge chunks out of the left front tire as it spun out of his jaws. Undeterred, he attacked the tire again and again, biting harder and louder. GRAAAWWP! And then GRAAAWWP! He was working himself into a frenzy.

Sharkbait came running out of the woods on the other side of the house, yelling at the top of his lungs, "Fr. Reiser! Fr. Reiser!"

The car stopped right in front of the house and Mr. Muscle sat, paralyzed, in the driver's seat, his eyes huge as he looked at Prince planted just outside his door, a perfect Mohawk rising above his back from his head down to his tail stump, baring his teeth and snarling at him through the glass with crazed eyes.

Sharkbait had nearly reached the rectory porch, when the back car door opened on the passenger side, nearest the rectory, ejecting a cloud of gray smoke, and Dapper Man leaped out, surprising Sharkbait and grabbing him by the arm. At that very moment the Right Arm of God, in the person of The Archangel, came stomping from the driveway into the clearing.

"Get your filthy hands off him!" he boomed, his volume cleaving the open air. His tone of voice left no doubt about his authority—he was clearly on a mission from God. Dapper Man froze, his head turned toward The Archangel, his mouth open. I could see him thinking, *'Who in the hell is that?'* while he contemplated The Archangel advancing on him and exuding the pure, unadulterated wrath of God.

Then all hell broke loose.

A vertical orange tracer striped the sky, terminating on the roof of the big Lincoln, as an M-80, containing the explosive charge of a third of a stick of dynamite, fell out of the heavens with a little backspin, all the touch that Toby could muster under the stress of the moment. It landed right on top of the car, then rolled erratically backward across the roof and fell onto the lid of the trunk. *BOOM!* It exploded with a deafening white blast, shattering the rear window of the Lincoln and spraying glass shards throughout the interior like grapeshot. *Boom!* came the echo from Illinois, just as Mr. Muscle, his eardrums now destroyed, leapt out of the car door, pulling his pistol from his waistband. Richard and I ducked down and watched as a second M-80 flashed past Mr. Muscle's head. Surprised by the orange tracer, he looked up to see where it had come from, then glanced down at the ground, and... BOOM! ...he also entered a new world of seriously impaired vision.

Prince, who hated the smell of gunpowder and hated Mr. Muscle, took that as his cue to spring into action, just as a third M-80, launched a tad aggressively by John with the hunting slingshot, tore right through the window screen on the front room of the rectory and passed out of sight inside. Two seconds later, an enormous BOOM! lit up the interior like a flashbulb, and P.J. came pouring out the front door, fastening his bathrobe, and staring in disbelief while Dapper Man used both arms to hold onto a kicking and struggling Sharkbait, and Mr. Muscle tried unsuccessfully to get his pistol up and aimed at Prince, who was driving home his disapproval with animal ferocity. P.J. wasn't motionless for long, however—he didn't like what he saw, and it galvanized him into action.

"Leave my son alone!" he roared, running toward Sharkbait, just as Mr. Muscle leveled his gun and fired. We saw the flame exit the muzzle, but the sound of the explosion was lost completely as a fourth M-80 detonated overhead, lighting up the entire area like a lightning flash, and further deafening us. I blinked. The concussion enabled Sharkbait to break loose from Dapper Man—he was headed for the cliff. *Oh my God! Use the pointer rocks!* He zipped into the woods without hesitation, Dapper Man in hot pursuit a mere arms-length behind him, hit the pointer rocks perfectly, First Base then Second Base, then launched himself blind into the escape net. Dapper Man, not to be outdone by the kid, launched himself, too—except he didn't mean to. He didn't know about the pointer rocks or the edge or the net already swinging away from the bluff top, so he just launched himself into the air two hundred feet above River Road. *Oops!*

Mr. Muscle was in serious trouble when we looked back—a machine gun wouldn't have helped him. Prince was uncontrollable. Mr. Muscle back-pedaled as fast as he could, trying to get his pistol leveled again, while an insanely enraged Prince drove into him with the speed and ferocity of a ninety-five-pound badger. We saw the muzzle flash again as Mr. Muscle disappeared into the border of the woods, but for some reason, it was pointed up in the air, and I realized I still had some hearing left because I heard the report, and then I heard Mr. Muscle screaming for three long seconds before he stopped abruptly. *The road to hell is paved with bad intentions.* Prince reappeared, walking back from the edge of the woods and wagging his entire rump as I ran into the clearing.

"Good boy, Prince!" I yelled. "Michael, check on Sharkbait, will you?" I said, running over to P.J., who was lying on the ground next to the car.

"Father, are you okay?" I asked, bending over him. My vision was limited in the failing light, but I could see the dark spill of blood pooling on the ground. *Maybe he cut himself when he fell. Maybe it's glass from the explosion.* But when I rolled him over and saw the chest wound, I knew it wasn't that—he wasn't okay at all. His eyes were open wide in shock, fixed and unblinking, and his mouth gaped cavernously.

"He's been shot, boys!" I yelled, feeling the entrance wound with my hand and applying pressure to the spot where he was bleeding. "We have to call an ambulance—right now—and the police will be here, too. Put everything away as fast as you can and come down here—now. Hurry! We have to talk." Richard knelt beside me and took over applying pressure to the wound, while I ran inside and called the ambulance, even though I was pretty sure it was already too late.

Summer of '63

Sharkbait reappeared—he was fine. The escape net had worked perfectly. The ambulance came and then the police cars—both of them.

As I got into the patrol car for the ride down to the station, I heard it again, clear as a bell—loud this time—it was Howlin' Johnnie—and he was close—it sounded like he was just on the other side of the woods. The policeman heard it, too—he stopped and looked around. I didn't tell him what it was. He probably thought it was just a coyote. Or a bobcat in heat. Toby and I looked at one another and nodded.

"Close the doors, boys," the policeman said, as Prince leapt into the back seat with us. As we drove the long steep road down the back of Castle Bluff, large raindrops splattered onto the car roof and windshield, as if the clouds had been seeded by the explosions on the blufftop. By the time we arrived at the police station, the rain had become a downpour.

88.
TELLING THE TRUTH

We had determined that it was necessary to tell about the treasure, but since Cottonwood Point had washed away, any future treasure hunters would be looking downstream—maybe even as far as Saverton Dam, with particular suspicion at any newly-developing sandbars. We were the only people on earth, except for Mrs. Washington, who suspected that the treasure had been off-loaded from the *Flying Eagle* at Cottonwood Point just before it exploded. That was still the Washington's family secret, and it was theirs to do with as they wished.

We got a lot of hostile stares as we walked into the Old Police Station. Richard's and my hands and arms were covered with blood up to our elbows, and the staff knew Fr. Reiser had been shot and taken away in an ambulance. We sat in the Chief's office while they called all of our parents and asked them to come down. While we waited, Richard borrowed a pen and a tablet and started writing down some notes. Mom and Dad were the first to arrive—Mom looking daggers and Dad looking concerned—and when I told them briefly that the mobsters had shot Fr. Reiser and we had tried to save him, she insisted on calling Fr. Jim, too. He came right down—he had already been notified that Fr. Reiser had been pronounced dead on arrival at the hospital.

Our statement took several hours—it was a lot to process. The Chief made us leave the door open so the rest of the officers and staff could hear the entire thing.

We told them the truth, or a lot of it anyway. We didn't mention the Big Ear or tell them we had been spying on P.J. or that we suspected him of working with the mobsters. No, apparently he had just been letting us play in the treehouse at his property out of the goodness of his heart. Same with the net, which we used as a giant swing. I glanced at Fr. Jim and saw his eyes narrow while he listened, but he didn't say anything.

Mom looked incredulous. "I thought you were all at Toby's for the night."

"Oh, no," I said as if there had been an unfortunate communication, "we were spending the night *with* Toby, but not at his house. We planned to sleep in the treehouse."

She thought about that for a second, then, "I knew you boys were playing in a treehouse down by the river, but I had no idea it was at Msgr. Reiser's rectory."

"He wanted us to keep it quiet—he thought some of the other kids might think he was playing favorites," I said, knowing this whopper would cost me significant extra burn time—I would just have to worry about that later. "He just had a good heart and liked to see kids having fun," I added. This was too much—both Richard and Toby suddenly put their faces in their hands and were apparently sobbing—they were practically hysterical. When they looked up, they both had tears in their eyes. Mrs. Piper and Mrs. Washington stood and patted their sons on the back, which only sent them into additional paroxysms. Then Sharkbait started crying. Mrs. Armani was crying, too. She stood over Sharkbait, soothing him. John and Michael looked on, wide-eyed. I would never hear the end of this one.

Joseph Welch

"He was such a good man," Mom said, "such a spiritual man." We all nodded, then buried our faces in our hands again.

"This is quite a tribute to your pastor," the Chief said, pushing up his glasses and wiping a tear from his own eye, "but I have to get the facts down for my report. Just how did this begin?"

"Here, Chief Malone, this might be helpful as a sort of timeline while you ask us questions," Richard said, sliding the notebook across the desk. The Chief was startled—he looked at Richard for a few seconds, then looked down at the paper. It took him several minutes.

"So," he said, "in a nutshell, it looks like a coupla men from outta town, who you call the 'mobsters,' rented rooms at the River's Rest, and the Piper boy somehow found out they were here to look for a treasure, and then young Washington here heard them in the library looking up the wreck of the *Flying Eagle*, is that right?"

"Yessir," Richard, Toby, and I said in unison.

"But what made you think there was a treasure on the *Flying Eagle*?" Chief Malone asked.

"Richard did the research, sir," I said. "Tell him, Richard."

So Richard told him a short version of the long story about Jefferson Davis taking the entire Confederate Treasury, plus $450,000 in bank gold, out of Richmond by train a week before the South surrendered, and how it was never found, and how two of Jefferson Davis' cabinet ministers had confirmed, one on his deathbed, that Robert E. Lee's *aide de camp* boarded a riverboat in Memphis with the treasure on April 11, 1865, and that was the night the *Flying Eagle* left Memphis and headed north, before it blew itself to smithereens four days later at the Mayfly railroad bridge, supposedly killing everyone on board, and about the creation of the sandbar at Cottonwood Point.

"How'd you find this out, son?" Chief Malone asked.

Summer of '63

"Looked it up in the library, sir," Richard replied. "And Mr. Mills helped me with the sandbar."

The Chief stared at Richard, as did everyone else in the room, and then he just shook his head.

"How old are you, young man?" he asked him. "Twelve, sir," Richard said. The Chief's mouth fell partway open.

"Good God A'mighty. Well, son, you've convinced me," he said, finally. Then he looked back down at the outline. I looked over at a completely unruffled Mrs. Washington; she didn't look a bit surprised, but I could tell she was pleased.

"Okay, now, the next thing on here, it says 'the Inquest ruled Tom Piper's death was suicide, but we knew it wasn't.' Why is that?"

"Basically, Tom had a good life and he was happy," Richard said. "He loved his parents, he loved his brother, he was extremely nice, outgoing, friendly, productive, a good worker. Basically, he wasn't a bit depressed—we all knew him well. And Toby saw him right before he died, and he was in a big hurry. A hurry to commit suicide? Seemed mighty strange to us. He told Toby he had to tell him something, but later. Plus he had stuff that he loved, a beautiful '57 Chevy and other stuff, and he didn't give any of that stuff away before he died." Mrs. Piper started to cry.

"Sorry, ma'am," Richard said. Mrs. Piper just nodded at him, a Kleenex in front of her face. Mr. Piper put his arm around her.

"And we found the pieces of the note that they tore the letters off of to put into Tom's pocket after he died to make his death look like suicide," Toby said, producing the Inquest baggie and the scraps. "They put these pieces in Tom's pocket after his death, and these other ones were stuffed into a crack in the floor of their room at the River's Rest. These are from a prayer that Fr. Reiser gave to all of us." It took several minutes to lay them all out on the desk and show the Chief how they fitted together, and how the edges didn't mate, but instead matched, because of the mistake the mobsters made.

"Alright," the Chief said, "I see that. But how does Cottonwood Point come into this?"

"Cottonwood Point was created by the Mississippi River in the years following the wreck of the *Flying Eagle*. The mobsters thought that the *Flying Eagle* had got caught there and caused that sandbar to build up and that if they dug down on that bar, they would find the wreck," Richard said. "I heard them talking about it to Mr. Mills at the title office. They said they were going to start a gravel mining operation, so they leased the land from Mrs. Armani and they dug every day, but they never mined any gravel—not a single shovelful."

"How do you know that?" the Chief asked.

"We watched them every day," I volunteered.

"Why? How were *you* going to profit from *their* treasure hunt?" the Chief asked.

"We weren't doing it for profit. We were doing it so Tom could get to Heaven," I said. Mrs. Piper sobbed loudly. No one said anything as Mr. Piper patted her. He had tears in his eyes.

The Chief rocked back in his chair, took off his glasses and rubbed his eyes, then leaned forward again. "Okay, I must be missin' somethin' here. You wanna explain to me how that was s'posed to work?" he asked.

"Tom couldn't be buried in hallowed ground because that *asshole* politician at the Inquest told the jury he was gonna be late for the Nineteenth Hole and didn't have time to listen to the evidence, so he just ruled his death a suicide," Toby said vehemently. No one corrected his language. Chief Malone looked nonplussed.

Summer of '63

"Suicides can't be buried in hallowed ground, according to Church doctrine," Fr. Jim explained.

"And if Tom can't be buried in hallowed ground, he can't get to Heaven," Toby said.

"So we had to prove Tom was murdered so he could get to Heaven," I said. "We've been watching them all day, every day, all summer. Tom was our good friend and a good guy, and he deserves to go to heaven. And his parents deserve to know he's in Heaven." That did it—Mrs. Piper convulsed in sobs. Mom and Mrs. Washington and Mrs. Armani all had tears streaming down their faces at this point. They all got up and went over to Mrs. Piper's chair and hugged her and patted her and put their arms around her. Dad and Mr. Piper just looked mad—I'm not sure I had ever seen my Dad that furious. Finally, Mrs. Piper quieted, holding a Kleenex to her face.

"What's the name of this politician?" Dad demanded angrily.

"I forget. But it's written on the wall of the public bathroom in Central Park," I said. Toby looked at me with tears running down his face and actually laughed.

"George Randall, the Coroner," Mr. Piper said.

"Okay, okay, I get it now; I guess I do," Chief Malone said. "So you boys have been watching them all summer long, every day, trying to prove they killed Tom, so you could change the verdict of the Inquest, so Tom could be buried in hallowed ground and go to heaven, is that right?"

"Yessir," all five of us said.

"Well, hell's bells, boys—it looks to me like Tom's goin' to heaven," the Chief said. He paused, then said, "But then what happened? It says here Sidney got mad at them and told them he knew they were after the treasure and they pulled a gun on him—is that true?"

"Yessir," Sidney and I both said. The Chief looked at me questioningly. "I was there, too," I explained, "but they didn't know it. After Sidney told them he knew they were really after the treasure, one of them tried to grab him, but Sharkbait, I mean, Sidney, cracked him on the head with his snake stick."

The Chief's eyebrows raised. "You did, huh, boy? Good for you—I hope you cracked him a good one."

"Yes, sir, I did," Sidney said, "twice." The Chief chuckled.

"What happened when they pulled the gun then?"

"The other one, the one we called 'Dapper Man,' said, 'no, you idiot—we can't shoot him—we have to make it look like an accident, like the other boy,' and Sharkbait ran into the swamp," I said.

"Like the other boy?"

"Yessir."

"Now, why do you call him 'Sharkbait'"?

"Sorry, that's his pirate name. We used to play pirates at Cottonwood Point," I said.

"'Sharkbait,' huh? That's a good name." Sharkbait glowed.

"Now the next thing on here is 'Mobsters Shot Fr. Reiser at the Rectory'—how did you get all the way up there and what happened?" You could tell he was getting tired and trying to get to the end.

So we told him about the race to the rectory, and the walkie-talkie messages about protecting Sharkbait because they were going to kill him, and how Michael brought Prince and we had the M-80s that Tom had gotten for us, and how we let 'em have it when they showed up and how Fr. Reiser yelled 'Leave that boy alone!'—all the others, including Sharkbait, looked at me when I said it—everyone who was there remembered exactly what he had really said.

And then we told him how Fr. Reiser ran toward Sharkbait, and Mr. Muscle shot Fr. Reiser and then Prince drove Mr. Muscle off the cliff, and how Dapper Man dived off trying to catch Sharkbait. Chief Malone's head just swiveled back and forth from one of us to the other during this account.

When it was all over he just shook his head. Then he said, "Now, boys, you know it's illegal to shoot those things off in town, don't you?" and we hung our heads and said, 'Yessir,' and he said, "But it's awfully good you had them to hand when you needed them and knew how to use them, or Sharkbait here might be dead, huh?"

We looked up, surprised. He was grinning at us.

"Don't worry, boys, that's the last that's gonna be said about that. Alright, boys, there'll be no charges filed against any of you, and I want to thank you for dealing with those two mobsters as you call them, but next time promise me you'll just call me up, okay? Will you do that?"

"Yes, sir!" we all said. "But sir," I said, "we were afraid since Tom had been ruled a suicide that you wouldn't believe us, and also we were afraid we didn't have time."

"I understand both of those things, son," he said. "And tomorrow mornin' I'm callin' the judge and tellin' him we need to reopen the Inquest right away so Tom's body can be moved and he can get to Heaven as soon as possible."

We all stared at him in disbelief. And Mrs. Piper...oh, you should have seen her...I can't even tell you....

When I looked back at the Chief, he was wiping tears from under his glasses.

Joseph Welch

An entirely different group left that station than the people who had arrived several hours earlier. Most of us had tears on our faces—Mrs. Piper was smiling and crying at the same time. The dispatcher did, too. She patted all of the women as we left and took Mrs. Piper by her arm and she and Mr. Piper helped her walk out the door and down the steps and put her in the car and she told all of us to call her if they could do anything at all for us.

89.
FR. JIM

I called Fr. Jim the next morning as soon as I finished my chores.

"Father, can we see you, please? We have some questions about this whole Fr. Reiser/mobster thing."

"Sure," he said, "how about 10:00 a.m. tomorrow?"

Toby and Richard came along with me to the old parish rectory in town. It was an ancient brick building with a side porch entry. Like many of the oldest brick buildings in Mayfly, it had been painted white when it was built, because the bricks were so soft they might have washed away otherwise. The housekeeper, an elderly widow who had raised seven children when her husband died at age twenty-nine, ushered us into Fr. Jim's office and closed the door.

"Father," I began, "there's a whole lot of things that don't make sense to us about this. We need to know if Fr. Reiser was in cahoots with the mobsters." Fr. Jim's head jerked backwards.

"What in the world makes you think he might have been?" he asked.

"Well, number one, I caught him there with Tom's body, immediately after he died—how did he happen to be there?"

"He told me he was saying his office when he came across Tom's body."

"Well, maybe," I said, "but he was searching his pockets—did he tell you that? And he was really, really angry, talking to him and saying, 'I warned you; I warned you' over and over. Warned him about what? Why would he be doing that if he didn't push him?"

"I know he had warned Tom about going up into the bell tower, because he knew Tom was drinking up there and he didn't think he should be drinking by himself in the first place, and he didn't think it was safe to be drinking up there; I assume that's what he was talking about. As far as looking through his pockets, I know he had taken back the key Tom used while he was helping around the church, and I assume he suspected that Tom had made his own key, and he was searching for it."

"Yes, but he was talking to him about all kinds of stuff. He sent me away, so I couldn't hear it, but I heard some of it—I just couldn't understand it," I insisted.

"I know he administered the last rites to Tom right after he died while he was lying there on the ground. The Latin prayer goes:

> *'Per istam sanctam unctionem et suam piissimam misericordiam adiuvet te Dominus gratia spiritus sancti, ut a peccatis liberatum te salvet atque propitius allevet.'*

Sound familiar? Maybe that's what you heard. In English, it's:

> 'Through this holy anointing may the Lord in his love and mercy help you with the grace of the Holy Ghost, and may the Lord who frees you from sin save you and raise you up.'"

Well. That was news to me. "He didn't mention any of that at the Inquest," I said.

"A priest will never volunteer information about spiritual matters with a congregant. Also, I'm sure he was embarrassed by one of his parishioners falling out of the bell tower, probably very embarrassed, especially if he knew he had been drinking up there. I know he went up and collected several liquor bottles from there and brought them down and threw them away."

"Why was he so weird with my parents?" Toby asked. "He would hardly even talk to them or look them in the eye at the Inquest or even at his funeral."

"I am sorry to hear that. Very unfortunate—I didn't know that. Fr. Reiser was not very good with people. The reason that occurs to me, however, is the same reason, I suppose: embarrassment—we're all only human, after all, and I suspect he was afraid they would blame him for Tom's death, for allowing him to go up into the belfry by himself, especially if they knew Tom was drinking up there."

"Then what was he doing at Tom's grave at midnight, the night he was buried?" Toby asked. I looked at him, astounded. This was the first time I had heard this.

"You mean that man was P.J., I mean, uh, Fr. Reiser?" I said to Toby. "I didn't know who it was, and I thought you didn't know who it was, either."

"I didn't, but there was always something vaguely familiar about him—I couldn't place it. I didn't recognize him until the night he got shot. But when he was lying there on the driveway in the dark and his eyes were wide open and his mouth was, too, I recognized him in a flash—immediately—no question at all—it was the same man and the same expression—I was sure it was him at Tom's grave that night." Then, turning to Fr. Jim, Toby said, "Why would he be there late at night? What was he doing?"

"Well," Fr. Jim said, "I've been meaning to tell you this, Toby, but frankly I've been putting it off. I haven't had a chance to speak with you alone, and this is a highly confidential matter. You know the doctrine that burial in hallowed ground is necessary to gain access to heaven. Well, Fr. Reiser was very upset that the Inquest ruling was suicide, because it meant he couldn't authorize Tom to be buried in hallowed ground. But he didn't believe Tom had committed suicide. And even if his personal belief was that Tom *had* committed suicide, he might have been wrong, just as he thought the Inquest people were wrong. So he consecrated Tom's grave in secret, that same night, even though the weather report was horrible—he didn't want Tom to be denied access to Heaven for a single minute if he could help it." I was shocked. I looked at Toby, whose mouth was wide open.

"But," Fr. Jim went on, "he couldn't go there during the daylight hours. Many of the Protestants in that cemetery—and they are mostly all Protestants—would have a cow if they thought a Catholic priest was consecrating their ground. So, he had to be circumspect. And he couldn't merely go after dark. It's not unheard of, as you boys are probably already aware, for young people to drink beer and go parking in cemeteries after dark, and he was aware that any suspicious activity on his part would very likely be reported. So, he set his alarm for 11:00 p.m. and then went to bed early, and got up and drove out the highway and then parked his car and walked into the cemetery. He was dressed incognito—he didn't even wear his Roman collar, and he had memorized the consecration prayer so he wouldn't be seen carrying his breviary. He was a ghost priest. He did it for Tom. But he didn't feel like he could tell anyone, not even your mother, since she was in a very fragile condition and would likely repeat whatever he told her. So now it's your secret. And I'm asking you not to repeat it to anyone, because it would cause scandal to the church if people knew that priests were going around consecrating protestant ground."

"What about my dad?" Richard asked. "He was buried in Korea. I have no idea if his grave is consecrated or not."

"Don't worry, Richard, the Army chaplains are very good at consecrating ground wherever our armed forces go. There is probably no place on earth which has not been consecrated for burial by Catholic priests, except in the U.S. I personally know two Army chaplains who have consecrated all of Korea, North and South, for Catholic burial. Maybe someday I'll introduce you to one of them." Richard smiled. "He's a good friend of mine and visits here sometimes."

"Thank you, Father—I'd like that," Richard said. His eyes were watering.

I never figured out exactly why I had such a visceral hatred for Fr. Reiser. Perhaps it was just as Fr. Jim said—he was not very good with people. I know he considered me one of his sheep, but I didn't want to be treated like one of his sheep—he acted so superior, so arrogant—I couldn't stand the idea that he thought he was better than I was, maybe for the simple reason that I thought I was better than he was. (Of course, this was before I knew I had what they now call Oppositional/Defiant Disorder—I had recognized the tendency in myself, but I always thought it was just a simple case of what some call "not suffering fools gladly" or what we call in Mayfly not putting up with assholes. Now I had to admit that the Fr. Reiser I was hearing about was definitely not the P.J. I thought I knew, the one I had so despised, the one I had loved to hate. Perhaps it was easier to think better of him now that he was dead, but, to my surprise, I was even glad that I had tried to save him.

"Did you know right before he died, he yelled 'Leave my son alone?'" Richard asked. "What did he mean by that? Is Sidney his son?" Fr. Jim blanched.

"What makes you think that?" he asked.

"Lots of things," Richard said. "Sidney's father is supposedly dead, but Mrs. Armani still goes by her maiden name. Also, Mrs. Armani's grandmother used to be the housekeeper for Fr. Reiser, but she got too arthritic, and then Mrs. Armani did it for a while and then moved to St. Louis."

Toby and I looked at Richard, dumbfounded.

"Your Dad told you," he said, looking at me, "that, when the old woman got too arthritic, her granddaughter took over for a while."

"I know," I said, "but what makes you think it was Mrs. Armani?" I asked, not making the connection.

"Your dad said the old woman's name was Mrs. Orba and she lived down close to the cement plant, and Mrs. Armani has a picture of her grandmother on the wall, and she told us her name was Mary Orba," Richard said.

Toby and I were stupefied, trying to remember those details. The room was silent.

"I guess we'll never be able to ask him," Fr. Jim said, finally. "And I don't think it's any of our business anyway, so I would implore you not to mention it to anyone or to ever ask Sidney or Mrs. Armani. 'Let him who is without sin cast the first stone.' Besides, you've heard him greet the congregation as 'my dear people' many times. I don't think it's such a stretch to call one of our young ones 'my son' or 'my daughter,' do you?" We just looked at him. I had never heard him call one of us his son.

I had two additional questions that had been bothering me for some time. I asked the first.

"Father, if you die in the state of Mortal Sin, you go straight to Hell, but it doesn't seem fair that a person who has an impure thought goes to Hell for all eternity, just the same as a person who tortures another person to death."

"Well," he said, "I know what you mean. Many of the rules that make up Church doctrine are rules that were made up by men, so they're not perfect. We like to think that these men have been guided by the Holy Ghost, but we have an awful lot of rules," he said, "and they are almost exclusively made up by men. When did Jesus say you had to go to Mass on Sunday or receive Communion during the Easter season or abstain from eating meat on Friday, all of which are Mortal Sins, according to Church doctrine, that will send you straight to hell? Or when did Jesus say that women were not allowed to become priests or that you will go to Purgatory for some sins and go to eternal Hell for others? When did Jesus personally claim that he was God, or that he was creating a new kind of matter through something our wise men over a thousand years later called 'transubstantiation,' and that he was only granting the power to create the transubstantiated matter to a tightly controlled class of professionals, who all had to be male? The Church teaches us to have faith in these things, and many people manage to do just that. However, if you don't have blind faith, you might think it takes a great deal of imagination, a great deal of elaboration, a great deal of wishful thinking, even, to believe that the words 'Do this in memory of me' accomplished all of that. All these matters have been argued over for centuries by men skilled in debating how many angels can dance on the head of a pin.

"Granted," he said, "some of the men who made up these rules were very wise and very good. Perhaps many of these men believed they had our best interests at heart when they made these rules up and thought they were speaking for God, but even so, there's no denying that these are rules made up by men. So, I can't tell you that these rules are not real or not correct or not good," he said, "but just bear that in mind—these rules were made up by men."

It seemed like he was trying to tell us more than he was saying.

"Can't we just read the Bible then?" Toby asked.

"Well, the Bible is...interesting. Much of it is what we call 'wisdom literature.' It contains lots of things that have nothing whatsoever to do with our relationship with God. And it was written by men, too, although we like to picture the Holy Ghost sitting on their shoulders telling them what to write, but I've never actually seen that happen—have you?" he asked, smiling. "In actuality, much of the Bible was passed down for generations by word of mouth, in something called 'the oral tradition,' like *The Iliad*. When things aren't written down, they tend to change over time, to become exaggerated—have you ever read 'The Iliad'? Or that game called 'telephone,' where you pass a whisper around the room? Often what comes back to the beginning isn't anything like the message that started. Scholars are still arguing about all the changes in the Bible. Prior to the Civil War, biblical scholars had identified more changes in the Bible than there are words in the Old Testament. Many of these were probably errors made by ignorant people, but many were made intentionally for political reasons, or gender warfare, or even just because the copying scribe thought that was the way it ought to be. And new methods of interpretation and new archaeological discoveries are showing us more and more all the time. So the Bible is not really a document that you would rely on for accuracy."

We were all silent for a while, mulling this over.

"Father," I said, finally, asking my second big question, "What about dogs? If I go to Heaven, will Prince be there with me?"

"If you want him to be with you in Heaven, then, absolutely, Prince will be in Heaven."

"What if I don't make it for some reason—will Prince go to Hell too?"

"No, of course not. Prince won't go to hell, whatever happens. He's a good dog."

"Thank you, Father," I said, completely relieved.

"And neither will you," he said. "Do you think God made somebody like you, somebody who tries to be good, just to trick you somehow so he can damn you to hell? I don't think so—that doesn't sound like God to me."

"Hot damn!" I said, once we had reached the sidewalk. "Prince won't have to go to Hell, whatever happens." And although I hadn't specifically asked, I couldn't really see him having to go to Purgatory, either.

Bad Billie joined us as we walked along Broadway on our way home, discussing the implications for our salvation, resulting from our meeting with Fr. Jim. He was still not convinced.

"Damn, boy," he said, "I wouldn't let anybody tell me what I had to believe, 'specially 'bout somethin' as important as God."

That afternoon, our Probate Judge, who had a reputation as a legal scholar, reviewed the Inquest findings and reopened the hearing to take additional evidence, "which had been newly discovered." He held the hearing immediately. Chief Malone, the primary witness, relying on Richard's timeline, recited the facts which "his investigation had revealed." The Court inquired of the three of us whether this account was "substantially correct," and then ordered that a new finding of unlawful killing by a person or persons unknown be entered on the record.

The next morning, the early Mass was held as a simple Requiem Mass presided over by Fr. Jim. Only the Pipers, Richard and Mrs. Washington, Sidney and Mrs. Armani, and my entire family were in attendance, as we prayed for eternal rest for Tom. Immediately thereafter, Tom's casket was lifted out of the ground at Riverside Cemetery and interred in the Piper family plot in the Catholic cemetery. The backhoe operator at Riverside was one Mister Gomer, who didn't recognize the three Fletcher boys, dressed as we were in suits and ties, until we nearly waved our arms off and called him by name.

"Who's that?" Mom asked.

"Just a really nice guy who helped us with our boards for the treehouse," I replied.

90.
THE SEMIs

The summer was rushing to a close. Two days later was the First Friday in August. It also marked the semi-finals for the Mayfly Summer CYO Tournament. I began the day by serving Mass, having my Confession heard by Fr. Jim, and then going to Holy Communion. At the end of my Confession, Fr. Jim told me something earth-shattering.

"Jamie," he said, serious and very sincere, "don't let impure thoughts depress you or come between you and Jesus. They're part of being human and being a man. This is the way God made you. Just do the best you can. God doesn't expect anything more. He didn't make you to be unhappy with the way He made you."

Thank you, Jesus! I practically skipped all the way home. But it wasn't so simple—in fact, it was something which I would mull over for many decades, trying to balance it with the Church's absolute condemnation of some of the most important and compelling human cravings and aspirations.

Fortunately, I didn't have to figure it all out right away. Once at home, I began to concentrate on the task ahead of me. Winning our first two games had qualified us for the Semifinals, which were to be held that evening, with the Finals the next night. Our semifinal opponent was Thomas Aquinas from Quincy, Illinois, which was a basketball powerhouse every year.

Before my eye injury, I believed we had the firepower to beat Thomas Aquinas, but things were different now. Lucas Crane had apparently determined to win the Future Famer trophy single-handed, whatever the cost to the team—his concept of teamwork was "Gimme the ball." Still, we were not without weapons—Toby had blossomed into a real player, and I could be counted on to take high-percentage shots when the opportunities arose.

I was grateful to Coach Hedges for changing my visual orientation on the court and insisting that I implement a side-to-side scanning motion and that I practice until it was second nature, even when I wasn't playing basketball. Defenders who thought they could use my eye patch to determine that I was unable to pass or drive in that direction were frequently stunned, although I had to be very careful about sudden double-teams arriving on my blind side, and I occasionally missed opportunities to pass the ball to open teammates—except Toby—I knew where Toby was and where he was going to be in any given moment.

Our team exchanged leads back and forth with Thomas Acquinas until the fourth quarter, when we were finally able to put together a six-point run and hold it, thanks to some fierce team rebounding and a blocked shot by Toby. I contributed two corner shots when Toby snatched offensive rebounds and then fired the ball out to me in the corner, and even made three free throws to keep us in the lead. We won by seven. Lucas Crane was five for eighteen on shots from the field and one for three on free throws. He was obviously becoming more and more frustrated by his poor shooting and could see the trophy slipping away from him unless he turned in a record-breaking game in the Finals. Normally, a player in a shooting slump will devote himself to passing, but it seemed like that never occurred to Lucas Crane. We were lucky to get a win.

91.
GO, MAY CATS!

The Championship Game was scheduled for 7:00 p.m. on Saturday evening. We were matched against the St. Clement Crusaders—Lucky's old team, which had traveled here from St. Louis to win the tournament and who had won it three out of the past five years. Once again, they were an impressive team, tall and quick and loaded with talent. Their postman was huge—it was hard to believe that he was the same age as our players.

The Mayfly Catholic team ("Go, May Cats!") was not allowed to have cheerleaders, much to our chagrin and the disappointment of the girls in our school. According to Mom, Sr. Ambrose had discussed it with P.J., and they were convinced that cheerleader gyrations, coupled with short skirts and fancy bunkies, constituted "an occasion of sin," leading to sins of impure thoughts as well as deeds. We hated both of them for that, but of course they were absolutely correct. I just had no idea how they knew—I was surprised that either of them could remember.

Once at a talent show when the high school cheerleaders were putting on an exhibition on our raised stage in their short pleated skirts with their pretty bunkies peaking out from time to time—if anyone noticed—*Lord be merciful to me a sinner*—Mom had looked over at P.J. to see if he was as horrified by the graphic nature of this display as she was and had been gratified to see that his eyes were shut tight to guard against those lovely images triggering impure thoughts, or worse.

"He's such a spiritual man," she said, recounting the event at our dinner table with deep disapproval, but satisfaction at P.J.'s reaction. *Puke. Gag me with a spoon.* There was no way humanly possible I could have closed my eyes during that performance. *Lord be merciful to me a sinner.*

But even though we weren't allowed to have cheerleaders, all the girls were at the game anyway, and so were all the parents and grandparents, not just from our team, but all the other teams as well. Everyone stayed for the Championship Game—the gym was packed—it was divided into swaths of team colors where the fans of teams that had already been eliminated sat together: sections of burgundy and gold and red and blue and black and green. Excitement was high.

We had trouble from the very first, when their giant won the opening tip, and they were off to the races. It was eight to nothing before we scored the first time, when I was able to use Coach Hedges' technique to steal the ball and then race to the other end for a layup. After that, we started clawing our way back, staying generally six points behind for ages, then finally narrowing the lead to four.

Lucas Crane was playing point guard, and I was stuck out on the left wing, where I never touched the ball unless I could grab a lucky rebound. "Lucky" was shooting like a fiend, virtually every time he touched the ball, but he wasn't hitting. That didn't matter to him—he kept shooting anyway. Our offense deteriorated into Lucas shooting and the rest of us crashing the boards, hoping for a rebound. By a great team effort, we were able to keep ourselves in the game with pure heart and scrappiness.

At half-time, we were down by two, but they won the tip-off, and were off and running up the score again, eventually leading by ten points before we were able to slow them down and start our comeback attempt.

At the end of the third quarter, we were still down by six points—we had not held the lead once during the entire game. Our desperation was building. Even though Lucas Crane was supposed to bring the ball down the floor, I started breaking free towards the inbounds passer, and my teamies started finding me on the inbounds plays, instead of giving Lucas the ball. It didn't matter—as soon as he touched the ball at the other end of the floor, he shot it. He was desperate by now, hurrying his shot and shooting off balance—you could tell even before he let the ball go that he didn't have a snowball's chance in hell of making it.

The rest of the team watched in dismay, then hit the boards fiercely on garbage detail, rebounding like wild animals, getting some much-needed offensive rebounds, then putting them back up, frequently getting fouled in the act of shooting. Since the three-point line had not yet been invented, the only way to make a three-point play in those days was to get fouled in the act of shooting and to make both the shot and the free throw. But we came back slowly, one point at a time.

Toby was ferocious. With fifty-four seconds left, and down by four points, my doofus friend looked anything but. He out-quicked their big man to a critical rebound, bent down to launch himself for the putback, and faked up so perfectly that their post man leapt onto his back, while Toby then continued muscling past him for the putback, making the basket and bringing us within two points of a tie.

And Toby still had a free throw coming, the biggest pressure shot of the game, and the biggest of Toby's young life. He stepped up to the line, made the Sign of the Cross, accepted the bounce pass from the referee, then used the Coach Hedges protocol: three dribbles, focus, then the shot. No hesitation—he popped the net. Now we were down by just one point.

The Crusaders threw the ball inbounds and began to move it down the court—they had ten seconds to cross the half-court line. If they couldn't cross the half-court line in that time, we would get the ball back. We picked them up man-to-man and dogged them the entire way down, trying not to foul. No luck—they advanced across the half line, then decided to hold the ball. When the clock wound down to approximately ten seconds, we would have no alternative except to foul them and hope for a missed free throw and a lucky rebound with time to move the ball the length of the court and then score.

The shot clock had not yet been invented, so there was no limit to how long they could hold the ball without shooting, unless we could tie one of their players up for five seconds in close defense while he held the ball, in which case the referee would call a jump ball. However, they were also required to penetrate past the hash mark with the ball every ten seconds, or we would get the ball back.

I had been watching the point guards' pattern of penetrating past the hash mark, counting seconds. *Eight seconds.* I timed his next move and sank off my man toward him just as he began his short dash inside, then slapped his dribble away and into the lane just as his bounce came up from the floor. Toby snatched it, holding it up and away in two hands, as the Crusaders streaked down the floor into their defensive position.

There were twenty-two seconds left. I looked over at our coach, who was frantically signaling for a time-out. "Time," I yelled, running up to a referee on the floor and giving him the hand signal as well.

"Okay, boys, listen up," Coach said. Sweat was pouring from his forehead and his shirt was wet. "Where's the chalk?" Our subs scurried to the bench and came back, handing him several pieces.

"Lucas, you throw the inbounds pass in—you're gonna throw it to Jamie in the backcourt." He was spitting as he yelled. "Critter, you and Jamie line up next to each other facing Lucas. Critter, you set a pick on the half-line side of Jamie's man to break Jamie loose into the backcourt for the pass," he said, drawing it out on his blackboard and fracturing his chalk in the process. One of the players handed him another piece.

"Jamie, you bring the ball down quickly, look around, count the seconds in your head from the time that you catch the ball—we have twenty-one seconds left, which is plenty of time, but start counting down from eighteen just to be safe—that'll give us a chance for a rebound if we need it—even if you score too quickly, they can't move the ball the length of the court and score in just three seconds. You're going to have to drive the lane—you know what your options are."

"Get your hands in here, boys," he said, holding one of his hands out toward us, palm up. We each placed one hand on his, the entire team, in a stack.

"Glory be to the Father," he said, as we all joined in fervently, "and to the Son and to the Holy Ghost, as it was in the beginning, is now, and ever shall be, world without end. Amen."

Then, "Go, May Cats!" we yelled, throwing our huddle hands high and breaking out as five of us returned to the floor, while the rest of the team remained on their feet.

92.
WHAT MIGHT HAVE BEEN

The Crusaders were in a man-to-man defense. Critter and I lined up facing Lucas Crane, who would throw the ball inbounds from the sideline; I was closest to our basket, Critter closest to the half line. Lucas slapped the ball hard and loudly, signaling the start of the play. Critter leapt toward my defender and set a perfectly tight contact screen against him. As Critter landed, I broke into the backcourt—it worked perfectly. I caught the inbounds pass unmolested—the clock started as soon as I touched the ball—and I turned toward our basket and started counting. *Eighteen thousand.* As I hustled over the half-court line—*seventeen thousand*—their point guard picked me up aggressively. *Sixteen thousand.* I drove the defender toward the free-throw line at three-quarter speed, anticipating a double-team at the top corner of the key. *Fifteen thousand.* He stayed with me, and the other guard sank over toward me for the double team—*fourteen thousand*—so I backed off a few feet in apparent indecision, scanning as I went. *Thirteen thousand.* He pursued me back out toward the top of the key, as I had hoped—*twelve thousand*—which allowed me to deal with the double-team pair separately. *Eleven thousand.* I feinted left, then drove right, searching out his left foot and trapping it with mine immediately outside and alongside his, which allowed me to cut past him towards the basket—*ten thousand*—then crossed over again, left, in front of the second man—*nine thousand*—

scanning my left while driving down an aisle which was now open four feet outside the left side of the lane. In that instant—*eight thousand*—I knew, although my sudden penetration had caused me to abandon my bird's-eye view of the court, that our forward would be running along the baseline from my left toward the opposite corner on my right, and their forward would now be collapsing toward me to prevent my taking it all the way in, that I was blind on that side, and would be forced to elevate too early, far out in front of their tall postman who was also coming at me from down low on the other side of the lane.

Sensing rather than seeing their big forward streaking from the baseline on my left, and knowing he could steal the ball on my blind side, I cut right again, hard, ninety degrees toward the center of the lane and the looming postman—*seven thousand*—a cross-over dribble to my right hand as I made the cut, then immediately shot it back under my left leg—*six thousand*—turning one hundred-eighty degrees back to my left, hard and fast, a real ankle-breaker for the in-streaking forward, as I passed him in the opposite direction, then continued, simultaneously switching the ball to my right hand, safe from blindside predators, not inward, toward the basket as they expected, but out toward my favorite corner, the spot I owned, the place where muscle memory took over, where I knew I could swish with both eyes closed. *Five thousand.*

But then it happened, suddenly—without warning, a bolt of lightning that changed my life forever—and I hadn't seen it coming.

"Spot!" It exploded from me clean and clear, like the crack of a pistol, like a mini-M-80 that rebounded off the concrete block walls of the gymnasium, clearly audible to every person in the building even over the frenzy of the crowd noise. *Four thousand.* Still dribbling away from the basket toward the corner, my right hand executed a quick-draw, palming the ball off the dribble and elevating it in a fraction of a second over the top of my right shoulder into a hard hook— *three thousand*—and I fired it behind my neck, with all my might, seven feet above the polished hardwood, to a spot I couldn't see, on a trajectory calculated to knock people off the far bleachers like bowling pins, to the place in the lane where I hoped Toby was, where I knew he would be, cutting toward the basket.

Only then did I turn and watch him, as did every person in that building: my goofus friend, the startled wide blue eyes, his mouth agape, his big, bony hands snatching the ball out of its jet-fighter trajectory toward the stands. With no hesitation, with the knowledge of three thousand repetitions, with the grace of certainty, in fluid motion toward the basket, brushing past their fire-breathing post man—*two thousand*—he launched off his right foot, his left arm curling out and away from the defender and up, all the way up, arcing high above his head, and then releasing the ball to roll gracefully, in slow motion off his fingertips, just before the final buzzer sounded, his backspin humming faster than the power of sight, the pure elegance of his execution completely dominating the sudden breathless silence, pregnant with possibility. And promise.

And with tragedy and eternal regret.

As long as I live, the memory of that shot will play in my mind, over and over, in stark and infinitesimal detail, in slow motion. And I will remember what was possible in that final expectant moment.

Because then it dropped, and it was all over.

And that sudden, timeless, whispered swish filled the gym with thunder. It blew out the walls. Pigeons lifted in alarm all the way down at the riverfront. And it wasn't just our lavish and golden triumph of victory—it was the splendor of its winning—its pure and abject beauty. And the profoundly deep and abiding tragedy of that shot was

Summer of '63

that, to their lifelong regret, no one who saw it would ever see its like again.

Toby had reached into his bag of tricks and pulled out a miracle. It shook the city, and the countryside around it. People shouted and screamed, holding each other by the shoulders and looking into wide-mouthed faces in disbelief. And then people began running onto the court, and—it was a little while before it started—some of those who were still in the stands were weeping—including Coach Hedges.

In the next several days, folks who didn't even like basketball related it like they had been there. For two weeks, everyone felt hard-compelled to describe it to everyone else, even to those who had actually seen it for themselves. But no one interrupted—they just nodded and smiled, and listened—they *wanted* to hear it, over and over again.

Now, over six decades later, people still talk about it, though not nearly so often, nodding gravely while they relate it—Toby's miracle shot, the magnificent perfection of that unexpected and inexplicable left hook.

Of course, Toby won the trophy. I was alright with that—I was happy for him. And the truth was, I had no use for it anymore. I was not a Future Famer—fame was no longer part of my future, at least not in basketball. I had been to the mountain. The basketball world that I had lived for so long, that I had created and practiced and finessed and eaten and slept and dreamed, held no more wonder for me.

And Toby deserved it—he had played a great game. He held their big post-man to eight points and collected twelve rebounds against him. He was our high-point man with eighteen points, most of them on put-backs after Lucas Crane's many misses. Lucas had gone five for twenty-two from the field, a measly twenty-three percent, and had

Joseph Welch

nearly thrown away our championship for personal glory. I was four for nine, plus three for three on free-throws.

I had played well—everyone told me so, even my brothers. They went on and on about the game situation, and my moves just before the pass, and what the defensive players did and tried to do. My little brother, Stephen, told me that the entire gymnasium jumped to its feet when I threw that pass. And Tim told me that on the way home, Mom said it was so selfless she didn't think I had it in me. My brothers were gratifyingly effusive—because they understood that pass—they understood what it took to make it, and what it had cost me.

In the living room the next day, just before our Sunday dinner, Dad told me that, in his entire life, he had never seen such a perfect pass. And Grandpa just sat there, nodding slowly, cigar in his mouth, and then he said, "I don't b'lieve I ever have either."

"You know," he said, after a pause, "I keep playin' it over in my mind, and I'm still not sure I even saw it. I guess the only person in the gym who really saw it was that red-haired boy, and he was the only one that mattered."

The Courier-Post newspaper account was lavish: "The Great Left Hook," the headline read. "Piper's Miracle Shot." There was even a sidebar titled simply "The Pass." It was okay—at least someone had noticed. It read, "Affectionately called 'Cy' by his teammates—short for 'Cyclops,' because he can only see out of his one good eye...." But it cemented my nickname—the name I am called to this day by nearly everyone in town.

93.
RICHARD'S DISCOVERY

We had spent the first week after Fr. Reiser's death in nearly constant contact with each other. We had sliced and diced the mobsters and P.J. and the big game and Toby's trophy and were interviewed once more by the police, as well as the local radio station and the TV news—our pictures were even on television!

The Mayfly Courier-Post ran a front-page news story about us, which read in part:

> Three members of the Mayfly Catholic Champion basketball team just solved a pair of murders, according to Police Chief Edward Hogan. Tom Piper, deceased older brother of Future Famer Trophy winner Toby Piper, was shoved to his death from the bell tower at Immaculate Conception Church on May 18 of this year. Although the cause of death was initially determined to be suicide, Tom's surviving brother, Toby, along with good friends Richard Washington, Jamie Fletcher, and Sidney Armani, suspected that Tom Piper had been murdered. Performing their own investigation in secret, the boys became suspicious of a pair of criminals from New Jersey who were in Mayfly to search for Confederate gold, which they theorized

had gone down with the *Flying Eagle* when it exploded and sank near the Mayfly railroad bridge on April 15, 1865. The criminals were a bad bunch—willing to kill people to keep the treasure secret. They murdered Msgr. Theodore Reiser at his rectory, but accidentally ran off the top of Castle Bluff while trying to kill young Mr. Armani, whom the criminals knew was also onto their scheme.

After a busy week of interviews, most of us spent several days in the treehouse talking it all over. For Toby, John, Michael and me, that meant lying around on our platform in Overlook Oak. Richard was often absent. He seemed restless, like he needed something else to engage his brain. We saw less and less of him and suspected he was inhabiting his favorite desk at the library.

On the last Friday afternoon of the summer, Richard came by the River's Rest. He had quit his job the week previous and told Toby he wanted to show us something.

"Where?" Toby asked.

"Cottonwood Point," Richard answered.

Toby radioed me, and I agreed to meet them. We rode our bikes down River Road to Sharkbait's house, and then the four of us climbed the trail up to The Projects overlook. Cottonwood Point was no more. The big flood roiled past it unimpeded. We looked at Richard curiously.

"Follow me," he said. We traveled across the face of the hill on an old deer path until it wound under a ledge of rock that jutted out toward the river. The path below it was dotted with scrub oaks and cedars. Directly ahead of us, the path ended in a bowl-like depression in the steep hillside, left by a recent landslide. The rock foundation of the bowl was still intact, but a huge earth divot had slid down the side of the steep hill, carrying several trees that still stood upright in the clump of earth. As we watched, Richard grabbed a limb from a gnarled oak and swung past the side of the hollow bowl. We held onto the limb and looked around the lip of the depression and found him standing on a limestone shelf that projected out below a narrow vertical opening in the cliff face. Richard looked at us to make sure he had our attention, then turned sideways and disappeared. Puzzled, Toby, Sharkbait and I swung over to the shelf one by one, poked our heads into the crevice, and saw that Richard had turned on a flashlight inside a passageway leading away from the bluff face. We squeezed through and followed him in.

The narrow passageway opened out into a cavern as wide as our living room. The bottom was smooth limestone. A bed of sand filled most of a shallow depression that ran along the left side of the room. A small clear trickle of water ran through the stream bed and out to the mouth of the cave.

"Ooh, nice place!" Toby said. "How did you find it?"

"I've been looking," Richard said. "I've been checking around the landslides." He pointed the flashlight at a flat rock laying in the middle of the floor, then bent down and lifted it up, revealing a small oval hollow. In the hollow was a white candle stub. We looked from the candle stub to Richard, but couldn't make out his face. *What does it mean?* He shone the flashlight across the room to the opposite wall. "Look," he said, pointing the flashlight beam at the middle of the wall. On the irregular limestone surface, scrawled in black, were letters of different sizes, crude but distinct: "Elijah + Janey 1864." I read it aloud.

"Who are Elijah and Janey?" Sharkbait asked.

"My great-grandparents," Richard said. "Their names are in our family Bible. Mom says they used to meet down here somewhere, before they were married. They were both slaves. They may have lived on your property."

"Holy smokes!" I said. "Does your mother know about this?" I asked.

"Not yet. I'm gonna bring her down here for her birthday," Richard said. "It's next Sunday. I'd like to take a picture of us standing in front of this wall if one of you guys could take it for us."

"Hell, yes!" Toby and I said at the same time.

94.
FLASHBACK: MAY 18ᵀᴴ, 1963

Clunk!—the sound was deadened metallic, but it came from high up on the wall in Room 111.

"Oh, shit!" Tom quickly lowered the device and stashed it in its hidey hole next to the door frame, as he exited the linen closet and closed the door behind him. Dashing toward the back stairwell, he passed Toby in the hallway.

"I've gotta tell you something, but later," he said, not even pausing. He turned left and ducked through the doorway which led into the back stairwell, then pulled some documents from his pocket and dropped them into the wood bin as he passed.

Hustling to the foot of the stairs and the back door which opened onto the alley, Tom almost ran over Crazy Carly in the basement hallway.

"Hi, Tom," she said, smiling. "C'mere a second," she said, trying to pull him into the laundry room, "I've got somethin' to show you." She looked offended when Tom shoved past her, jerking his arm out of her hand *en route* to the door. She pursued him.

"Come on, Tom—what's wrong with you? Why are you always in such a hurry, Tom? I don't bite—unless you want me to." Without pausing to answer her, Tom burst out the door, turned left, and ran up the alley.

Joseph Welch

Toby stood quietly on the top stair, waiting for Crazy Carly to clear out, so he could return to his basement eavesdropping station. When he heard the door to Room 111 open, he crept slowly and quietly down the stairwell.

The two men in Room 111 had heard the mirror hit the metal register grill high up on the wall. They looked at each other questioningly for a couple of seconds, then Mr. Muscle went over to the wall, pressed his ear against it, and listened. Nothing. He looked at Dapper Man and shrugged. Both men remained still, listening. Finally, Dapper Man quietly crossed the room and opened the door into the hallway, but saw no one. He walked several feet down the hall to the linen closet and opened the door. Nothing but linens, neatly stacked on the shelves.

At the exact moment that Tom exited the back door, Gunnar Green was driving past the front of the River's Rest in his Dad's car. He didn't have a driver's license, but he did have the car keys—he had fished them out of his old man's pocket while he lay passed out on the living room floor. Gunnar had already been out west to the A & W drive-in and was now driving slowly east on Broadway, posing with his right hand on the wheel, his left arm propped on the bottom of the open window, just looking cool and trying to get a look at whoever saw him. Just then, he happened to see Tom leave the back of the River's Rest parking lot and run into the alley.

"There's that skinny little bastard," he thought, mistaking Tom for Toby and sensing opportunity. "Surprise, surprise," he said aloud as he continued driving east on Broadway. "Ah'm gonna knock the shit outta that kid," he added, determining to drive down Hayden Street and intercept him in the alley. The memory of Toby hitting him in the front of his thighs as hard as he could with a baseball bat was still fresh in his mind—he had huge bruises on both thighs to remind him.

Meanwhile, Crazy Carly had been musing about Tom. Her plan to get him to marry her in a hurry was not working very well. She had seduced Tom shortly after she learned she was pregnant, and she wasn't sure how much longer she had before she started showing. At least now she could tell him it was his, if it came to that, but it would be much better if they got married before he even knew she was pregnant. To do that, she needed to change the game, and fast.

"Headed to the church again," Carly thought. *"I don't know why he goes there when there's nothin' goin' on, but I can play that game, too—I just need to offer him some other options."* In a sudden flash of resolve, she ran upstairs, told Mrs. Piper that she had "a personal matter" she had to take care of, and then left by the back door, walking up the alley toward the church.

Meanwhile, the mobsters had been looking around their room.

"Where's the treasure article?" Muscles said.

"It was right here. The hydrology report is gone, too," Dapper Man said. "That skinny son of a bitch must've taken them—where'd he go?"

"I didn't see him, boss, but I think he hides out in the church." Dapper Man stopped moving and looked at Muscles with his eyebrows raised.

"What makes you say that?" he asked, quietly.

"I've seen him goin' in there all times of the day, and even after dark," Muscles said, "when there's no services goin' on."

"Let's take a little walk," Dapper Man said. "I'd rather talk to him there where his parents aren't around." The two men headed out the front door, walking the half block up Broadway toward the church.

Up in the choir loft, Ray Lee Po was preparing for a quiet night, and was halfway down the stairway from the choir loft on his customary evening visit to the vestibule restroom when Tom suddenly materialized in front of him, charging up the steps like a bat out of hell.

"'Scuse me, Ray Lee," he said as he pushed past him, not only looking at him and speaking to him, but actually patting his shoulder in what he thought was a reassuring gesture on his way to the bell tower. Ray Lee was so aghast he didn't know what to do. His mouth hung all the way open and his eyes were the size of saucers.

He continued lumbering to the restroom, unbuttoned one of the straps of his bib overalls, and sat down on the toilet. He was paralyzed. No one had touched him in decades—not even a doctor or a dentist.

Outside, Gunnar Green crept down Haydon Street at a snail's pace in his father's car, then turned right into the alley, just as Crazy Carly arrived at the top of the church stairwell above him. She quietly opened the door and walked into the sacristy. Closing the door quietly, she crossed the room and stood in the doorway to the sanctuary, looking around the church. The air smelled of incense and candle wax. The dimmest of light from the darkening sky shone through the stained-glass windows. A single flame glowed inside a red glass candle pillar on a tall bronze stand next to a shiny gold cabinet door in the sanctuary. There was no one else in the church.

Feeling like a burglar, she retraced her steps, walked out the same door she had come in, and closed it behind her. Seconds later, the mobsters walked in the front door of the church. They pushed open the big padded swinging door separating the vestibule from the church proper, stood there for a few seconds, and looked around. No one—nothing moved. Off to their right, in the back of the church proper, a stairwell led up to the choir loft. Dapper Man stepped into the church proper, turned to his right, and went up the stairwell. The choir loft was empty. He walked to the east side of the loft and tried the door to the bell tower. It was locked. Meanwhile, Muscles, who had remained looking around on the first floor, opened the door to the restroom in the vestibule and surprised Ray Lee Po as he sat on the toilet. Ray Lee Po was a very large man with sunken eyes, his mouth slack, and an eight-day beard. At that moment, his overalls were pooled on the floor around his very hairy lower body. It was difficult to say which of them was more astonished. Muscles quickly shut the door, then opened a second door on the east side of the vestibule, behind which was a darkened stairway leading up.

"Boss, looky here," Muscles whispered as Dapper Man came back into the vestibule from his trip up to the choir loft.

"Let's look around the main floor first—if we don't find him, we'll go up the stairs," the little Dapper Man whispered. Muscles nodded and closed the door quietly. The two of them went to the front of the church, past the communion rail, and proceeded to check the sacristy and the altar boys' robing room. Nothing. Silence. They returned to the vestibule and entered the tower stairwell on tiptoe, closing the door quietly behind them.

After Crazy Carly walked out of the sacristy and down the outside stairs, she stood for a few moments next to the alley in thought, hoping Tom would materialize, before realizing she had neglected to check the vestibule in the front of the church. She walked back along the west side of the church toward Broadway, traversed the narrow passageway between the church and the school, then walked up the wide front stairs, pulled open one of the big oak doors, and went inside. The vestibule was dark. She pushed open one of the swinging doors into the church proper and stood there for a moment in the gloaming, looking around carefully, then retraced her steps toward the front door. She stopped when she saw a light gleaming under the door to the restroom. She crossed the vestibule and opened the door to the vision of Ray Lee Po sitting on the toilet with his overalls pooled around his feet and looking like he would murder her. Shocked, she instantly apologized, closed the door, and left the church as quickly as she could. As she hurried down the steps, turning to look behind her to make sure she wasn't being followed, an old woman with a fat dog passed by on the sidewalk below her. Carly didn't even notice her, intent as she was on getting away from that demented-looking man on the toilet.

Gunnar Green sat for a few minutes in the alley with the nose of his father's car pointed west toward the River's Rest, his bright lights on, looking for Tom. Finally, somewhat dampened by his disappointment, he drove past the motel and continued his joy ride.

"Hey, boy—you've got somethin' that belongs to us." That was what Dapper Man meant to say to Tom. As it turned out, though, he never got a chance.

Tom was sitting on the windowsill with his legs dangling down over Hayden Street when the tower door banged open. The dapper little man and his muscular bodyguard burst onto the floor of the bell tower at almost the same moment. Tom was so startled that all he could do was twist his torso around and look at them. Recognizing the precariousness of his position, he hurriedly reached up and inside the top of the stone window frame to pull himself back inside as he leaned his torso out in the opposite direction to gain purchase to swing his legs inside. Unfortunately, however, his hand touched a bat—he was so horrified and revolted that he let go as if he had touched a hot iron. Even more unfortunately, all his momentum and his body weight were outside the tower. His mouth opened in a gasp as he vanished from sight. The two men heard his body hit the ground. Shocked, they rushed over to the window and stared down.

"Oh, hell," Dapper Man said. "We could get the chair for this."

"What are you talkin' about, boss?" Muscles asked. "We never touched him."

"Doesn't matter—we'll never prove that—who's gonna believe us? It looks bad, and we both have a prior history," the dapper man said. "Let's get out of this tower—fast."

They hurried back down the stairs, pushed one of the huge front doors open slightly, and checked the area for witnesses. No one was around, so they hurried around the corner onto Hayden Street. The body was lying on the Hayden Street sidewalk. The dapper little man again checked for witnesses, then rapidly bent over the body and went through Tom's pants pockets, trying to avoid the widening pool of blood. He came up with a small black case, which he unsnapped to find a rosary.

"What the hell?" he exclaimed, then hurriedly stuffed it back into Tom's front left pants pocket. Next, he moved quickly to Tom's shirt pocket, where he removed a long strip of paper folded back on itself twice. Opening it, he squinted in the light of the corner street lamp and read, "Lord, be merciful to me, a sinner." He stood staring at it, then started to fold it up, then stopped, dead still. "Wait—maybe we can use this." Holding the strip at arm's length, his eyes traveled down the length of it as he nodded, then tore three pieces off. He crumpled the rest of the fragments from the strip and handed them to his ape-like companion.

"Get rid of this," he said. His bodyguard tossed them into the street. "Not here, idiot!" he hissed. "Pick them up and put them in your pocket. Get rid of them later."

He again eyeballed the three fragments he had culled from the long note. Handing the last of the three retained pieces to his companion with a "Hold this," he stacked the first two together facing into one another, then tore down the right side, simultaneously tearing a small section off the back edge of the first piece and the front edge of the second piece, both held together so that both edges bore a single tear—

they were now identical. He then removed the first fragment and handed it to his companion in exchange for the third, saying, "Now hold this one and give me the other one" before facing the second and third fragments into each other and holding them together while simultaneously tearing the back edge of the second fragment and the front edge of the third fragment. Reclaiming the first piece from his companion, he then carefully placed them in order, crumpled all three fragments together, and quickly bent over the body to stuff them into Tom's shirt pocket.

"What's goin' on, boss?" asked the bodyguard.

"Let's get out of here," replied the dapper little man. "Let's go back through the church and out the side door to the alley." As they entered the alley, they saw Mrs. Buben and Buddy coming down the narrow passageway between the church and school.

"Do you think she saw us?" the dapper man asked.

"I doubt it," Muscles said.

Moments later Fr. Reiser walked up Haydon Street from the old rectory. He had just finished saying his office and was walking around the property before he turned in, when he saw a bundle laying on the ground near the corner....

95.
TRIBUTE MASS

Msgr. Reiser's Funeral Mass was scheduled for Friday, the first week after classes resumed. The entire school was in attendance, as well as much of the parish. The church was packed—standing room only—even the side aisles were filled with folding chairs. The Mass was concelebrated by 18 priests of the diocese, who completely overflowed the capacity of our sanctuary. The main celebrant was the Bishop. Of course, it was a High Mass, complete with all of the pomp and ceremony the Church could provide—the music was beautiful, and there was plenty of incense, which I fully appreciated.

The Bishop delivered the sermon personally. Even though I had softened considerably on Fr. Reiser since his death, I still knew him as "P.J.," certainly not one of my most beloved friends, and I had a bit of a hard time listening to all the accolades about his selflessness and care for his flock.

I was doing fine, however, remaining neutral, until the Bishop came out with his "Greater love than this hath no man, that he lay down his life...." Suddenly, my eyes started tearing up and my nose was running—I had to sniff. Toby looked over at me, stunned.

"Get a grip on yourself— you didn't even like him!" he hissed out of the corner of his mouth.

"I know," I sniffed back, "I was thinking about Prince."

"Prince! What are you talking about? He didn't die!"

"I know," I said, "but he might have."

96.
AFTERWORD

As I travel back in memory now to that time and place, some of it bad, much of it good, a number of things are striking to me in retrospect.

We were triple-dosed with religion: we got it in church, we got it at school, and we got it in spades at home. It started with Original Sin at birth—that was a sin we were all steeped in, but never got to enjoy. We had all kinds of additional sins to deal with, a veritable multiplex, but the rest of them didn't start until age seven—they were all freebies until then.

What a difference between six and seven! When I was six, I was a happy-go-lucky First Grader, with no moral conscience and no need of one—I was certain I was pure as the driven snow, and intended to stay that way. I had no doubt that my behavior was pleasing to God. When I learned about Mortal Sins and Venial Sins, I resolved that I would never in all my life commit a Mortal Sin under any circumstances. I studied diligently, however, and by the time I entered Second Grade, I had received enough religious education to realize that, previously unknown to me, I was committing multiple Mortal Sins every day! It turned out that those incredibly moving photographs in the Sears catalog were actually "Occasions of Sin,"—and Mortal Sins at that! And that wasn't all—even thinking about them was also a Mortal Sin! Thus began my Dark Night of the Soul, imprisoned in deep despair that I could ever find my way back into a permanent State of Grace, and knowing that the Gates of Heaven would be barred to me and Eternal Damnation all but assured—unless I had a "lucky" death, which in my case meant dying as I exited the church building after going to Confession.

There was no safe or permissible sexual outlet. There was no room in Church dogma for sexual curiosity or experimentation or joy or discovery or the normal trajectory of growing up—there was nothing but complete prohibition and a heavy price to pay for violations.

Despite the magnitude of the stakes for which we played (eternal bliss vs. eternal damnation), it was a wonder we weren't better boys than we were—it seemed like all the religion we got—all our religious training and "upbringing"—failed to make us any better. But it certainly made us creative: "Is it still a sin if I don't actually touch it?"

Today I have more questions than I used to, but perhaps that is only my Oppositional/Defiant Disorder kicking in. Who knows, perhaps one day the veil will be lifted, and I will be filled with such faith, hope, and charity that these questions will seem uninformed, half-baked, illegitimate. After all, what do I know? *Judge not, that ye be not judged.* I still pray for faith, but I'm not sure I can trust the glib answers.

I still pray for the Poor Souls and wonder if Fr. Reiser is among them, even though I doubt that he is. I imagine Fr. Reiser served his sentence out during his life on earth, putting up with little shits like us.

The church is kept locked up these days, except for those who have signed up in advance for "an hour of Adoration." In the Summer of '63, I could stop in "just for a visit" whenever I liked—at any time of the day or night. I used to love praying there, where it was peaceful, in the silence and the dim light, the sun diffused by the stained glass, inhaling the traces of incense and old wood and wax. *Eternal rest grant unto Tom, oh Lord*—and by now, of course, my dear brother, Mark, and my grandparents, and both of my parents, as well as a long and growing list of others to pray for. *Oh, and Lord, please be merciful to me, still a sinner.* I so hope and pray that God is not through with me yet—because if She is, I'm definitely a goner.

And Fr. Reiser? It turns out I misjudged him, terribly. I have no doubt that he is Sharkbait's father, and I certainly can't blame him for that. I don't know anyone who could have been around Angela Armani in her teens and not have been completely overwhelmed by her. *Let him who is without sin cast the first stone.* And what if it's not a sin? What if it's just the way that God made men? Imagine your entire world being rocked by a pure and unimaginable natural love, and then being forced to abandon it, and her, and your son, to adhere to a rule made up by men, who insisted they knew for a fact that their invented rules were the will of God.

Fr. Reiser was in a tough situation when Angela moved back home—trapped between his duty and the rules of his Church. Despite the scandal that he risked, he did the best he could, because he didn't think he had a choice—he was "a priest forever." Renouncing his vows meant eternal damnation—no wonder the poor guy was perpetually angry.

In Fr. Reiser's living room was a framed picture of the Sacred Heart of Jesus. When it was taken down, a thick brown envelope was discovered glued to the back of it, on which he had written "Sydney" in blue ink. Inside the open envelope was a stack of twenties, as well as two crisp one hundred dollar bills lying on the top. It was all he was allowed to do for him.

We also found out that he had secretly purchased the Armani mortgage from the bank. Mr. Mills said he had done it to protect a parishioner, because he was worried the little family could be foreclosed on if she missed a payment. He had arranged for the bank to continue collecting the monthly payments, depositing them into an investment account for Mrs. Armani. Every time she made a mortgage payment, she increased her savings, unbeknownst to her. Fr. Reiser left the mortgage to her in his will, which canceled it outright. I never heard the amount of the investment account he left them at his death, but years later the president of the Mayfly National Bank told me confidentially that it was "significant."

Oh, and Crazy Carly had her baby. He was short and round, born with a headful of jet-black hair. She named him "Rocko, after his father," she said. He looked nothing like Tom.

I'm not sure where Bad Billie is today—probably wore himself out.

About my big boyhood plans and dreams, the all-encompassing impulse that drove most of my actions, the need to achieve fame—it was all nonsense, ephemeral stuff, wisps of wishes. It wasn't necessary or even important to become the Heavyweight Champion of the World, or the best basketball player in the history of Mayfly, or the best at anything. It was important that I worked hard toward my goal and that I achieved some success. Success without the effort required to achieve it would have been hollow. But I knew I had given it my best, and I could live with that. Apparently, what I thought of myself was the primary determinant in what others thought of me. It was amazing but true that other people seemed to adopt as their appraisal of me the value I placed on myself.

People still yell "Cy" at me from across the street. They love to say it—even the children. And every time I hear it, I know that it is a compliment, a reference to That Pass in that one big game...long, long ago...and I know that they remember....

And that's mostly all I can recollect about the Summer of '63.

97.
DEEP FLASHBACK: THE LAST VOYAGE

A fat moon rose low and round between floating banks of clouds. Stray wisps of mist partially cloaked the great river, alternately dimming and brightening as they drifted across the dark water.

A thousand moonlights winked and shifted in the surface ripples left by a slight breeze, as the *Flying Eagle* with its skeleton crew worked its way upriver, and into legend....

Made in the USA
Monee, IL
26 February 2025

13028495R00351